JONATHAN DRAWS
THE LONG BOW

LONDON : GEOFFREY CUMBERLEGE
OXFORD UNIVERSITY PRESS

THE SPECTER WHALEMEN

From *The Old American Comic and the People's Almanac, 1841*, Boston: S. N. Dickinson, n.d.

(See pp. 66–67, below)

Jonathan Draws the Long Bow

BY

RICHARD M. DORSON

1946

HARVARD UNIVERSITY PRESS

CAMBRIDGE, MASSACHUSETTS

PRINTED AT THE HARVARD UNIVERSITY PRINTING OFFICE
CAMBRIDGE, MASSACHUSETTS, U.S.A.

TO

HOWARD MUMFORD JONES
KENNETH B. MURDOCK
F. O. MATTHIESSEN
PERRY MILLER

.

PREFACE

ANY AUTHOR or collector dealing with American folklore must face a double ambiguity in the boundaries of his subject. By "American" I mean the main stream of United States culture; by the form of "folklore" I treat, folktale, I mean fictional matter that enjoys traditional life in either oral or printed circuits. Since only New England folktale is here involved, a further definition is necessary: a tale is credited to New England if two of three conditions are fulfilled — if its place of publication, its locale, or its main character is regional. In this study direct oral sources of folktale are bypassed; the aim has been to locate, arrange, and present folktales lodged in print. Although abundant leads to living tradition have enticingly opened, their pursuit is a complementary task. Even with this major reservation, the survey claims no measure of completeness; to take obvious examples, the text fails to mention Sam Hyde or Mike Martin or "The Devil and Daniel Webster." Still it is hoped that the scheme of presentation has brought within its compass a meaty sampling of New England popular tales and legends.

The resources of libraries have built this book. For unusual favors I am indebted to the staff of the Harvard University Library; to Mrs. Marion Cobb Fuller of the Maine State Library; to Miss Agnes Lawson of the Vermont Historical Society; and above all, to Mr. Clarence S. Brigham and the staff of the American Antiquarian Society. Courtesies were also extended me by the Billings and Wilbur Libraries at Burlington, the Public Libraries of Bangor, Lewiston, Hyannis, and New Bedford, the Maine and New Hampshire Historical Societies, the Berkshire Athenaeum at Pittsfield, and the office of the *Rutland Herald*. A Sheldon Traveling Fellowship from Harvard University for the academic year 1942–1943 provided financial assistance for the undertaking. Besides the aid of Harvard faculty members mentioned elsewhere, I have benefited greatly from the folklore erudition of Professor Kenneth H. Jackson. A net of college friends has caught me tips: thanks, Sully, Topper, Pete, Gresh, Holly, Symmey. Pleasant shoptalks with Mr. Cornelius Weygandt, Mr. Robert P. T. Coffin,

Preface

Mr. Walter Hard, Mr. Charles E. Crane, Mrs. Guy E. Speare, Miss Marion Blake, Professor Leon W. Dean, and Professor H. Walter Leavitt linger in my mind. My wife, who typed some 1500 pages of transcripts and the entire original manuscript, besides assisting with the research, filing, checking, and editorial assembling, is virtual co-author of this work.

In transcribing stories I have not retained the numerous misprints that creep into newspapers and similar ephemeral publications; in citing local histories I have consistently abbreviated names of states.

R. M. D.

East Lansing, Michigan
September, 1945

viii

CONTENTS

CONTENTS

JONATHAN DRAWS
THE LONG BOW

I

NEW ENGLAND STORYTELLING

AMERICAN CULTURE, late to arise in the history of civilizations, exhibits a folklore with distinctive qualities. While the popular tale is an international form, and storytelling a universal pastime, national characteristics and historical conditions color and shape folkstories. Not all peoples have the flair for legendry; nor do different societies necessarily produce similar tale types. In the United States the practice of narrating stock fictions becomes a firmly fixed social trait; but such tales run to the comic anecdote and local legend, the tall story and trickster yarn, rather than to the creation myths, prose sagas, animal fables, aetiological tales, *Märchen*, and *novelle* familiar in medieval, classical, and primitive cultures. Elizabethan superstitions, frontier humor, rural character types, outdoor occupations, Indian place histories, and geographical landmarks have largely determined the content and flavor of American homespun yarns, which grow from a people born in the seventeenth century, when talk traveled by print as well as by mouth, pagan gods had died, science was diminishing wonder, and emigrants crossing the sea exchanged old associations for new. Americans wove the fresh materials of their experiences and livelihoods into story stuff dyed with Old World supernaturalism and New World extravagance, and by the devious routes of folklore channels, stories passed into a popular currency, and crusted into a traditional lore.

For a survey of native legendary tales preserved in print, New England offers special advantages. A long and rich regional history favors the growth of folk tradition. Wide rural areas and a varied geography encourage abundance and diversity of folktale coinage. Extensive cultural activity, as expressed in many publishing mediums, provides numerous nets for trapping oral flotsam. A prolific art literature, including much that is regional, should reveal links with folk literature. And yet, in spite of the promising auspices, New England has remained fallow ground for folktale search, although literary and in-

3

tellectual historians periodically furrow her higher levels of creative expression.

Oral storytelling. The habit of storytelling took early root in colonial New England. Pioneer families crowded around the hearth fire at the close of the day entertained themselves with tales of mystery and marvel, begotten from the actual scenes in their wilderness life upon which inherited fancies were easily grafted. In all the New England states the custom is recorded; lacking books, loving horrors, bred in demonology, and surrounded by dread animals and savages, colonial Americans turned naturally into vivid spinners and eager consumers of folkyarn.[1]

Cradled and nurtured in the wonder-laden atmosphere of a new world and stimulated by a brimstone theology that clothed evil in human form, this native flair for storytelling found continuous expression and ready opportunity with the nation's growth. The center of story diffusion shifted from isolated pioneer cabins to congenial haunts in the village where men met to drink, fraternize, and yarn, or to gathering places in the open air where they relaxed from common work. Inns and taverns on the post road blossomed into undiscriminating fraternities, as farmers assembled to discuss crops, politics, and village affairs; around the evening blaze a garrulous clique of oldtimers often ringed, to match tough stories or recall other days.[2] Outdoors as well as in yarning flourished; the development of economic pursuits intimately bound with the woods, the fields, and the sea gave fresh impetus to the manufacture of story and the embroidery of personal experience. Farmer folk at husking bees, stripping ears around

[1] For reference to such storytelling activity in each New England state, see the following: Cyrus Eaton, *Annals of the Town of Warren in Knox County, Me.* (Hallowell, Me., 1877), p. 156; Mrs. Bathsheba H. Crane, *Life, Letters, and Wayside Gleanings, for the Folks at Home* [Newfane, Vt.] (Boston, c. 1880), pp. 36–37; Warren R. Cochrane, *History of the Town of Antrim, N.H.* (Manchester, N.H., 1880), p. 316; Shebnah Rich, *Truro — Cape Cod* (Boston, c. 1883), pp. 185–186; Samuel T. Livermore, *Block Island* [R.I.] (Hartford, Conn., 1886), pp. 88–89; Samuel Orcutt, *History of Torrington, Conn.* (Albany, 1878), p. 172.

[2] See e.g. Ethel S. Bolton, *Shirley Uplands and Intervales* (Boston, 1914), p. 84; Frank C. Angell, *Annals of Centerdale, R.I.* (Central Falls, R.I., 1909), pp. 97–98; Joseph O. Goodwin, *East Hartford: Its History and Traditions* (Hartford, 1879), pp. 112–113; George M. Curtis, "Meriden's Early History," *An Historic Record and Pictorial Description of the Town of Meriden, Conn.* (Meriden, 1906), pp. 339-340.

the cornpile, beguiled appreciative audiences by drawing the long bow.[3] Veteran hunters startled neophytes with lucky escapes and dizzy chases for bear, wildcat, rattlesnake, deer, and moose, that expanded under the stress of competition and the stimulus of awe.[4] Old salts along the wharf front or retired sea captains idling in the country store enriched the constant story fare of coastal New England: phantom ships seen at sea that heralded a wreck; ghosts sighted on the water of kinfolk who had died at home, or harbingers of their approaching death; smugglers and pirates and secreted treasure.[5] Still today in rural areas undisturbed by cityways, the grocery or corner store caters to eloquent fictionists, and the occupational groups of outdoor men have continued to dispense tales without interruption to the present time; potato farmers, blueberry pickers, guides and game wardens and fishermen hug the stove wintry evenings in forums productive of artistic tales.[6]

In the sessions and fests of yarn spinning, locally celebrated spellbinders customarily held forth. Instead of the company equally sharing the narrations, after the fashion of the *Decameron* and the *Canterbury Tales*, usually a master orator dominated the assembly, or attracted one by his simple presence. Obscure, even anonymous, these fabulists enjoyed a passing celebrity that received mention in town annals.

He was our oldest man in town, and his stories of olden time were the wonder of my childish imagination. He had served in the war of our revolution; and nothing delighted the old man more than to find a good listener to his long stories

"While thrice he vanquished all his foes,
And thrice he slew the slain."

If one might believe him, his feats had been more marvelous than those of Munchausen himself. He was none of your hesitating, half story-tellers, ever distrusting your faith, and doubting how far he should go; but a bold, hearty liar, plunging at once into the very fulness of your credulity.[7]

[3] L. Whitney Elkins, *The Story of Maine: Coastal Maine* (Bangor, Me., c. 1924), pp. 168–169; W. R. Cochrane and George K. Wood, *History of Francestown, N.H.* (Nashua, N.H., 1895), p. 473.

[4] Charles A. J. Farrar, *Wild Woods Life* (Boston, 1884), pp. 194–195; T. S. Gold, *Historical Records of the Town of Cornwall, Conn.* (Hartford, 1877), p. 192.

[5] Samuel Roads, *The History and Traditions of Marblehead* [Mass.] (Boston, 1880), p. 35; Charles E. Trow, *The Old Shipmasters of Salem* (New York and London, 1905), pp. 21–30.

[6] See Henry Buxton in the *Bangor Daily News*, Nov. 30, 1938.

[7] Nathaniel S. Dodge, *Sketches of New England* (New York, 1842), p. 61.

Our town in those distant days, had its men of eccentric character, its story teller, one who was especially gifted in the power to entertain by the recital of scenes and adventures which it was not essential for the hearer to believe in order to enjoy. The elder Farnsworth, who had a family of sixteen children, was an inveterate taker of snuff, and could likewise tell a good story,

> "Such as of Salmon in his boots,
> Full sixty pounds he drew,"

and once in an encounter with a bear, after fighting for two hours on a large stump of a tree, he — not the bear — came off conqueror and killed a bear and a cub.[8]

There were always men who had the gift of storytelling. Perhaps some of their relations would be termed in these modern days "fish stories." Old Hutta Dyer had the reputation of being the Prince of Yarners. Whenever he seated himself to smoke his pipe, whether under the trees or the sheds, there the boys gathered also.[9]

This champion of the deceitful word appeared to greatest advantage in his citadel, the general store. Surrounded by shelves of tinned goods and barrels, smoking, chewing, and spitting in a densely clouded atmosphere, discreetly reaching for the free cheese and crackers, the congregation hung admiringly on the narratives of its central raconteur: the scene might be in Rumford, Maine.

Every country store had its "chairman." Across the river from Rumford Corner "Uncle" (they were always "Uncle" or "Squire") Charles Kimball occupied the chair in the Kimball store. He was a gallant talker and easily kept the field against all comers. Conversation was thus an art in those days and skilfully weaving their tales, they did their best to hand down the art of tale-telling through the ages, as did the Arabs in the Arabian nights, — tales told round the evening camp.[10]

Or in Ira, Vermont.

As has been said, Peter Parker was a storyteller and rhyme-maker, but in addition he was a great boaster, always priding himself on his physical valor. Unhappily not all of his delightful lies have been preserved, though if they had they would doubtless make Baron Munchausen look pale by contrast. . . . In his day he presided as king of yarn-spinners before the varied gathering at the country store in Ira, where collected the best pioneers

---

[8] George N. Gage and others, *History of Washington, N.H.* (Claremont, N.H., 1886), p. 67.

[9] Rich, *Truro — Cape Cod*, p. 255.

[10] Arthur Staples, *The Passing Age* (Augusta, Me., 1924), p. 76.

and the best liars of the community to match their wits against one another, an agreeable pastime when time hung heavy on everybody's hands in the cold wintry days.[11]

Or in New Castle, New Hampshire.

Capt. John is the story-teller of New Castle; an artist of the naive kind; a poet without verse. . . . He has been on whaling voyages and trading voyages; tempests, wrecks, pirates, pestilence, starvation and thirst, prodigies in the heavens and in the seas, adventures and perils in strange ports, hair-breadth 'scapes, he knows, and has experienced all that a sailor can and live. . . . Of a winter's day, in the village store, he sometimes begins in the morning, adjourns for dinner, continues through the afternoon, adjourns for supper, and concludes in the evening, one narrative all the day long. . . . He recalls past generations of men and women, their manners and the remarkable incidents in their lives; how they used to smuggle rum and coffee, their quarrels, their jests and songs, their extempore rhymes, their house-raisings, their dress, opinions, superstitions and peccadilloes. . . . His memory is not only longer than that of others, but of a different order; it is like a tree full of foliage compared with the stark and winter bough of common memory.[12]

Or in Matinicus Island off the Maine coast.

When you go over to Matinicus, if you have been well advised, you will search out a certain man and talk with him. His name is Mark Young and he is known to all the world as Uncle Marky. Unlike all the world he has business of two kinds. He keeps a store and goes a-fishing. He is a descendant of one of the oldest families on the island and has a character all his own. A man of 57, perhaps, with bright blue eyes that almost pop out of their sockets when he makes a point in his talk; medium height and build, with a quick, alert step and manner; nervous and energetic. . . . His face is burned bronze red, and his iron-gray hair bushes out from under his black felt hat as a fisherman's hair should do. His most characteristic feature is the little chin beard that bobs and wobbles when he talks as the words come tumbling over each other among his teeth. But the best thing about Uncle Marky is not his looks. He can tell you stories from the beginning of one day till the end of the next, and never stop for a breath, or wait for a word.

On a quiet bright Sunday morning the genial spirits of the village were gathered at Uncle Marky's store. The reporter sat on the head of a pork barrel and waited. That store is in its way a curiosity. To get into it you walk up an incline made of the garbroad-strake of some wrecked vessel, and when you get there you see four pork barrels set in a row. Over them

[11] John P. Lee, *Uncommon Vermont* (Rutland, Vt., c. 1926), pp. 50–51.

[12] John Albee, *New Castle* [N.H.]: *Historic and Picturesque* (Boston, 1885), pp. 38–39.

hang five or six seine nets, waiting till somebody has the bad luck to lose his in a gale. Behind these is the counter. It is made of a single plank set on the tops of two flour barrels, but it serves its purpose as well as if it were carved mahogany. Behind it there is a marvelous collection of cans, boxes and pasteboard packages, and a coffee mill screwed to the wall.

The roof of this remarkable place of business is unshingled, and there are 100 holes at least that a man can put his fist through.

"Say, uncle," said a fisherman from a salt box, "why don't you get a bunch of shingles and nail 'em on?"

"Eh, what's that?" sputtered Uncle Marky, "shingles? don't need no shingles on that roof. When it's dry I don't want none, and when its wet the boards swell, so's the cracks is all stopped up." [13]

Among the outdoor pursuits congenial to yarning, the same peerless fabricator appeared and exacted admiring tributes to his sturdy inventions. He might be a Vineyard hunter who elaborated on deeds of dubious verity, but retold wherever gunners gathered; [14] a Swampscott skipper who had seen wondrous sights; [15] a lumberjack in the north woods, of Paul Bunyan hue; [16] a farmer of West Winterport, Maine, whose tales of threshing and teaming reached such heights they dwarfed pine trees to the size of alder bushes.[17] A mountain guide, Roy Dudley, long-time dweller at Chimney Pond on Mount Katahdin, Maine, until his accidental death in 1942, surpassed in fame the average rural raconteur. Mountain climbers annually revisited his cabin to hear his fund of whimsical tales about Pamola, god of the mountain, who smoked forest fires in his pipe and was troubled by porcupines nesting in his ears. Dudley recast gloomy aboriginal legends [18] into humorous yarns adapted to his audiences, featuring the antic strength of Pamola, whose traces survived in geological formations interpreted with tall-tale genius.[19]

[13] Joseph W. Porter, "The Wayfarer Papers," from the *Bangor Commercial* (Maine Historical Society, bk. III, p. 36).

[14] Joseph C. Allen, *Tales and Trails of Martha's Vineyard* (Boston, 1938), pp. 200–203.

[15] Robert Carter, *A Summer Cruise on the Coast of New England* (Boston, 1864), pp. 103–108.

[16] Stanley F. Bartlett, *Beyond the Sowdyhunk* (Portland, Me., 1937), pp. 11–19.

[17] Henry Buxton, *Bangor Daily News*, Nov. 30, 1938.

[18] See Fanny H. Eckstorm, "The Katahdin Legends," *Appalachia*, XVIII (December 1924), 39–52.

[19] H. Walter Leavitt, *Katahdin Skylines* (Orono, Me., 1942), pp. 52–55, 69–72; R. M. Hayes, "Barnstorming Mt. Katahdin," *In the Maine Woods, 1936* (Bangor, Me., 1936), p. 47. Professor Leavitt has retold me some of Dudley's stories.

Besides the steady gush of entertaining popular tales, a further stream of oral lore to carry floating motives and fictions may perhaps best be described as folk history. Early episodes, uncommon personalities, and memorable happenings that belong to the life of the town linger in the memories of aged townspeople, in a sense community historians, who relay them to youthful interested groups somewhat in the manner of the Icelandic sagamen or the shanachies of Ireland. Where the oral preservation of history is customarily associated with an ancestor cult, for the reason that the aristocratic families in feudal society made the history,[20] in the United States the unit of growth and the sense of clan have been supplied by the township, and according to this unit oral and printed histories have been constructed. Democratic participation in and guidance of town affairs have no doubt inspired a filial pride and loyalty roughly akin to that in an Irish sept; united with the usual storytelling urge, it produces this folk history, whose recitation has been variously noted. In the absence of more formal agencies, persons with the capacity for remembering and the talent for relating provided the conduits along which historical traditions passed into the knowledge of succeeding generations.[21] Counterparts of such folk historians exist in other countries as trained savants with a definite function in society, performed by the printed archives of the modern state. The parallel element here, however, rests not in the value but in the enjoyment of the telling, both by narrator and by auditors — enjoyment in the story appeal of history made live by close detail and grim suspense.[22]

In the manner that seems to be universal with the oral descent of even purportedly authentic narratives, fictive matter intruded and coalesced with the primary mass. This process has been clearly observed in the Celtic and Icelandic prose sagas which, beginning with a nucleus of family history, in the course of time accumulated magical,

[20] See Alexander H. Krappe, *The Science of Folklore* (New York, 1930), ch. 6, "The Prose Saga"; Bertha S. Phillpotts, *Edda and Saga* (London, c. 1931).

[21] See e.g. Francis E. Blake, *History of the Town of Princeton* (Princeton, Mass., 1915), I, 326; Cornelius Weygandt, *The White Hills* (New York, c. 1934), p. 12; James R. Jackson, *History of Littleton, N.H.* (Cambridge, Mass., 1905), I, 166.

[22] See e.g. the history-telling of "Marm" and Rachel Quin, in Fannie S. Chase, *Wiscasset in Pownalborough* (Wiscasset, Me., 1941), p. 625.

supernatural, and heroic incidents and fictions; these impurities may have existed independently in oral tradition and been attracted to the larger body, or they may have formed through the imaginative contributions of the tale bearer. In a somewhat analogous fashion, the momentum of an expanding town history, whose early chapters filter through the communal memory before being committed to print, approximates the force of saga; and the final literary recording in many instances includes accretions gathered from popular lore. "A town history to be exactly in order, it is said, must have an Indian legend, a witch episode, a haunted house, a bear, fish and snake story." [23] Many New England town histories do contain such stray items, included half apologetically in isolated chapters that they might not disturb "the easy and dignified flow of the historic narrative." [24] Yet perhaps, since social pressure did not compel the existence of sagamen or shanachies, more tales were lost than survived.[25]

Besides salvaging many perishable traditions by working them into the living chronicle of the town that some day might become fixed in print, the community historians distorted, or repeated the distortion of, their material. Such changes took opposite directions, the glorifying of pioneer heroes and the ridiculing of odd characters. Hero-making expressed itself in the extension to legendary size of awe-provoking personalities in the early history of the town; the scale might be limited, but the process was familiar and universal.

Most famous among the names of the old sea captains of Bristol is that of Simeon Potter. . . . His wealth was acquired in "privateering," and tales of his captures upon the sea, and especially of his wild marauding descents upon foreign coasts, were familiar as household words to the ears of the Bristolians of three-quarters of a century ago. Those tales lost nothing in the telling and in them Potter came to be endowed with attributes he never possessed. This was especially the case with his stature. Like Charlemagne he continued to grow taller with each fifty years after his death. He came in time to be pictured as a giant in size and strength,

[23] Lucy R. H. Cross, *History of Northfield, N.H.* (Concord, N.H., 1905), Pt. I, p. 218.

[24] Henry R. Stiles, *The History of Ancient Wethersfield, Conn.* (New York, 1904), I, 679.

[25] *The Centennial Celebration of the Town of Campton, N.H.* (Concord, 1868), p. 25, and Frederic P. Wells, *History of Barnet, Vt.* (Burlington, Vt., 1923), p. 60, for example, mention the disappearance of early fireside stories never committed to print.

a man whose success was largely due to the might of his arm, and not to any especial mental ability.[26]

Magnification and conventionalizing of episode tentatively reworked the historical tapestry of the struggle to settle, a struggle which involved heroic conditions and conceivably might in an earlier age have grown into a folk epic. In the battle with the red men for the possession of a continent lay an epical theme, in the single combats between eminent leaders lay its leading motives; but the civilization so soon industrialized looked on its birthing with an unpoetic realism that stunted the unconscious effort for epic scale.

Traditional narratives expand by repetition. The accounts of the engagement with the Indians which have been quoted are dressed in the familiar uniform, and wear the service stripes of frequent use. The two accounts are contradictory in substance and in detail, but are constructed on familiar models. The duel between the captain of the soldiers and the chief of the Indians has embellished the narrative of many engagements in the Indian wars. In every instance the soldier is grazed but unharmed, and the poor Indian, pierced by a bullet, leaps to a stated altitude and expires. It is remarkable that these historic bullets, leaping from muzzle pointing to muzzle, and traversing in opposite directions the same course, have not met midway, smiting each other to the earth, much to the dismay of the opposing marksmen. In honor of Captain Baker one is sorry that Walternummus leaped only four or five feet high. Paugus, when shot by Chamberlain, leaped six feet high and died in the air.[27]

Denied an outlet in the glorification of its heroes and epochal scenes by the ridicule of unbelief, folk creation turned the native faculty for ridicule to account, and spun its tales about the village idiot instead of the intrepid settler. The initial urge to glorify had been there, but a compressed American history did not permit the slow, centuries-long weaving of sober heroic legend, nor the long retrospective glance that favors credence; so the tales remained in scattered fragments or small heaped pockets of jokes and anecdotes, a permanently arrested development of folk saga. In the town stories and growing legends there were few romantic heroes, but many scapegraces, scalawags, drunkards, dolts, crones, ne'er-do-wells, hermits, and fanatics. They rarely transcended the bounds of town or at most county notoriety, but their

[26] Wilfred H. Munro, *Tales of an Old Sea Port* (Princeton, N.J., 1917), pp. 37-38.
[27] Ezra S. Stearns, *History of Plymouth, N.H.* (Cambridge, Mass., 1906), I, 9.

attributes were fixed and in their total they provided a rich backlog of circulating jests from which the regional comic stereotypes of the Yankee, the Hoosier, the Puke, the Cracker, and the Pike drew inspiration. Those town histories that faithfully transcribed the living saga of the folk duly noted these "characters" and preserved their idiosyncrasies.[28]

Such gossip about antics and sayings of the odd folk prominent in tight little communities addicted to the marvelous added a further stream of oral narratives to the real and imagined incidents in town history. A whole cycle of tales might group about a particular character. "Who has not heard of old Grimes?" began an account in a literary weekly of a village scapegrace, and the town history prefaced its similar string of anecdotes by saying, "Stories enough to fill a volume have been told of his tricks and crimes, some of them true, but many of them probably without foundation in fact." [29] Even a popular song was handed down about Old Grimes. Singular actions and phrases of eccentric characters remained in currency beyond the lifetimes of their progenitors and casually mixed with apocryphal absurdities.[30] Most heroic tales about local strong men, while supplying an antiphonal chord to the scapegoat theme, developed within the structure of comic folk saga. Accounts of herculean deeds were repeated in oral history not as faithful recollections, though that was their starting point, but as wonder-inspiring reconstructions; and in the telling their wondrousness increased to ludicrous proportions. Folk history built, but native humor sabotaged, American epics.

In various ways, then, active springs of oral story have fertilized and irrigated the native soil. But only half — perhaps less than half —

---

[28] A very extensive list of references could here be given. One character whose reputation exceeded the purely local is Timothy Dexter of Newburyport, Mass. (see e.g. John P. Marquand, *Lord Timothy Dexter*, New York, 1925). For a character whose witticisms have been amply recorded, see G. T. Ridlon, *Saco Valley Settlements and Families* (Portland, Me., 1895), pp. 410–418 [Uncle Daniel Decker].

[29] *Saturday Rambler*, July 22, 1848 (vol. III); J. M. Stowe, *History of the Town of Hubbardston, Mass.* (Hubbardston, 1881), p. 173.

[30] See Wells, *History of Barnet, Vt.*, p. 61, and Robert Davis, "Some Characteristics of Northern Vermont Wit," *Proceedings of the Vermont Historical Society*, n.s., V (December 1937), 327–328. A fine study of a Middlebury "character" by the same author is in "Heroic Buffoon," *ibid.* (March 1939), 3–12.

the credit for spreading American popular tales and legends belongs to vocal avenues.

Literary storytelling. New England traditional narrative has also been perpetuated or even been initiated in literary form — that is, in ways quite other than the unbroken oral descent whose interception is sought by scientific folklorists. Literary tales may represent one or many removes from an oral tale or may merely be suggested by popular motives; their treatments are colored by the purposes of the composers and the circumstances that govern their appearance. Important resting places of New England folktale, like the town histories, the *Yankee Blade, The Jonny-Cake Papers* of "Shepherd Tom" Hazard, Clifton Johnson's *What They Say in New England*, the ballads of Holman Day, the compilations of Charles M. Skinner, all vastly dissimilar in character, bear quite different relations to verbal sources. But if Johnson directly records, Skinner reconstructs, Day versifies, Hazard recalls, and the *Blade* stylizes tales, the variable elements of tradition and composition in such materials matter less than their common traits of storytelling design, familiar plots, and continual handling. American popular literature extends beyond simple copies of oral fictions; for circulation in print as well as by tongue has mothered native story.

In the absence of methodical field collecting in the seventeenth, eighteenth, and nineteenth centuries, verbal traditions seeped into print through various connective channels, often opened by literary, antiquarian, or commercial vogues; conversely, the printed mediums have themselves originated and distributed fictions that might eventually find their way into oral movement. The effect of printing on the flow of American folkstories is seen in two main currents, the horizontal propagation of popular tales and the vertical propagation of popular legends.

To estimate the importance of the literary tale in American folklore — particularly in folk humor — we have only to remember that its richest repository is the pre-Civil War newspaper. Irrespective of region, the chatty and intimate dailies and weeklies that entertained as well as informed the reading public in the middle decades of the nineteenth century prove well-stocked arsenals of folk stuff.[1] This literary jelling of fugitive, refurbished, or invented humorous items not only preserved and presented comic tales; it also resulted, from the practice of the "exchange," in their wide dissemination. In a period when the swarm of ephemeral and established papers and periodicals far outran any possible original sources of supply, when the mutual aid of the exchange permitted organs to pilfer, snatch, and clip at will, and when the chief filler lay in rural jokes and anecdotes, a good story never died. Given its initial appearance in some leading journal like the New York *Spirit of the Times* or the Boston *Yankee Blade* which could boast a number of regular contributors, the successful yarn began a prolonged series of travels; it bobbed up all over the country; it even recurred in the same paper; it might end up in a book. This rotation of favorite pieces occasionally provoked caustic comment from editors.

It is amusing to watch the progress of newspaper articles, and light stories, as they travel the grand rounds, and the changes of attire which they from time to time assume as they once in some half a dozen years or oftener start forth anew before the public, and travel the whole newspaper circle, with as bold a swagger as tho' they had never been seen before.[2]

The *Yankee Blade* petulantly complained about the use of one of its prize stories by eager pilferers who gave no exchange credit.

This capital story, written for the "Blade," is going the rounds of the newspaper press, but alas for literary property! Some credit it to "Scott's Weekly," and some give it no credit at all. The "Bangor Democrat" is one of the former. We rarely notice such things, but this is *such* a good one," that we really must insist upon its being allowed to be "our thunder." Help yourselves, gentlemen, to everything on our table, but don't forget the landlord.

[1] See e.g. Levette J. Davidson, "Colorado Folklore," *Colorado Magazine*, XVIII (January 1941), 7–8; Eston E. Ericson, "Folklore and Folkway in the Tarboro (N.C.) *Free Press* (1824–1850)," *Southern Folklore Quarterly*, V (June 1941), 107–125; Philip D. Jordan, "Humor of the Backwoods, 1820–1840," *Mississippi Valley Historical Review*, XXV (June 1938), 25–38 [chiefly Ohio]; Randall V. Mills, "Frontier Humor in Oregon and Its Characteristics," *Oregon Historical Quarterly*, XLIII (December 1942), 339–356.

[2] The *Rutland [Vt.] Herald*, March 1, 1831, quoted from the *New York Commercial Advertiser*.

Since the complaint appeared December 4, 1847, and the story, "A Yankee in a Cotton Factory," was originally published on October 2, borrowing had evidently proceeded apace. We find the "good one" in the *Spirit* for October 16, two weeks after its birth, and eleven years later, September 5, 1858, in the *New York Atlas.*

As one result of the staggering proportions of American publishing activity made possible by the mechanism of the exchange, humorous fictions were carried to many places in the decades between 1830 and 1860, and given abundant opportunities for oral life.[3] These printed anecdotes and sketches form a legitimate body of popular tales, where they enjoyed extensive currency among separate audiences and publics and contained, in their tricks, characters, and long bows, general folk motives. After the Civil War the focus of journalistic humor moved from the back country to the city, from communal and anonymous to individual creation, and the horizontal diffusion of folk anecdotes via the exchange practically ceased.

In the post-Civil War years another phenomenon of American publication served to stimulate the spread of folk story, the vigorous production of local history that kept alive the traditional past. Along this bridge of continuous republication a local legend passed from its remote inception, perhaps in colonial times, into the awareness of twentieth-century generations whose strong regional attachments attracted them to the curious, quaint, and picturesque roots of their community. Where the reprinted tale appeared in many places during a limited time span, the local legend was anchored to place by physical landmark or historic site but it extended vertically in time over the centuries. A town history incorporated a tradition current orally, or previously printed in colonial narratives, or in local newspaper articles that formed the basis of the history; subsequent enlarged editions or complete new undertakings of the history repeated the legend; if sufficiently intriguing, it might enter county or even state histories, and find larger publics in commercial guide and travel books, or Saturday

---

[3] Over 300 different exchange credits for humorous items reprinted in one newspaper from 1848 to 1858 can be found in the (mimeographed) *Index to the Burlington Free Press in the Billings Library of the University of Vermont*, vols. I to III (The Historical Records Survey, Montpelier, Vt., 1940). Many papers are listed more than once, and obviously not all credits are indicated.

and Sunday supplements of urban newspapers that appealed to regional audiences.

Thus legendary feats of the "powwow" Passaconaway have been relayed in print during nearly the whole course of American history, and ramified from historical to popular writings. The marvelous sorceries of this Penacook "bashaba" received notice in William Wood's *New England's Prospect* (1635) and Thomas Morton's *New-English Canaan* (1637); later historians, drawing from these early works, invariably repeated the marvels, and the fame of the sachem descended through the years, entered the romantic associations of the White Mountains, one of whose peaks it named, found a place in Whittier's ballads, and ultimately was enshrined in literary collections of native legends. Myth gathered about the figure; he became identified with the Indian saint Aspenquid, whose burial on Mount Agamenticus in Maine evoked a funeral offering of 6711 animals; in Penacook belief — or settlers' translation — he sped off the peak of Mount Washington enveloped in a fire cloud to attend a Council of the Gods in heaven. Town, county, and state histories, memorial statues and buildings have honored the chieftain who could make water burn and the trees dance.[4]

Perpetuation and radiation operate visibly with the legend of the wizard Kaler. This first appeared in a Hallowell, Maine, newspaper, repeating oral tellings, in a series of articles on local traditions; the articles eventually were published in book form; the town history duly contained the legend; a Portland newspaper carried it in 1940; clipped from the paper and posted on the bulletin board of the Hallo-

[4] *Wood's New England Prospect*, Publications of the Prince Society (Boston 1865), pp. 92–93 [Pissacannawa]; *The New English Canaan of Thomas Morton*, Publications of the Prince Society (Boston, 1883), pp. 150–151 [Papasiquineo]. Charles E. Beals, *Passaconaway in the White Mountains* (Boston, c. 1916), pp. 23–27, 47–51, gives a number of references. Whittier devotes section II of his poem "The Bridal of Penacook" to "The Bashaba" (*The Complete Poetical Works of John Greenleaf Whittier*, Boston, 1883, p. 19 and note 21, p. 438). For popular treatments, see Samuel A. Drake, *A Book of New England Legends and Folk Lore* (Boston, 1901), pp. 129–130, 359–360; G. Waldo Browne, *Real Legends of New England* (Chicago, c. 1930), pp. 39–40; Charles M. Skinner, *Myths and Legends of Our Own Land* (Philadelphia and London, 1896), I, 212–213. Henry J. Shaw has discussed, with full references, the relationship of Passaconaway and St. Aspenquid in *Sprague's Journal of Maine History*, XI (April-June 1923), 76–82; and in "Agamenticus and the Myth of St. Aspenquid," *Piscataqua Pioneers: Proceedings of the 26th Annual Meeting, York Village, Aug. 14, 1930*, pp. 15–31.

well hotel, it there attracted the attention of the writer in July, 1942, and no doubt that of many other guests.[5] Here the legend has completed a cycle of literary transmission from newspaper to books to newspaper, but the arc of diffusion has considerably enlarged from a purely local one-town audience to a reading public embracing several counties, a change that reflects the larger regional community established by modern means of travel and communication.

To suggest the many available avenues of printed media through which a local legend may proliferate, the tale of the Windham Frogs can be traced as a serviceable example. The fabulous incident of the Windham Frog Fright found a congenial launching place in the Reverend Samuel Peters' highly suspect history of Connecticut in 1781.[6] The incident, which seems to have had a real basis in fact, since Dr. Stiles commemorates it in a contemporary letter of 1754,[7] relates the mistaking by the Windhamites of a traveling army of noisy frogs for a French and Indian invasion, and their precipitate flight from their beds in various stages of undress; the names of two prominent citizens, Elderkin and Dyer, were distinctly heard to be called, in a supposed invitation to treat; in the morning an armed scouting force discovered numerous dead frogs on both sides of a ditch running through a nearby pond. Details varied in later tellings, for the tellings were many; the county history in 1874 painted their growth:

The story flew all over the County with innumerable additions and exaggerations. . . . Nor was the report of the Windham panic confined to its own County. Even without the aid of newspapers and pictorial illustrations, it was borne to every part of the land. It was sung in song and ballad; it was related in histories; it served as a standing joke in all circles and seasons. Few incidents occurring in America have been so widely circulated. Let a son of Windham penetrate to the uttermost parts of the Earth, he would find that the story of the Frog-fright had preceded him.

[5] *"Van Ho"* in the Hallowell *Register*, Dec. 21, 1889; Edward P. Norton, *Legends and Otherwise of Hallowell and Loudoun Hill* (Augusta, Me., 1923), pp. 3–7; Emma H. Nason, *Old Hallowell on the Kennebec* (Augusta, Me., 1909), pp. 290–292; "Old Kalf of Hallowell was a Very Queer Man," *Portland [Me.] Express*, July 3, 1940; referred to in "Hallowell, Mellow with History," *Kennebec [Me.] Journal*, Jan. 8, 1940.

[6] *The Rev. Samuel Peters' LL.D. General History of Connecticut*, Samuel J. McCormick, ed. (New York, 1877), pp. 129–131.

[7] Quoted in Ellen D. Larned, *History of Windham County, Conn.* (Worcester, Mass., 1874), I, 562. Peters placed the date erroneously at 1758.

The Windham Bull-Frogs have achieved a world-wide reputation, and with Rome's goose, Putnam's wolf and a few other favored animals, will ever hold a place in popular memory and favor.[8]

In the published report of the bicentennial celebration (1893), a twelve-page poem celebrated "The Epic of Windham."[9] A monograph on various treatments of the episode mentions "The Bull Frog Fight, A Ballad of the olden time," printed in forty-four verses in the *Boston Museum*, 1851, and a composition by one Ebenezer Tilden entitled, "A True Relation of a Strange Battle Between Some Lawyers and Bull-Frogs Set Forth in a New Song, Written by a Jolly Farmer of New England."[10] In the periodicals of the 1850's the tale floated on the swell of popular humor, in ballads and in prose; one newspaper reprinting observed in preface, "Our readers who have in years gone by read the old ballad of the 'Frogs of Windham,' we doubt not will be glad to peruse it once more in these latter days, and those who have never seen it, will doubtless be pleased to do so now."[11] Peters was castigated for embellishing the simple facts "with as much of fable and reproachful comment as with his vindictive and malignant purpose";[12] but no sooner was the narrative sobered up than a yet more extravagant rendering appeared.[13] Eventually the legend found its way into regional lore;[14] and Tom Hazard for once stepped outside his beloved Rhode Island to include it in his recollected folktales.[15]

This celebrated local legend, besides traveling as a unit through oral and printed repetitions, is further linked to folklore movement in deriving its chief entertainment value from a common tale motive. "The facility with which imagination may identify the croaking of

---

[8] Larned, I, 562–563. This authority asserts that not thirst but some malady caused the frogs' outcries.

[9] *Windham's Bi-Centennial 1692–1892* (Hartford, Conn., 1893), pp. 95–107.

[10] Lillian M. Higbee, *Bacchus of Windham and the Frog Fight* (Willimantic, Conn., 1930), pp. 13–25.

[11] "The Frogs of Windham," *Burlington Daily Free Press*, May 12, 1853.

[12] "Something More About Frogs," *Portfolio*, Dec. 20, 1856 (vol. II).

[13] The Windham Bank-Bills, and Connecticut Frogs," *Spirit of the Times*, XXVI (Jan. 24, 1857), 591.

[14] Skinner, *Myths and Legends of Our Own Land*, II, 40–41; Charles B. Todd, *In Olde Connecticut* (New York, c. 1906), pp. 128–132; Clarence M. Webster, *Town Meeting Country* (New York, c. 1945), pp. 94–95.

[15] Thomas R. Hazard, *The Jonny-Cake Letters* (Providence, 1882), pp. 401–403.

frogs with articulate human speech is illustrated very pleasantly by the following anecdote," added one commentator on the Windham Frog Fight, and relates how a Frenchman in the Revolutionary War mistook a croaking bull frog for a British soldier. Informed of his mistake, he asked, "If he was de bull-frog, how de dibil he know my name?" [16] A New England comic almanac carries a tale of an incorrigible thief who relinquished his stolen goods upon hearing a chorus of frogs cry out repeatedly, "De-liver-up." [17] Clifton Johnson reports from Northampton, Massachusetts, that a confirmed sot, Moses Pomeroy, carrying as was his custom a rum-laden jug across the meadow, heard warnings from the frogs and in fright threw the jug far out into the pond; and how a lazy boy in Hadley, named Edward Good, turned back from an errand because frogs in a swampy meadow on the way kept hollering, "Ketch Eddy, ketch Eddy! Eat him up, eat him up!" [18]

Folktale diffusion. Interaction of oral and literary storytelling habits could be expected to expedite the processes of folklore movement. That interaction existed, and stimulated the diffusion, revision, and persistence characteristic of folktales, readily marshaled evidence can testify. The tales cross into new centuries, the legends travel to new localities, by unseen intermediate routes.

Long-lived tales provably owed vitality to both verbal and printed renditions. Sometimes the same tale resurfaced intact in plot and setting but in changed stylistic dress. Strangely out of keeping in a collection of somber and romantic place legends, one trickster tale crept into Skinner's *American Myths and Legends* (1903), titled indicatively "A Travelled Narrative," and prefaced with this comment:

There is one narrative, formerly common in school-readers, in collections of moral tales for youth, and in the miscellany columns of newspapers, that is thought to have been a favorite with Aristophanes and to have beguiled the Pharaohs when they had the blues. . . . Every now and again it reappears in the periodicals and enjoys a new vogue for a couple of months.

[16] *Portfolio*, Dec. 20, 1856 (vol. II).

[17] "Regulation Reckon's Ackeount o' a Nat'ral Thief, an' the Fascination o' Bull-Frogs," *Jonathan Jaw-Stretcher's Yankee Story All-My-Nack*, 1852 (Boston, n.d.).

[18] "The Warning of the Frogs," "The Cannibal Frogs," *What They Say in New England* (Boston, 1896), pp. 248–249, 246–247.

Many villages clamor for recognition as the scene of the incident, but as Rutland, Vermont, makes a special appeal, it may as well have happened there as anywhere.[1]

The story related the reprisal of a storekeeper on a loafer who had filched a square of butter and concealed it under his hat; simulating hospitality, the storekeeper pressed him to stay and seated him close by the stove until the butter had melted and run down his forehead. Some sixty years before, January 23, 1841, the *Spirit of the Times* had carried the sketch, crediting the *New Orleans Picayune*; the plot and the Vermont locale are the same, but with the embellishing touches of dialect, verbal inflection (indicated by italicizing), and small physical details at which the frontier humorists excelled, the story is dressed in the mannerisms of the literary tall tale. Another robust trickster yarn concerns a sheepstealer who facetiously asks the ram in the flock the price of his wethers before taking them, and then speaking for the ram fixes a price; the owner, who has secretly spied the mischief, in the morning sends (or brings) the ram to his neighbor's door with a bag on his horn to collect the money. In the *Rutland Herald* of March 7, 1844, this episode is announced as having actually occurred in Connecticut some years previously; but a like claim is made for the story on its appearance over a century before in the *Boston Evening Post* of February 26, 1739. Stylistic differences again favor the earlier version, whose crisp Elizabethan idiom suggests the manner of English chapbooks.

Comic yarns not only linger in newspapers, almanacs and jokebooks, but crop up still in the mouths of storytellers. The American hunting classic, the big bag of game with one shot, frequently recurs in nineteenth-century publications, and is still being gathered in current oral texts; we can trace its course in New England from the Old Farmer's Almanac of 1809 to a verbal rendering given the writer in 1942.[2] A tall yarn about a hardheaded Negro who tried to butt through a grindstone that has been wrapped to resemble a cheese is printed

---

[1] Charles M. Skinner, *American Myths and Legends* (Philadelphia and London, c. 1903), I, 54–55. Woburn, Mass., also makes a claim; see Parker L. Converse, *Legends of Woburn* (Woburn, Mass., 1892), p. 123.

[2] See R. M. Dorson, "Jonathan Draws the Long Bow," *New England Quarterly*, XVI (June 1943), 253–259; Robert Kempt, *The American Joe Miller* (London, 1865), p. 104, no. 300.

in the *Exeter News Letter* of July 6, 1841, credited to the *Boston Post*, and in the *Yankee Blade* for August 20, 1842; adapted to a local character, it turns up in the *Berkshire Hills*, April 1, 1905; and folklore collectors of the present day discover a thick-skulled Negro in Florida with comparable butting propensities.[3] In a waggish prank carried by the *Yankee Blade* in 1852, a customer confuses the storekeeper by asking for a bottle of beer, which he then returns for a loaf of bread; when payment is demanded, the consumer points out that he has not drunk the beer, and has returned it to pay for the bread. Local tradition in Middlebury, Vermont, in 1939, ascribes the same game, with doughnuts and cookies, to a town character.[4] During the research on the present study an onlooker glanced over the writer's shoulder at the volume of the *Yankee Blade* for 1851 spread before him, observed a sketch titled "The Ill-Looking Horse," and without reading below the title proceeded to relate the same tale as it had been told him by a fellow farmer in Connecticut; details differed in the two versions — in one the Yankee fools, in the other he is fooled — but the plot is fixed: a shrewd trader cautions a prospective buyer that his horse doesn't look very well; the purchaser replies that he can judge the looks of the horse for himself, but discovers after the sale that the animal is blind, and that the trader had given fair warning. As this juxtaposition of literary and oral variants ninety years removed would indicate, "The Ill-Looking Horse" has traveled widely by print and by mouth.[5]

Probably no really popular American tale has escaped the influence of both methods of storytelling. Observe the well-known New England yarn, "Thar She Blows!"; this tale, which describes a humorous colloquy between a seaman and his skipper over the sighting of a whale, apparently originated in New Bedford, but in time it drifted to many parts of the world.

[3] *Florida: a Guide to the Southernmost State*, Federal Writers' Project (New York, 1939), p. 132.

[4] "A Knotty Case," *Yankee Blade*, May 8, 1852 (vol. XI); Robert Davis, "Heroic Buffoon," *Proceedings of the Vermont Historical Society*, n.s. VII (March 1939), 10.

[5] For the two texts mentioned above, see Chapter III. The *Blade*'s form (credited to the *Boston Post*) is given in the *Burlington Daily Free Press*, May 29, 1868; for latter-day variations, see the *Northern*, II (March 1923), 16, "Pete's Bargain Horse"; Marion Blake, "A Hopeless Plight," *Burlington Daily Free Press and Times*, Jan. 27, 1936; "Defense," *Yankee*, III (July 1937), 15.

Jonathan Draws the Long Bow

I publish *Thar She Blows* with considerable foreboding. It is not an entirely original story. It has passed, by word of mouth, up and down the New England coast for almost a hundred years. But it has rarely appeared in print. And like that other famous American saga, *Frankie and Johnnie*, it has taken on or lost color with each telling. There are many, many versions; each of them different in some degree from the others. And each and every teller claims that his is the only true and original version.[6]

So in every record of the telling, controversy has arisen. A number of years ago the New Bedford "Mercury" and the New York "Sun" swapped variants, and scores of correspondents contributed versions. One had heard it told in Chile, another had heard it on the Dead Sea, the Grand canal, in the foc's'le of a schooner in the doldrums of the South Atlantic trades, on the taffrail of the yacht "Wanderer," on the wharves at New Bedford and Nantucket.[7]

Even in this instance, where the story has obviously prospered in oral currency, the mechanical assistance of printing evidently contributed to its further propulsion.

If tales survive in time, so legends move in place. In the Rhode Island folk memories of "Shepherd Tom" Hazard, a disastrous string of mishaps befalls Timothy Crumb: he goes swimming, is chased by a bull, stung by hornets in the tree he has climbed, forced to take an impromptu ride on the bull, and is finally tossed on top of the deacon's daughter — whom he has been courting. Virtually the same elaborate sequence overtakes Mike Fink, legendary hero of Mississippi keelboatmen, in Tennessee.[8] This procedure of readapting a personal or place legend to new environments can be clearly discerned in a New England happening of some frequency: a sleepy horseman crosses over a bridge at night and in the morning is shocked to learn its planking had been washed away and he has ridden on the stringer. The verity of this incident was proclaimed by one town historian who complained of its adoption by other localities.

We have seen published, we think, later accounts of similar feats performed in the darkness of night by horses bearing their unconscious riders

[6] Paul Johnston, *Thar She Blows. An Early New Bedford Whaling Yarn* (New York, 1931), introduction.

[7] *History of New Bedford*, Zephaniah W. Pease, ed. (New York, 1918), p. 68.

[8] Hazard, *The Jonny-Cake Letters*, pp. 119–122; *Yankee Blade*, Nov. 17, 1855 (vol. XV); and Walter Blair and Franklin J. Meine, *Mike Fink: King of Mississippi Keelboatmen* (New York, c. 1933), pp. 93–97, 276 item 18.

in safety over bridge timbers; but of the truth of such accounts there is much room to doubt, and it is not impossible that this one, which is as true as it was remarkable, may have been the only original of all such reported stories.[9]

Thompson protested with justice, for the same account, invariably attached to a stated person in the town, is found in Newburyport, Massachusetts, Henniker, New Hampshire, Parsonfield, Maine, and Great Barrington, Massachusetts; Timothy Dwight set down the anecdote in his travels, and tells how the rider fainted on learning of his narrow escape.[10]

In the extremer cases of mutation, a central motive alone survives to form the nucleus of a separate narrative. A newspaper clipping recently brought to light from an old scrapbook related an outrageous experience of a traveler in Vermont in the 1890's who saw old people in a mountain hamlet frozen and stored away for the winter as a food-saving measure, then thawed out in the spring in time to plant the corn. Reprinted in the *Rutland Herald* and *Yankee* magazine, the story enjoyed new life; the *Boston Sunday Globe* for May 28, 1939, copied it from the *Herald*, and in 1941 Charles E. Crane used it for a chapter in his book, *Winter in Vermont*. Nothing is known of the original appearance of the account; but the *Yankee Blade* on May 8, 1852, states, "There is a story going the rounds of the press that a young man was brought to life lately, after having been frozen eleven months among the Alps." Here the motive of refrigerated human beings may have been transferred from an Alpine to a native setting; coincidentally the separate tales which it unites pass through similar cycles, nearly a century apart, of the horizontal transmission characteristic of the American press.

[9] Daniel P. Thompson, *History of Montpelier, Vt.* (Montpelier, 1860), p. 158.

[10] *New Hampshire Folk Tales*, Mrs. Moody P. Gore and Mrs. Guy E. Speare, compilers (n.p., 1932), pp. 145–146; Leander W. Cogswell, *History of the Town of Henniker, N.H.* (Concord, N.H., 1880), p. 381; *A History of the First Century of the Town of Parsonfield, Me.* (Portland, Me., 1888), p. 239; Merle D. Graves, *Bubblin's An' B'ilin's At The Center* (Rutland, Vt., 1934), p. 165; New Hampshire's Daughters, *Folk-Lore Sketches and Reminiscences of New Hampshire Life* (Boston, c. 1911), p. 37; Charles J. Taylor, *History of Great Barrington, Mass.* (Great Barrington, 1882), pp. 217–218; Timothy Dwight, *Travels; in New-England and New-York* (New Haven, 1821), II, 380.

In this chapter a few sample illustrations must suffice to support general theses. The custom of imaginative storytelling, under American conditions, has continuously flourished in New England from the seventeenth century to the twentieth. Much of this accumulating deposit of popular story has found its way, sometimes with stylistic embellishments, into print. The circumstances of American publishing have materially influenced the span and spread of native folktales and legends. Although these fictions inevitably show Old World inclusions and parallelisms, on the whole they differ markedly from those of earlier cultures, for they grow as bellying native talk of things seen, done, or heard on good authority. But, like all folkstories, they travel, endure, bob up in new forms, and disclose old traits.

II

SUPERNATURAL STORIES

A LARGE PROPORTION of American popular fictions depend for their entertainment value on the allure of the unearthly. The mass of tales thus loosely grouped together embraces wonders of colonial days when the hand of God displayed itself in marvelous providences, gossip of witches bruited in every town and hamlet, imagined interviews and contracts with Satan inspired by seventeenth-century respect for the personality of the Fiend, and accounts of specters, visions, omens, and prophecies documenting the secret human awe of occultism. These tale types interlock with others: haunted crime spots, while a ghostly phenomenon, fall within the bounds of place legend, and indeed most of the spectral beings are identified in individual tales with specific places; in their later usage spooks and the Devil succumb to humorous treatment. Native humor developed later than inherited superstition as a molder of the popular fancy, but their separate courses have overlapped rather than succeeded each other.

Marvels and prodigies. The first two centuries of American history were congenial to the play of fancy and the distortion of fact. A mystery-laden wilderness and an omnipresent deity who upset natural causes at will conspired to inflame colonial minds with lurid conjecturings and mirages. These wonders can be glimpsed in the literature of colonial travels and history and, after 1704, in newspapers; but whether preserved by the early historians or imbedded in the weekly gazettes, recounted marvels and prodigies catered to an avid colonial appetite for the sensational and supplemented oral movement, for later historians repeated the earlier ones and the papers reprinted each other's choice finds. In the voyages of Josselyn, Winthrop's Journal, the histories of William Hubbard and Cotton Mather, as in Herodotus, passages and even whole sections described memorable occurrences heavily strewn with fantasy;[1] so in the eighteenth century press items to thrill and shock dominated the inside columns reserved for domestic news. Bizarre accidents occasioned by discharged guns, lightning bolts, falling timbers, or upset carts, untimely deaths from strange malaises, drownings, burnings, and murders were solemnly noted in unsparing detail; and then there were monstrous births and malformations, mystifying natural phenomena, or grotesque incidents of daily life. In such a garden of mysteries germinated rank fictions, the first American popular tales.

Even the slender printing resources of the seventeenth century trap weird relations that circulated in men's talk. John Josselyn, in writing about his voyages to America in 1638 and 1667, sets down a story-telling scene from his first visit rich with large tales.

At this time we had some neighbouring Gentlemen in our house, who came to welcome me into the Countrey; where amongst variety of discourse they told me of a young Lyon (not long before) kill'd at *Piscataway* by an *Indian*; of a Sea-*Serpent* or *Snake*, that lay quoiled up like a Cable upon a Rock at *Cape-Ann*; a Boat passing by with *English* aboard, and two *Indians*, they would have shot the *Serpent*, but the Indians disswaded them, saying, that if he were not kill'd out-right, they would be all in danger of their lives.

One Mr. *Mittin* related of a *Triton* or *Mereman* which he saw in *Casco-bay*, the Gentleman was a great Fouler, and used to goe out with a small Boat or Canow, and fetching a compass about a small Island (there being many small Islands in the Bay) for the advantage of a shot, was encountred with a *Triton*, who laying his hands upon the side of the Canow, had one of them chopt off with a Hatchet by Mr. *Mittin*, which was in all respects like the hand of a man, the *Triton* presently sunk, dying the water with his purple blood, and was no more seen. The next story was told by Mr. *Foxwell*, now living in the province of *Main*, who having been to the Eastward in a Shallop, as far as *Cape-Ann* a Waggon in his return was overtaken by the night, and fearing to land upon the barbarous shore, he put off a little further to Sea; about midnight they were wakened with a loud voice from the shore, calling upon *Foxwell*, *Foxwell* come a shore, two or three times: upon the Sands they saw a great fire, and Men and Women hand in hand dancing round about it in a ring, after an hour or two they vanished, and as soon as the day appeared, *Foxwell* puts into a small *Cove*, it being about three quarters floud, and traces along the

---

[1] James A. K. Thomson, *The Art of the Logos* (London, c. 1935), analyzes the inclusion of traditional tales by Herodotus, in a way that invites comparison with the early New England historians.

shore, where he found the footing of Men, Women and Children shod with shoes; and an infinite number of brands-ends thrown up by the water, but neither *Indian* nor *English* could he meet with on the shore, nor in the woods; these with many other stories they told me, the credit whereof I will neither impeach nor inforce, but shall satisfie my self, and I hope the Reader hereof, with the saying of a wise, learned and honourable Knight, *that there are many stranger things in the world, than are to be seen between* London *and* Stanes.

September the Sixth day, one Mr. *John Hickford* the Son of Mr. *Hickford* a Linnen-Draper in *Cheapside*, having been sometime in the province of *Main*, and now determined to return for *England*, sold and kill'd his stock of Cattle and Hoggs, one great Sow he had which he made great account of, but being very fat, and not suspecting that she was with pig, he caused her to be kill'd, and they found 25 pigs within her belly; verifying the old proverb, As fruitful as a white sow. And now we were told of a sow in *Virginia* that brought forth six pigs; their foreparts Lyons, their hinder-parts hogs. *I have read that at* Bruxels, Anno 1564, *a sow brought forth six pigs, the first whereof (for the last in generating is always in bruit beasts the first brought forth) had the head, face, arms and legs of a man, but the whole trunck of the body from the neck, was of a swine, a sodomitical monster is more like the mother than the father in the organs of the vegetative soul.*[2]

Josselyn, like a good folklorist, is immediately reminded of parallels. Elsewhere in the same vein he likens an Indian flood myth of the White Mountains to the Bible story of Noah's ark, tells of apparitions visited on the red men by evil spirits, and gives reports of eerie witch magic.[3] So too John Winthrop, in *The History of New England from 1630 to 1649*, records the sighting of a wraith that spoke audibly amid sparkling flames, a spectral ship that floated over the harbor at New Haven, and a malignant witch whose execution was attended with a violent tempest — all wonders vouched for by the testimony of many people.[4] The manner in which an untoward natural phenomenon (today readily explained as an avalanche) excited men's fancies and tongues and in time became entrenched as a local legend can be seen in the "ominous accident" of 1670 known as the Overturned

---

[2] John Josselyn, *An Account of Two Voyages to New-England* (London, 1675), pp. 23–25, in *Massachusetts Historical Society Collections*, 3d series, III, 228–229.

[3] Josselyn, *Two Voyages to New-England*, pp. 134–135, 132–134, 182; *Mass. Hist. Soc. Colls.*, 3d series, III, 301, 300, 332.

[4] *Winthrop's Journal "History of New England," 1630–1649*, James K. Hosmer, ed. (New York, 1908), II, 155–156, 346, 344–345.

Hill. Josselyn mentioned it in his *Chronological Observations*; John Winthrop, the governor of Connecticut, described it in detail to a correspondent in England, as it had been told him by "creditable persons," in a letter read before the Royal Society of England and eliciting a request for a still "fuller account of this wonder"; Hubbard and Increase Mather referred to the oddity, and town histories in the Maine area where it occurred transcribed these earlier accounts. Winthrop couched his description in precise terms; a hill near the Kennebunk River, of specified dimensions, was carried some eight rods over the tree tops and set upside down in the river — no earthquake was reported at the time. The scientist who records this "strange and prodigious wonder" concludes "the natural causes . . . a matter too hard for me to comprehend; but the power of his Almighty arm is too manifest to all who weigheth the hills in a balance, and in whose presence the heavens drop, the hills are melted like wax. Sinai itself is moved." [5]

Similarly the Mathers, Increase and Cotton, scrupulously noted and collected data on physical upsets wrought by the Supreme Being in disregard of natural laws. But however scientific their procedures or theological their motives, the fearful tales they assembled in print preserved folk history and agitated oral romance.[6] Cotton Mather

[5] John Josselyn, *Chronological Observations of America* (London, 1674), pp. 277–278 (*Mass. Hist. Soc. Colls.*, 3d series, III, 395); William Hubbard, *A General History of New England from the Discovery to MDCLXXX* (Boston, 1848), p. 646; Increase Mather, *Remarkable Providences illustrative of the earlier days of American colonisation* (London, 1890), pp. 228–229; *Correspondence of some of the founders of The Royal Society of England with Governor Winthrop of Connecticut, 1661–1672* (reprinted from *Mass. Hist. Soc. Proceedings*, 1878), p. 48, which refers to Winthrop's letter and gives a reply by Henry Oldenburg dated April 11, 1671; Charles Bradbury, *History of Kennebunk Port* (Kennebunk, 1837), pp. 37–39; Edward E. Bourne, *The History of Wells and Kennebunk* (Portland, 1875), pp. 120–122. This last is the quoted source.

[6] Book VI of the *Magnalia* (1702) expands *An Essay for the Recording of Illustrious Providences* (1684), so that the work of father and son is of one piece. Many of their providential case histories become local legends (see especially ch. 7, "Thaumatographia Pneumatica, Relating the Wonders of the Invisible World, in Preternatural Occurrences"). E.g., Cotton Mather presented documentary testimony in his history that a spectral band of French and Indians besieged the garrison at Gloucester in 1692 (*Magnalia Christi Americana*, Hartford, 1855, II, 620–623); the narrative subsequently enters military history ("Niles's History of the Indian and French Wars," *Mass. Hist. Soc. Colls.*, 3d ser., VI, 231–232), local history (John J. Babson, *History of the Town of Gloucester*, Gloucester, 1860, pp. 212–213), and finally is accounted legend (Charles M. Skinner, *Myths*

both drew upon and contributed to folk gossip when he added to a sermon "An Appendix touching Prodigies in New-England."

In the Summer of the Year, 1688, just before the first eruption of our unhappy *War*, we had growing in *Boston* a Cabbage Root, out of which there sprouted three very wonderful Branches, one of them exactly resembling a *Curtlace*, another of them, as exactly resembling a *Rapier*, and a third, extreamly like to the *Club* used by the *Indians* in their Barbarous Executions. I was my self *one* among the Multitudes that visited this *Curiosity*, with no little surprise at the odness of it; and the *Characters* of it in my thoughts have grown more *Serious* and *Solemn*, since the *Consequences* of it have been so agreeable. I do not imagine my self herein impos'd upon, as *Lycosthenes* who wrote of *Prodigies*, was in the Business of his *Bearded Grapes*; but it would be *crambe bis cocta* for me to offer the Reader what Exemples parallel hereunto are mentioned by the exquisitely Learned, and Curious *Authors* of the Renowned German *Ephemerides*.

Moreover, it was credibly affirmed, that in the Winter of the Year 1688, there fell a *Red Snow*, which lay like Blood on a spot of Ground, not many miles from *Boston*; but the Dissolution of it by a Thaw, which with in a few hours melted it, made it not capable of lying under the contemplation of so many *Witnesses* as it might have been worthy of. The *Bloody Shower* that went before the suffering of the ancient *Britains* from the Picts, (a sort of People that painted themselves like our *Indians*) this Prodigy seem'd a second Edition of.

And in the opinion of the most Critical Observers, throughout the Countrey, they were *prodigious*, or at least, *Uncommon* SIGHTS and SOUNDS, which on the first of *October*, in the Year, 1689. We were entertained withal, and not unlike those which *Pliny* mentions as *presages* to the *Cimbric* Wars of old. For on that Day, in the Morning, while the *Sky* was too clear, to give us a suspicion of any thing like Thunder approaching, there suddenly Blazed a *Flame*, in the fashion of a *Sword*; which Blaze after a continuance, far longer than that of an ordinary *Lightning*, expired in a smoke that gave Terror unto the Beholders of it. But hereunto succeeded immediately very terrible and Repeated Noises, exactly like *Volleys* of *small Shot*, not without *Reports* like those of Great Guns superadded thereunto. *This* was a *Scaene* which all the Colonies of this large Countrey, and Thousands of People, at once were Spectators of, carrying in it, *something*, beyond the *known Laws* which ordinary *Meteors* are Conform'd unto. And herein was indeed One Circumstance, that gave Demonstration, of something *Rare* and *Great* in this Occurrent; That persons which were Distant from one another many scores of Miles above an

---

and Legends of Our Own Land, Philadelphia and London, 1896, I, 238–241). The New Haven specter ship similarly passes from Winthrop to Cotton Mather to Whittier to Skinner, and is transposed from uncommon fact to familiar fiction.

Hundred, yet at the same Time, both *Saw* and *Heard* the whole of what is now related.[7]

A more secularized society by the eighteenth century no longer accepted fanciful story as God-made history. Hutchinson in his history of Massachusetts relegated Winthrop's flame spirit to a footnote, with a patronizing comment.

From manuscripts and printed accounts I could collect as many prodigies in one part of the country and another, at different times, as would fill a small volume. Guns fired in the air, great quantities of clay cast up in form of bullets out of the earth, and the like; but I shall take no notice of any other than this, which is related by one of the best historians with great seriousness, as if he had no doubt of the truth of it.[8]

But if Hutchinson considered such matters unworthy of credence, and so of mention, they continued to travel along the humbler levels, oral and literary, of eighteenth century popular rumor. "Gossip and scandal had free play and there was a love of the marvellous and easy belief of the most incredible things which gave spice to many quiet lives and secluded homes. . . . Omens and portents and prodigies were much in evidence. The newspapers of the mid-century give us glimpses now and then of the tales that were circulated and credited."[9] Mysterious defections from the ordinary course of natural laws came under the heading of news, if not of providences — even in the baking of puddings.

We are at present amus'd with a very odd Story from Martha's Vineyard, which however is affirm'd for a Truth by some Persons lately come from

[7] *The Way to Prosperity* (Boston, 1690). Thomas J. Holmes provides a modern parallel to these phenomena in an Associated Press dispatch for Aug. 29, 1936, just prior to Mussolini's invasion of Ethiopia: "Mark on Eggs Seen as Omen of War" (T. J. Holmes, *Cotton Mather: A Bibliography of his Works*, Cambridge; Harvard University Press, 1940, III, 1207).

[8] Thomas Hutchinson, *The History of Massachusetts* (Salem, 1795), I, 120n. The historian referred to is not Winthrop but Hubbard, who has repeated (*General History of New England*, p. 425) Winthrop's apparition story. Kenneth B. Murdock has pointed out that Hubbard was much more reserved than his fellow historians in accepting providences ("William Hubbard and the Providential Interpretation of History," *Proceedings of the American Antiquarian Society*, vol. 52, pt. I (1942), pp. 15–37); Hutchinson in criticizing Hubbard's credulity therefore signalizes the complete break with Puritan historiography and its unintended leaning toward folklore.

[9] Thomas F. Waters, *Ipswich in the Massachusetts Bay Colony* (Ipswich, 1917), II, 271–272.

thence, *viz.* That at a certain House in Edgar Town, a Plain Indian Pudding, being put into the Pot and boil'd the usual Time, it came out of a Blood-red Colour, to the great Surprise of the whole Family. The Cause of this great Alteration in the Pudding is not yet known, tho' it has been Matter of great Speculation in that Neighborhood.[10]

The following remarkable Phaenomenon it is said may be depended on for truth, as several Persons of undoubted Veracity were Witnesses to the Fact, viz. "That a Woman at Walpole, one Day last Week, made two Loaves of Bread, consisting wholly of Indian Meal, mixed with clear Water; when she took them out of the Oven, one of them was as red or of a deeper red than if it was mixed with Blood, except one Streak thro' the Middle of it was white as natural; and the other Loaf of natural Colour, except a Streak in the Middle as red as any of the other Loaf; which was very affecting to the Baker and many others to behold." — (*We have lately heard of several other very strange Stories from the Country, but for want of more authentic Information we shall defer publishing them for the present.*) [11]

Speculation on such matters led to a plausible explanation.

They write from Plymouth, that an extraordinary Event has lately happen'd in that Neighborhood, in which, some say, the Devil and the Man of the House are very much to blame. The Man, it seems would now and then in a Frolick call upon the Devil to come down the Chimney; and some little Time after the last Invitation, the good Wife's Pudding turn'd black in the boiling, which she attributed to the Devil's descending the Chimney, and getting into the Pot, upon her Husband's repeated Wishes for him. Great Numbers of Peoples have been to view the Pudding, and to enquire into the Circumstances; and most of them agree, that the sudden Change must be produc'd by a Preternatural Power. But some good Housewives of a Chymical Turn assign a Natural Cause for it. However, 'tis thought, it will have this good Effect upon the Man, that he will no more be so free with the Devil in his Cups, lest his Satanick Majesty should again unluckily tumble into the Pot.[12]

Into the news columns filtered pranks played on innocent mortals by invisible beings.

We have the following odd affair related to us by a Gentleman of this town, who was an eye witness to it, viz. That on Monday the 16th of March last, the Rev. Mr. Barrett of Hopkinton, in this province, was walking in the high-way in that town, near the house of Mr. John Abbe, with

[10] *New-England Courant*, Mar. 19-Mar. 26, 1722.
[11] *Boston Evening-Post*, May 25, 1767.
[12] *New-England Courant*, Feb. 1-Feb. 8, 1725.

a Great Coat round his shoulders, but on a sudden he missed it, and after looking some considerable time, he saw it at about one hundred yards from him, hanging on a tree, near thirty feet from the ground. — We must reasonably suppose that it was taken off by some *invisible* hand, as it was a very calm time, and not wind enough to blow off his hat. — The coat was taken down and weighed by some Gentlemen then present, and found to weigh above five pounds. *Oh! Strange!* [13]

The hand of Calvin's God still struck infidels with sudden reversals of natural laws.

Another strange Report has also been current for some Time past, and we imagine of equal Truth with the above, viz. That a Man near Albany, contrary to the Advice and Entreaties of his Friends, lately went out to Work in his Field on the Lord's Day with a Pair of Oxen, and were all turn'd into Statues where 'tis said they remain immoveably fixed as Examples of God's Judgment against Sabbath breakers. [14]

Or perhaps His Voice had been heard to command.

A report prevails that some unaccountable noises were lately heard near Hartford; and 'tis said, via Derby, that a few men being lately at work in a wood they were terrified with an extraordinary Voice, commanding them to read the seventh chap. of Ezekiel. [15]

Dreams and prophecies enlarged the roll of unaccountable phenomena and accentuated the mysterious design of ordered events.

We hear from Wrentham, That on Friday the 19th of April past, an Occurrence somewhat remarkable happened there; Mr. John Day of that Town having rais'd a large House and cover'd it; one of his Sons dreamt for three several Nights, that the Roof thereof was blown off, and had but just related his Dream to one of his Brethren, when it was fulfill'd, a sudden Squal of Wind, or rather a Whirlwind, just circumambient about the said House, carry'd off half the Roof of it Spars and all, except those of the gable End, and taring it into two parts, one part fell to the Ground, and the Nails being violently forc'd out, it shatter'd to pieces; the other part was in a strange manner blown up into the Air a considerable highth, where it was turn'd bottom up, & then fell on the Garret Floor entire. [16]

[13] *Boston Evening-Post*, April 20, 1767, supplement; *New Hampshire Gazette*, April 24, 1767. From Providence.

[14] *Boston Evening-Post*, Dec. 31, 1764. The report alluded to concerned a traveler attacked on the road by the landlord he had stayed with the preceding night.

[15] *Boston Evening-Post*, Aug. 4, 1766.

[16] *Boston News-Letter*, May 2-May 9, 1734.

We hear from Hebron, in Connecticut, that on the 7th instant, Mr. Joseph Allen, of that place, being on horseback with a midwife who had attended his wife, he fell from his horse and expired. — It is remarkable he was telling the woman, *that he had a calf died yesterday very strangely, by turning round two or three times and then dying*; upon his so saying, he sallied upon his horse and expired. A physician being near, he immediately attempted bleeding him, but in vain.[17]

We have an Account from Nottingham, of an exploit performed there lately by a little Girl about Eleven Years old, as follows; The said Girl dreamt that she had killed a Deer in the Woods, after she awoke & got up, she sharpned a little knife, and went out, taking her Dogs with her, and in a short Time came upon the Track of a great old Buck, which she followed with her Dogs about a Mile, when the Dogs seiz'd him, and the Girl got hold of him by the Ear, and would have got upon his Back, but he shook her off, upon which she took her Knife and first cut the Ham String, and then his Throat.[18]

The prodigy slid into the tall tale in an easy transition when marvels of daily life became divorced from supernatural agencies, divine or diabolical.

We hear from Barnstable, that the Wife of a Man in that County was lately delivered of two Children; & besides this Event, which undoubtedly gave him much Pleasure, his Negro Woman, the same night, was also delivered of a Child. He was likewise remarkably successful in the Generation of his domestic Animals, viz. his Cow had two Calves, his Mare a Colt, his Sow a considerable Number of Pigs, his Bitch a Number of Puppies, his Cat kitten'd, and one of his Hens hatch'd a Brood of Chickens — all in one Night.[19]

Witches and wizards. Minions of Satan in covenant with the Fiend to do his bidding, an army of village hags and crones fed petty revenge and vented sour spite through witchery of objects, animals, and persons. A flurry of tattling rumors elevated to unwelcome prominence crabbed spinsters, widows, and goodwives whose errant actions enlivened folk history and sometimes spiced court records. Resident in over a hundred New England communities, witches everywhere performed similar mischiefs and succumbed to identical reprisals. As the Yankee magnetized popular fancies in the humorous mood of the nineteenth century, so did the witch in the superstitious mood of the

[17] *Boston Evening-Post*, May 4, 1761.   [19] *Boston Evening-Post*, Nov. 12, 1764.
[18] *Boston News-Letter*, Aug. 9-Aug. 16, 1733.

eighteenth. Both were stock figures manipulated in a series of characteristic practices by facile imaginations; but where the type Yankee evolved as the composite image of a salty native breed of rural characters and achieved an independent fictional existence, the bogey witch figure lay already implanted in men's minds, whence it draped its sinister form-fitting cloak over likely individuals.

In popular tales the witch most often appeared as a vengeful wielder of magic. Denied a favor or request, she plagues the property of the refuser. When Moll Cramer asked in vain for a piece of pork, a blight fell upon that man's kine and they could never be fattened again.[1] Zechariah Davis forgot to bring Goody Davis the "small passell of winges" he had promised her, whereupon his calf fell to dancing and roaring, would not suck, sat on his tail like a dog, and remained in fits until he died.[2] Not granted any of the ten fine pigs in the litter, the witch cursed her neighbor and shortly they all jumped over the fence and ran away.[3] The sale of walnuts displeased a certain elderly lady in old Haverhill; that night neither vendor nor his wife could sleep for the rattling of walnuts on the kitchen hearth; in the morning all were piled up in a pyramid on the hearthstone, returned by the witch.[4] Refused conveyance, an old woman curses the traveler, whose horse when next approaching the meeting place balks and will go no further.[5] A man disliked by Dame Tucker drove past her house, when she ran out to the road and snapped her fingers at the oxen, upon which the yoke fell off and the man was obliged to turn back.[6] When Susanna Trimmings would not lend her cotton, Goody Walford threatened her; Susanna was struck as with a clap of fire on the back and could not speak until her husband unlaced and pinched her.[7] Dissatisfied with a horse trade between her husband and Samuel Dag-

---

[1] William Cothren, *History of Ancient Woodbury, Conn.* (Waterbury, Conn., 1854), I, 160.

[2] Walter Harriman, *The History of Warner, N.H.* (Concord, N.H., 1879), p. 548.

[3] John M. Currier, "Contributions to New England Folk-Lore," *Journal of American Folk-Lore*, IV (July-September 1891), 254–255 [Grafton County, N.H.].

[4] William Little, *History of Warren, N.H.* (Manchester, N.H., 1870), p. 432.

[5] C. C. Lord, "Manners and Customs in Hopkinton — No. 4," *Granite Monthly*, II (June 1879), 283.

[6] Frank H. Craig, *Sketches of the Town of Topsham, Vt.* (Bradford, Vt., 1929), p. 67.

[7] John Albee, *New Castle [N.H.] Historic and Picturesque* (Boston, 1884), p. 83.

gett, Mrs. Esensa was heard to remark that the horse had "always been a plague, and would never do the Daggetts any good." Not long after the horse was mysteriously untied in the stable, and could never thereafter be confined within the barn with even the most complicated horse knots; people came from all parts of town to see the animal.[8] Informed by Mrs. Emerson that she and her daughters were too busy to prepare a breakfast for her, the old woman with the evil eye prophesies they will do little work that day; until nightfall the front door will not open, passers-by do not hear their calls from the window, and poor Sally misses her tryst with her lover.[9]

In the majority of enchantments fire could be fought with fire; proper treatment of the bewitched object or animal severely affected the witch. Most frequent case of domestic witchery, the butter that would not come, called for various related remedies. A hot poker plunged into the churn brought a loud scream; the butter then came, and Mrs. Kimball was reported to have a bad burn on one of her legs.[10] A heated horseshoe dropped into the cream burned out the witch.[11] Sally Tripp died just as the butter yielded to a furious pounding of the dash.[12] A heated crane hook dipped into the churn brings the butter, and shortly a woman dies with a terrible burn on the back of her neck in the shape of a crane hook.[13] A farmer fires his musket through the recalcitrant churn and soon the butter comes; but that day, at the time of the shooting, an old woman was taken suddenly with a fit and died without any apparent cause.[14] Strangely on one occasion immersion of a red hot "cops pin" brought no butter and caused no inconvenience to the suspect.[15]

[8] John L. Sibley, *A History of the Town of Union, Me.* (Boston, 1851), pp. 228–229.

[9] *New Hampshire Folk Tales*, Mrs. Moody P. Gore and Mrs. Guy E. Speare, compilers (n.p., 1932), pp. 153–157 [Barnstead].

[10] George F. Plummer, *History of the Town of Wentworth, N.H.* (Concord, N.H., 1930), p. 345.

[11] Cothren, *History of Ancient Woodbury, Conn.*, I, 160.

[12] "Old Witch Legend Still Clings to Part of Falmouth," *Portland [Me.] Telegram*, Oct. 7, 1934.

[13] Gore and Speare, *New Hampshire Folk Tales*, p. 172 [Meredith, N.H.].

[14] Samuel Orcutt, *A History of the Old Town of Stratford and the City of Bridgeport, Conn.* (New Haven, Conn., 1886), I, 146.

[15] Lucy R. H. Cross, *History of Northfield, N.H.* (Concord, N.H., 1905), pt. I, pp. 221–222.

Special ways of handling witches were preserved by tradition. Needles, pen-knives, or bradawls placed in the tracks of a witch caused cessation of motion until they were removed[16] or words were uttered.[17] Sweet bays under the threshold deterred Rachel Fuller who crowded in on the side of the door left free. [18] When medicines had no effect on a sick woman, the doctor had her bled and threw the blood into the fire; immediately the patient began to improve while old Mrs. Rice had her hands terribly burned just at that time.[19] Rusty pins and needles might be boiled in the blood of the afflicted.[20] A strapping girl witch-tortured without relief was finally freed by the expedient of lopping off the head of a live rooster into a kettle of boiling water.[21] A Salem sailor recommended to Aunt Peggy of Beals Island, Maine, a method of combating the witch who had killed her sheep: scorch the sheep over a hot fire; a boat would come over three times for something, but she should refuse to give the article. The day following the third refusal the witch died.[22] Other tales relate the demand of the witch's messenger for an article possessed by the exerciser; when the witch is burned out of the cream, her child comes rushing over for medicine, and upon its refusal she dies.[23] An elaborate remedy of ancient repute was resorted to by a farmer who had seen witches dancing along the crane in the fireplace at midnight and whose cattle were afflicted. From tallow and beeswax he moulded an image of the offending woman, hung the effigy before the fireplace, and as it melted stuck it full of thorns from the thorn-apple; at the same hour the woman whose spell had plagued the cattle fell down stairs and broke her neck.[24] (In their

[16] *Granite Monthly*, II (June 1879), 284; Gore and Speare, pp. 161–162, 174; William R. Bliss, *The Old Colony Town and Other Sketches* (Boston and New York, 1893), pp. 109–110.

[17] *Journal of American Folk-Lore*, IV (July-September 1891), 254 [Grafton County, N.H.].

[18] Joseph Dow, *History of the Town of Hampton, N.H.* (Salem, Mass., 1893), I, 85.

[19] Silvanus Hayward, *History of the Town of Gilsum, N.H.* (Manchester, N.H., 1881), p. 162.

[20] "Old Time Witch Stories of Berwick Reveal Widespread Belief in Sorcery," *Portland [Me.] Herald*, June 24, 1935.

[21] Harry H. Cochrane, *History of Monmouth and Wales* [Me.] (East Winthrop, 1894), I, 216–218.

[22] *Maine: A Guide 'Down East,'* Federal Writers' Project (Boston, 1937), pp. 233–234.

[23] Gore and Speare, pp. 171–172 [Lee].

[24] Frederic P. Wells, *History of Newbury, Vt.* (St. Johnsbury, Vt., 1902), pp. 337–338.

turn witches tormented victims by sticking pins in their effigies.) [25]

The malignant powers of witches in many instances brooked no interference. In their more sportive moods witches delighted to reverse or upset the natural order of things. Black Marea twisted about the heads of a flock of geese so that they were forced to travel backwards and could not pick grain or gravel off the ground; to fatten them for market the farmer had to place food on their backs.[26] The witch of Charmingfare upset loads of hay on level ground and detached the revolving wheels from the wagon of a farmer she disliked.[27] The witch of Whitingham turned the cattle and everything else in the barn wrongside up.[28] The witch of Weare made the tongue pin of an ox team seventy-five miles away pop out every time the team got under way.[29] Besides wringing off the necks of hens and chickens, upsetting a calf and bleeding sheep to death, a witch in York caused household utensils to jump into the fire and spoons to disappear from the table.[30] In Simpson Hollow an unknown hand, suspected to be Granny Bates, perpetrated strange pranks on the Wilbur family, slashing clothes on the clothesline, hiding beads, and placing odd articles in the dye tub.[31] Witches in Norton unloosed tied cattle, turned oxen's yokes, and made wheels part from passing wagons.[32] After riding all night with Aunt Jinny to the poorhouse, the officer found himself in front of her house in the morning.[33] Black witch art drew a calf through a barn knothole and wedged it into a hollow log.[34] A favorite form of witch-cunning compelled passing teamsters to stop at the tavern operated by the charmer or her husband and buy liquor — or so they claimed.[35]

[25] Bliss, *Old Colony Town*, p. 110.

[26] *Portland Herald*, June 24, 1935.

[27] F. B. Eaton, *History of Candia* [N.H.] (Manchester, N.H., 1852), p. 118.

[28] Clark Jillson, *Green Leaves from Whitingham, Vt.* (Worcester, Mass., 1894), p. 111.

[29] Cornelius Weygandt, *November Rowen* (New York and London, 1941), p. 42.

[30] Edward C. Moody, *Handbook History of the Town of York* [Me.] (Augusta, Me., n.d.), pp. 183–184.

[31] Clifton Johnson, *What They Say in New England* (Boston, 1896), pp. 242–244.

[32] George F. Clark, *A History of the Town of Norton, Mass.* (Boston, 1859), pp. 532–533.

[33] *More New Hampshire Folk Tales*, Mrs. Guy E. Speare, compiler (Plymouth, N.H., 1936), p. 206.

[34] Francis Chase, *Gathered Sketches, New Hampshire and Vermont* (Claremont, N.H., 1856), pp. 116–120.

[35] Warren R. Cochrane, *History of the Town of Antrim, N.H.* (Manchester, N.H.,

In most virulent form witchery caused torture and death. Mammy Red of Marblehead, besides venial habits of curdling the milk in the milk pail and turning butter to blue wool, wished that a bloody cleaver might be found on the cradles of infant children, and whenever the cleaver was distinctly seen the children sickened and died.[36] When the Godfreys' child died, wife and daughter testified that Rachel Fuller came in with face daubed with molasses, and when the mother drew the sick child's hand away, Rachel smote the back of her hands together and spat in the fire.[37] Witch-riding served as a pastime and means of transport but also inflicted torment. Tangible evidence of the practice lay in witch bridles, brightly colored strings full of curious knots;[38] flung over straw, they caused ponies to appear;[39] thrown upon the face of a sleeper with an incantation, they harnessed his spirit.[40] Broomsticks were used as steeds; Witch Webber averred she had stubbed her toe when broom-riding over the roof of a barn on Dimond Hill, and upon investigating the owner found a few shingles had been detached.[41] The witch of Windmill Hill, beleagured in her house, assuredly escaped up the chimney on a broomstick, for the house was empty save for a handleless broom when courageous ones entered.[42] Not only Witch Bentham but her thirteen-year-old daughter were believed to ride tandem with the devil on nightly journeys.[43]

But the preferred mounts were human. A rheumatic invalid explained his lameness by saying that old Sally Tripp turned him into a horse and drove him up and down Hurricane Hill every night beating him

1880), pp. 315–316; Charles J. Smith, *Annals of the Town of Hillsborough, N.H.,* (Sanbornton, N.H., 1841), p. 29.

[36] Samuel Roads, *The History and Traditions of Marblehead* [Mass.] (Marblehead, 1897), p. 33.

[37] Dow, *History of the Town of Hampton, N.H.,* I, 84.

[38] Edwin Emery, *The History of Sanford, Me.* (Fall River, Mass., 1901), p. 519; *Granite Monthly,* II (June 1879), 283.

[39] Bliss, *Old Colony Town,* pp. 106–107.

[40] John M. Currier, "Contributions to the Folk-Lore of New England," *Journal of American Folk-Lore,* II (October-December 1889), 292.

[41] Gore and Speare, p. 167 [Hopkinton, N.H.].

[42] Fannie S. Chase, *Wiscasset in Pownalborough* (Wiscasset, Me., 1941), pp. 622–623.

[43] C. Bancroft Gillespie and George M. Curtis, *A Century of Meriden* (Meriden, Conn., 1906), pt. I, pp. 257–258.

with a whip.[44] The mysterious rifling of the Noyes' cupboard was cleared up long after by a Scotch teamster who recalled how he had been
changed into a horse, ridden to the Noyes' house and chained to a post
with other horses while a party of witches entered and helped themselves to wine, bread, butter, preserves, tarts, pies, and even some sweet-
tasting medicine.[45] After Skipper Perkins demanded a sixpence for the
fish old Betsey Booker asked of him, her eyes followed his boat out of
the harbor, and the skipper caught no fish that day. That night a violent
storm arose, and the hag penetrated into the skipper's house with a train
of witches who stripped him bare; in a trice old Betsey bridled and
mounted him, while her sisters clung to her back and prodded their
steed to make him speed the more. All night they rode to York and
back again through the shrieking gale, and Skipper Perkins nursed his
hurts abed for three weeks.[46] In West Barnstable a Mr. Wood charged
Liza Tower Hill with putting a bridle and saddle on him and riding
him many times to Plum Pudding Pond in Plymouth, where witches
held nightly orgies.[47] Captain Sylvanus Rich, gale tossed at sea, fell
deadly ill and his flesh rotted away; he swore to the crew that every
night an old woman who had sold him a bucket of milk before the voyage entered the cabin through the lazaret, saddled and bridled him,
and drove him over the hills and through the woods of Truro. When
the ship and the captain were both nearly done for, a rescue vessel overtook the drifting wreck, and Captain Rich was no longer plagued by a
spectral old woman riding the ocean billows in tiny eggshells.[48] Sometimes the witch-rid victim suffered no more than self-delusion; in the
morning visitors of the tormented one found the bedpost gnawed and
the bedclothes in violent filth and disarray from the convulsions of a
nightmare.[49] Tuggy Bannock spied a prize creeper sheep dressed in an
improvised garment to compensate for the loss of its wool, and hasten-

---

[44] *Portland Telegram*, Oct. 7, 1934.
[45] Little, *History of Warren, N.H.*, p. 433n.
[46] Whitney Elkins, *The Story of Maine* (Bangor, 1924), pp. 170–171.
[47] Amos Otis, *Genealogical Notes of Barnstable Families* (Barnstable, Mass., 1888),
p. 101.
[48] Shebnah Rich, *Truro — Cape Cod, or Land Marks and Sea Marks* (Boston, c. 1883),
p. 184.
[49] *Yankee Blade*, Jan. 22, 1853 (vol. XII); Little, *History of Warren, N.H.*, p. 439.

ing home to brew a witch broth, related how she had been witch rid by ole Mum Amey, whom she recognized by her red and blue blanket.[50]

One power above all others distinguished the village witch, that of transformation. Sundry were the animals and birds whose forms housed an evil spirit — cats, dogs, rabbits, cows, horses, bulls, hogs, sheep, crows, pigs. When the enchanted animal was beaten or bruised, the ill effects displayed themselves on the body of the witch: a pig kicked, she limps; a horse struck on the head, she appears with a patch over one eye; a sheep beaten, she goes into fits; a cat scalded, her back is afflicted with St. Anthony's fire; a large black bug knocked to the floor with a stick, she falls downstairs and breaks her leg.[51] Josselyn told of "a Witch that appeared aboard of a Ship twenty leagues to Sea to a Mariner who took up the Carpenters broad Axe and cleft her head with it, the Witch dying of the wound at home." [52] Burning the tips of the ears and tails of a bewitched horse, cow, or pig undid the charm, and usually caused death to the witch.[53] Impervious to ordinary bullets, the bewitched bird or animal succumbed to silver pellets. A swimming black cat is shot at sea with a silver button, and on land the witch dies.[54] A crow hovering over soldiers at Louisburg is wounded with a silver sleeve button, and Peg Wesson, who had threatened them, falls with a fractured leg in Gloucester, the button imbedded in her flesh.[55] A lost hunter who could not frighten a rabbit away loaded his musket with a silver sleeve button and shot it; the witch was killed and the pathway appeared plain

[50] Anna S. Nugent, "The Witch Sheep," *Facts and Fancies Concerning North Kingstown, R.I.* (North Kingstown, 1941), pp. 47, 49; Alice M. Earle, *In Old Narragansett* (New York, 1898), pp. 103–119.

[51] Craig, *Sketches of . . . Topsham*, p. 67; Daniel F. Secomb, *History of the Town of Amherst, N.H.* (Concord, N.H., 1883), p. 471; Gore and Speare, p. 168 [Peterborough, N.H.]; Speare, p. 206 [Hillsborough, N.H.]; Rebecca I. Davis, *Gleanings from Merrimac Valley: Sheaf Number Two* (Haverhill, 1886), pp. 41–42.

[52] "Josselyn's Account of Two Voyages to New-England," *Mass. Hist. Soc. Colls.*, 3d series, III, 332.

[53] Sibley, *History of the Town of Union, Me.*, p. 229; Edgar Gilbert, *History of Salem, N.H.* (Concord, N.H., 1907), pp. 348–349; Gore and Speare, p. 170. [Salem, N.H.]; Little, *History of Warren, N.H.*, pp. 433–434.

[54] Donald G. Trayser, *Barnstable, Three Centuries of a Cape Cod Town* (Hyannis, Mass., 1939), p. 325.

[55] James R. Pringle, *History of the Town and City of Gloucester, Mass.* (Gloucester, 1892), p. 62; Henry C. Leonard, *Pigeon Cove and Vicinity* (Boston, 1873), pp. 77–78.

before him.[56] A farmer whose oxen stopped when a black cat jumped on the reach pole, shot it with a silver button; some days later a woman fell on a stump, breaking her hip, and the button was found in her body.[57] Another farmer shot in vain at a circling bird, then ripped a silver button from his shirt and fired it with success; an old woman in a cabin five miles away grasped her side and fell dead.[58] A youthful hunter whose point-blank shots at a dignified raccoon had not the least effect at last cut a young witch hazel, sharpened and fitted it to the bore of his gun, and discharged it full into the face of his adversary. The coon was never seen again, but an elderly and unpopular lady in the neighborhood was rumored to be badly wounded in the face by some unaccountable accident.[59] Beatings restored bewitched objects to obedience: a driver whips the wheels of his cart, which then moves while an old woman nearby is covered with wales; the owner of a bewitched house strikes a beam with an axe, freeing the spell and laming the witch.[60] Witches were not always caught. Blows and bullet did not avail against the witch of Hopkins Hill in Rhode Island who, when attempts were made to break the magic circle around her rock, turned aside the plow and appeared successively as a crow, a beldame with a cocked hat, and a black cat which vanished into the ground.[61] Goody Walford changed from her costume of white linen hood, red waistcoat and petticoat, green apron and black hat into a yellow cat that defied shooting and disappeared.[62]

A certain class of witches, less common than the ordinary vexatious meddlers, specialized in necromancy, curses, prophecies, and powers of second sight. A condemned witch clutched a stone on the way to the gallows that ever after bore the fingerprints of Goody Basset.[63] Sen-

[56] Leonard A. Morrison, *The History of Windham in New Hampshire* (Boston, 1883), p. 242. Told of "Old Rif," said to be the last slave in New Hampshire.

[57] *Rhode Island: A Guide to the Smallest State*, Federal Writers' Project (Boston, 1937), p. 109 [Exeter].

[58] Skinner, *Myths and Legends of Our Own Land*, II, 48 [Haddam, Conn.].

[59] *The History of Medway, Mass.*, E. O. Jameson, ed. (Millis, Mass., c. 1886), p. 15.

[60] *History of Medway*, p. 16; Davis, *Gleanings from Merrimac Valley*, p. 47.

[61] Skinner, *Myths and Legends*, II, 32–33; Clarence M. Webster, *Town Meeting Country* (New York, c. 1945), p. 81.

[62] Albee, *New Castle Historic and Picturesque*, pp. 82–84; Harriman, *History of Warner, N.H.*, pp. 546–547.

[63] Orcutt, *History of . . . Stratford and . . . Bridgeport, Conn.*, I, 246.

tenced to die by Colonel Buck, the witch placed a curse upon him that took the form of an indelible leg mark on his monument.[64] An old woman fell helplessly on the ground alongside a brook; two passing boys jeered and stoned her, but a third carried her home and cared for her. Her prophecy that they will come to no good while he will be rich and respected is borne out.[65] When five drunken youths burned the house of Granny Hicks for turning into a woodchuck and bewitching a baby, Granny stood on a stump and prophesied the manner of their retributive deaths.[66] Molly Molasses of Wiscasset, Maine, was believed to possess the power of a shaman or witch doctor and be able accurately to prophesy coming events;[67] "Tammy" Younger, a tusked, snuff-taking, tobacco-smoking favorite of Cape Ann seamen enjoyed wide repute as a fortuneteller, and at her funeral was honored with a silver-plated coffin.[68] A vagrant fortuneteller, Jeffrey Martin, blasted crops, dried milch cows, and struck barns with lightning; when Chloe Wilbur refused him a drink, he foretold that her husband would have a withered left arm and her oldest son would drown in a seething river. When both predictions had come true, Chloe acknowledged, "Joe lived in constant terror of the Curse all his life." [69]

One witch of prophetic gift transcended all others in renown.

The celebrated witch Moll Pitcher died at Lynn, Mass. in 1813. This person has been more celebrated than any other witch of modern times. Not only was her name known in most towns throughout the United States but her fame extended to Europe. Many persons came from places far remote, to consult with her on affairs of love or loss of property, or to obtain her surmises respecting the vicissitudes of their future fortune. Every youth who was not assured of the reciprocal affection of his fair one, and every maid who was desirous of anticipating the hour of her highest felicity, repaired at evening to the humble dwelling of Moll Pitcher, which stood on a lonely road in Lynn, near High Rock, with a single habitation nearly opposite, at the gate of which stood two bones of a whale. Her skill was principally exercised for the discovery of things

---

[64] *Maine: A Guide 'Down East,'* p. 274; *New England Magazine,* XXVII (September 1902), 111–113.

[65] Gore and Speare, pp. 260–265 [Lancaster, N.H.].

[66] Gore and Speare, pp. 158–159 [New Hampton, N.H.].

[67] Chase, *Wiscasset in Pownalborough,* pp. 24–25.

[68] George W. Solley, *Alluring Rockport* [Mass.] (n.p., n.d.), pp. 99–100.

[69] Abbie P. Gardner, "The Ancient Curse," *Facts and Fancies Concerning North Kingstown, R.I.,* pp. 39–41.

lost; and she never was very malicious in her witcheries. When a gentleman once offered her a large sum if she would inform him what ticket would draw the highest prize in a lottery, "Do you think," said she, "if I knew, I should not buy it myself?" [70]

Twice told fireside tales sometimes pictured Moll in conventional guise, an old woman who bewitched her neighbors' cattle and passing teamsters' horses that she might receive a few pennies for her timely medical assistance, and who finally was punished by having an ear cropped.[71] Again she looms as a personality of some distinction: local witches flew to Lynn to attend convocations of the weird sisters at which Moll presided;[72] in turn she visited alien localities which remember her in folk history. A local legend of Brookline, New Hampshire, memoralizes a prophecy made by Moll near the Devil's Den.

In connection with this cave and Little Muscatanipus hill, the writer many years ago heard the late Samuel Talbot relate the following legend; which he claimed to have heard when a boy, many times told by his father, Ezra Talbot, who lived on the west slope of the hill. It is a witch story; and one of the few of that kind which have survived here from the early days of the town. It dates back to a period in the country's history immediately following the close of the Revolution, when New England was flooded with witch stories in which the celebrated Moll Pitcher was the heroine; her reputation as a witch having been established from the fact that, owing to the insufficient methods then in use for the dissemination of news, the brave deeds which, as a soldier in man's clothing, she performed in the Patriot army while fighting by the side of her husband in its ranks, were, in their transmission throughout the country, so changed, and the real facts so altered and distorted, as to impress the general public with the idea that she was endowed with supernatural powers.

But to return to the story. Moll Pitcher once made a visit to this town, where she was for a brief period the guest of one of its citizens. One day while walking out with her host and a party of his friends, prompted, perhaps, by a desire of pleasing him and them as a slight return for their hospitality, she suddenly stopped in a small cleared space near the den, and, standing erect with uplifted hands, began to mutter what appeared to them to be incantations. As the moments passed, her gestures became more and more violent, and her language more wild and incoherent. Suddenly, to the great surprise, and, very probably, to the consternation of her audience, an old sow with a litter of twelve pigs issued from the surrounding woods

---

[70] *The American Comic Almanac, 1837* (Boston, n.d.).

[71] Mrs. Bathsheba H. Crane, *Life, Letters, and Wayside Gleanings for the Folks at Home* (Boston, c. 1880), p. 36.

[72] *Granite Monthly*, II (June 1879), 283.

and began to run around her in a circle. Twelve times they circled around her form and then disappeared; vanishing as suddenly as they came. With their disappearance the witch resumed her normal condition, and proceeded to inform her astonished hearers that the day would come when silver and gold would be dug out of that hill by the cart load. The witch's prophecy is as yet unfulfilled; but the citizens of today are still able to point with pride to the cave, and also to the hill, the most important concomitants necessary to its fulfillment.[73]

Where witches, save for Moll Pitcher, possessed little individuality and could easily have exchanged roles in separate wispy tales, wizards had colorful detail. Simeon Smith differed little from the common witch in most of his artifice but stamped himself in village tradition with considerably more distinction.

The archwizard and head necromancer of our town was no doubt Simeon Smith. He, it was commonly believed, had supernatural powers and thereby made his neighbors very uncomfortable times.

"Wonderful were the feats he could perform. Sometimes, from sheer malice, he would saddle and bridle one of his neighbors and gallop him all over the country round. The butter would not come, and he was in the churn. The cat mewed and tore wildly about the house, and he was tormenting her. The children behaved strangely and he had bewitched them. Smaller than a gnat, he could go through the keyhole; larger than a giant, he was seen at twilight stalking through the forest. He could travel in the thin air and, mounted on a moonbeam, fly swift as a meteor over the woods and above the mountains." [74]

Simeon first gained his reputation by hastily leaving the meeting house one Sunday to announce that a great Revolutionary battle was then in progress; in his fits of second sight he sat abstracted on his motionless horse, perhaps gazing upon fiendish revels. An ardent rebel, he bewitched deaf Caleb, son of Merrill the Tory, and caused him to run up the sides of house or barn like a squirrel and traverse ridgepoles of the highest roofs with the greatest ease. Finally, to relieve Caleb from his tortures, neighbors corked the boy's urine in a bottle by the hearth; immediately Simeon was taken with a violent bleeding at the nose, until the urine ran out through a cut in the cork. When the torments continued, Caleb's blood was placed in the bottle and a small

[73] Edward E. Parker, *History of Brookline, N.H.* (n.p., n.d.), pp. 34-35. The New England witch is here confused with Molly Pitcher, the Revolutionary War heroine of Pennsylvania.
[74] Plummer, *History of . . . Wentworth, N.H.*, p. 344.

sword inserted in the cork. Next morning Caleb gleefully informed his family by signs that Simeon was dead; such indeed was the case, and examination of the bottle found that the sword had penetrated the cork to the blood. The wizard was buried under an apple tree according to his request, and thenceforth boys never stole from that tree again — possibly because the apples were crabbed and bitter beyond belief.[75]

In the coastal town of Marblehead a rival sorcerer became notorious, "old Dimond," who possessed the black art of divination. Persons traveled long distances to benefit by his advice, for good or for ill, but the seer used his powers with justice: he charmed a thief who had stolen firewood from a poor widow, and made him walk all night with a heavy log of wood on his back; to an aged couple robbed of their money he revealed the name of the culprit and the site of the cache. On stormy nights old Dimond took his stand on the burying hill, and roared above the tempest his orders to imperiled ships at sea, orders that none fearing shipwreck dared disobey.[76]

Indian traditions of the renowned Passaconaway, "Child of the Bear," infiltrated into folkstory of the white man. Like all powwows this sagamore, whose dominions embraced the land from Merrimac River to Cape Porpoise, inherited his powers from the Indian devil: powers to make water burn, rocks move, trees dance; to raise a green leaf from the ashes of a dry one, produce a live snake from the skin of a dead one; to heal sickness and cause death by incantations. Bright plumes covered his head, bear and catamount skins robed his body, a necklace of fishbones dangled on his chest; in the chase he outsped the moose and the mountain cat, wrestled with bears and choked rattlesnakes; his heavy club shook the earth, no warrior could bend his bow, his feathered arrows disappeared in the sky. In a hickory sledge drawn by wolves he raced up sacred Mount Agiochook (Washington) to see his spirit father, king of the Penacooks, and rode off the mountain top skywards in a cloud of fire.[77]

[75] Little, *History of Warren*, N.H., pp. 226, 436–439.
[76] Roads, *History and Traditions of Marblehead*, pp. 42–43; and *History of Essex County, Mass.*, D. H. Hurd, compiler (Philadelphia, 1888), II, 1069. The frontispiece to Joseph S. Robinson, *The Story of Marblehead* (Boston, c. 1936), shows old Dimond hurling his orders across the sea.
[77] See p. 16, n. 4; also John Farmer and Jacob B. Moore, *Collections, Historical and*

Probably the most extraordinary exercise of New England wizardry occurred at Hallowell, Maine, credited to a character well known in the folklore of the town. This native legend is unusual in containing a magic motive.

OLD KALF OF HALLOWELL WAS A VERY QUEER MAN

Old Kalf was a queer character. He owned the laziest horse in Kennebec County. But Old Kalf was a very wise man. He had the reputation of being a wizard at making good and bad weather, love philters, and amulets. He could cure sick cattle. In short, he could perform any magic art at your command.

It's the old timers of Hallowell holding one of their frequent street corner chats and recalling another legend of Loudon Hill. This venerable group of men gather for a meeting upon the slightest notice and you have to be fairly well informed to be on hand when they start spinning a yarn from the few threads left by the generation before them.

At the time Old Kalf came to Hallowell — 50 years ago — nearly all the residents of Loudon Hill were seafaring men. . . .

All the time Old Kalf, or Mr. Kaler, as he was sometimes called, lived in an old house near the main road from Hallowell. The dusty road led to Gardiner where there was a large settlement. Down the Kennebec River still farther, at Pownalboro and Fort Richmond, lived the "aristocracy of the county," one old timer recalled.

One warm misty evening in May over 150 years ago, Uncle Kaler heard some horses speeding up the hill. The old man was startled when they stopped at his door. Upon opening it, a man's voice came from the darkness, "Is this Mr. Kaler?"

"It is. I'm at your service," Kalf answered.

"Well, my name is Bridge and this lady with me is Miss Cushing of Pownalboro. We are on our way to Hallowell to be married. Her relatives do not approve of the match and are following us hot foot. Listen!"

Away down the river could be heard the long drawn bay of hounds.

"You see, old man, our horses are about used up and if something isn't done they will overtake us, and that will mean all kinds of trouble. You have the reputation of being a wind-jammer and wizard. Here are a hundred Spanish milled dollars for the worst weather you can produce, and if it does the business, another hundred when I come back," the impatient young man exclaimed.

Miscellaneous, and Monthly Literary Journal (Concord, 1823), II, 89–90. Town histories that paraphrase or quote the seventeenth-century account of Thomas Morton are Jeremiah P. Jewett, *History of Barnstead* [N.H.] (Lowell, Mass., 1872), p. 22; Nathaniel Bouton, *The History of Concord* [N.H.] (Concord, 1856), pp. 21–22; Charles Bradbury, *History of Kennebunk Port* [Me.] (Kennebunk, 1837), pp. 39–40; C. E. Potter, *The History of Manchester, N.H.* (Manchester, 1856), pp. 54–55; Little, *History of Warren, N.H.*, pp. 51–54.

Old Kalf made no reply but went to a chest, took out a small canvas bag, and gave it to the stranger, saying "Go back a little way on the road, cut open the bag, squeeze out the contents, throw the bag away and then come back and resume your journey."

The young man hurriedly did what he was told and returned, breathlessly exclaiming, "If you have played us false ——"

"Rest easy," said Old Kalf. "Hark!" And away in the southwest could be heard a low grumbling like distant thunder. It increased and deepened suddenly, until it seemed as if a cyclone was tearing through the forest.

"What will happen," cried the young lady, who had been standing wide-eyed as if terrified and speechless.

"A cloud burst in the hills. It will take a sharp hound to follow your tracks in five minutes. Go in peace, and good luck with you from a man who can make good luck," said Old Kalf.

Away they sped through the gathering storm and darkness.

Under the rolling thunder and nearly deafened by the roar and crash of the raging torrent he had conjured, the old man went into the house saying to himself, "I'm afraid I made that bagfull too strong. But I don't know that I am sorry, for it would never do to have the young people caught."

The dawn broke clear and beautiful, according to the tale. But where a peaceful little brook had flowed through a green pasture the day before, and a little mill had clattered merrily, grinding out a few grists brought by the neighbors, there was now a deep gorge gullied down to bed rock and choked with uprooted trees and brush.

The mill was gone, and the big boulder that formed part of its foundation had been swept away, far out in the river. It can be seen today and is known as Mill Rock. . . .

One by one the old timers leave, the impromptu meeting adjourned. They head for home, minds and hearts full of memories of the "good old days." The Hallowell Old Timers' Club will meet again some day.[78]

The Devil. If the unseen hand of God raised prodigies in the wilderness, his arch-enemy left very visible footprints. Gargantuan outlines of a cloven hoof seared into rocks all over New England testified to the very corporeal nature of Satan; and popular fictions, taking their cue from the verbal portraits of evangelical Christianity, pictured him as a physical personality with constant attributes, a sly, wily, unscrupulous prowler for hell recruits. In the tales a personal visit by the Fiend to individuals whose moral frailty made them likely prey for his lethal barter — souls for gold — brought disaster or near disaster in its wake. An eighteenth-century newspaper presents a contemporary notice of such a visit.

[78] *Portland* [*Me.*] *Express*, July 3, 1940. Paragraph headings have been eliminated.

47

Last Wednesday Morning, one Mr. Willard, at Braintree, being delirious (and his Watchers going to Sleep) he untied himself, and got out of Doors, took an Ax which he found, and Struck himself on his Head, but it happened to slide off on one side, and did not hurt him very much; afterwards he held the Edge of it upwards, knocked his Neck on it, and jam'd, and cut it terribly. He says the *Devil* told him to eat an Apple, which he did, by which Time the People happened to find him, or 'tis thought he would have killed himself. He said that Mr. *Devil* shall not serve him so again.[1]

The motive of the visit from the Fiend customarily lay in closing an unsavory league or contract with the visitant, or collecting upon a contract previously arranged.

A Person in *Connecticut* a few days since who was suspected of stealing, was kept in custody the night after he was apprehended, guarded by three men — The thief spent the forepart of the night in walking and appeared exceedingly dejected — on being enquired of, informed the guard, that he had made a league with the Devil, and that he expected he would call for him immediately — wished them not to be frighted, as he presumed he should go in a flame of fire and brimstone by the way; while the person was walking he strewed gun-powder about the room in different directions; and when the time arrived, that he had previously informed them that the Devil was to call for him — he by some means conveyed fire to the powder, by which means the room appeared to be in flames, and while the guard were in the greatest consternation and surprise — *The Devil carried off the Prisoner!* [2]

Sometime plain evidence that the Evil One had wreaked his vengeance stupefied the credulous. One instance involved

a colored magician, who, it is rumored, dealt in the "black art," and was "in league with the devil" for a certain number of years. He told fortunes, discovered lost property, and performed strange feats; but whether this was done through his incantations or otherwise, a certain moroseness of character, a something so weird and mysterious about him, tended greatly to strengthen the impression and aided him in securing from the people whatever he demanded. Everybody was afraid of him, and gave him a wide berth. When, after one of the most terrific storms known in the place, in which the pitchy darkness of the night was almost incessantly lighted up by flashes of lightning, followed by deafening peals of thunder, he was found in a lonely wood, frightfully torn in pieces, stripped limb from limb, and strewn about the forest, it was believed his life lease had ended, and he had surrendered himself, soul and body, to the Evil One, in ac-

[1] *Essex* [Salem] *Gazette*, Aug. 6-Aug. 13, 1771.
[2] *Hampshire* [Northampton] *Gazette*, Oct. 7, 1789.

cordance with the stipulations in the league, greatly to the relief of the ignorant and superstitious.[3]

When such stark circumstantial evidence was coupled with the contractor's admission of the unholy transaction, who could doubt the Devil's agency?

Down the hill toward the Grist Mill there was a cider mill. One day Rufus Goodrich of Rocky Hill came along and stopped to refresh himself with cider. He said he had sold himself to the devil, and he said there would be thousands at his funeral. As he went on his way, he invited all to be present. A few days afterward it was noticed that something was wrong in the barn of a neighbor. Swarms of flies were buzzing in and out. Investigation discovered the body of the poor man, wedged between two upright posts back of the hay-mow.[4]

Rarely did tales vouchsafe a direct view of the dread personage. Mayhap the glimpse of a tail or a cloven hoof warned the unwary against the blandishing stranger,[5] or similar telltale signs.

In another part of the town, was an old gentleman of rubicund visage and jovial temperament, who came in early times from some of the eastern seaport places. One evening when the clouds hung in thick masses in the sky, and a sudden gust of wind now and then shook his house to its foundations, "suddenly there came a tapping" at our friend's door, on going to which, he saw, standing on the step, a tall and swarthy individual. The old gentleman observed that his eyes were like coals of fire. Half suspecting who his visitor was, he asked him in, and with an extreme sense of propriety, invited him to drink. A mug of flip, hissing hot, slipped down his throat, as though he was used to it, and he left seemingly in a high state of satisfaction. There is said to have been a strong smell of brimstone about the premises for some time after. Of course the reader must judge how much of this story is true, and how much owing to the excited imagination of the worthy old gentleman, who took a drop now and then.[6]

Liquor and the Devil formed an effective partnership. An elderly toddy-loving lady named Bailey, of Salisbury, New Hampshire, one stormy night entered into a contract with the Prince of Darkness, and naively related to her household the details of the transaction, even to

[3] Mrs. Bathsheba H. Crane, *Life, Letters, and Wayside Gleanings, for the Folks at Home* (Boston, c. 1880), pp. 49–50.
[4] Catharine M. North, *History of Berlin, Conn.* (New Haven, 1916), pp. 24–25.
[5] Prentiss Mournian, *In Those Days* (New York, 1939), pp. 23–26, 258–262.
[6] F. B. Eaton, *History of Candia* [N.H.] (Manchester, N.H., 1852), p. 119.

showing the wound on her finger pricked that she might sign and seal the document with her blood. Thoroughly agitated, the minister and his congregation determined to frustrate the bargain; on the day appointed for the collection of Mrs. Bailey's mortal and immortal parts, a multitude of persons surrounded the old lady, an immediate inner circle of twelve ministers from adjoining towns, then a larger group of deacons, elders, and other members of the church. Singing, praying and supplication against the tempter proved successful for he did not call.[7]

But when the devil was not exorcised, woe betide the covenanter. In Brighton, Massachusetts, in Governor Belcher's time, rascally Tom Walker walking through a pine wood stumbled across a swarthy fellow, who promised him Captain Kidd's treasure in return for the usual concession. Walker declined, but his wife on hearing of the offer immediately departed to take advantage of it, and all that Tom ever found of her was a dried liver and a withered heart. Meeting the dark one again, he at length closed a deal whereby he would use Kidd's money to start a loan office in Boston and practice usury. Walker prospered until one day he invoked the devil's name when unprotected by his Bible and was whisked off in a trice. That night his house burned to the ground.[8] Neither bolts nor latchets could bar the house of his victim to the Evil One, who abducted his property in full view of onlookers. When Old Soddy lay dying, scarlet with sins and openly confessing allegiance to his infidel master, Ma'am Soddy and the neighbor women dozed by the fire and waited for the Devil to claim his own. From the bed of coals poked the head of a glittering serpent, which slithered across the floor, leaped onto the quilt, and whirled into a heap on the pillow, with its head hanging over the face of the invalid. Old Soddy gave his death rattle, and the snake whizzed back up the chimney with a piece of something that looked like dried apple in his jaws.[9] In the old-time Maine

[7] John J. Dearborn, *The History of Salisbury, N.H.* (Manchester, N.H., 1890), pp. 430–432. "The incidents recorded below were taken from the diary of the late Asa Reddington, of Waterville, Me., who was a revolutionary soldier" (p. 430).

[8] Washington Irving, *Tales of a Traveller* (New York, 1825), II, 216–238; "The Devil and Tom Walker." This literary tale passes into folklore; cf. Skinner, *Myths and Legends of Our Own Land*, I, 275–279. The same evolution occurs with William Austin's story of "Peter Rugg, the Missing Man" (1824); see Amy Lowell, *Legends* (Boston and New York, 1921), pp. xiii, 238–252, "Before the Storm: the Legend of Peter Rugg."   [9] Prentiss Mournian, "Old Soddy," *Yankee*, VI (October 1940), 13.

logging camps both supernatual and humorous folktale seems to have
flourished among a heroic and elemental society. From the Penobscot
loggers comes a Faustian yarn to immortalize Jack the Ripper. Tradition
affirmed that any axeman could meet familiarly with the Devil by re-
pairing to a lonely spot seven nights running at the same hour and
minute; on the seventh night the Devil would appear. A husky farmer whose attempts at riding the logs made him the camp goat sought
out the Devil in this way; young Jack closed a bargain with the stranger
in the velvet doublet licked by blue flames, who guaranteed, for the usual commitment, that Jack would outsmart any lumberjack on the Kennebec or the Penobscot for a five-year period, and would be warned
of impending danger by a flash of blue flame. Sure enough, Jack became the most famous lumberjack in the region; his comrades might be
crushed in log jams but blue fire signaled him in time; when he
chopped, an invisible axe chopped with him and cut chips so large
two men had to lift each one. But one snowy night Jack disappeared,
and all that searchers ever found of him was his charred axe handle
and his axe blade which had turned blue as if from great heat, in a
lonely cavern filled with brimstone fumes.[10]

Many of the contract stories, however, delighted in denying the
devil his due, through various wiles and chicanery. A well-known
gambler and horse racer of Woburn, Massachusetts, Sam Hart, received a visit from a glittering-eyed stranger who bet three to one on
his black horse against Hart's mare. During the race the breath of the
hotly pursuing black horse seemed to smoke, and suddenly divining
the character of his adversary, Sam headed for the Baptist church.

> As I can't follow you on that Holy Place,
> Like a decent devil, I'll give you the race;
> With three hundred in gold, and my bonnie Jet Black
> On whom you can bet safely on any race track.

With his new acquisition Sam won every race in which he entered —
though people said he would go to hell for winning on a sure thing.[11]

[10] Ernest E. Bisbee, "Jack the Ripper," *The State O' Maine Scrap Book* (Lancaster, N.H., c. 1940).
[11] Parker L. Converse, "Sam Hart's Race. A Legend of the First Baptist Church, 1809," *Legends of Woburn* (Woburn, Mass., 1892), pp. 95–99.

For putting up the farmer's barn the Devil was to have his soul when he died. The only proviso stated that the work must be done before the first rooster crowed in the morning, else the bargain was off. Before daylight the farmer went out to his shed, made a crowing sound, and was answered by the rooster — thereby cheating His Infernal Master.[12]

Duping the Devil had its dangers, illustrated in the dealings between Old Nick and Jonathan Moulton, a personage notorious in the historical and supernatural traditions of Hampton, New Hampshire, and wider areas.

About a century ago, there lived in Hampton, one General M———N. After him was a town named *Moulton*-borough, situated near the Winnipiseogee lake, in the interior of the State. — General M———N owned much property elsewhere; but particularly in Hampton and Moulborough — it is said every house and all the land in the villages belonged to him. It was a mystery to all who were acquainted with him, how he had acquired so much property, as it was said when he first came into town, he was not better off than other men. He assumed all at once so much importance among the good farmers with whom he had before been on a level, that they were wont to look upon him with distrust, though they felt more than ever the necessity of treating him with every possible respect.

The land on which he had erected his house, was fenced off in such a manner that it resembled the singular form of a common flatiron. . . . He lived here for some time, but I do not know how long. It was pretty generally understood, about this time, among the old folks, that he was any thing but honest, from this fact, that if he saw a farm which he liked, by some quarrel, which he managed to bring before the determination of a court, he would be sure by some peculiar contrivance, to get into it his own hands. And finally such was the prejudice created in the minds of the farmers against the old General, from these and numerous other acts equally surreptitious by which he managed to augment his property to the distress and embarrassment of his neighbors, that they cried out against him for a cruel, hard hearted man, and said that if he were not leagued with the devil, he could not meet with such invariable success in these dishonest schemes, nor could he have amassed such a fortune. No man in the State of New-Hampshire was known to be so rich as General M———N.

But it came to pass, that the old General's house caught on fire and was consumed.

The old man was seen, during the conflagration, [at] the uppermost chamber, tugging away at an old straw bed, which he was trying to get

---

[12] Clifton Johnson, "Cheating the Devil," *What They Say in New England* (Boston 1896), pp. 241–242.

out of the window; while at the same time valuable plate was known to have been destroyed in the lower part of the house, and which might have been saved. The old man's mind was bewildered, and he knew not what he was about. "Ah!" exclaimed the idle spectators, "if you had let alone the poor — if you had not taken the beds from under them while, perhaps, in sickness, because they could not punctually pay their rent — if you had not taken away the poor man's farm, the widow's portion — you might have retained the presence of mind which would [have] enabled you to distinguish straw from silver when destruction cometh!"

When asked the reason that they did not endeavor to save the old man's effects, which were burning up before them, the inhabitants replied, "He is leagued with the devil, to whom he has sold both his soul and body after death — on condition that he (the general), should be provided with a certain quantity of gold and silver, which should be periodically rained down the chimney into an old boot. The boot," continued they, "was cut off at the bottom by the General, who was not faithful even to the devil — when the latter cried out from the top of the chimney, 'Is not that c——d boot full yet?' 'No!' said the General — and the room was filled, instead of the boot, with gold and silver. When Satan had discovered how he had been imposed upon, he was exceedingly wroth at his unprincipled confederate, and in revenge he burnt his house, when all the General's gains were consumed. — But they became friends again, and were seen walking together."

Well, as I heard it, it was "Jimmy Squaretoe," the little man-in-leather, who was seen in company with the General, after they had become reconciled.

It was not long after this circumstance that the old General died, and was buried — yes, the *coffin* was buried, or was ready to be, but the body of the defunct General was not, to all accounts. The deceased, as usual, was laid out and put into the coffin, but on the succeeding day, when all was arranged for the dread solemnities of a great funeral, on lifting the lid to take a last farewell peep — lo! the coffin was empty! The little man-in-leather, to the fulfilment of his bargain, had taken possession of his prize, and with it, perhaps, flew to the infernal regions, though it is said that the little man-in-leather is still occasionally seen in different parts of the town.

And the flat-iron lot on which stood the General's house still bears the imprint of a cloven foot, symbol of a curse that lingers on the land. In 1820 a gentleman bought half an acre of the lot and built himself a splendid house thereon — although old Lyd Blazedell warned him that Jimmy Squaretoe had bewitched the property.[13] Sure enough,

---

[13] Warren Brown, *History of the Town of Hampton Falls, N.H.* (Manchester, N.H., 1900), I, 540, states that Lydia Blaisdell claimed she had seen the Devil flying away with the soul of Jonathan Moulton.

misfortune dogged the Academy opened by Mr. S.; he and his creditors failed; students mysteriously took sick; the young preceptor met
with a sudden death; and Mr. S. was finally obliged to sell his house
at great sacrifice. So was fulfilled the prediction of the witch Lyd:
"Mr. S — — N, I am sorry for you — but Jimmy Squaretoe and General
M — — N, will not suffer with impunity, any encroachment on their
land, which stands accursed for the league, and the cutting off of the
bottom of a certain boot!" [14]

In a suspiciously similar fashion the miser Thomas Bagnall in-
curred the wrath of Satan by failing to observe his part of the bargain.
The Devil had promised to fill his pot with gold every Friday night
provided a few coins were left at the bottom; when Mrs. Bagnall
poured treacle in the pot, the coins would not rattle, and the Devil
came no more. Bagnall grew more merciless toward his creditors,
until the medicine man Squidrayset began to prophesy against him,
saying that Bagnall was responsible for the lean maize and empty
snares of the tribe. The vengeance of the tribe was visited on Bagnall, and the Devil cast off the garb of Squidrayset — not, however,
before dropping the earthen pot in the loam of Richmon's Island,
where a farmer's plow uncovered it in 1855.[15]

While the Devil of unholy legend did not disappear from the New
England scene with the advent of nineteenth-century popular humor,
the stories in which he continued to perform his familiar antics
stemmed from abroad. German, French, Irish, and Welsh literary
legends, far more elaborate than the colonial oral fictions, contributed
to the entertainment needs of almanacs and journals, and in a sense
supplied continuity between the earlier supernatural and the later

[14] *Exeter* [N.H.] *News-Letter*, July 3, 1843 (vol. XIII). The crystallized version of
Jonathan Moulton and the Devil is in Samuel A. Drake, *The Heart of the White Moun-
tains* (New York, 1882), pp. 11–14, and *A Book of New England Legends and Folk
Lore* (Boston, 1884), pp. 322–328; *New Hampshire Folk Tales*, Mrs. Moody P. Gore
and Mrs. Guy E. Speare, compilers (n.p., 1932), pp. 184–190; Skinner, *Myths and
Legends of Our Own Land*, II, 22–25. Accounts closer to oral sources are in Samuel
G. Drake, *Annals of Witchcraft in New England* (Boston, 1860), pp. 156–157; *Some
Descendants of John Moulton and William Moulton, of Hampton, N.H., 1592–1892*,
Augustus F. Moulton, compiler (n.p., n.d.), p. 18; Gore and Speare, pp. 190–195,
which mentions the "Flatiron lot."
[15] Herbert M. Sylvester, *Cascoe Bay* (Boston, 1909), pp. 318–333. The discovered
pot of gold coins also gave rise to buried treasure legends.

comic tales. The personality of the Evil One, so conspicuous in international folktale, attracted American readers even in colonial times; among the early books that circulated in Massachusetts the story of *Dr. Faustus* ranked astonishingly high in popularity,[16] and must have influenced American storytelling. In these imported tales place mattered little for their plots revolved around common, constantly used motives; save for foreign names they could as well have passed for native productions. A poor cobbler outwits the Devil by selling his soul for wealth and at the expiration of the term handing him a sole — according to the spelling of the scroll.[17] An ingenious sharper named Cut Legs entered into an agricultural partnership with Satan and "wooled" him three times successively: when their crop was corn, he proposed to take the tops and leave the Devil the roots; when it was potatoes, he agreed to reverse the procedure; when in disgust the Devil decided to dissolve the partnership and collect his share of the pigs, Cut Legs claimed all the pigs whose tails he had twisted to indicate they were his, and the Devil could find only one old sow without strength enough to keep the kink in her tail.[18] After a chance meeting with Morgan Jones the Devil kept under cover for some time, for Morgan, who was carrying a fowling piece, offered him his baccy pipe to smoke, and when the Fiend put the muzzle in his mouth, Morgan pulled the trigger. "Puff!" said Satan, pulling the gun out of his mouth, "D———d strong baccy, Morgan!" and looking huffed he walked off not to return.[19] Sometimes a harassed community contracted with a wealthy mysterious stranger for funds to build a church or a bridge in return for the first human soul to enter or cross the structure; the Prince of Darkness is foiled when a wolf or a dog is

[16] Harold S. Jantz, "German Thought and Literature in New England, 1620–1820," *Journal of English and Germanic Philology*, XLI (January 1942), 15. For a story within a novel of a German demon and a Yankee who concluded a compact, see J. P. Brace, *Tales of the Devils* (Hartford, 1850), pp. 69–74.

[17] *The Comic Token for 1836* (Boston, n.d.), pp. 27–28.

[18] "The Origin of the Twist in Pig's Tails," *Spirit of the Times*, XIV (May 4, 1844), 109. Mr. Richard Chase of Profitt, Virginia, has told me this tale as he heard it orally.

[19] "Morgan Jones and the Devil," *Spirit of the Times*, XVI (July 4, 1846), 228. This appears as a twentieth-century American tale in O. C. Hulett, *Now I'll Tell One* (Chicago, 1935), pp. 23–24.

first to do so.[20] In the legend of Luttrel's mill the avaricious Colonel tricked Old Nick in much the same manner as did Jonathan Moulton; in spite of all his exertions Satan could not fill the room with gold until, pausing to rest, he noticed that the stream of guineas disappeared through a hole in the floor into a room below where the Colonel was shoveling them into a closet. Amused at such cuteness, the Devil made no immediate protest but on his day of collection the Colonel barely escaped the reckoning by a feverish clasp on the Holy Book.[21] Such literary stories contained ingenious examples of trickster cunning readily congenial to native tastes.[22]

In the native comic fictions of the nineteenth century Satan emerged as an approachable personality who formed a pivotal figure in tricks, hoaxes, and tall yarns. In a vision Thomas Mudgett dreamt that the Devil came to him and threatened to destroy him unless given an impossible task. On the first assignment the Devil easily picked up a rock as large as a house and threw it into Squam Lake. On the second, he plucked a thick oak out of the ground and sailed it after the rock. Thomas thought carefully over the third task and finally asked Satan to show him a bigger liar than Gus Petty. The Devil confessed himself licked.[23] When at a revival meeting in a Maine saw-mill village, about 1860, Elder Blodgett related a dream of seeing Dan'l Ames in hell, Dan'l, who was saved annually, had an adequate rejoinder. Dan'l solemnly arose and stated that he had been dreaming of late also; he had died and gone to Hell, but the Imp had pleaded lack of room, and referred him to Old Satan himself. After they had swapped hellos, Sate explained, "Wall now," says he, "I'm mighty sorry; but the rooms in this section of Hell are all full. But we are enlargin'. We had to enlarge fer we're expectin' Elder Blodgett and his whole congregation.[24] Denied allowance for tea and snuff by the selectmen of

[20] "Satan Outwitted," *Saturday Rambler*, March 16, 1850 (vol. 5); "The Devil's Bridge," *Yankee Blade*, Mar. 6, 1852 (vol. II).

[21] Samuel Lover, "The Devil's Mill," *Burlington Daily Free Press*, July 11, 1848.

[22] Numerous references to international tales of the Devil tricked are given in George L. Kittredge, *Witchcraft in Old and New England* (Cambridge: Harvard University Press, 1929), p. 206, notes 19–22.

[23] Cornelius Weygandt, *The White Hills* (New York, c. 1934), pp. 352–353.

[24] Arthur G. Staples, "On 'A Maine Sawmill Village, 70 Years Ago'," *Lewiston* [*Me.*] *Journal*, May 25, 1931.

Granville, Massachusetts, Molly Swett, town pauper, related to them a dream she had the night before. She had died, and found herself on large plain bounded by a high hill on which stood a palace. Moll climbed the hill and knocked at the gate, but an answering angel informed her no Granville people were admitted, and suggested she try a gloomy building with iron doors and grated windows at the foot of the hill. Accordingly Moll turned her steps there, and was met by a furious looking demon whose mouth flashed fire and nostrils belched smoke. But to Moll's plea for shelter the demon replied he had no room, for the place was full of Granville people. Despairingly the traveler asked, "Where then, *can* I go?" "Back to Granville!" "And then, *then*, the big tears gathered in my eyes, *I cried!*" [25]

The intimacy, even insolence, with which the new order treated the old is seen in the Yankee's visit to Hell.

The introduction of the Yankee to his infernal majesty is peculiar,—
"How d'ye dew, folks," said the stranger, puffing away at a long cigar; "is the boss devil to hum?"

His majesty looked sulphur and saltpetre at the intruder.

"Reptile?" he exclaimed, in a voice of thunder, that rumbled and reverberated in a pit without a bottom, "who are you that dare intrude upon our sacred privacy?"

"Whew!" said the stranger, "don't tear your shirt!—Why, what on airth is the use o' your goin' off at half cock, in that way? Why do you jump afore you's spurred?—there ain't such an almighty occasion for you to get your dander so awfully riz, jest as if you was goin' to bust yer biler. Seein' that yer climate's rayther of the warmest, it would only be doin' the civil thing if you said,—'Mister, toe the mark and take yer bitters'."

"Worm!" thundered Satan.

"Worm!—I guess not," drawled out the stranger with imperturbable calmness.

"Drag him hither!" roared the Arch Enemy to his attendant furies.

"No, mister, not so fast; I've got my ticket from the regular agent, and I don't choose a berth so near the *engine!*" [26]

Even the old theme of the covenant received a jocular twist in the newer crop of traditional story.

Captain Jeremiah Snaggs lived up the Cape and he did not die in the odor of sanctity. The story is he tried to escape the devil by various devices.

[25] "The Story of Molly Swett," *Portfolio*, May 24, 1856.
[26] *The New-England Almanac, 1855* (New London, n.d.), p. 29.

He dodged the devil in Barnstable, he eluded him in a hollow tree in Orleans, he escaped from him in Wellfleet by putting a jack-o'-lantern which looked like him in a tree, but in Provincetown the devil caught up with him.

"Well," said Captain Jeremiah, "you caught me fair and squar'. Whar do we go from here?"

"Go?" said the devil. "Nowhar. Ain't we to Provincetown? " [27]

In the popular Cape Cod yarn of Ichabod Paddock and the unconquerable whale, the olden superstitions receive salacious and disrespectful handling. In desperation the famous whaler dove through the open mouth into the belly of his adversary, there to meet the Divil and a beautiful companion playing cards — for him. The girl won, and thereafter Ichabod spent nights in nocturnal orgies with the maiden, until on one of his rare visits home his wife gave him a silver whaling iron which inadvertently (from Ichabod's point of view) killed the monster and the witch he harbored.[28] Such seventeenth century motives as the devil-witch alliance, the soul purchase, and the silver weapon appear in this fiction, but the transition from a supernatural to a humorous base is complete; this is a tall tale, a smutty tale, a nineteenth-century tale.

Specters and apparitions. Ethereal visions of recognized or unfamiliar faces and forms glide into several phases of New England storytelling, colonial marvels, local folk traditions, and trickster humor; and the printed fictions can be only a fraction of those repeated in whispered hearsay and hushed avowal. Spectral sights usually signified some tragic occurrence, past or future; approaching deaths or committed murders were revealed by wraith-likenesses and supernatural manifestations. Such phenomena were comprehensible to Indians and white men alike; Josselyn personally verified some of the strange apparitions witnessed by the aboriginal inhabitants of the new land.

They acknowledge a God who they call *Squantam* but worship him they do not, because (they say) he will do them no harm. But *Abbamocho* or *Cheepie* many times smites them with incurable Diseases, scares

---

[27] Mary H. Vorse, *Time and the Town: A Provincetown Chronicle* (New York, 1942), p. 76. Cf. Elizabeth Reynard, *The Narrow Land* (Boston and New York, 1934), pp. 298–301: "Always the flight ends in Provincetown, and the conclusion is the same; but different Captains and different towns are used for the starting-point." (p. 326).

[28] Jeremiah Digges, *Cape Cod Pilot* (Provincetown, Mass., 1937), pp. 80–84.

them with his Apparitions and panick Terrours, by reason whereof they live in a wretched consternation worshipping the Devil for fear. One black *Robin* an *Indian* sitting down in the Corn field belonging to the house where I resided, ran out of his *Wigwam* frighted with the apparition of two infernal spirits in the shape of *Mohawkes*. Another time two *Indians* and an *Indess*, came running into our house crying out they should all dye, *Cheepie* was gone over the field gliding in the Air with a long rope hanging from one of his legs: we askt them what he was like, they said all wone *Englishman*, clothed with hat and coat, shooes and stockings, &c. They have a remarkable observation of a flame that appears before the death of an *Indian* or *English* upon their *Wigwams* in the dead of the night: The first time that I did see it, I was call'd out by some of them about twelve of the clock, it being a very dark night, I perceived it plainly mounting into the Air over our Church, which was built upon a plain little more than half a quarter of a mile from our dwelling house, on the Northside of the Church: look on what side of a house it appears, from that Coast respectively you shall hear of a Coarse within two or three days.[1]

John Winthrop recorded an eerie set of apparitions, connected with an unexplained accident of 1643, that after three centuries of repetition would acquire the status of a local legend.

About midnight, three men, coming in a boat to Boston, saw two lights arise out of the water near the north point of the town cove, in form like a man, and went at a small distance to the town, and so to the south point, and there vanished away. They saw them about a quarter of an hour, being between the town and the governour's garden. The like was seen by many, a week after, arising about Castle Island and in one fifth of an hour came to John Gallop's point. . . . The 18th of this month two lights were seen near Boston, (as is before mentioned,) and a week after the like was seen again. A light like the moon arose about the N. E. point in Boston, and met the former at Nottles Island, and there they closed in one, and then parted, and closed and parted divers times, and so went over the hill in the island and vanished. Sometimes they shot out flames and sometimes sparkles. This was about eight of the clock in the evening, and was seen by many. About the same time a voice was heard upon the water between Boston and Dorchester, calling out in a most dreadful manner, boy, boy, come away, come away: and it suddenly shifted from one place to another a great distance, about twenty times. It was heard by divers godly persons. About 14 days after, the same voice in the same dreadful manner was heard by others on the other side of the town towards Nottles Island.

These prodigies having some reference to the place where Captain

[1] "Josselyn's Account of Two Voyages to New-England," *Mass. Hist. Soc. Colls.*, 3d ser., III, 300.

Chaddock's pinnace was blown up a little before, gave occasion of speech of that man who was the cause of it, who professed himself to have skill in necromancy, and to have done some strange things in his way from Virginia hither, and was suspected to have murdered his master there; but the magistrates here had no notice of him till after he was blown up. This is to be observed that his fellows were all found, and others who were blown up in the former ship were also found, and others also who have miscarried by drowning, etc., have usually been found, but this man was never found.[2]

Cotton Mather in his contemporary reporting of the Salem witch-craft trials, *More Wonders of the Invisible World* (1692), uncovered a spectral communication remarkable not only as a richly detailed native instance of the murder revelation, like that delivered to Hamlet by his father's ghost, but also in being transoceanic.

A Narrative of an APPARITION *which a Gentleman in* Boston, *had of his Brother, just then Murthered in* London

It was on the *2d of May*, in the year 1687, that a most ingenious accom-plished and well disposed Gentleman, Mr. *Joseph Beacon* by Name, about five a Clock in the Morning, as he lay, whether Sleeping or Waking he could not say, (but judged the latter of them) had a View of his Brother then at *London*, altho he was now himself at our *Boston*, distanced from him a *Thousand Leagues*. This his Brother appear'd unto him in the Morning about five a Clock at *Boston*, having on him a Bengal Gown, which he *usually* wore, with a Napkin tyed about his Head; his *Countenance* was very Pale, Gastly, Deadly: and he had a *Bloody Wound* on one side of his Forehead. *Brother!* says the affrighted *Joseph. Brother*, answered the Apparition. Said *Joseph, What's the matter Brother? How came you here?* The Apparition replied, *Brother, I have been most* barbarously *and* injuriously *Butcher'd, by a Debauch'd, drunken Fellow, to whom I never did any wrong in my Life.* Whereupon he gave a particular description of the Murderer; adding, *Brother, this Fellow changing his Name, is at-tempting to come over unto* New-England, *in Foy or Wild: I would pray you on the first Arrival of either of these, to get an 'Order from the Gov-ernour, to Seize the Person whom I have now described; and then do you Indict him for the Murder of me your Brother: I'll stand by you and prove the Indictment.* And so he vanished. Mr. *Beacon* was extreamly astonished at what he had seen and heard; and the people of the Family not only ob-served an extraordinary Alteration upon him, for the week following,

[2] *The History of New England from 1630 to 1649*, James Savage, ed. (Boston, 1853), pp. 184–185. Cf. Edward R. Snow, *The Islands of Boston Harbor: Their History and Romance* (Andover, Mass., 1935), p. 198.

but have also given me under their hands a full Testimony, that he then gave them an Account of this Apparition.

All this while, Mr. *Beacon* had no advice of any thing amiss attending his Brother then in *England*; but about the latter end of *June* following, he understood by the common ways of Communication, that the *April* before, his Brother, going in haste by Night to call a Coach for a Lady, met a Fellow then in Drink, with his Doxy in his Hand: Some way or other the Fellow thought himself Affronted with the hasty passage of this *Beacon*, and immediately ran into the Fireside of a Neighbouring Tavern, from whence he fetch'd out a Firefork wherewith he grievously wounded *Beacon* in the Skull; even in that very part where the Apparition show'd his Wound. Of this Wound he Languished until he Dyed on the Second of *May*, about five of the Clock in the Morning at *London*. The Murderer it seems was endeavouring to Escape, as the Apparition affirmed, but the Friends of the Deceased *Beacon*, Seized him; and prosecuting him at Law, he found the help of such Friends as brought him off without the loss of his Life; since which there has no more been heard of the Business.

This History I received of Mr. *Joseph Beacon* himself, who a little before his own pious and hopeful Death, which follow'd not long after, gave me the Story written and signed with his own Hand, and attested with the Circumstances I have already mentioned.[3]

A similar occurrence of the vengeance message may be found in the folk history of Ipswich, Massachusetts.

SPECTRE ACCOUNT. We give the subjoined, as a matter of history, without pretending to settle the question about apparitions.

"1729, Dec. 1st. Last week, one belonging to Ipswich came to Boston and related, that, some time since, he was at Canso, in Nova Scotia; and that on a certain day there appeared to him an apparition in blood and wounds, and told him, that at such a time and place, mentioning both, he was murdered by one, who was at Rhode Island, and desired him to go to the said person, and charge him with the said murder, and prosecute him therefor; naming several circumstances relating to the murder; and that since his arrival from Canso to Ipswich, the said apparition had appeared to him again, and urged him immediately to prosecute the said affair. The above-said person, having related the matter, was advised and encouraged to go to Rhode Island, and engage therein, and he accordingly set out for that place on Thursday last."[4]

While the spectral portent of imminent or occurring death, like the post-murder apparition, is not confined to particular place, period, or

---

[3] *Salem Witchcraft*, Samuel P. Fowler, ed. (Salem, 1861), pp. 415–417.
[4] Joseph B. Felt, *History of Ipswich, Essex, and Hamilton* (Cambridge, 1834), pp. 208–209. Credited to the *New England Journal*.

people, its presence among superstitious New England folk swelled the floating body of colored oral fictions. An old family account book preserves a spectral omen, seen in 1735, of the kind no doubt endlessly relayed in family gossip.

Thursday 29 (1735) of october my wife went into a chambur that was lock to seek candels that was in a half bushel under a bed and as shee kneled down and tock her candels and laid them on the beed and as shee thrust back the half bushel there came out a childs hand she saw the fingers the hand a striped boys cife or sleve and upon shurch there was no child in the chamber on thursday a fort nite aftar my stepen son henery died. the next thursday Ebenezar died the next monday morning his eldest son Stephen died.[5]

Folk history contains its authenticated visionary frights. Reminiscences of an elderly inhabitant of Black Hall, Connecticut, treasure a storytelling scene at a Thanksgiving party in 1857, with a ghost tale text.

"Then in the evening we all went to Aunt Ellen's, talked, chattered and danced by the firelight. . . . Aunt Ellen's ghost story was a very real one to me. It seemed removed from the vision theory, as there was another witness.

"Aunt was sleeping in a room alone, one of her children occupied a small one opening from hers, but with no other exit. A friend Mrs. ——— was living in Ohio, at last accounts well and happy. Auntie had no more reason to think of her than usual. She was waked from sleep by the sight of her friend passing through her room into the one where the child slept. In a moment the child screamed 'there is some one in my room'— They knew afterward that the friend was dead, but how things corresponded I never knew."[6]

Cavendish, Vermont, claims a unique spectral tale. Sights of other men's ghosts are legion. "But never since the world began has it been told before that a man met his own ghost." Sam Connor told the story that he was crossing a swamp and saw a man coming towards him from the opposite direction. "It was as when a man walks towards a long mirror and sees his image coming with equal pace to meet him at the glass." He had seen his own double. The image spoke to Connor and

[5] Ms. Account Book (Essex Institute), opp. p. 67, quoted in Clifford K. Shipton, *Sibley's Harvard Graduates*, V (Boston, 1937), 334.

[6] Adeline B. Allyn, *Black Hall: Traditions and Reminiscences* (Hartford, Conn., 1908), pp. 83–84.

told him that in a year from that time he would die. A year to the day he was working at a barn raising. The men present would not allow Connor to have anything to do with the building because of the danger involved in putting the heavy timbers into place. But while they were all gone to the house for supper, "Connor, because it was his fate and there is no escaping fate, went up on a frame to fix a brace — fell back, and the prophecy was fulfilled." [7] In spite of its vaunt to uniqueness, this folktale has a parallel among a number of phantasmal incidents that afflicted a house in Portland, Maine. The son of the tormented family, on going to his room to change his clothes, "perceived his double sitting at the dressing table engaged in arranging some portion of his toilet. There was no mistaking the appearance of the figure. Every feature corresponded exactly to his own. On approaching the apparition it melted away." The young man saw it frequently thereafter. "Like Banquo's ghost, it has even seated itself at the dinner table, although it did not partake of any food." The same family, whose high character is vouched for in the account, observed a phantom seamstress, who vanished and reappeared at different times, but could be accurately described. "Her hair was dressed in the style of about twenty-five years ago, while from her hands, that were clasped in front of her, depended an old-fashioned sunbonnet. The woman wore an intense, earnest expression, but nothing of a ghostly character was noticed except that she was rather pale, and her eyes seemed a little fixed." No ill consequences seem to have attended these spectral visits.[8]

In the mid-nineteenth century newspapers, where so many idle stories lodged, spectral narratives of this sort mingled with the commoner comic types. Colonial superstition could not be invoked to explain away these attested visions, which transpired in the midst of an urban and technological society; and a gap of two centuries showed no slackening off in preternatural phenomena, nor in the interest accorded their description.

[7] "Sam Connor's Ghost," *Scribbler*, I (Mid-Summer, 1901), nos. 14 and 15.

[8] Scrap Book AC 040, P831 (vol. 7, p. 25), in the Maine Historical Society, Portland, Me. The text, which credits the *Portland Advertiser*, bears the headline, "A Haunted House in Portland — A Phantom Seamstress at Work — A Young Man Visited by his Double."

Jonathan Draws the Long Bow

A very curious case of spectral visitation occurred a few days since to the occupant of a chamber in one of our city hotels — a hotel which certainly has never previously made any pretentions to being haunted, and none of whose guests, permanent or transient, have ever before been heard to complain of company from the other world. The gentleman to whom the adventure occurred is a well-known resident of this city, whose word is fully entitled to credence. He has occupied the chamber in which he saw the spectre for some months. It is inaccessible save by one door, which he asserts was securely locked on the night in question. The window could not be reached, save by a winged being, from the outside, and as he found the blinds inside fastened after the spectre had disappeared, he feels entirely sure that he was the victim of no practical joke. He arrived at midnight from a neighboring city, where he had been engaged in business all day, and went straight to his room and to bed, without turning out the gas, as he desired to read one or two letters which had arrived during his absence. Having finished those, he turned the gas flame almost out, leaving a tiny jet like the ray of a star athwart the darkness; and lost himself in sleep. He awoke suddenly just as the city hall bell was striking two, and feeling cold, pulled the clothing more carefully around his person.

As he half rose to do this he became conscious of a presence, and an indistinct feeling of fear overcame him. Near the foot of the bed was a tall, slender, indefinite form, like a "pillar of cloud," which advanced quietly toward him. It had no human shape, was noiseless, but as it advanced, the gentleman grew deathly cold, felt overpowered, and desired to cry out. He was broad awake — he knew that; but he could not stir. He thought of optical illusions and wondered if this was one; but the thing, whatever it was, advanced slowly to the head of the bed, and the chill around him became frightful. His blood was congealing; he felt that he must do something or die. Summoning all his courage, he instantly rose, trembling in every limb, and walked to the shape. It stood between him and the gas jet, distinct now — an outline gradually developing into human proportions. Each second added to its development. He walked directly through it, caught at the gas pipe, turned on the full flame, and saw nothing! But he is firmly convincd that had he remained in bed he would have been found dead there the next morning, as the approach of the spectre gradually absorbed his life. He is a cool-blooded man and not a believer in spiritualism; but he is most positively sure he has seen a ghost — and rejects all theories of night-mare, nervousness and illusion as ridiculous. There be many ghost-stories, but this one has the advantage of being true, if any human testimony is to be believed.[9]

Even a railroad station could be the scene for spectral disorders.

[9] *Burlington Daily Free Press*, May 19, 1869, credited to the *Springfield* [*Mass.*] *Republican*, May 14.

A RAILROAD HAUNTED

The Boston papers publish the following as a strange but well authenticated story:

The engineer of the freight train on the Boston and Lowell Railroad, which leaves Boston about three o'clock in the morning, has on several occasions discovered a red light swinging at a furious rate at the Woburn Station where the train stops for water. The light would sometimes be in front and sometimes in the rear of the train. When the engineer would stop his train and send someone to learn why the signal to stop was made, the messenger would be greatly surprised to see the light vanish. Investigation has proved that no person was there with a lantern, and the brakeman and conductor concur also in having beheld the phenomenon, which, so far as known, is without visible cause. Some laborers living on the line of the above station state that a few mornings since they were coming down the road in a hand car, when they suddenly heard the approach of an engine and train, and knowing that no train was due in the vicinity at that hour, they became greatly frightened, and, jumping out of the car, threw it off the track to await the train which they thought was coming at a rapid pace upon them, but which, it is needless to say did not come.[10]

In certain cases the mystery surrounding phantoms dissolved before a neat and plausible backdrop of circumstantial clues. Such evidence explained the startling occurrence testified to by Hazen Whitcher and D. M. Norris in a factual deposition taken before a Justice of the Peace in Grafton County, New Hampshire. As they watched at the deathbed of their neighbor, Samuel Mann of North Benton, both heard a deep lengthened groan, which emanated from no visible source.

Mr. Whitcher stepped to the fireplace to get the light, to see what the noise came from or what caused it. As he took the light and turned around toward the bed, we both saw the room lighted up all at once, with an unearthly crimson colored light. It almost extinguished the light of the candle, so that its light was very feeble, apparently almost out — and immediately we both saw a strange looking man standing between us and the bed, looking apparently at Mr. Mann — his dress we cannot describe, his whole face we did not see. His clothes were dark, but cannot give the fashion or make, nor say whether he had on boots or shoes or hat, or not.

We were both transfixed . . . as the strange man stood before us, his back toward us, and his face toward Mr. Mann, Mr. Mann appeared much excited and agitated; he rolled on the bed, and threw his arms about and opened his eyes wide open, and appeared frightened and to gaze upon the apparition, then he tried to cover up his head.

[10] *Burlington Daily Free Press*, Feb. 12, 1870.

To his astonished neighbors the dying man then confessed to having assisted his employer, some forty years before, in murdering a man and disposing of the body. He said no more, but sank down, groaned and died; when he had ended his confession the stranger had gone, but how he left the watchers could not tell.

To this affidavit the editor printing the story added relevant information, as told by old-time residents of the vicinity. Some forty or fifty years before, a joiner named Hodgdon had worked in Landaff, New Hampshire, on a house for Jonathan Noyes, and even lent him funds for its completion. One evening after the job was done Hodgdon called on Noyes, who owed him some $400 — and was never thereafter seen. Although some excitement arose, it soon died away, since the man was a stranger, and Noyes explained he had gone to New York, and the matter was forgotten until the deathbed revelation of Mann brought it back to mind. Then some recalled that when Noyes himself lay dying, a few years back, he intimated that he had something to disclose before he could die in peace; but Mann had visited him for a whole day, and no disclosure was ever made. Noyes expired in the greatest mental agony, and apparently under fearful remorse of conscience, for he frequently exclaimed, "O God! forgive me that one sin." [11]

What lay behind the strange misanthropy and moods that afflicted Captain Reuben Joy in his last years? Papers found among the belongings of his second mate seemed to contain the answer. An experienced whaler in the days when Nantucket was the chief whaling seaport of the nation, Joy often rounded Cape Horn in the *Betsey Ann* to cruise for whales off the coast of Chile. On his thirteenth voyage, he had about filled his cargo space with oil and was preparing to return home, when a school of spermaceti whales was sighted. Boats were lowered, chase was given and several monsters harpooned; the boat of the first mate, Mr. Ray, was drawn some distance by its whale, and long after the return of the other boats had still failed to reappear. Search was made the rest of the day, and the ship hove to that night; but the next day instead of continuing the hunt Captain Joy suddenly ordered the *Betsey Ann* to make for home, silencing remonstrances with the statement that the

[11] *Exeter News Letter*, July 26, 1842 (vol. XII), from the *New Hampshire Statesman*.

ship was now shorthanded, and doubtless the missing boat had been stove in by a whale. Rounding the Cape on the return voyage, the *Betsey Ann* fell in with an outgoing Nantucketer; letters were brought on board, and her captain spoke briefly with Reuben Joy. Part of their discourse reached the ears of the second mate, who heard the visiting captain remark that the widow Barnard had died; in anguished voice Joy exclaimed, "Then I have damned my soul for nothing." But on that he checked himself and quickly steered the conversation into other channels. Meaning lit the mind of the listening mate; young widow Barnard had mocked the old Captain, but encouraged the advances of young Ray.

On Joy's next cruise a chase developed about the spot where Ray had been lost, and the Captain again led one of the boats. While killing a whale (according to his later words) he perceived another boat draw near, and on looking closer recognized it as the long lost one: horrible to behold, its crew were skeletons whose bones rattled as they moved about, while ever and anon the shrill cry of "Stern all! ease off — veer the line — pull ahead" floated over the waves in sepulchral and gibbering tones. Joy sank down in the box of the boat and his men, who seemed not to have observed the specter whalemen, pulled back to the ship. Captain Joy ordered the crew to trim the sails, while he went to the masthead and seated himself on the highest crosstree. At a vast distance he glimpsed a speck on the ocean, which he took for one of the boats still out, but after the ship had sailed in its direction half an hour, he beheld once more the fleshless bones of the specter crew. The skeleton at the head of the boat seemed to see the Captain, for he flourished his long lance in his bony hands, pointed it towards him in derision, and tossed it in the air with a screeching laugh. The Captain hurried down to his cabin; but on subsequent voyages he continued to see the spectral whalemen, and in other parts of the Pacific. On his last voyage he saw the ghastly crew whenever he put off for whales; in despair he returned home with the hold half empty, retired to Siaconset in utter solitude, and died alone and friendless. Only the second mate, to whom he confided his scourge, knew his dread secret.[12]

[12] *The Old American Comic And The People's Almanac*, 1841 (Boston: S. N.

Supernaturalism yielded to comedy in many ghost stories, which hinged on false scares and alarms provided by spurious specters. Folk history narrated such misadventures: luminous ghosts turn out to be a basket on a knoll blown in and out of sight by the wind, or a sheeted joker walking a plank; ghostly noises are produced by a dead limb scraping on the roof, cows locked in the church, a dying cat, or a hen with frozen feet that bump eerily on the floor.[13] In the literary weeklies of the 1840's and '50's ghost hoaxes intrude; a visitor to Salem sleeps in a haunted house on a dare, and meets a gigantic bloody specter who promises to reveal the hiding place of treasure for which he was murdered — but it is all a dream; the redoubtable Timothy Treadwell is challenged to cut off a branch from the yew tree in the churchyard at midnight, and there meets a vocal ghost — but it is only a prankster.[14] If spectral fictions partially succumbed to the vogue of folk humor, their appeal to credibility has not necessarily languished. In many cases the ghost tale becomes established as a local legend because persistent repetition of the story or renewed appearances of the unaccountable sights and sounds keep fresh the eerie tradition.[15]

Dickinson, n.d.), pp. 7, 9; *The People's Almanac*, 1841 (Boston: James Fisher, n.d.), p. 36.

[13] William Little, *The History of Weare, N.H.* (Lowell, Mass., 1888), pp. 581–582; *New Hampshire Folk Tales*, Mrs. Moody P. Gore and Mrs. Guy E. Speare, compilers (n.p., 1932), pp. 220–223.

[14] *Yankee Privateer*, Sept. 27, 1856 (vol. V); *Yankee Blade*, June 24, 1854 (vol. XIII).

[15] Marion Lowndes, *Ghosts That Still Walk* (New York, c. 1941), includes four accounts of New England houses whose haunted character endures in local memory. Cornelius Weygandt mentions twentieth-century ghost sights in *New Hampshire Neighbors* (New York, c. 1937), p. 242.

III

YANKEE YARNS

WHEN THE insatiable native urge for story manufacture turned for plastic material to prominent eccentricities of the New England character, it molded a fixed symbolic image figure around whom anecdotal fictions swarmed and clustered with easy abundance. The Yankee was a creation of paradoxes: he was both storyteller and story hero; many times an unspeakably witless and "verdant" boor, just as many he stood portrayed as a sly and scheming knave; an "original" completely regional in projection and design, he did not differ fundamentally from backwoods and backmountain types throughout the land. From the interplay of type caricature and inventive flair arose a noteworthy new form of subliterary tale, the Yankee yarn, which embraced a medley of folk jokes, anecdotes, and humorous sketches. Yankee yarns incorporated and preserved local turns of speech, the twists, epithets, and inflections of New England rural talk that colored and pointed oral narrative art. They reported, borrowed, and created situations appropiate for their central actor, sharp trades, dupes, "saws," "sells," and endless clownish antics that resembled in plot but differed in tone from Old World tales of rogues, scalawags, and dolts. They emphasized salient traits of rural personality, uncontrollable curiosity, dismal naivete, impudence, low cunning, parsimony, and loutishness. Fed into humor-hungry newspapers, periodicals, almanacs, and jokebooks that entertained the nation in the middle decades of the nineteenth century, these yarns supplied literary mediums with a prolific fund of native story, often grounded in actual scenes and characters, making use of familiar motives, and enjoying wide vogue. But whether actual, embroidered, or imagined, scenes of Yankee escapades conformed to set lineaments in the popular fancy about what Yankees were and how they should act; individual tales swelled into a folk biography of a type buffoon whose performances always ran true to character.

Besides this general indebtedness to popular sources for its themes, the Yankee yarn as a form touched folktale in three ways. Its constant hero, the comic Yankee, represented a generic folk motive. Often yarns employed or contained a storytelling situation which presented, and perhaps copied, an oral tale.[1] And, as always happens when whirlpools of storytelling activity attract drifting motives and fictions, stock tales bobbed up that had been and would be told in many places at different times. Students and historians of American humor who discuss only literary Yankee humor bypass the extensive folk literature of Yankee yarning.

Greenhorns. Preëminently the comic figure was a fool, an ignorant countryman, baffled by urban ways, befuddled by modern machinery, legitimate game for dupes and hoaxes. The industrial age had passed him by; mechanical contrivances caused Jonathan surprises and grief.

A YANKEE IN A COTTON FACTORY

Dear Blade, — Did you ever see, read, or hear tell of *"A Green 'Un"* in a cotton mill?

Pray don't answer rashly; don't lose yourself among "Yankees in Coal Screens," "Yankees in Hot Baths," "Yankees in Restorateurs," and answer unadvisedly — *yes!* Mine is a Yankee in a *new phase.* His dilemma is a *Yankee Fix* — "*sui generis,*" — *a live Yankee in the card room of a cotton mill!*

"The plain unvarnished facts in the case," as politicians say, "are these:" — A raw, straw-hatted, sandy-whiskered, six-footer — one of the purely uninitiated — came in yesterday from Greene, with a load of wood, for the Factory Company. Having piled his wood to the satisfaction of the "Squire," he bated his team with a bundle of green grass brought all the way from home for that purpose. Then, after investing his available capital in the purchase of root beer and gingerbread at Ham's, he started to see the "city," filling his countenance rapidly with bread, and chewing it vigorously as he went.

He reviewed the iron foundry and machine shop, and was just opposite the warp-mill as the "hands" were going in from dinner. The girls were hurrying in as only factory girls *can* hurry, and Jonathan, unaccustomed to such an array of plaid shawls and hood bonnets, deposited his goad stick upon the stairs, and stalked in *"to see what the trouble was."*

The clatter of the machinery and the movements of the operatives soon

[1] Yankee actors like Dan Marble and George H. Hill made a specialty of telling Yankee stories between the acts of their plays or on the lecture platform, and many were printed in newspapers and humor books. See their biographies, *passim*: William K. Northall, *Life and Recollections of Yankee Hill* (New York, 1850); Jonathan F. Kelley, *Dan. Marble: A Biographical Sketch* (New York, c. 1851). Dr. Valentine became especially known for his Yankee monologues, popular both in oral and later printed form.

absorbed his whole attention. Being, however, of an inquiring turn of mind, and seeing much that was calculated to perplex one whose observations in mechanics had been mostly confined to threshing machines and corn shellers, he began to push vigorous inquiries in all directions. In this way he made himself acquainted successively, with the external and internal economy of the *"Picker," "Beater," "Lap-winder," "Doubler,"* and *"Speeder."* By two o'clock he had extended his researches as far as the *"Breakers"* and *"Finishers."*

He reached the latter just as the card-stripper was "Stripping the flats." In this operation the cylinder of the card is exposed to view, and is seen revolving with a very pretty buzz. Not satisfied with contemplating the "poetry of motion" at a safe distance, our hero must needs introduce himself between the cards to get a nearer view. This movement brought his "nether habiliments" into dangerous proximity to the gearing of the next card, and "thereby hangs a tale."

"You, I say! She goes pooty, don't she Bos?" said Jonathan, enquiringly. "She don't do anything else," responded the stripper. "But you must be very careful how you move around amongst this *hard ware.* 'Twas only last week, Sir, that a promising young man from Oxford — a student at the academy here — was drawn into that very card, Sir, and before any assistance could reach him, he was run through, and manufactured into No. 16, super extra, cotton warp yarn."

"I s-s-swow! I believe yure joking!" stuttered Jonathan.

"Fact, Sir," continued Stripper, "and his disconsolate mother came down two days ago, and got five bunches of that same yarn, as melancholy relics."

"By the mighty! That *can't* be true!"

"Fact, Sir, fact! and each of his fellow students purchased a skein apiece, to be set in lockets, and wore in remembrance of departed worth!"

"Is *that* a fact, now! *was* he really carded, spun, and set in lockets?" A sense of personal danger here shooted across our hero's mind; he began to retreat precipitately without waiting for an answer.

There was not much room to spare betwixt himself and the gearing of the card behind. Another step backwards completed the ceremony of introduction. His unwhisperables being of large *"calibre,"* the process of snarling them up into a hard knot was no ways slow. Our hero "gave tongue" instanter, and by the twentieth gyration of the *embodiment,* the music was melodious. His *"explosive tones"* were scientific, and did honor to his knowledge of dynamics. Gen. Scott himself could not have protested more forcibly against an "attack on his rear."

"O-h! M-u-r-d-e-r!! — Let go! — you h-u-r-t. Blast your picter — Let go! Aint ye ashamed! Git out — Taint pooty. Darnation seize ye! Let alone on me, can't ye! — do!"

The gearing by this time had wound him up so that he was obliged to stand on tiptoe. His hands were revolving vigorously behind him, but he dared not venture them near the "seat of war," lest they too should be drawn into *hostilities.*

The card stripper threw off the belt, but the momentum of the cylinder kept it revolving, and our hero, supposing it in full operation, burst out anew:

"Oh, stop her! stop her! won't ye? Stop her, do — I aint well, and I orter be at home. Father wants the steers, and mother's going to bake! Stop the tarnal masheen — can't ye? — do! Aint ye got no feelin' for a feller in distress? Oh dear! I'll be carded and spun, and made into lockets! Je-RU-*sa-lem*!! How I wish I was to Greene!"

The card was stopped at last, but Jonathan's clothes were so tangled in the gearing that it was no slight task to extricate him. Like Othello, "*he was not easily moved*," and it was only by cutting out the whole of the "*invested territory*" that he was finally released.

"What *are* you about here?" said the overseer, entering.

"Nothin' Sir, only *Stripping flats*," answered the stripper.

Our hero not caring to resume his "pursuit of knowledge under difficulties," a pair of overhauls were charitably loaned him, and he *scattered* suddenly towards Mill Hill, giving a series of short kicks with either leg, on his way, as if to assure himself that he had brought away his full complement of limbs, from the "cussed machine!"

Lewiston Maine.[2]

Inevitably the bewildered rustic found himself cozened by city sharpers.

NEHEMIAH FLUFKINS'S VISIT TO THE CITY OF NOTIONS

Nehemiah Flufkins was one of those unfortunate specimens of the genus homo, that seem by some accident to have barely escaped shooting out of the ground in the form of a cabbage, and to have been born with all the outward semblance of humanity. Spite of his awful greenness, Flufkins was an observant chap, anxious to look about the world, and, to use his own words, be "some pumpkins." He came to Boston one day to see the elephant, and innocently suffered all manner of tricks to be played upon him, such as paying twenty-five cents to go inside the Common, a charge made by a cunning boy, who discovered that Flufkins had "just come down." Another of the "b'hoys," who had received his cue from the lad who charged the entrance fee to the public Common, stopped Nehemiah as he came out and passed down Tremont street, and politely tapping him on the arm, he said:

"Fifty cents fine, sir," at the same time holding out his hand for the money.

"Fifty cents! Creation, what fur?"

"The mayor's house, sir."

[2] *Spirit of the Times*, XVII (Oct. 16, 1847), 396, by "Gamboge." Credited to the *Yankee Blade*. For the popularity of this sketch see Chapter I, *Literary storytelling*. Cf. the motive of the man manufactured into carpet cloth in Jim Blaine's "The Story of The Old Ram" (Mark Twain, *Roughing It*, New York and London, c. 1913, II, 126).

"Wot of that?" asked Flufkins, looking at the house designated by the other.

"You have passed it just now, *without taking off your hat!*"

"How yer talk. S'posin' I did?"

"Why, that's fifty cents fine in Boston."

"No!"

"Certainly; and unless you pay it, I shall be obliged to take you to the Police Office."

"W-h-e-w! Well here's a half. Let's see which house it is," said Nehemiah, taking off his hat.

"That's it, sir, the next but one to where we stand."

"Wall, I won't git caught agin, anyhow," said the innocent Flufkins, as he walked back and forth before the house of a green grocer, and fixed the spot in his mind!

Scarcely had Nehemiah Flufkins turned another corner, before he was stopped by a third person, who had got the hint from the other two operators.

"What's the matter *now!*" asked Nehemiah, "I haven't passed *another* mayor's house, have I?"

"No, but you forgot your landing fee."

"Landin' fee — what's that?"

"Why, head money."

"Head money! Do yer have tu pay for keepin' yer head on?" asked Nehemiah, innocently.

"No — you don't understand, my friend. I perceive that you must be a stranger to the city."

"Wall, I guess I am."

"You see the law is, that any person arriving in town for the first time, shall pay seventy-five cents head money."

"Du tell."

"Yes. What route did you come by."

"Fitchburg railroad."

"That's it!" exclaimed his persecutor, as though he had made a discovery.

"What's it?" asked Nehemiah.

"Why, you are the fellow the police are after."

"After me, what fur?"

"For slipping away without paying your head money."

"Wall, look a' here, nabor, it's pretty expensive business, 'pears to me; but there's three quarters, will that fix it?"

"Yes, that is all right — you are free now to look about the town," said the other, walking away with a suppressed chuckle.

"Thank ye," said Flufkins; "only to think of the perleece after me! Well, that *was* an escape."

If there was one thing above another for which Nehemiah had a weakness, it was smoking. At home, his pipe was in his mouth half the time, and seeing some cigars in a window, he felt the desire come over him, and so he walked in, purchased a "long nine," lit it, and walked out into the street, smoking as he went along, looking into the shop windows in Washington street. The fact was, Nehemiah was now really breaking a city ordinance, and laying himself liable to a fine. It was not long before a policeman, with his badge of office on his hat, accosted him.

"Sir, you must put out that cigar and walk with me," said the officer, with an air of decision that staggered Nehemiah.

"What fur?" stammered Flufkins.

"Smoking in the street."

"Is there a fine fur that tew?"

"Yes, sir."

"How much?"

"Five dollars."

"Creation! Five dollars. I haven't got but six left."

"Can't help it, you must go with me."

"Look a' here — hold on!" said Nehemiah; "I don't want to go no whar."

"But you must," said the officer, at the same time looking about him slyly, and seeing no one very near, he added: "If you choose to pay *me*, why it will save your being locked up."

"*Locked up?* Creation! Here, there's five dollars," said Nehemiah, handing the officer the money, who pocketed the change, and walked away — leaving Mr. Flufkins standing alone seemingly afraid to move backwards or forwards, for fear he should incur another fine.

And this was the case; Flufkins was afraid to move lest he should break some other unknown law of the city. He thought the matter over, as well as he could in his confused state of mind, and remembering that he had just one dollar left, enough to carry him home in the cars, he looked all about him for a moment, to see that no one was by to stop him, and then "scratched gravel" like a new one, back towards the depot. As he approached the grocer's house, that had been pointed out to him as the mayor's, he pulled off his hat and only ran the faster, until he was out of sight of it.

At the head of Hanover street, he was partially stopped by some one who wished to ask the way to some other part of the city, being, like himself a stranger — but Nehemiah had eyes and ears for only one thing, and misunderstanding the question, halloed out:

"Can't help it if *'tis* a fine to run; I haven't got no money." And he dashed on like mad towards the railroad station.

Nehemiah didn't let on much about his visit to Boston, but merely said he didn't stay long, it was so pesky expensive.[3]

City merchants habitually sold the verdant.

[3] *Yankee Blade*, April 12, 1851 (vol. X). Credited to *Flag of our Union*.

Yankee Yarns

THE YANKEE'S CHRISTMAS VISIT

The day preceding Christmas, a 'green 'un'—green from head to foot—was seen rushing up Washington street, with his hands thrust into his pockets. In passing Jone's, Shreve's and Brown's, he was suddenly brought to a stand by the brilliancy of jewelry displayed in their window.

'Tarnation seize me, ef them rings hain't harnsome enough for my Sall! Dang it, ef I don't, *neow*, buy the hoop what'll dew for Sall's finger wen we're hitched, next plantin' time, by Parson Crout.'

Upon this determination, our verdant stepped into the magnificent store, and walked up to the show-case of diamond-jewelry, at the same moment, relieving his hands from their prison, pointed to the most expensive ring within reach of his vision—worth at least five hundred dollars.

'What'll ye take for that are?' asked the Yankee.

'What will you give?' responded Mr. Jones, understanding the customer he had to deal with.

'Dang it ef I know!—guess 'bout ninety five cents is all dad would allow me tew gin, as he sold hisself short uv apple sass tew git the tin tew pay my way up tew Bosting.'

'Cannot afford the ring for that money—it cost twice as much as you offer,' said Mr. Jones.

'Yeou git out—dang it ef I'll be cheated any how; but Sall must have the ring. Luff the hoop eout here, an' let a feller kersamine it.'

At this gentle request, Mr. Jones removed the ring from its rich case, and held it towards the Yankee, who was evidently determined upon a purchase.

'Neow, I tell yeou wot it is, Mr., I can't gin all creation for Sall's weddin' ring, cos I got tew git the beddin' an' other fixins; but ef ye'll take ninety-five cents for the tarnal bright leetle critter, I'll tuk it right off your hans, an you'll hev the fun uv gitting red uv one uv yer hoops, an' the money fer it tew, right in yer fist.'

At this last generous proposition, Mr. Jones took the ring as if to do it up for his customer. At the same instant, the thought flashed across the mind of the Yankee that he was paying 'too dear for the whistle.'

'Tan't bruck nor nothin'—an' them leetle glass beads what's druv inter the top, won't come eout nor nuthin,' Mr.?'

'I don't warrant it, my friend,' replied Mr. Jones.

'Thunder, ef I don't see Sall bust fore I buy a hoop fer her what don't come warranted.'

With this last speech, the Yankee gave his hat an additional slap and walked out of the store, muttering to himself—

'Can't come it over this ere chap, any heow.' [4]

No matter what precaution the skinflint purchaser oberved in selecting his wares, he seemed destined to be miserably hoodwinked in the tiniest investment.

[4] *Yankee Blade*, Jan. 5, 1856 (vol. XV).

A YANKEE SPECULATION

The other day, being in the vicinity of the old Cradle of Liberty, we paused to witness the operations of a cute Yankee at a refreshment stall. —

The object of our attention was a stalwart, red-cheeked youth, with fox-skin cap, blanket coat and woolen mittens, and might have come down from Vermont with a load of venison and poultry. It was evident from his manner that he had got through with his business, whatever it was, and was now a man of leisure. The chapman displayed his most tempting edibles, for he saw before him a customer amply able to extend a liberal patronage. The Yankee looked over his whole stock in trade, and priced nearly every article he had.

"How much is that ere candy a stick?" he would say.

"Two cents."

"Wall — but by hullsale?"

"Ten cents a dozen."

"Wall — but *seein it's me?*"

"Sein it's you, you may have a dozen sticks for sixpence."

"Do you think I'm made of gold, you shaver?" retorted the Yankee. — "Never mind — drive on — How's doughnuts?"

And he fixed upon a plate of these delicious Yankeeisms his avid and devouring eyes. Here he stood on safe ground; — some of the other 'fixins' were beyond his comprehension — but he 'knew' doughnuts as well as he "knew beans."

"How's doughnuts?"

"Dougnuts has riz," replied the vendor with an air of profound importance and intelligence.

"The continuance of the Mexican war," he added, raising his right arm oratorically and transforming himself into a human teapot, "the proposed loan — and the dread of a drain of specie, has caused a raise of breadstuffs — flour has riz and doughnuts has gone up."

"What's all that are nonsense about the Mexican war, you d——d old jackass?" said the Yankee — "How's doughnuts?"

"One cent per nut," replied the vender lowering his arm and tone.

"Mought a fellow take his pick?" inquired the customer, hesitating with his cent in his left mitten.

"Oh! — certing — certing" — replied the dealer.

The Yankee deposited the specie, and seized on a doughnut which he had before selected with his eyes. It was a sockdollager as big as a Baldwin apple.

"Anything else?" inquired the vendor, as he swept the coin into his drawer, and noted the sale on his slate.

"Not to-day," replied the Yankee with a gleam of satisfaction, and he withdrew with his prize. We were curious enough to follow him — we watched him as he set his teeth into the immense mass. Alas! for the vanity of human hopes. That doughnut was an imposition — a sham — a mere batter bubble blown into the semblance of solidity.

Loud were the imprecations of the Yankee.

"Taken in! by thunder!" he exclaimed. "Consum the fellur's impudence. These Boston chaps do beat the devil! He done me out of that ere cent as slick as grease upon a cartwheel. Might have bought an apple with it — might have bought two sixes — might have bought a world of notions — and car'd home presents to the family — and now I'm bust and bubbled and bamboozled. It's *tu* bad!"

And we left him "fit to weep" and "not to be consoled!"

Poor fellow! [5]

In the big city the theater had, ever since Royall Tyler wrote *The Contrast* in 1787, mystified and confounded the unitiated countryman.

ONE OF THE "AUDIENCE"

One night last week, a tall, gaunt-looking fellow, from up the country, stopped before the Howard Athenaeum, just as the crowd was passing in, to witness the performances of the Ravel Family, and having satisfied himself that it was a "meeting 'ous," he stepped over to the entrance. As he was passing the door-keeper, "Ticket, sir!" announced rather peremptorily by that functionary, set the stranger aback somewhat.

"A wot?"

"Your ticket."

"I haint any."

"Where is it?"

"I gin it to the rail-road chap."

"I mean your entrance ticket *here*."

"I tell yer I haint any."

"You can get one below, sir."

Our friend went down to the office, where he applied for a ticket of admission.

"I want a good seat, sir."

"Fifty cents, sir."

"Look here — I can't go the *half*, stranger, but I'm good for a quarter."

An upper circle ticket was furnished him, and our verdant gentleman mounted the stairs. He had leisure to gaze upon the crowd but for an instant, when Javelli made one of his daring springs upon the tight rope.

"Gee — Whittaker!" exclaimed the stranger — "wot's that?"

But his surprise was drowned by the applause which followed, and Javelli threw one of his famous somersets, alighting upon the cords on his feet.

"That's the devil, sartain," said Johnny Raw — "it aint nobody else. — This is the pers'asion I like! Go it, hoss! you're one of 'em! Thunder and

[5] *Spirit of the Times*, XVII (Feb. 12, 1848), 598. Credited to the *Yankee Blade*.

airthquakes, look at 'im! Wal, blister me ef I don't come to town, and
'tend *this* meetin' three times a week, *sure*." [6]

Public conveyances afforded fruitful opportunities for shameless display of Yankee gaucheries.

THE PUBLIC TOOTH-BRUSH

As the splendid steamer Connecticut was passing Blackwell's Island, on
her way from Norwich to New York, a few days since, a gentleman might
have been seen performing his ablutions in one of the marble basins in
the wash-room in the forward part of the boat. While he was in the midst
of his task, a tall and verdant specimen of the incipient Yankee traveller
entered the apartment, and, after staring about a few moments to assure
himself, commenced a conversation with his fellow passenger.

"I saay yeou — kin anybody wash himself in this here cooky?"

"You have a perfect right to avail yourself of the accommodations of the
boat. You can help yourself to the water."

"Yaas; but this here pumpkin shell has got a hole in the bottom, and
the darned fassit's knocked all askew. I swow, yeou, is that are brasscock
made of solid silver? I swanny, this wash hand dish looks jest like marble!"

The gentleman quietly placed the stopper in the right place, and "turned
on" the water for our hero, who soon "made himself at home" pretty generally. The former, however, in a short time missed his tooth-brush, and
on looking around, was astonished to perceive the Yankee applying it
vigorously to his tobacco-stained ivories.

"My dear friend, you have made a very great mistake in using my
tooth-brush," said the gentleman.

"Your *what?* — your bresh? You don't mean to say that this here's your
tooth-brush?"

"I do, sir; but it is of no consequence now. You are welcome to the
brush."

The Yankee looked puzzled at first, as if he suspected a trick, but at
length he exclaimed:

"Here, yeou, take your confounded thingumbob! But I should like to
know what in thunder has become of the *tooth-bresh that belongs to the
boat!*" [7]

Tricksters. On the reverse of the shield, the Yankee appeared as a
scheming knave and fertile prankster who matched his wits against a
suspicious world, both for business and for pleasure. Ingrained in the
Yankee fable lay the conception of a wily, cozening trickster, poised
under a mask of ingenuousness and seeming good will for a shrewd deal

---

[6] *Spirit of the Times*, XVII (Oct. 23, 1847), 406. Credited to the *Boston Times*.
[7] *Yankee Blade*, Oct. 18, 1851 (vol. XI).

or an act of mischief. Down-easters logically became itinerant vendors of miscellaneous wares, relentlessly pursuing the sale or the swap.

THE YANKEE FOX SKIN

'Mornin', Squire!' said 'down east,' giving a nod and a wink to Lyman and Towle, as those gents stood in their store one morning, 'up and dressed,' for business.

'How are you, Sir?' said the merchants.

'Pooty well, con-siderin the state of things in ginerawl. I say, yeou sell skins here, don't yeou?'

'We do, occasionally,' was the response.

'Well, so I calkelated; buy Fox Skins teou, I reckon?'

'Sometimes. Why, have you got some for sale?'

'Some. Ye-s, guess I hev *one*; its some teou, I tell yeou.'

'Let's look at it,' say one of the merchants. The owner of the skin tugged at the capacious pocket of his 'yaller over-cut,' a few minutes, and out came a pretty considerable, sizeable bang-up of a venerable reynard.

'There it is, a perfect bewty it is, too. Aint it?'

'Seen many finer ones,' says Towle.

'Praps yeou hev, and praps yeou haint; but I deou think it is a rare bewty —slick and shiny as a bran new hat.'

'When did you get this skin?' says the merchant.

'When did I git it. Why, when I killed the darn'd critter, of course.'

'Yes, we know, but was it in the fall or summer, or when?'

'Oh! ye-s; well, I reckon, 'twar'nt fur from 4th July, any way, fur I'd jest clean'd up my old shooting piece, for p'rade on the glorius annivarsity, and along comes the old critter and I jest giv him a rip in the gizard that settled his harsh, mighty sudden I tell yeou.'

'Fox Skins,' said the merchants, 'are not very good when taken in hot weather, the fur and hair is thin, and not fit for much in summer.'

'Well, neow I reckon, since I come to think it over, 'twar'nt hot weather, when I shot the critter; no, I'll be darned ef it was; made a thunderin mistake 'beout that, fur 'twas nigh on to Christmas, was by golly, fur I and Seth Peurkins wur going to a frolic. I remember it like a book, cold as sixty, snowin awful, was, by ginger!'

'Well,' says the merchants, — 'was the Fox very fat?'

'Fa-t! O! Molly, warnt it fat? Never did see such a fat feller in all my beorn days. Why yeou, the fa-t came clean through the critter's hide, run down his legs, 'till the very airth was greasy where the darn'd varmint crawled areound. Did by Peunkins!'

'Too fat then, we guess, to be good,' said Towle. 'Fat skins, Sir, are not so good as those taken from an animal not more than ordinarily fat.'

'Well, guess war'nt so darn'd fat nuther; come to think abeout it, 'twas another Fox our Siah shot last fall; *this* old critter, warn't so darn'd fat, not overly fat — fact, I guess, it was reyther poor; kind of lean, treemenjus lean; poor old varmint was abeout to die of pure starvation; never see such a darn'd eternal starved, lean, lank famished live critter, on the lord's yearth before!'

'Very poor, eh?' says Lyman.

'Very poor? I guess it was; so almighty poor that the old critters beons stuck clean eout, almost threough his skin, had'nt killed it jest when I did, it would died afore it got ten rods further along. Fact! by Golly!'

'Ah! well,' says the merchants, 'we see the skin is poor, very poor; the fur is thin and loose, and would not suit us.'

'Wunt suit yeou? Neow look ahere yeou,' says the Yankee, folding up his versatile skin, — 'I dunt kind o' like sich dealing as that, no heow, and I'll be darn'd to darnation, ef you catch me a tradin' Fox Skins with *yeou* again, there aint no lumber in the state o' Maine!' And the holder of the skin vamosed! [1]

Not often, however, did the ubiquitous Yankee pedlar fail to consummate a successful deal.

A Yankee Trick. 'I calculate I can't drive a trade with you to-day,' said a yankee pedlar, at the door of a merchant.

'You calculate about right then, for you cannot,' was the reply.

'Wal, you need'nt get huffy about it — now here's a dozen genuine razor strops, worth all of two dollars and a half — you may have 'em for two dollars.'

'I tell you I don't want any of your trash; so be off.'

'Wal, now, I declare! I bet you five dollars if you make me an offer for them strops, we'll have a trade yet.'

'Done!' said the merchant, placing five dollars in the hands of a bystander. The Yankee deposited a like sum — when the merchant offered him a picayune for the strops.

'They are yourn,' said the pedlar, as he quietly pocketed the wager, amid the shouts of a laughing crowd.[2]

In an appendix occasionally supplied, the pedlar climaxed this act of guile with a further outrage. To show his goodheartedness, he offered to trade the razor strops back. There they are, good fellow, said the relieved merchant; now give me the money. The Yankee gave him the sixpence.[3]

That an innocuous offer customarily concealed some ingenious twist, other dealers with the Yankee pedlar learned to their sorrow.

[1] *Spirit of the Times*, XVIII (Feb. 17, 1849), 614, by Yankee Hill. Credited to *Aurora Borealis*. Also in *Union Jack*, Mar. 10, 1849 (vol. II).
[2] *Rutland Herald*, Nov. 16, 1843.
[3] *Granite State Magazine*, IV (October 1907), 179–180.

THE "CUTEST" YANKEE TRICK OUT

A Connecticut broom pedler — a shrewd chap from over among the steady habits, wooden clocks, school masters and other fixens, drove through the streets of Providence, heavily laden with corn brooms. He had called at several stores and offered his load, or ever so small a portion of it; but when he wanted the cash and nothing else in payment, they had uniformly given him to understand that they had got brooms enough, and that he might go further. At length, he drove up to a large wholesale establishment on the west side, and once more offered his wares.

"Well," said the merchant, "I want the brooms badly enough, but what will you take in pay?"

This was a poser. The pedler was aching to get rid of his brooms; he despised the very sight of his brooms; but he would sooner sell a single broom for cash than the whole load for any other article — especially that which he could not as readily dispose of as he could brooms. After a moment's hesitation, however, he screwed his courage to the sticking point — it required some courage, after having lost his chance of selling his load half a dozen times by a similar answer — and he frankly told the merchant he must have cash. Of course the merchant protested that cash was scarce, and that he must purchase, if he purchased at all, with what he had in his store to pay with. He really wanted the brooms, and he did not hesitate to say so; but the times were hard, and he had notes to pay, and he had goods that must be disposed of.

Finally, he would put his goods at cost price, for the sake of trading, and would take the whole load of brooms which the pedler had labored so unsuccessfully at other stores to dispose of.

"So," said he to the man from Connecticut, "unload your brooms, and select any article from my store, and you shall have them at any price."

The pedler scatched his head. There was an idea there, as the sequel shows plainly enough.

"I tell you what it is," he answered, at last, "just say them terms for half the load, and cash for t'other half, and I'm your man. Blowed ef I don't sell out ef Connecticut sinks with all her broom stuff the next minute."

The merchant hesitated a moment, but finally concluded the chance a good one. He would be getting half the brooms for something that would not sell as readily; as for cost price, it was an easy gammon in regard to it. The bargain was struck, the brooms brought in, and the cash for half of them was paid over.

"Now, what will you have for the remainder of your bill?" asked the merchant.

The pedler scratched his head again, and this time more vigorously. He walked the floor, whistled, drummed with his fingers on the head of a barrel. By and by, his reply came — slowly and deliberately.

"You Providence fellers are cute, you sell at cost, pretty much all of you, and make money. I don't see how 'tis done. Now, I don't know about your goods, barrin' one article, and, ef I take anything else, I may be cheated. So, seein' as t'wont make any odds with you, I guess I'll take brooms. I know them like a book, and can swear to what you paid for 'em."

And, so saying, the pedler commenced re-loading his brooms, and having snugly deposited half of his former load, jumped on his cart with a regular Connecticut grin, and without cursing his imprudence and his own stupidity, drove off in search of another customer.[4]

A Yankee role to rival the clock pedlar was the equally infamous horse jockey.

THE ILL-LOOKING HORSE: A PUN THAT WAS NO JOKE

A Frenchman, near the Canada line, in Vermont, sold a horse to his Yankee neighbor, which he recommended as being a very sound, serviceable animal in spite of his unprepossessing appearance. To every enquiry of the buyer respecting the qualities of the horse, the Frenchman gave a favorable reply — but always commenced his commendation with the depreciatory remark — "He's not look ver good." The Yankee, caring little for the looks of the horse, of which he could judge for himself, without the seller's assistance, and being fully persuaded, after minute inspection, that the beast was worth the moderate sum asked for him, made the purchase and took him home. A few days afterwards he returned to the seller, in high dudgeon, and declared he had been cheated in the quality of the horse. "Vat is de mattaire?" said the Frenchman. "Matter!" said the Yankee, "matter enough — the horse can't see! — he is blind as a bat!" "Ah!" — said the Frenchman — "Vat I vas tell you? — I vas tell you he vas not *look* ver good — *be gar*, I don't know if he *look* at all!"[5]

[4] *Yankee Blade*, Jan. 24, 1852 (vol. XI). Credited to the *Providence Post*.

[5] *Yankee Blade*, Aug. 2, 1851, credited to the *Boston Post*. Cf. an oral text given me by William S. Piper in Worcester, Mass., Feb. 10, 1943, as he had heard it some thirty years before when a farmer in the Connecticut Valley.

"A fellow went to a Yankee farmer and mentioned that he was in the market for a horse, and the farmer said he didn't know but he had one he might sell. So he trotted out a horse after some dickering. The would-be purchaser asked him what the faults of the horse were. The farmer said, Well he didn't know that the horse had any particular faults outside of not lookin' so good. The purchaser having examined the animal was satisfied as to the condition of the feet, knees, mouth and so forth, decided to pass up the matter of looks, and so they struck a dicker. Some days later a very irate man came into the farmer's yard and yelled, 'What d'you mean by selling me a blind horse, after you guaranteed that he was sound?' 'Well,' he answered, 'I don't know as I made any guarantee — all I said was, as far as I know, the animal didn't have any particular faults except that he didn't look so good.'"

For other horse trades hinging on a literal statement see "A Horse Trade," *Burlington Daily Free Press*, May 17, 1848; "Faults Pompey Couldn't Remember," *ibid.*, June 23, 1860; "Hoss Trade," *Yankee*, II (January 1936), 47; Cornelius Weygandt, "Thee'd be Pleased to See Her Go," *November Rowen* (New York and London, 1941), p. 251.

Yankee Yarns

The deceptive qualities of horses continually provoked the Yankee trick.

WHY HE DISPOSED OF THE HORSE

Mr. Sellum is a horse-jockey; that is, when he is not more profitably employed, he is not ashamed, so he says, to "try his fort'n in that respectable calling." He dropped in at Bailey's Bazaar a few weeks since, and very soon after Sellum arrived, a superb-looking charger, mounted by a graceful rider, pranced up the court and entered the arena, to be sold at public vendue.

"There he is, gents," said the auctioneer, "there he is! a splendid beast — look at him and judge for yourselves. There's an ear, a forearm, a nostril, an eye for you! That animal, gentlemen, was 'knocked down' to a gentleman under the hammer, less than three months ago, for two hundred and eighty dollars. But I am authorized to-day to sell that horse — let him bring more or less. He's a beauty; fine figure, splendid saddle beast, natural gait fourteen miles to the hour, trots a mile in 2:42, and altogether he's a great horse" (which last remark no one could doubt, for he weighed eleven hundred pounds). "How much am I offered for that beautiful horse?" continued the auctioneer. "Move him around the ring once, John. That's it — elegant motion ———"

There the horse stopped short, and refused to budge another inch, though John buried the rowels to the shoulder into his ribs.

"Give me a bid, gentlemen, if you please — that horse must be sold."

"Twenty dollars," was heard from one corner of the room.

"Twenty dollars!" screamed the auctioneer, with a seemingly ironical laugh. I'm offered the stupendous sum of twenty dollars, gentlemen, for that animal. Are there no sausage-makers in this congregation? I'm offered only twenty dollars! But, gentlemen, as I said, the horse is here to be sold, so I shall accept the bid.

"Twenty dollars. I'm offered twenty dollars —twenty dollars, twenty — twenty — give me thirty? — twenty dollars, twenty — did I hear thirty? Twenty dollars — give *five*? Twenty dollars — did I hear five? — twenty — give two and a half? Twenty dollars — say *one*? Shall I have twenty-one? Twenty — if that's the best bid, down he must go, gentlemen! Twenty dollars — going! Twenty, only — who's the fortunate buyer?"

"Sellum, John Sellum," said our friend.

"John Sellum, twenty dollars," says the auctioner; "you've got a horse as *is* a horse, Mr. Sellum."

And the fortunate John bore his magnificent charger away in triumph. A few days subsequently, an old acquaintance met John in the cars, and inquired about his purchase.

"Got that horse yet, John?"

"No, I sold him."

"So soon — what for?"

83

"Wal, nothin' in particular, but I didn't fancy the critter, all things considered."

"He was sound, wasn't he?"

"Wal, I reck'n he wasn't; that is to say, I calk'late he wasn't. Show'd very good pluck, till I got him down into Washington-street, after I left the Baz-a-r, but just opposite the Old South, he fell slap down on the pavement."

"Pshaw! you don't say so!"

"Yaas. Blind-staggers — wust kind. But I didn't mind that, so I took him home, and nussed him up a little. Put him in the gig next day — wouldn't start a peg! Coaxed him, draw'd him, run a hot wire in his ear, wollup'd him, and so forth, and finally bilt a fire under him. All no use; cunning cuss — sot rite down on the pile o' lighted shavins, and put it out."

Here his friend smiled.

"That wusn't nuthin', tho'. Went to git inter the wag'n, and he started 'fore I gathered up the ribbins. Went 'bout three rods for'ard, and stopped again quicker'n lightnin'. Throw'd me out over his head, inter the hoss-trough — kicked hisself out o' the shafts, and run a mile afore we ketched him. Brought him back, put him in the stall — low stable — got out of his reach, an' then begun to whale 'im. Then he kicked up again; knocked the flooring all through overhead, stove his shoes off, broke his halter, and then run back inter the stable floor. Trap-door happened to be open, and down went his hind legs, clean to the hips. There I had him foul."

"Yes, you did," replied his friend.

"I got a piece o' plank, an' I lam'd 'im for 'bout ten minits, w'en I be hanged if he didn't *git mad!* and kicked hisself out o' the hole. Next mornin' found him swelled up big as four hogsheads. Rub'd sperrets o' turpentine all over 'im, an' the ungrateful rascal kep' tryin' to kick me for 't. Give him nothin' to eat for eight days, an' the swellin' went down again! Took him out o' the stable, and found him lame, *behind.*"

"Very likely!"

"But, on a closer examination, see he was full as lame *for'ard*; one balanced t'other, so's he couldn't limp. One eye had been knock't out in the fight, but the headstall kivered that misfort'n. Brushed 'im down kerefully, and put on the shiny harness. Led him down the street, an' met an old gent in search of a 'spirited' beast. Asked me if I wanted to sell?

" 'No *sir!*' sez I.

" 'Wot'll you take for 'm?' sez he.

" 'He's high strung,' sez I.

" 'No matter,' sez he, 'I want a good 'un.'

" 'Isn't he 'ansome?' sez I.

" 'He is,' sez he; 'wot's he wuth?'

" 'I never warrants hosses,' sez I. 'Ef you want 'm jest as he is — you're a good judge o' hosses, no doubt?' sez I.

" 'Wal, I am' sez he.

" 'Very well, then; you may hev 'm for two hundred dollars,' sez I.

"The old gent peeked into his mouth, stroked his neck, looked very knowin', and replied —

" 'I'll give you a hundred and fifty?'

" 'Split the difference,' sez I.

" 'Done!' sez he.

" 'The hoss is your'n,' sez I.

"He give me the money, took the animal, an' that's the last I've heern o' him or that hoss."

"Possible!" exclaimed his friend.

"Yaas. Under all the suckemstances, I thort it wa'nt best to keep the beast, you see, so I let him go."

"Where are you going now?" asked his friend.

"To York."

"When do you return?"

"*Not a present*," said Mr. Sellum, slily — and I reckon he didn't.[6]

Yankees and horses enjoyed affinity not only in the proverbial trade but also in trotting races. One set of stories depicts the trickster entering a seedy nag into the race, undismayed by the contumely of contestants and spectators.

"SLEEPY DAVY." — A SPORTING SKETCH

The substance of the following sketch of "life on the road" may already have been printed, though I never met with it. I heard it related with most capital gusto and "marked emphasis," by a knight of the ribbons, while journeying through New Hampshire, lately — where good horse stories are very current at all seasons.

I had taken a seat on the box with the driver of the mail coach from B— to E—, no rail having as yet been laid down to the latter place — and upon handing him my cigar-case, I found him at once good-natured and communicative. Three miles from our starting, we came out of the woods upon a piece of hard, granite-ized road, over which the coach-tires rang right merrily, as the team bounded forward, seemingly accustomed to a much better pace thereabouts, than I had hitherto observed *en route*.

The nigh leader was (or rather *had been*) one of the "pelters" that we sometimes read about in sporting chronicles; a hammer-headed, strong-sinewed chestnut, of fabulous age, but a nag of unquestionable bottom, with as many "points" as joints! He was evidently a good 'un to go," *malgre* his protruding withers and manifold windgalls; and as he put out on striking the smoother road, I remarked that he was certainly "some pumpkins."

[6] *Spirit of the Times*, XXI (July 5, 1851), 232, by the "Young 'Un" (George P. Burnham).

"G'lang Davy!" said our driver, rather insinuatingly, as I spoke — and throwing the snapper of his long whip as gently upon his flank as an expert disciple of Walton could possibly drop his trout-fly upon an unbroken stream, old "Davy" straightened out his traces, and laid himself to his business with a will that set the rest of the team into a rollicking gallop, instanter.

For a mile or more, we dashed on at railroad speed, and the performance was really very credible. The road soon became rough again, however, and our Jehu became tamer.

"That's a good hoss, sir — that Davy," ventured the driver.

"So I think. Have you driven him here long?" I inquired.

"Over ten year, sir, in all weather, every day but Sundays, back and forth, and never lost a trip with him."

"Is it possible?"

"Fact sir. But Davy's an old 'un. Ten years ago he'd done with whole corn, anyway."

"Whole corn?" I asked — "how?"

Jehu smiled at my innocence.

"Grinders used up sir; that's all."

As I did not understand, he continued: —

"Teeth gin out sir. Couldn't eat corn — he was old, *then*. So we feed him on meat. G'lang Davy!"

"And how old must a horse be, in this condition?" I asked.

"Sixteen, p'raps."

"Then Davy must have seen over a score of year, at least."

"Five-and twenty, sir, sure! G'lang Bess! He's seen the time when he could slay 'em, though — the best on 'em too."

"He travels well," I added.

"Well, sir, that's noth'n now. You see he hitches a little behind. He's a bad spavin. More'n fifteen years ago he had his legs well under him, and was a sure card. We've got eight miles to go yet, and I'll tell you a story about him, if you like."

I readily assented, and he continued, thus: —

"As I said, it was a near a score o' years ago, that a big race was got up in York State, where half a dozen o' the best nags in the country were up for trial, and a pile of money was ventur'd on the result. There was a heap o' bragging, too, on the ground, and you'd better believe the cattle they brought to the course, that time, were fast 'uns. They didn't talk o' nothin' but two-forties, two-fifties, and three-minitters, for six weeks afore the race; and when they all got together, it was a good show, sartin — bet your life on it.

"Well — arter the first race was over with the running horses, all at once there came up to the Judge's stand a drunken man; that is, he wasn't *very* drunk, but *pooty* drunk, you know — just about as tight, (supposing he could carry off a gallon o' licker,) as two quarts 'd make him."

"Half-cocked." I suggested.

"Edzactly; I see you understand. Well, he come up, an' says to the

Judge, 'Hain't you, ic, narry *trottin'* 'osses, yere?' But the head Judge says to him, 'Go 'way, my good man; you're slightly 'neebr'ated; and if you don't git out the way, you'll get knocked down by the horses.'

"But the feller wouldn't! He wanted to know if they hadn't narry trottin' horse, you see. 'I ain't afeered, ic, o' being knocked down by nun o' your trottin' 'osses, says the feller. 'Well, then, I'll send for a p'liceman,' continued the Judge, politely — 'an' he'll knock you down quicker'n *scat!*' So the drunken man sidled up to the Judge ag'in, and said he, 'I can beat your *trottin'* 'osses all to rags. Ef you've got any, fetch 'em on!' *Then* the Judges took a little more notice of the feller, you see

"The drunken man paid an entrance fee, at once, and shortly afterwards staggered in on to the track, leading a shocking looking beast, with an old black saddle on him, and a yaller bridle with blinders on it; Of course, the crowd yelled and hurra-ed like sixty — but the man was too much 'neebr'ated to care much for that; and, what was wuss, it was clear that his licker was a workin'; for, if anything, he grew a little drunker every minute. However, he came up to the stand with his beautiful nag.

"The next race was announced. Three mile heats — best two in three — open to all comers, without distinction — for $1000 a side. It was a bad show for the poor feller, anyhow. He hadn't but a hundred dollars, and the horses were coming up for trial. Suddenly his *brother* came out of the crowd, all covered over with dust, and out of breath — just arrived — heard he was there, drunk and fooling away his money, and begged him to go home with him. No! The feller was goin' to have a trot with the "big bugs." His affectionate brother assured him (and the crowd) that he would lose every dollar he had — but he would trot, anyhow. So, he give his note, and his brother let him have money enough to "anty up" with the betting men all round; who took his seven or eight hundred dollars at large odds aginst his chances.

"You never saw so bad a looking creeter as that man's hoss was. He hitched along behind his drunken owner, with his nose down between his knees, his tongue lolling half out of his thin jaws, his eyes nearly closed, and his tail clinging close to his body, while the 'boys' were in high glee at the prospect of the approaching fun. The bets were all closed, and those who watched the *man* thought that the excitement had rather helped him — for he really wasn't so drunk as he had appeared!

"You should have been there, sir, to have seen that horse the instant the bugle sounded, calling the animals to the post! Ha! ha! Well, it's no matter. The drunken man vaulted into the saddle, and ten men couldn't have held his horse. At the word 'go!' he jumped into a gait such as the two-forty jockies never dreamed of!"

"*What!*" I exclaimed in amazement.

"Yes, *sir*," continued Jehu, enthusiastically, "that drunk, that stupid horse, that dear brother, was all a *guy*. The lazy nag took the pole at the start, and before the second mile had been reached, he had it all his own way, *followed* only by ten or eleven of the best horses in York; while he pelted right through the three miles, inside of eight minutes, winning the first heat splendidly!"

"Well — what followed?"

"What followed! Why, one half the horses that chased him in on the first heat, to be sure. When the Judge said 'go!' the second time, I tell you he was there — and *went!* Ha! ha! ha! It's no use talking, he laid 'em all out — coming home the last mile in two-thirty-two — only three of the whole crowd saving their distance. Ger'*lang* Davy! He's an old 'un now, sir!" continued Jehu, again applying the snapper to his nigh leader.

"But you don't mean to say," I required, "that *this* is the animal you have described?"

"Oh, yes, sir, that's *him;* Davy — 'Sleepy Davy,' we call him, sir."

While I was lost in thinking of the changes in poor Davy's career during the previous twenty years or less, the stage-horn sounded from the terminus of our route, and the coach rolled up right gallantly, at a twelve mile gait, before the door of the tavern where we "changed horses." [7]

One form of "saw" common in Yankeeland relied on the literal statement of a contractual agreement. According to the letter of the bargain, the outsmarted party had to confess himself done brown and accept the stipulated terms.

ART OF A YANKEE PAINTER

A person who kept an inn by the roadside, went to a painter, who for a time had set up his easel not a hundred miles from Ontario, and inquired for what sum the painter would paint him a bear for a signboard. It was to be a real good one, that would attract customers.

"Fifteen dollars!" replied the painter.

"That's too much!" said the inn-keeper; "Tom Larkins will do it for ten."

The painter cogitated for a moment. He did not like that this rival should get a commission in preference to himself, although it was only for a signboard.

"Is it to be a wild or tame bear?" he enquired.

"A wild one to be sure."

"With a chain or without one?" again asked the painter.

"Without a chain!"

"Well, I will paint you a wild bear, without a chain, for ten dollars!"

The bargain was struck, the painter set to work, and in due time sent home the signboard, on which he had painted a huge brown bear of a

---

[7] *Spirit of the Times*, XXIV (July 29, 1854), 279–280, by the "Young 'Un." Cf. "The Thirty-Nine Dollar Mare," *Yankee Blade*, Jan. 21, 1854 (vol. XIII). The same tale plot is used by Holmes in his poem, "How the Old Horse Won the Bet" (*The Complete Poetical Works of Oliver Wendell Holmes*, Boston and New York, 1899, pp. 289–301).

most ferocious aspect. The signboard was the admiration of all the neighborhood, and drew plenty of customers to the inn; and the inn-keeper knew not whether to congratulate himself more upon the possession of so attractive a sign, or on having secured it for the small sum of ten dollars. Time slipped on, his barrels were emptied and his pockets filled. Every thing went on thrivingly for three weeks, when one night there arose one of those violent storms of rain and wind, thunder and lightning, which are so common in North America, and which pass over with almost as much rapidity as they rise. When the inn-keeper awoke next morning, the sun was shining, the birds singing, and all the traces of the storm had passed away. He looked up anxiously to ascertain that his sign was safe. There it was sure enough, swinging to and fro as usual, but the bear had disappeared. The inn-keeper could hardly believe his eyes; full of anger and surprise, he ran to the painter, and related what had happened. The painter looked up coolly from his work.

"Was it a wild bear or a tame one?"

"A wild bear."

"Was it chained or not?"

"I guess not."

"Then," cried the painter, triumphantly, "how could you expect a wild bear to remain in such a storm as that of last night without a chain?"

The inn-keeper had nothing to say against so conclusive an argument, and finally agreed to give the painter fifteen dollars to paint him a wild bear with a chain, that would not take to the woods in the next storm.

For the benefit of our unprofessional readers, it may be necessary to mention that the roguish painter had painted the first bear in water colors, which had been washed away by the rain; the second bear was painted in oil colors, and was therefore able to withstand the weather.[8]

Retributive practical jokes formed a fruitful section of Yankee tricks.

A MELTING STORY

One winter evening, a country store-keeper in the Mountain State was about closing his doors for the night, and while standing in the snow outside putting up his window-shutters, he saw through the glass a lounging, worthless fellow within grab a pound of fresh butter from the shelf and hastily conceal it in his hat.

The act was no sooner detected than the revenge was hit upon, and a very few moments found the Green Mountain store-keeper at once indulging his appetite for fun to the fullest extent, and paying off the thief with a facetious sort of torture for which he might have gained a premium from the old inquisition.

"I say, Seth!" said the store-keeper, coming in and closing the door after him, slapping his hands over his shoulders, and stamping the snow off his shoes.

[8] *Yankee Blade*, Dec. 16, 1854 (vol. XIV).

Seth had his hand upon the door, his hat upon his head, and the roll of new butter in his hat, anxious to make his exit as soon as possible.

"I say, Seth, sit down; I reckon, now, on such an e-*tar*-nal night as this, a leetle something warm wouldn't hurt a fellow; come and sit down."

Seth felt very uncertain: he had the butter, and was exceedingly anxious to be off, but the temptation of 'something warm' sadly interfered with his resolution to go. This hesitation, however, was soon settled by the right owner of the butter taking Seth by the shoulders, and planting him in a seat close to the stove, where he was in such a manner cornered in by barrels and boxes that while the country grocer sat before him there was no possibility of his getting out, and right in this very place sure enough the store-keeper sat down.

"Seth, we'll have a little warm Santa Cruz," said the Green Mountain grocer, as he opened the stove-door and stuffed in as many sticks as the space would admit. "Without it you'd freeze going home such a night as this."

Seth already felt the butter settling down closer to his hair and jumped up declaring he must go.

"Not till you have something warm, Seth; come, I've got a story to tell you, too; sit down, now;" and Seth was again pushed into his seat by his cunning tormentor.

"Oh! it's tu darn'd hot here," said the petty thief, again attempting to rise.

"Set down — don't be in such a plagey hurry," retorted the grocer, pushing him back in his chair.

"But I've got the cows tu fodder, and some wood tu split, and I *must* be agoin'," continued the persecuted chap.

"But you mustn't tear yourself away, Seth, in this manner. Set down; let the cows take care of themselves and keep yourself *cool*, you appear to be fidgetty," said the roguish grocer with a wicked leer.

The next thing was the production of two smoking glasses of hot rum toddy, the very sight of which, in Seth's present situation, would have made the hair stand erect upon his head had it not been well oiled and kept down by the butter.

"Seth, I'll give you a *toast* now, and you can *butter* it yourself," said the grocer, yet with an air of such consummate simplicity that poor Seth still believed himself unsuspected. "Seth, here's — here's a Christmas goose — (it was about Christmas time) — here's a Christmas *goose* well *roasted* and *basted*, eh? I tell you, Seth, it's the greatest eating in *cre*ation. And, Seth, don't you never use hog's fat or common cooking butter to baste with; fresh pound butter, just the same as you see on that shelf yonder, is the only proper thing in natur to baste a goose with — come take your *butter* — I mean, Seth, take your toddy."

Poor Seth now began to *smoke* as well as to *melt*, and his mouth was hermetically sealed up as though he had been born dumb. Streak after streak of the butter came pouring from under his hat, and his handkerchief was already soaked with the overflow. Talking away as if nothing was the matter, the grocer kept stuffing in the wood into the stove, while poor Seth sat bolt upright, with his back against the counter, and his knees almost touching the red hot furnace before him.

"Darnation cold night, this," said the grocer. "Why, Seth, you seem to perspire as if you were warm! Why don't you take your hat off? Here, let me put your hat away!"

"*No!*" exclaimed poor Seth at last, with a spasmodic effort to get his tongue loose, and clapping both hands upon his hat, "No! I must go: let me go out; I aint well; let me go!" A greasy cataract was now pouring down the poor fellow's face and neck, and soaking into his clothes, and trickling down his body into his very boots, so that he was literally in a perfect bath of oil.

"Well, good night, Seth," said the humorous Vermonter, "if you *will* go;" adding, as Seth got out into the road, "neighbor, I reckon the fun I've had out of you is worth a nine pence, so I shan't charge you for that *pound of butter!*" [9]

An appropriate reprisal to a certain malicious practical joke passed into folktale.

THE TWO JOKING FARMERS OF OLD CONNECTICUT

In the Land of Steady Habits, in the good old days of the early pilgrims and the reign of Blue Laws, there dwelt on the banks of the Connecticut two sturdy farmers, by the names of Thompson and Jones, whose eccentric and fun-loving characters formed a striking contrast with all their stern, straight-jacket neighbors. Their farms were adjoining each other, and they always lived on intimate and friendly terms. They would borrow and lend hoes, harrows, and plows, exchange day's works at haying time and harvest, go to each other's huskings, and join their teams together to break the roads and haul out wood in the winter. Their great peculiarity, which marked them so distinctly from their neighbors, was their love of fun and fondness for practical jokes.

As the other neighbors were so dissimilar in their habits and feelings, that they would hold but little intercourse with these "sons of Belial," Thompson and Jones were naturally thrown more exclusively upon each other for society, and their hard practical jokes were consequently played off upon each other with the utmost good humor, and he that could joke the hardest was the best fellow.

Thompson had a valuable sheep, which was a little prone to gadding, and which grew rather fond of neighbor Jones' clover field. Jones had turned the sheep out several times, and remonstrated with Thompson against the intrusion and the trespass. Thompson only laughed, and told Jones he must keep a better fence or poorer feed. His sheep was a sheep of

[9] *Spirit of the Times*, X (Jan. 23, 1841), 555. Credited to the (New Orleans) *Picayune*.

excellent taste and sound judgement, and certainly ought not to be blamed for looking out for number one.

Jones didn't feel exactly satisfied with this reasoning, and resolved, if the trespass were repeated, to inflict summary punishment on the trespasser. On looking out early the next morning he beheld the sheep again in the clover field. He drove the sheep into his barn-yard and caught her. Then taking a sharp knife, he run it through one of the hind legs between the tendon and the bone near the gambrel joint, and taking up the other leg, thrust it through the incision he had made. He then turned the sheep out and sent it hobbling home on three legs.

When Thompson went out to his barn in the morning he discovered his poor sheep in this sad predicament, and having relieved her from the unpleasant embarrassment, he started off to give Jones a piece of his mind.

"Now, neighbor Jones," said Thompson, "I think you are too bad. I can bear a joke as well as any body; but I'll tell you what 'tis, this is carrying the joke too far by a great sight. Here my sheep now is almost spoilt by having one hind leg stuck through t'other. Now, Jones, how could you be so unhuman?"

"Me? neighbor Thompson," said Jones; "I had no hand in it. Why should you accuse me? The fact was, your sheep was in my clover-field again this morning, and I went out to set the dog on her to drive her out; but she was so smart in looking out *for number one*, that she turned and run like fury, and as she jumped over the fence she came down a little on one side, and stuck one leg right through t'other, herself. I hadn't no hand in it, neighbor Thompson. That's a wonderful smart sheep of yourn. Why, when she had only three legs, she out-run my dog with four."

Thompson being unable to obtain any satisfaction, pocketed the joke, hard as it was, and went home. Now Jones had a long-legged, long-sided hog, about a year old, a mischievous, unprincipled animal, that went about poking his nose into everything, and meddling with matters that he had no business to. And it so happened, that early next morning, Thompson found Jones' hog in his garden rooting up the vegetables. He caught the hog, and with a sharp knife slit his mouth open on both sides clear to his ears. He then turned the grunter out and sent him home very much chop-fallen. Jones now in his turn was in a rage. He bound up the animal's head as well as he could, and then started off to give Thompson "a real setting out."

Thompson saw Jones coming, full of fire and fury, and he sat down on a log before his door, and quietly took out his jack-knife and went to whittling. Jones came up, breathing hard with indignation.

"Now, Thompson," said he, "you and I are done. I'll tell you what 'tis, if you are going to turn savage, I'll quit. I'll have nothing to do with any body that's more cruel and more brutal than a savage. Now, Thompson, you've ruined that hog of mine. He isn't worth a sixpence. He isn't fat enough to kill now, and I never shall be able to fat him, now you've cut his mouth open from ear to ear. I tell ye, Thompson, you and I are done."

"Why neighbor, how unreasonable you are," said Thompson very gravely; "the most unreasonable man that ever I knew, to accuse me of such a thing as that. Why, the case was jest this, neighbor Jones. Your hog was walking out early this morning, and he came down this way, and as he was going by my barn-yard, he happened to look through the fence and see my poor sheep running about with one leg stuck through t'other, and upon my word, neighbor Jones, he split his mouth from ear to ear a laughin'." [10]

Saws and sells in profuse variety interlarded Yankee storytelling; in one case on record, the narrator himself served the trick.

JEMMY DELANY'S STORY

Jemmy Delany was a capital story-teller, and in the days when he was in his prime, it was a fashionable amusement for the bloods about town to congregate together to while away the winter evenings singing songs, telling stories, and passing the bottle. But that was a long time ago, — long before the advent of temperance notions; and Maine laws have made such things nearly obsolete.

Besides being a capital story-teller, Jemmy Delany was also a capital humorist; and often instead of telling his story, as his companions usually expected, he would elude their solicitations by some ingenious specimen of waggery, which was always sure to "bring down the house" with "Bravo! Jemmy — we will excuse you this time!"

One fine sparkling winter evening found Jemmy seated with a jolly lot of bloods, under just such circumstances as we have already alluded to; and the rule of the evening was, that each member of the circle should sing a song, tell a story, or order a fresh bottle of wine. After a couple of hours were spent in this manner, it came Jemmy's turn to "do service."

"Tune up, Jemmy — give us one of those capital songs," says one.

"Pshaw," says the next man; "you know Jemmy's forte lies in telling stories!"

"Yes — yes — give us a story," is the general cry.

After two or three preliminary "hems," and another pull at the little bottle of wine, Jemmy cast an inquiring glance around. "I really don't know as I have anything I can tell you that I have not told you before. The fact is, I think you are pressing me rather too closely."

"Oh, never mind," says one, "we are not very particular this time; give us something good now; you have such a way of embellishing an old story that its repetition under such circumstances — — — "

"Yes, yes," interrupted a second, "give us one of your old stories, if you can't think of anything new!"

---

[10] Seba Smith, *Spirit of the Times*, XVII (March 20, 1847), 38. Cf. "Anecdote of an Old Tar," *Union Jack*, July 1, 1848 (vol. I); G. T. Ridlon, "Angry Neighbors," *Saco Valley Settlements and Families* (Portland, 1895), pp. 378–379.

"Well, well," adds Jemmy, with an air of modest submission, "I will endeavor to satisfy you. It is possible some of you may have heard the story about the man who had his arm bit off by a bear?"

"No! no!" was the reply on every side, "that will do — give us that."

"Ah! that being the case, I may be able to interest you. To commence, then, some ten years ago, I knew a man who was attacked by a bear in the woods; and he had his arm bit off by the ferocious animal before he could make his escape. But," says Jemmy, looking around, "I think you have all of you heard the story?"

"No! no!" was the echo. "Go on, and give us the story."

"Really, gentlemen," says Jemmy, "I protest I do not, after all, consider the story of much interest, and I am sure you have heard it."

"But we have *not* heard it, and we insist upon hearing the story."

"Well, well," says Jemmy, with an appearance of great reluctance, "if I must, I must. I'll just commence back at the beginning: *Some ten years ago, I knew a man who was attacked by a bear, in the woods, and he had his arm bit off by the ferocious animal, before he could make his escape —* now gentlemen," says Jemmy, appearing to interrupt himself, "I am perfectly sure you *must* have heard this story; and indeed — — — —"

"Oh! nonsense!" roared one of the bloods, interrupting Jemmy, "never mind if we have heard it; just give it to us again; what if we have heard it, we can listen to it again — for my part, I never heard it, and you will particularly oblige me, to say nothing of the rest of the company, if you will be kind enough to favor us with the story."

They were all anxious for the story, and Jemmy being pressed on all sides, at last consents to give them the story.

"Hem! Hem! — now don't interrupt me, if you please."

"No, no — go ahead!"

"Well, gentlemen, (allow me to commence at the beginning,) *Some ten years ago, I knew a man who was attacked by a bear in the woods, and he had his arm bit off by the ferocious animal, before he could make his escape! —* " seeming again to interrupt himself, Jemmy turns a look on each of his expectant listeners. "Really, gentlemen, I insist you must all of you be familiar with the story; I am *positive* I have told it to you; several times, I think." And Jemmy "drew a bead" on a smile.

The idea seemed to enter each head at once that they *had, all* heard the story! In fact, Jemmy's story was, *"some years ago he knew a man who was attacked by a bear in the woods, and he had his arm bit off by the ferocious animal, before he could make his escape."*

Jemmy had free tickets at the bars around town, on the strength of that story, for the next six weeks.[11]

Originals. Where he was not involved in gulls or frauds, either as hoaxer or the hoaxed, the Yankee still displayed his uniform stripings of

[11] *Yankee Blade*, Oct. 28, 1854 (vol. XIV).

eccentric manner and conspicuous oddity. Always the downeaster impressed society as being a "character."

AN ORIGINAL CHARACTER

Whoever travels through any of the New England States, and twigs as he journeys, the eccentricities of some of the natives, cannot but be amused with the following graphic sketch, and may derive many new ideas in respect to etymology and diversity of character,

Some years since an acquaintance of ours set out on horseback from the eastern part of Massachusetts for the Green Mountains in Vermont. While travelling through the town of New Salem his road led into a piece of woods some five miles in length, and long before he got out of which, he began to entertain doubts whether he should be blest with the sight of a human habitation; but as all things must have an end, so at last the woods, and the nut brown house of a farmer greeted his vision. Near the road was a tall rawboned, overgrown, lantern jawed boy probably seventeen years of age, digging potatoes. He was a curious figure to behold. What was lacking in the length of his tow breeches was amply made up for behind; his suspenders appeared to be composed of birch bark, grape vine sheepskin; and as for his hat, which was of dingy felt — poor thing, it had once evidently seen better days, but now, alas! It was only the shadow of its glory. Whether the tempest of time had beaten the top in, or the lad's expanding genius had burst it out, was difficult to tell; at any rate, it was missing — and through the aperture red hairs in abundance stood six ways for Sunday. In short, he was one of the roughest specimens of domestic manufacture that ever mortal beheld. Our travelling friend, feeling an itching to scrape an acquaintance with the critter, drew up the reins of his horse and began:

"Hallo, my good friend, can you inform me how far it is to the next house?"

Jonathan started up — leaned on his hoe handle — rested one foot on the gamble of his sinister leg, and replied —

"Hullo yourself! how'd dew? Well I jess can. Taint near so fur as it used to be afore they cut the woods away — then 'twas generally reckoned four miles, but now the sun shrivels up the road and don't make more'n tew. The fust house you come to though, is a barn, and the next is a hay stack; but old Hobsin's house is on beyant. You'll be sure to meet his gals long afore you get there; tarnil rompin' critters, they plague our folks more'n little. His sheep git in our pasture every day, and his gals in our orchard. Dad sets the dog arter the sheep and me arter the gals — and the way we makes the wool and the petticoats fly, is a sin to snakes."

"I see you are inclined to be facetious, young man — pray tell me how it happens that one of your legs is shorter than the other?"

"I never 'lows any body to meddle with my grass tanglers, mistur; but seein' it is you, I'll tell ye. I was born so at my tickler request, so that when I hold a plough, I can go with one foot in the furrer, and t'other on land, and not lop over; besides, it is very convenient when I mow round a side hill."

"Very good, indeed — how do your potatoes come off this year?"

"They don't come at all; I digs 'em out and there's an everlastin' snarl of 'em in each hill."

"But they are small, I perceive."

"Yes, I know it — you see we planted some whoppin' blue noses over in that 'ere patch there, and they flourished so all firedly, that these 'ere stopt growin' just out of spite; 'cause they know'd they couldn't begin to keep up."

"You appear to be pretty smart, and I should think you could afford a better hat than the one you wear."

"The looks aint nothin'; its all in the behavior. This 'ere hat was my religious Sunday-go-to-meetin' hat, and it's just as chock full of piety now as a dog is full of fleas. I've got a better one to hum, but I don't dig taters in it no how."

"You have been in these parts sometime, I should guess."

"I guess so tew. I was borned and got my bro'tin up in that 'ere house; but my native place is down in Pordunk."

"Then you said that it is about three and half miles to the next house?"

"Yes, sir; 'twas a spell ago, and I don't believe it's grow'd much shorter since."

"Much obliged. Good bye."

"Good bye to ye — that's a darn slick horse of yourn."

There, reader — there is a Jonathan for you of the first water. You don't find his equal every place.[1]

Among the categories of gawking originals, none surpassed in popularity the rustic swain.

A full-blooded Jonathan, residing in a certain town in New England, once took it into his head to "go a courtin;" he accordingly saddled the old mare, and started off to pay his devoirs to one of the buxom lasses of the neighbourhood. After "stayin" with his "gal" until daylight began to streak the east, he made preparations to depart. Just as he was seating himself in the saddle, his fair one, who stood in the door, (and who, by the way, was marvellously fond of having "sparks,") wishing to have him come again, stammered out, *"I shall be at home next Sunday night, Zeb."* Zebedee, taking out his tobacco-box, and biting off a quid of pigtail in less than a second, honestly answered. *"So shall I, by gaully!!!"* [2]

Amorous Yankees furnished humor in native literature from the Jonathan of *The Contrast* to Zekle in *The Biglow Papers*; in fleeting anecdotes and sketches, courting scenes were equally staple. His natural

---

[1] *Spirit of the Times*, XIII (Dec. 23, 1843), 506; also the *Exeter News Letter*, June 15, 1841. The motive of the short leg used for traveling around a hill distinguishes the "Sidehill Gouger," a mythical beast in twentieth-century native tall tales.

[2] *The American Joe Miller* (Philadelphia, 1847), p. 149.

gaucherie accentuated by attempts at tenderness and gallantry, Jonathan a-courting presented an absurdly clumsy spectacle.

FARMER SMITH AND MA'AM JONES

Widower Smith's wagon stopped one morning before widow Jones' door and gave the usual country signal, that he wanted to see somebody in the House, by dropping the reins, and sitting double, with his elbows on his knees. Out tripped the widow, lively as a cricket, with a tremendous black ribbon on her snow white cap. Good morning was said on both sides, and the widow waited for what was further to be said.

'Well ma'am Jones, perhaps you don't want to see one of your cows, no how, for nothing, any way, do you.'

"Well, there Mr. Smith, you couldn't have spoke my mind better. A poor, lone woman like me, dose'nt know what to do with so many creatures, and I should be glad to trade if we can fix it.'

So they adjourned to the meadow. Farmer Smith looked at Roan — then at the widow — at Brindle —then at the widow —at the Downing cow — then at the widow again — and through the whole forty. The same call was made every day for a week, but Farmer Smith could not decide which cow he wanted. At length, on Saturday when widow Jones was in a hurry to get through with her baking for Sunday — and "ever so much" to do in the house, as all farmers wives and widows have on Saturday, she was a little impatient — Farmer Smith was as irresolute as ever.

'That 'ere Downing cow is a pretty fair creature' — but he stopped to glance at the widow's face and then walked round her — not the widow, but the cow.

'That 'ere short horn Durham is not a bad looking beast, but I don't know —' another look at the widow.

'The Downing cow I knew before the late Mr. Jones bought her;' Here he sighed at the allusion to the late Mr. Jones, she sighed, and both looked at each other. It was a highly interesting moment.

'Old Roan is an old milch, and so is Brindle — but I have known better.' A long stare followed this speech — the pause was getting awkward, and at last Mrs. Jones broke out —

'Lord Mr. Smith, if I'm the one you want, do say so!"

The intentions of widower and the widow Jones were duly published the next day as is the law and custom in Massachusetts; and as soon as they were "out published," they were married.[3]

Temperamental decisions sometimes upset matrimonial plans.

A YANKEE calling himself Sam Hopeful, who has written some very good things, tells right out in meeting why he never married after three attempts. He says:

[3] H. Hastings Weld, *Burlington Daily Free Press*, May 19, 1848. Also *Union Jack*, July 1, 1848 (vol. III); *Exeter News Letter*, July 12, 1842.

"I once courted a gal by the name of Deb Hawkins, and had made up my mind to get married. Well, while we were going to the deacon's I stepped into a mud puddle and spattered the mud over Deb's new gown made out of her grandmother's old chintz petticoat. When we got to the deacon's he asked Deb if she would take me for her lawful and wedded husband? 'No!' says she. 'Reason,' says I. 'Why,' says she, 'I have taken a misliken to you.'

"Well it was all up then, but I gave her a string of bead, a few kisses and some other notions and made it all up with her. So we went to the deacon's a second time. I was bound to get even with her this time, so when the deacon asked me if I would take her for my wedded wife I says, 'No, I should do no such thing.' 'Why,' says I, 'I have taken a misliken to you.'

"Well, it was all over again, but I gave her a new apron and a few other trinkets, and we went up again to get married. We expected that we should be tied so fast all natur couldn't separate us; but when we asked the deacon if he would marry us he said, 'No, I shan't do no such a thing.' Why, what on airth is the reason?' says we. 'Why,' says he, 'I have taken a misliken to both of you.'

"Deb burst out crying, he burst out scolding, I burst out laughing, and such a set of busters you never did see; and that is the reason I never got married. My chance is gone." [4]

HARD OF HEARING

A Love Story

A young Jonathan once courted the daughter of an old man that lived "down east," who professed to be deficient in hearing, but, forsooth, was more captious than limited in hearing, as the sequel will show.

It was a stormy night in the ides of March, if I mistake not, when lightning and loud peals of thunder answered thunder, that Jonathan sat by the old man's fireside, discussing with the old lady, (his intended mother-in-law,) on the expediency of asking the old man's permission to marry "Sal." Jonathan resolved to "pop it" to the old man the next day. Night passed, and by the dawn of another day, the old man was found in his barn-lot, feeding his pigs. Jonathan rose from his bed early in the morning, spied the old man feeding his pigs, and resolved to ask him for Sal.

Scarce had a minute elapsed, after Jonathan made his resolution, ere he bid the old man "good morning." Now Jonathan's heart beat; now he scratched his head, and ever and anon gave birth to a pensive yawn. Jonathan declared that he'd as lief take thirty-nine "stripes" as to ask the old man; "but," said he aloud to himself, "however, here's go it, a faint heart never won a fair girl," and addressed the old man thus: —

"I say, old man, I want to marry your daughter."

[4] *Harry Hazel's Yankee Blade*, Aug. 24, 1872 (vol. X). Cf. "Three Chances for a Wife," *Life and Recollections of Yankee Hill*, William K. Northall, ed. (New York, 1850), pp. 142–143, where the same plot is set in Ireland.

Old Man — "You want to borrow my halter. I would loan it to you, Jonathan, but my son has taken it and gone off to the mill."

Jonathan — Putting his mouth close to the old man's ear, and speaking in a deafening tone — "I've got five hundred pounds of money!"

Old man — Stepping back as if greatly alarmed, and exclaiming in a voice of surprise — "You have got five hundred pounds of honey, Jonathan? Why, it is more than all the neighborhood has use for."

Jonathan — (Not yet the victim of despair, and putting his mouth to the old man's ear, bawled out) — "I've got gold."

Old Man — "So have I, Jonathan, and it's the worst cold I ever had in my life." So saying, he sneezed a "wash up."

By this time the old lady came up, and having observed Jonathan's unfortunate luck, she put her mouth to the old man's ear, and screamed like a wounded Yahoo:

"Daddy, I say Daddy — you don't understand; he wants to marry our daughter."

Old man — "I told him our calf halter was gone."

Old Lady — "Why daddy, you don't understand — he's got gold! — he's rich!"

Old man — "He's got a cold and the itch, eh! What's he doing here with the itch, eh!" So saying the old man aimed a blow at Jonathan's head with his walking cane — but happily for Jonathan, he dodged it. Nor did the rage of the old man stop at this, but with angry countenance, he made after Jonathan, who took to his heels; nor did Jonathan's luck stop here, he had not got out of the barn yard, nor far from the old man, who run him a close race, ere Jonathan stumped his toe, and fell to the ground, and before the old man could "take up," he stumbled over Jonathan and fell sprawling in a mud hole. Jonathan sprung to his heels, and with the speed of a John Gilpin, cleared himself. And poor Sal! she died a *nun. Never had no husband.*[5]

Place a Yankee in a witness box, and an original scene would be bound to ensue.

WADLEIGH'S TRIAL FOR SLEEPING IN MEETING

Justice Winslow. — *What* do you know about Wadleigh's sleeping in meeting?

Witness. — I know all about it; 'taint no secret, I guess.

Justice. — Then tell us all about it; that's just what we want to know.

Witness. — (scratching his head). — Well, the long and the short of it is, John Wadleigh is a hard working man; that is, he works mighty hard doing nothing; and that's the hardest work there is done. It will make a feller sleep quicker than poppy-leaves. So it stands to reason that Wadleigh would naterally be a very sleepy sort of person. Well, the weather

---

[5] *Yankee Blade*, March 1, 1851 (vol. X).

is sometimes naterally considerable warm, and Parson Moody's sarmons is sometimes rather heavy-like.

"Stop, stop!" said Justice Winslow. "No reflections upon Parson Moody; that is not what you were called here for."

Witness. — I don't cast no reflections on Parson Moody. I was only telling what I know about John Wadleigh's sleeping in meeting; and it's my opinion, especially in warm weather, that sarmons that are heavy-like, and two hours long, naterally have a tendency —

"Stop, stop! I say," said Squire Winslow; "if you repeat any of these reflections on Parson Moody again, I'll commit you to the cage for contempt of court."

Witness. — I don't cast no reflections on Parson Moody. I was only telling what I know about John Wadleigh's sleeping in meeting.

Squire Winslow. — Well, go on and tell us all about that. You weren't called here to testify about Parson Moody.

Witness. — That's what I am trying to do, if you wouldn't keep putting me out. And it's my opinion, in warm weather, folks is considerably apt to sleep in meeting; especially when the sarmon — I mean especially where they get pretty tired. I know I find it pretty hard work to get by seventhly and eighthly in the sarmon myself; but if I once get there, I generally get into a kind of a waking train again, and make out to weather it. But it isn't so with Wadleigh; I've generally noticed that if he begins to gape at the seventhly and eighthly, it's a gone goose with him before he gets through tenthly, and he has to look out for another prop for his head somewhere, for his neck isn't stiff enough to hold it up. And from tenthly up to sixteenthly he's as dead as a door nail, till the amen brings the people up to prayers, and Wadleigh comes up with a jerk, just like opening a jack-knife.[6]

Interrogated Yankees might provoke with their indirection, but inquisitive Yankees outraged all propriety with impudent investigations.

[6] *Spirit of the Times*, XVII (July 10, 1847), 228. This is a condensation of a longer account which appeared in the *Yankee Blade*, March 25, 1847, bearing the title "John Wadleigh's Trial" and giving this information: "Under this caption a droll story of the old Puritan times in New England, by Seba Smith, is going the rounds of the press from Calais to Matamoros. It was written originally for the N. Y. Illustrated Magazine." This is reprinted in Smith's collection of popular pieces, *'Way Down East: or, Portraitures of Yankee Life* (Philadelphia, 1890), pp. 5–28. For a memoir on the Rev. Samuel Moody of York, Me., see Charles C. P. Moody, *Biographical Sketches of the Moody Family* (Boston, 1847), pp. 54–94; the author writes (p. 69): "His eccentricities were very striking, and under this head we might place nearly his whole memoir." Cf. Clifford K. Shipton, in *Sibley's Harvard Graduates*, IV, 358: "The more eccentric manifestations of 'Father' Moody's religion grew into a folklore that succeeding generations loved to hear and tell around Maine firesides." Humorous anecdotes about Moody are in the *Idiot, or Invisible Rambler*, vol. I, no. 45 (Nov. 14, 1818), and *Harry Hazel's Yankee Blade*, vol. VI, no. 41 (July 25, 1868).

This Moody is not to be confused with Rev. Joseph or "Handkerchief" Moody, also of York, around whom Hawthorne constructed his tale, "The Minister's Black Veil."

Yankee Yarns

AN INQUISITIVE YANKEE

A gentleman riding in an eastern railroad car, which was rather sparsely supplied with passengers, observed in the seat before him a lean slab-sided Yankee, every feature of whose face seemed to ask a question: and a little circumstance soon proved that he possessed a most "inquiring mind." Before him, occupying the entire seat, sat a lady, dressed in deep black; and after shifting his position several times, and manoeuvring to get an opportunity to look in her face, he at length "caught her eye." He nodded familiarly to her, and asked, with a nasal twang utterly incapable of imitation.

"In affliction?"

"Yes, sir," replied the lady.

"Parents? — father or mother?"

"No, sir," said the lady.

"Child, perhaps? — a boy or gal?"

"No, sir, not a child," was the response, "I have no children."

"Husband, then 'xpect?"

"Yes," was the curt answer.

"Hum — cholery? — a tradin'-man, mebbe?"

"My husband was a sea-faring man — the captain of a vessel — he didn't die of cholera — he was drowned."

"Oh, drowned, eh?" pursued the inquisitor, hesitating for a brief instant — "save his chist?" he asked.

"Yes, the vessel was saved, and my husband's effects," said the widow.

"Was they?" asked the Yankee, his eyes brightening up.

"Pious man?" he continued.

"He was: a member of the Methodist church."

The next question was a little delayed, but it came.

"Don't yeou think you got gre-a-a-t cause to be thankful that he was a pious man, and saved his chist?"

"I do," said the widow, abruptly, and turning her head to look out of the car window. The indefatigable "pump" changed his position, held the widow by his "glittering eye" once more, and propounded one more query, in a little lower tone, with his head slightly inclined forward over the back of the seat.

"Was you cal'latin to git married agin?"

"Sir!" said the widow, indignantly, "you are impertinent!" And she left her seat and took another on the other side of the car.

"'Pears to be a little 'huffy!'" said the ineffable bore, turning to our narrator, behind him.

"She needn't be mad — I didn't want to hurt her feelins. What did they make you pay for that umberel you got in your hand? It's a real pooty one!" [7]

[7] *Yankee Blade,* March 13, 1852 (vol. XI). Credited to the *Knickerbocker.*

IV

TALL TALES

I F NO FOLKTALE TYPES are unique to the United States, some are con-
spicuously associated with American creation, and none more so than
the tall tale, the "long bow," the "large," "hard," and "tough" story.
In New England tall-tale production has easily kept pace with, if not
outdistanced, other sections and found abundant expression in ante-
bellum journalism, folk history, local-color writings, and other printed
conveyers of constantly flowing popular tales.

Munchausens. Sources and reservoirs of our native folk humor have
been many local story vendors with capacious memories, facile tongues,
and soaring fancies, and sometimes ear-witness records have preserved
their art at first hand. A sober antiquarian may recall a shiftless catchall
for stray tales.

Amasa Abbey was a character in his day. He was always merry and full
of fun, and was never annoyed because he was poor. Life and merriment
was worth more to him than riches. He was not a bad neighbor, nor was
he much given to the improvement of mankind. He had a fund of the most
improbable stories, a few of which will bear repeating. He probably told
them for amusement and not in any vicious spirit. One was that he had an
old horse unfit for duty, so one cold day in December he killed him and
hung his skin on the fence to dry, and on the same day he killed several
sheep and hung their skins on the same fence; that in the evening the old
horse pushed his nose through the kitchen window and whinnered as if cold
and hungry, whereupon Abbey rushed out into the dark to replace his skin
upon the animal, and by mistake put on the sheep skins, "and don't you
think," continued Abbey, "that horse lived and the next year I sheared forty
pounds of wool from him." Another one of his stories ran as follows: Abbey
said he went hunting deer one day and the game run round and round the
brow of a hill and he could not hit him with his gun, so he placed his gun
between two sapling trees and bent the barrel into a circular form and then
shot at the deer. The ball went round and round the hill until it hit the deer
and killed him. Still another which the writer remembers well: He said he
was out fox hunting, and having started up a young fox, and the dog being
in close pursuit the fox run against a small tree and split himself right in two
in the middle; that in coming together two legs were up and two down, but
nevertheless the fox ran away first on two legs which were down, and when

they got tired he would change over and run on the other two legs until they were tired, and in this manner the fox got away. He also said the trees were so large where he came from in Massachusetts that one day he started to cut one down to make into shingles, and chopping two weeks he started to go round the tree and see how large it was; that he found a man on the other side of the tree who had been chopping for three weeks and neither had heard the noise of the other's axe.[1]

Within the dragnet of the humorous journals an instance of some fluent narrator was sure to be caught.

TOUGH STORIES
Or, Some Reminiscences of "Uncle Charles"

One of the oddest and most eccentric geniuses that ever fell under our notice was "Uncle Charles," — an old, grey-headed man, of about three score and ten, who resided some years ago in a little village with a big name, about twenty miles from the Capital of Maine. Many amusing anecdotes are told of this "rare specimen of originality," some of which, though not excessively funny, and costing us some trouble to "lick them into shape," may yet yield some amusement to the reader. Uncle Charles enjoyed a favorable reputation as the biggest li—teller of "whoppers" in all his diggins," and he had so long been in the habit of telling tough stories, outraging all probability, that he at last believed all his fabrications true. No matter how monstrous or incredible the narrations of his neighbors, who, understanding his "weak spot," taxed their inventive powers to "draw him out"; their tales were but diminutive vegetables, compared with those of Uncle Charles. In fact, it was given in by all the villagers, that as a regular out-and-out-story-teller, he "flogged down" all competition — distancing Major Longbow "all hollow," beating Sam Hyde into "shoe-strings," and leaving Munchausen *"no whar."*

One day in a tavern bar-room a conversation was started about the strength and compass of the human voice. Some one remarked to the company that Uncle Charles could "holler" as loud as any person he ever heard. "Yes," responded the old man, catching as greedily as a pike at the chance of "drawing his bow," "that's a fact. I recollect a good many years ago, before there was a bridge at Augusta, of going there with Capt. S———t. We were nearly *an hour and a half* a going, and didn't reach the river till after dark. The ferryman was on the other side, and the horn

[1] *Proceedings of the Orleans County [Vt.] Historical Society*, from November 1889 to Jan. 1, 1891, no. 2, pp. 50–51. Cf. the last story, "One Jonathan's Munchausens," *The Galaxy of Comicalities* (Philadelphia), I (Nov. 27, 1833), 69 (credited to the *Newburyport Herald*). A Yankee, to illustrate the magnificent growth of pine trees in Maine, described one on which half a dozen woodcutters had worked energetically for six months. Deciding to take a spell on the opposite side, they traveled for a day, when to their surprise they discovered a dozen woodcutters who had been working lustily for over a year.

couldn't be found. The Captain thought if I hollered the ferryman would hear me. I did so once or twice, *just as easy as I could*, — but no answer. I then just let out my voice, and cuss me, if I didn't make a *roar*! Capt. S. clapped his hands on both his ears, and begged me, for gracious sake, not to try it again, for I should alarm the whole village. He said a thunder clap was nothing to it — and he'd heard pretty loud thunder in his days. It ee'namost knocked him down, and did stagger him back a rod or two. The ferryman came over quick enough, I tell you. He said he never heard such an awful, unearthly sound come out of a man's mouth before. It frightened, he said, three or four horses hitched in the streets, so that they broke loose and smashed up the wagons — and good many thought it was a cannon firing off, or else an earthquake. Two or three squares of glass were broken out in one of the houses nearest the water. About a week afterwards, Mr. Plaisted, who lives on Plaisted's hill, in Gardiner (six miles below Augusta), was at my house and enquir'd 'if I was not at Augusta last Thursday evening, hollering for the ferryman?' He said he heard me as plain as if I had been only down at Major Gay's. I didn't ask him how he knew it was *my* voice, for I supposed he had heard me try my lungs before."

All this was said with as much seriousness and gravity as if it were an actual verity, which all the hearers would readily swallow. Indeed, Uncle Charles fully believed everything he told, and however big or tough the stories he manufactured out of "whole cloth," no one could ever detect in his countenance the slightest indication that he was conscious of cutting off even "a hem," as Fuller would say, "from truth's garment."

It happened one day that a boy of C—— village fell through the ice in the pond, and being alone, came very near perishing. By dint of much struggling, he succeeded in crawling out. Uncle Charles, hearing the story, had a very vivid recollection how, when he was himself a little shaver, he "nearabout" lost his life in the same way. "I was skating on the pond," said he, "in the spring of the year, after the sun and rain had made the ice very weak. After cutting 'curlicues' and 'monkey shines' till I was pretty tired, I concluded to turn towards our landing, about a mile off. I had hardly skated a rod, before the ice broke under me, and down I went, like soap suds into a sink. Thinks I, I'm a gone coon this time, sure as snakes. I struggled there more than an hour trying to get out — sometimes crawling up a little, and just getting my knees on the edges of the ice, then breaking it and going down ker-souse again into the water. At last I found 'twas a desperate case — so I hollered with all my might; but no help came near me." (Uncle Charles must have forgotten his other "hollerin" story — or perhaps his lungs had not acquired their extraordinary, bull-of-Bashan capacity at this time.) "Now, thinks I, I must kick the bucket, that's a sartin fact. All at once, however, I happened to think of a hole in the ice by our landing, where we watered the cattle. I just let myself sink to the bottom of the pond, and walked coolly along towards the hole. My skates troubled me so much that I sat down on a rock and took them off. I then walked on without much trouble. I soon saw the light through the hole, but it turned out to be much farther off than I had guessed 'twas. I got directly under it, and giving a tremendous spring, came up safely on to the ice. I should think I laid there as much as ten minutes, though, before I could catch my breath. My head got some bad bumps under there, too — for, in walking where the water was shoal, I couldn't help hitting it, now and then, against the ice. One of the swellings on the back of my head was bigger than your double-fists; and I couldn't wear my hat for more than a week."

Another of Uncle Charles's favorite stories, was about a snake, which he chopped in two in the woods one day, with an axe. A week afterwards, he met the same identical snake with the two parts grown together again, and slipping along over the leaves as nimbly as ever.

Speaking of poultry, Uncle Charles said he had once three hens that had laid no eggs all summer. "In the fall," continued he, "my barn being full of grain, I let them have what they would eat, and they became so fat upon it, that, during the winter, sitting upon the roost, they *burst open, making a loud report, like a pocket pistol!*" [2]

In nostalgic chronicles of a township biography might appear the familiar oracle.

JOTHAM STORIES

The old-time New England farm hand . . . has passed, but Jotham remains. He has told the tales of his grandfather's exploits as a hunter so many times that he not only believes them himself but is equally sure that everyone else believes them. . . . I do not doubt Jotham's grandfather told them of his grandfather and that they belong to neither but are local folk lore, pasture sagas, changelings born of the queer union of east wind and blueberry blooms, brought up by hand — farm hand. . . . Jotham usually caps his list with the following:

"I guess the greatest wild goose hunting grandfather ever did was the time the big flock got caught in the ice storm. It came in November, a foot of soft snow and then one of those rainstorms that freeze as soon as the rain touches anything. Every twig on the trees that storm was as big as your wrist with ice and there was an inch or two of clear ice on everything and more coming all the time, when grandfather heard a big flock of wild geese honking. They didn't seem to be going over, but their voices hung in the air right over the big steep hill from the barn up into the back pasture. After they'd been honking up there for some time grandfather went up to see what it was all about, but he didn't take his gun. As he climbed the hill through the wet snow he heard 'em plainer and plainer, and when he got to the top he saw a most 'strodinary sight. There was a good-sized flock, ninety-seven geese, to be exact, that had got so iced up that they had to settle on the top of the hill.

[2] *Spirit of the Times*, XVII (April 24, 1847), 105. From the *Yankee Blade*.

"The ice had formed on their feathers as they flew and they were so weighted down they couldn't fly and they were getting more and more iced up every minute. Granddad didn't care to go back for his gun for fear some of the other nimrods in the neighborhood would come on the scene and bag the game first, but there wasn't any need of a gun. All he had to do was drive 'em home. They were terribly iced up, but their legs were still free and he chased 'em about for some time before he got 'em started down hill. But once over the edge of the hill the weight of ice on 'em turned 'em right over and over, and so they rolled on down. It was a wet snow and as they rolled they took up more and more of it till by the time they came slap up against the side of the barn every single goose was sealed up in the middle of a hard, round snowball. They all stopped there and all that grandfather had to do was to pile them up, and there they were, in cold storage for the winter. Every time the family wanted roast goose they went out and split open a snowball. The folks in granddad's time used often to freeze their fresh meat and keep it out in the snow all winter, but he was the only one that I ever heard of that stored wild geese in that way."

There are worse tales and more of them, but I fear that cold type chills out the subtle aroma of probability with which Jotham always manages to invest them. One needs to hear them told with the fragrance of a barn full of newmade hay in the nostrils, the swish of the northeaster to accompany the voice in his ears, and with his eye on the distant hillside pastures all hung with mysterious draperies of mist to make a proper background of quaint shadows of romance. Then he can really appreciate the folk lore that goes with us by the familiar title of "Jotham stories." [3]

If a journalist were present when old salts congregated, he added another figure to the gallery of native spellbinders.

YARN-SPINNING

It happened to us once upon a time, to be at "Wood's Hole" in Martha's Vineyard. There were several vessels, wind-bound in the roadstead, the captains of which used to spend their afternoons at the hotel on shore in the edifying occupation of yarn-spinning. It was a rich treat to us to be present, toasting our shins before the old fashioned wood fire, and picking up the crumbs of wisdom which fell from the table of those wide-world voyagers. There was one brown, hard-featured man among them, whom we well remember. He was a man of the most positive order. He was a firm believer in himself, and had an up and down way of expressing an opinion or telling a story, which caused others to believe devoutly in him also. This unlimited faith in his own resources, led him, doubtless, into self-delusion, for he used to relate all his adventures, — which we could not help believing at the time, but which we now see must have been strongly tinctured with fiction, — with an air of the most profound conviction and sincerity.

[3] Winthrop Packard, *Old Plymouth Trails* (Boston, c. 1920), pp. 203–204, 211–213.

One afternoon — it was a raw, sleety day, with a fresh gale from the south east, and a thick mist in the atmosphere which prevented our seeing beyond the water's edge — we had built a larger fire than usual, and provided our pockets with a double quantity of short sixes. It was *the* afternoon for yarn-spinning.

We had just got comfortably seated, when the boy of the establishment came in and informed us that "father was stuck with his wagon in the yard close by, and wanted help." We accordingly went out into the wet, and travelled about half a mile to the place. Our hard captain, whose name was Benson, took the leadership by general consent. He stationed one man at the horse's bridle, another alongside with a whip, and a third in the rear to push. He then crawled beneath the vehicle, a huge cart, weighing not less than half a ton, sunk in the sand to the axletrees, and placing his back to the bottom of the team, so as to get the greatest pressure between his shoulders, gradually straightened himself up, at the same time completely extricating the unfortunate vehicle, while his subordinates performed their parts, and so got things upon a better footing.

After our return to the house, some one complimented Captain Benson upon his strength of muscle.

"Humph!" said the captain, "you never heard how I served the bull on old man's farm, I guess."

There was a general ignorance on the subject.

"Well, you see, I was at work one day carting rocks from pasture, when a party of men and women folks undertook to cut across. The old bull not liking the idea of such familiarity with his feeding ground, let after 'em head-bent for Dublin. Brimstone, such a screaming and scampering! I down stick and after him. Ketching him by the tail, I fetched him to the ring bolt short metre. 'Run,' says I to the neighbors, 'I'll hold him.' But the old bull was a little blamed smarter than I thought for. He gin a powerful twitch just as the last one got over the wall, and after 'em, and shiver my timbers, if he hadn't left his tail in my hands, taken out as clean as new rum out of a quart pot!"

We all agreed that that was certainly a wonderful feat.

"I was young then," continued the captain musingly, "and at times a little wild. I had been down to a dance house one evening, and was going home, a very leetle 'how fare ye,' when I noticed a bright light in a neighbor's parlor. Now for a little fun, thinks I. There was a barber's shop close by, with a long striped pole planted in the ground in front. To whisk this up, and let it drive into the parlor window, was just as easy for me as to say Jack Robinson. It happened that they were just serving up ice cream and other frozen vittles, and such a shock as the old red and white pole gave 'em coming through the window — they thought it was an earthquake playing the eccentric. Oh, Lord!"

The captain, however, had one crowning feat of bodily strength, the narration of which was reserved for the last.

"I was once," said he, "in company with a juggler who swallowed jack-knives. I had with me a favorite Newfoundland dog, who from a desire of proving that some things could be done as well as others, snatched a knife out of the fellow's hand and swallowed it. I asked him, the juggler, to get it back, but he said it couldn't be done. 'Here's trying,' said I, 'at any rate,' and I run my hand clean down his throat till I felt something hard. I gave a pull, and burn my timbers if I didn't turn the quadruped inside out. I had somehow or other got hold of the inside of his tail, and this operation kinder brought his head in an opposite direction, and the way he footed it was a caution to cripples."

In the course of that wonderful afternoon Captain Benson told a great many stories, or as we should rather say, spun a good deal of yarn. As they were, however, somewhat of the long bow order, we shall not further enlarge upon them. But there is one which now comes to our recollection so exquisite of its kind, that we hope to be excused for relating it. The conversation had turned upon far sightedness.

"I am not very far sighted," observed the captain, "but I rayther think I *am* quick at hearing, shipmates. A good many years ago I was in London, and was one day standing with a friend along side of St. Paul's. 'Look here,' says he, pointing to the steeple, 'do you see that little mouse running along on the weather-cock?'

" 'No,' says I, 'I don't see nothing, but I can hear him trot quite distinctly.' "

So much for our souvenirs of "Wood's Hole." [4]

A leisurely traveler relaxing in port might encounter an extraordinary sea adventurer.

A MARINE MUNCHAUSEN

In the evening we received visits from several Swampscott skippers, whose vessels, like our own, were wind-bound in the port. One of these men sat with us till midnight, spinning the most monstrous and incredible yarns, which he narrated with a serene gravity that would almost have persuaded the hearer to believe any lie. He was a marine Munchausen of the first water, and his adventures were nearly as wonderful as those of the renowned Baron himself.

You could mention no island that he had not visited, from Borneo and Madagascar down to No Man's Land, or Pitcairn, or the Isle Royale of Lake Superior. He had sailed on all seas except Dr. Kane's Open Polar Sea, and that he reluctantly admitted he had only seen at a distance. He had conversed with all potentates, from the Czar Nicholas to the King of the Cannibal Islands, and kindly gave us each a couple of cigars, which he said were from a box presented to him by his friend the Captain-General of Cuba, a very choice and rare brand that could not be got for any money even in Havana. The last part of this assertion was probably true. No such cigars were ever seen in Cuba, for they were obviously of Connecticut

[4] *Yankee Blade*, Oct. 25, 1851 (vol. XI).

tobacco, and we had ourselves bought some of the same choice kind at a shop in the main street of Gloucester for two cents apiece.

We spoke of snakes. On this topic he spread himself amazingly. He had often seen the sea-serpent, and once when cruising for swordfish off Nantucket, had harpooned the monster from the deck of his vessel, and had been towed out to sea a hundred miles in thirty minutes, when the line broke and the creature got away.

"Rattlesnakes? Yes, sir; I *have* seen rattlesnakes. Some years ago, I grew tired of the sea, and took a farm in Illinois. I had a meadow on the prairie of three hundred acres, and when it came haying-time rattlesnakes were so thick there, that of seven Irishmen I sent to mow it one morning, five were bitten so that they died instantly, and the other two were only saved by keeping them constantly drunk with whiskey for more than a month. That job cost me a barrel of good Bourbon, beside the funeral expenses of the dead men."

"And you lost your hay?" said the Professor.

"Not at all. I had seen too much of snakes to be bluffed off in that way. I had a pair of boots which had been given to me at Buenos Ayres by General Rosas, of the kind worn by the Gauchos on the Pampas when they go out to hunt the jaguar. They are made of the toughest bull's hide, doubled, and I was confident that if they could resist the jaguar's claws they could the fangs of the rattlesnake. They came up to my hips, and I put them on one fine morning, and taking a scythe, went into the meadow and began to mow. The snakes came at me, a dozen at a time, and whenever they struck their fangs into the tough leather it held them fast. I took no notice of them, but kept on mowing till they hung in such numbers about my legs that the weight became troublesome, and then I stopped mowing and cut them off with the scythe. I had to do this about once in half an hour, and when I went home to dinner there were so many heads hanging to the boots that you could scarcely see the leather. The boys picked off enough to fill a peck measure heaping full, and when I came home to supper they got off as many more. I kept this up for a fortnight, and by that time, I can tell you, snakes were getting rather scarce in that particular meadow."

"What became of them boots?" inquired our Pilot, who had listened to this narrative with much apparent interest.

"Them boots," said the visitor, lighting one of the Captain-General's Havanas with much deliberation, and rolling the weed slowly between his lips, evidently to gain time for invention, — "them boots saved my life not long afterwards. You see, I soon got tired of farming and went to sea again. I bought a brig in New York and started on a trading expedition to the west coast of Africa. Off the Cape de Verdes we had about the worst storm I ever saw in my life, and were driven ashore in the night a little south of Cape Blanco, where the Great Desert comes down to the sea. The brig struck a reef running out under water a considerable distance. The next day a whole tribe of Arabs appeared on the beach making signals to us.

I went ashore to see what they wanted, and as I did not like to expose the boat's crew to harm, before going I put on them identical boots, which I had always kept with care, in order that I might wade from the boat to the beach. As the water was shallow, the boat could keep a good way out beyond the reach of the javelins and spears of the Arabs, who did not seem to have any fire-arms. As soon as I landed I was seized and hurried off over some sand-hills to their camp. Knowing enough of the language to understand most of what they said, I soon found that they meant to entice my crew on shore, make slaves of them, and plunder the ship. As a part of this plan, they treated me civilly for a time, only taking off my boots, which seemed to strike their fancy in a way that I could not at first comprehend. But I soon found that they were almost wholly out of provision, though they had plenty of water, and that they meant to make soup of the boots. They accordingly put them into a big iron pot, over a fire, and in about an hour invited me to partake of the broth. I declined, and they ate it themselves. In half an hour afterwards every mother's son and daughter of them was as dead as Julius Caesar. There was rattlesnake poison enough in them boots, sir, to destroy all the Arabs of Arabia. The next day we got the brig off without material damage, and we found gold-dust enough in the camp of the Arabs to make every one of the crew a rich man. That was on the whole the most successful voyage I ever made.

"But speaking of snakes, if you want to see snakes you must go to the East Indies. I was once lying at anchor in a little port on the coast of Sumatra, waiting for a cargo of pepper. The weather was intensely hot, and we left all the hatches open at night. I got up early one morning and found the gunwales of the ship nearly down to the water's edge. Supposing that we had somehow sprung a leak and were sinking, I roused up the men and sent a couple of them down the main hatchway to see what the matter was. They did not come back, and after waiting a few minutes I sent the mate, who looked in cautiously with a lantern, and reported that there was a serpent in the hold, and that he had probably swallowed both the seamen, as the feet of one of them were sticking out of his mouth. From the depth to which his weight had sunk the ship he was evidently a big one. Prompt measures were necessary. I directed the men to rig a tackle and fall, on the main yard, and let down a stout rope with a running noose right over the hatchway. I then mustered all our fire-arms and gave the snake a volley to rouse him. He soon reared his head out of the hold, I dropped the noose over it, the men ran him up, while the mate and I with axes chopped him in two. He was so long, sir, that it took the whole forenoon to haul him out by sections, cut him up, and throw the pieces overboard." [5]

Hunting and fishing. Hunters who cocked a long rifle in the daytime habitually drew the long bow of evenings. Breathtaking shots and

[5] Robert Carter, *A Summer Cruise on the Coast of New England* (Boston, 1864), pp. 103–108.

awesome bags threaded their discourses, which issued from many quarters but seemed always to embrace strangely similar performances. The dubious hunting yarn, like other native story types, can be found in the eighteenth-century press.

One Josiah Prescott, of Deerfield, in the Southwest part of Nottingham, being out a hunting on the 26th of November last, about three miles from his house he spy'd a MOOSE, at about 100 yards distance, he immediately fired at her, and shot her down dead; upon that there arose up two more at a little farther distance; he immediately charg'd his gun again, and shot down the second; and while the other was smelling of his mate, he charg'd again, and shot down the third; and while he was charging his gun again, a fourth came up towards the others, and he shot her dead also: two of them were old ones, the other two young ones. One of the old ones was ten feet high and ten feet long; the other eight feet high and ten feet long; the other two were about six feet high and eight feet long. After this extraordinary exploit was over, he was joined by a partner, who being at a little distance, heard the guns, came up to his assistance; and in going home he got help to dress the Mooses: A wild Cat they also killed on their return. — This is fact.[1]

Many hunting brags play variations on fixed motives: the crooked shot, the fired ramrod, the immense results of a single fortuitous discharge. New England marksmen, like those in the South and West, have been obliged to shoot at elusive targets from a curved gun barrel.

SOME PIONEER STORIES

One of Thomas Moore's stories is substantially as follows:
"I was going on foot to Winchester, N. H., on a time, and when I had reached a spot on the Connecticut river where I had been accustomed to cross on a ferry boat, I found the boat had been carried away by a freshet or flood. Not being much of a swimmer, I undertook to ford the river. I fearlessly waded in, carrying a gun loaded with powder and ball in my hand. I soon found my head under water, but I kept on wading, the water rushing and roaring, meanwhile, over me; but nothing daunted, I continued to wade until I reached the opposite bank. My legs had become so heavy that it was with the utmost difficulty that I could pull myself ashore. When I was fairly landed, I took off my clothes and found I had some twenty or thirty pounds of fresh shad in my trousers and clinging to my boots. I climbed up a peeled poplar tree, on which I hung my clothes to dry. Looking around me, I discovered a haystack in the field with a fence around it. On the topmost rail of that fence sat a row of quails. I immediately set my wits to work to know how to kill all those quails at one

[1] *Boston Evening-Post*, Dec. 21, 1767. From Portsmouth, N.H.

shot, having but one charge of powder and ball with me; that I had preserved dry in my gun by corking it at the muzzle. I finally run my gun
under a rock and bent it to a curve, crawled on my hands and knees as near
to the stack of hay as I dared, pointed the muzzle of my gun to the nearest
quail, and whiz! went the ball, hitting the first quail and sweeping every
bird clean off the fence and laying them dead on the ground. But I found
the ball coming after me, for I was close up to the fence when I fired. I
ran like a white-head round the stack, the ball continuing after me, and
seeing it gaining on me I caught up a slab and turned it off. Thus I secured a rich harvest of shad and quails."

Mr. Moore didn't stop to explain how the ball passed out of the curved
gun without bursting it, but left his auditors to wonder at the marvel he
had told them.[2]

Slow-burning powder postponed but made only more glorious the
inevitable triumph.

OLD GAWGE AND THE NINETY AND NINE

Old Gawge took a heroic draft of lemonade. "Ah-h-h!" —he smacked his
lips. "I ain't had a drink like that since the Spring my brother John come
offa the drive an' fell over the cow-yard fence." Then he settled down to
business:

"Wal, sir," he said, "they wan't nary shotgun in the back country whar
I was riz. My fambly was addicted to the old Winchester 44–40, which
were, an' still is, a great gun fer deer an' b'ar. But when it come to ducks,
I fixed me up a scattermaran that had the old 44–40 skun forty ways fer
Sunday. She was a old Revolutionary War flintlock musket with the bar'l
sawed off half way betwixt the muzzle an' britch. My load was a handful
or so of powder, paper waddin', an' as many rocks, dried beans, nails, and
sech like as I could cram into her.

"Course, she wouldn't allus fire when you pulled the trigger, 'specially
if the weather happened to be a mite damp, but when she DID go off —
gracious Peter! It took the rest of the forenoon fer to tote the ducks home!

"Wal, sir, this partic'lar mornin' I'm a-tellin' you about, I riz long before
the sun, did the most of my chores, loaded up ol' Betsy Ann, an' traipsed
down to the lake an' rowed out to a island while 'twas still dark. 'Twas
early in the Fall an' they was consid'rable of a mist, which put me to
some trouble fer to keep my powder dry.

[2] *Centennial Celebration of the Settlement of Chelsea, Vt.* (Keene, N.H., 1884),
pp. 113–114. Cf. Nixon Waterman, "Bill Smith's Whopper," *Granite State Magazine*,
II (July–December 1906), 266–267 (curved shot kills 999 pigeons); *Granite Monthly*,
XXIV (May 1898), 253 (still repeated story of a Goffstown, N.H., character, whose
bent gun shoots a deer around a mountain); Winthrop C. Packard, *Old Plymouth Trails*
(Boston, c. 1920), pp. 204–208 (circular shot kills 762 yellow-legs); Joseph C. Allen, *Tales
and Trails of Martha's Vineyard* (Boston, 1938), pp. 202–203 (shot around a haystack
hits gunner's stern).

"Without makin' no more noise than a weasel in a chicken coop, I pulled the boat up on shore an' crep' across that island to a leedle small cove on t'other side, whar the ducks held their lodge meetin's.

"Gosh all hemlock you should of see the sight which met my eyes! The sun was jest beginnin' fer to rise, an' that thar cove was fuller of ducks than a Grange hall on a strawberry festervule night! They was young ones, old ones, big ones, leedle ones an' meedjum-sized ones: all colors, shapes an' descriptions! 'Jeepers!' thinks I, 'I'm goin' to need help luggin' them ducks home, sure as leedle green apples'll give you the tummy-ache!"

"Cautious as a tomcat at a dog show, I creeps a leedle closter, kneels down, pours a leedle powder in the pan, an' aims right spang into the middle of them ducks. Then I braces myself, closes my eyes, and pulls the trigger.

"Nawthin happens.

"I wait a leedle while an' nawthin still happens, so I opens my eyes an' takes a peek at Betsy. The powder in the primin' pan ain't went off. I snaps the flint a couple times an' she sparks all right, but it seems like that ain't enough fer to set the powder off 'cause she's mebby a leedle mite damp.

"But this don't bother me a mite. I aims ol' Betsy again an' scratches a match an' holds it onto the pan. Z-z-z! The primin' percolates fine an' dandy this time, but it don't set off the charge. So I fills up the pan an' tries again. I kept tryin' till my primin' powder was all gone, but 'twas no use."

Here Old Gawge favored me with a meaning look: "But I didn't git on the rampage an' begin cussin' an' threatenin' like some folks I knows on. Nossir, I had too much sense fer that, even if I was leedle more than a boy. I jest riz onto my feet an' quietly went back to my boat and started to row fer home.

"Wal, sir, I hadn't got more'n a few rods offa that island when I hears a sizzlin' noise. I looks down at my feet an' thar is ol' Betsy Ann jest a-smokin' an' a-frothin' at the mouth, a-rarin' to go! The sun had riz by now an' out on the open water it had been hot enough fer to dry that powder charge out.

"Judas Priest! Now I want to tell you, mister, the way I turned that boat round and rowed fer that island again was a caution! I knew ol' Betsy was a-goin' to speak her piece right plumb sudden, an' I wanted to git her aimed at them ducks afore she started talkin'.

"I beached the boat an' run across that island to the cove so fast the trees looked like a card of matches, an' all the time ol' Betsy Ann was a-splutterin' away like as if she couldn't hold in no longer.

"Wal, sir, to make a long story short, I jest did manage to git back to that thar cove an' draw a bead when 'Boom!' ol' Betsy Ann let a roar out of her an' a peck of rocks, dried beans, nails, and lead-foil from tea packages scattered in amongst them ducks, while I went rump-over-tea kittle in the opposite direction, on account of not havin' a chancet to git set fer ol' Betsy's kick.

"Purty soon I got myself picked up, found they was no bones busted, an' begin a-countin' of them ducks. I counted ontil my fingers was all used up an' then begun a-countin' on my toes ontil they was all used up too, when I begun all over ag'in."

Suddenly Old Gawge halted and poked a club-like finger into my chest. "I'll bet you couldn't guess how many ducks I got with that one shot if'n you was to go to Tophet fer it," he said.

"One cripple scared to death by the noise and another paralyzed just by seeing your face," I replied, just a bit sarcastically.

Old Gawge sniffed disdainfully and turned to Paxton. "S'pose you guess," he invited.

Paxton thought a moment. He takes games very seriously, Paxton does. Once he won first prize of a fifty-cent cigar lighter in a charades contest. "Seven?" he asked hesitatingly.

Old Gawge spat disgustedly. "Nossir!" he snorted. "They was ninety an' nine ducks layin' dead in that cove when the smoke rolled away!"

Paxton and I stared open-mouthed for sixty seconds. Then I reached for and downed a liberal libation. A lemon seed choked me and it was several more seconds before I could recover my breath. "Why," I inquired of Old Gawge when I could talk again, "why didn't you call it a hundred?"

The old sinner assumed an expression of injured dignity. "I said ninety an' nine 'cause that's jest prezactly how many I counted," he said firmly. "Do you think fer one minute that I would up an' make a liar out of myself jest fer one measily duck?" [3]

Lacking bullets, the hunter inserted his ramrod into the gun and fired with prodigious consequences.

LARGE STORIES

We have all heard of "fish stories," and it is generally understood that they are rather difficult to swallow. There are some, however, who have acquired such a facility in manufacturing them, that they deem it derogatory if they allow themselves to be surpassed in telling them.

Of this class were Jem B. and Joe P., two old cronies, who whilom flourished in a neighboring village.

They were seated in the village store one evening, when Jem, after a preparatory hem, designed to call the attention of the company, commenced as follows, —

"I say, boys, did I ever tell you what a time I had shooting pigeons over our house one night last winter?"

"No, no," said a chorus of voices, "Come, tell it!"

[3] Walter H. Martin, *Sun-Up* (September 1932), pp. 9, 17. Cf. "Slow, But Dreadful Sure," *Burlington Daily Free Press*, Aug. 1, 1848. Slow-burning powder forms a separate motive independent of the wonderful shot; see Edmund Wheeler, *The History of Newport, N.H.* (Concord, N.H., 1879), p. 228, where a store lounger tells how he saw a live coal dropped into the gunpowder keg, and half the powder burned up before he could rush to the river and back with a pail of water.

"You see," said the old man, "my old woman and I were seated round the fire-place one night in the kitchen, when we heard a fluttering up above."

"What's that?" asked Jemima.

"I do not know," said I; "it sounds like pigeons."

"So I got my old musket, and charged it up pretty well, and pointing it up chimney, I found there was a screech and a crashing noise, and a dozen as plump pigeons as you could wish to see, fell upon the hearth. Two fell into the pot that was boiling over the fire, and we had them for breakfast next morning. We didn't have to buy any butcher's meat for a week afterwards."

"Ahem!" commented Joe, "that's pretty fair luck, but it isn't a circumstance to what happened to me once. I'll tell it, if you haint no objection."

"Go ahead, Joe, we are all anxious to hear you."

"Well, I'd been out hunting one afternoon — had dreadful luck — fired away all my shot, and hadn't brought down anything yet. I began to be discouraged, and was thinking of going home, when all at once a lot of robins, there were fifty of 'em, and all in a row, flew by.

"Here was a capital chance to shoot; but the worst of it was I had no shot. So I did the best I could. I put in the ramrod, and charged it up pretty well. I took aim and fired, and, wonderful to tell, I took the first robin through the eye, and it passed through the whole row of 'em, so they fell to the ground all strung on the ramrod as neat as could be. I shouldered 'em, and carried 'em home."

"How many robins did you say there were?" asked a bystander.

"Just fifty."

"And they all were strung on the ramrod?"

"Sartin. Have you any thing to say agin it?"

"O, no, certainly not. Only it must have been a *plaguy long ramrod*, that's all." [4]

One foe in particular challenged the prowess of the New England huntsman, and legion were the stories that described fierce brushes, grapples, and encounters between a woodsman and a bear.

A BEAR HUNT IN VERMONT

I have just been reading 'Sketches of the Eccentricities of David Crockett' the great hunter of the west. But this same David Crockett is no part of a priming to a Varmount hunter, who stands six feet four without shoes or stockings — one of your regular built busters, who wasn't born no how any way, but the thunder shook him out of a rock; — who will tear up a live oak tree with one hand, and wring off a bear's neck with the other, who will carry home panthers in his vest pocket, and eat wild cats with a spoon. David used to make a good four hours' job of killing a bear, but a Var-

[4] *Yankee Blade*, Jan. 28, 1854 (vol. XIII). Cf. Winthrop C. Packard, *op. cit.*, pp. 208–210; Joseph C. Allen, *op. cit.*, p. 202.

mounter don't want over fifteen minutes if the bear is any thing less than nine feet long — a genuine Varmounter — one who come out of the Green Mountains in a thunder-storm, and who proved his manhood by slinging a panther over the mountain by the tail when he was eight years old, is a model for a modern hunter — a backwoodsman is n't a shaving to him — he is no more to be talked of in the same day than a popgun and a thunder clap. Varmounter never uses a dog — he is his own dog. Give him a gun and he asks no odds — there's no varmint that crawls the earth who can match him.

Zeb Short — he was only six feet two, used to be laughed at, by the regulars, and he was no fool — he used to say he could take a backwoodsman by the heel, and shake his liver out in no time. And yet he was considered but a boy. I once saw Zeb have a 'tusle' with a bear, which sent my blood dancing but didn't seem to stir him out of his ordinary course. We were out hunting one morning — I was a novice in the business, but Zeb had seen play, when we came on the track of a bear. Zeb primed his smooth bore — he never saw a percussion, — and trailed on. I followed at a respectful distance, determined to have a shot. After tramping through woods, slumping through sloughs, and shoving through under-brush we came in sight of him — the largest fellow my two eyes ever looked on. I was for letting into him at once, but Zeb says he 'dont waste your powder man, I want to shoot him just under the off ear, that's the spot,' so I held up. He went on as fearlessly as if he was treading his own kitchen with his shooting iron in his right hand until he was within three paces of the monster. The bear turned round and took a steady look at him. Zeb raised his gun to his shoulder and snapped. 'Confound this powder — it's as slow as a woman.' The bear walked towards him and Zeb snapped again. No fire. The bear was now within two lengths of the gun, and Zeb kept snapping. He began walking backwards still snapping the old flint, but his gun would n't go. 'Shall I shoot Zeb?' ' No if the gun wont go I'll knock him down with the butt of it.' Just as he had spoken, his foot caught in the brush and over he went flat on his back — and dropped his gun. The bear was on him in an instant.

I raised my gun — but Zeb sung out 'fair play,' and I dropped it, trembling all over. There he was, rolling round on the ground grappling with the fierce animal which was at least four times his weight, and not a weapon about him. I thought it was all over with the poor fellow. Presently he got one hand in the bear's mouth and grappled his tongue. The bear writhed like a serpent, and chawed away on his arm as if it had been a stick. The cold drops run off my forehead and I was about to fire, when he pulled his hand from the bear's mouth, ripping out his tongue by the roots. The bear bounded up in agony and run. Zeb was up in a twinkling. 'I guess you'll never holler much more' said he, and seizing his gun gave chase. They ran about a hundred yards, and I after them, when they both together went plump into a slough. I could not help him — they were both rolling round so in the mud I could not tell which was the man and which the bear. 'What shall I do Zeb' said I almost paralyzed, 'Be striking a fire man' said he as he spit out the mud, 'I want to eat some of this fellow.' I could do nothing but look at him. There he was floundering in the mud with a great bear and nothing but his hands to help him. I considered him a dead man. But I was mistaken. As soon as the bear turned so that he had a chance, he gripped him by the back of his neck and pushed his head, arm's length down into the slough — 'There you varmint suck mud for breakfast.' The monster floundered like a vexed tiger. 'You may as well take it easy,' said Zeb 'its no use kicking.'

Here was a sight a man don't see every day of his life. A genuine Varmount hunter holding a bear down in the mud with main force, by the head as he would a child. Zeb looked on while the bear kicked, as coolly as if he were wringing the neck of a chicken. Up to his middle in the mud, and with a grave face holding the bear down as far as he could reach.

But my story is longer telling than it was doing. Suffice it Zeb held him there till he was perfectly quiet, and dragging himself out of the mud left the bear, tail up, in the slough. Winding his handkerchief round his arm, which was horridly mangled, he reported himself ready to continue his hunt.

This is but one instance reader, of a bear hunt in Vermont, and I can vouch for its truth, but it is enough to give you an idea how they manage things up there. I wonder what David Crockett would have done if he had been in Zeb's place, with all his alligator and steam boat. Why Zeb could tie a bear in a double bow knot round him and heave both where they would never see daylight again.[5]

Stories with a fishy smell have from old pervaded New England shores and lakes. A letter from Hampton, New Hampshire, in 1756, may well have inaugurated the practice.

We have had something remarkable and uncommon among us this Week: Last Tuesday two or three young Men were coming up from *Shaws*-Island across the Marsh, and heard a rustling in a little salt-pond, and upon looking in, spy'd a vast number of fine large Mackrel swimming about; they immediately waded in, and they were so thick that they threw Numbers out with their Hands: One of the Men ran to the nearest House, got a Pigeon Net, and drew out 400 presently. The next Day in that and another Salt Pond, they catched upwards of 1000, as fine large Mackrel as I ever saw . . . . It causes much Speculation, for there never was a Mackrel known thereabouts, nor are they yet taken in our Sea, being not yet come in in any Plenty.[6]

---

[5] *Pearl and Literary Gazette*, III (Dec. 21, 1833), 79; also in *Galaxy of Comicalities*, I (Feb. 22, 1834), 162–163. For a selection of New England bear tales, see R. M. Dorson, "Just B'ars," *Appalachia*, n.s., VIII (December 1942), 174–187.

[6] *Boston Evening-Post*, June 28, 1756.

Ante-bellum newspaper humor testifies to the rising swell of a sturdy native fish lore.

A FISH STORY

The Claremont Eagle tells a story of a son of Deacon Bradley. Who is Deacon Bradley? No matter. His son was fishing one day up Sugar River, and having a bite, pulled up a two quart jug out of the water, which he broke, and a large dace was discovered within! The young gentleman was puzzled to know how the dickens it came there — he scratched his head, and finding no solution there, he ran home and asked his father for one. 'Why,' said the Deacon, who was somewhat illiterate, 'the fish was *converted to the jug!*' The Claremont Eagle then says:

The fact is, as stated. A jug got lost in the stream and a small dace made his way into its smooth mouth. The current threw the jug bottom upwards, the fish in the meantime growing in size, and by the time the jug keeled over again, he was too large to effect an egress. — The bait on the hook dangled near the mouth of the jug, and near the mouth of the fish, and swallowing it, he was drawn out of the water, with his house over his head. Perhaps he was able to thrust his head out of the mouth of his earthen vessel, and by paddling with his fins within, to move about a little, like a man with irons on his arms, and nibble at a few little delicacies. The circumstances, however much it may smell like a fish story, is as recorded, whatever speculations in regard to it may be indulged. It is one of the most singular things we ever heard.[7]

Among Maine guides the startling fish adventure has become a standard accessory.

THE SNAKE AND THE FROG

Thirty years ago, my first year of guiding I was just a youngster, and stories told in those days made an everlasting impression. Last Sunday while reading the guide stories in the Sunday Telegram this one came to my mind.

"Gramp" who lived in the days when two-masted schooners plied between Sebago Lake and Boston, carrying farm produce and lumber up and rum, molasses and tobacco back, was one of the group of fishermen and he told the following story:

"You know where the Otter Ponds are, well, this morning it was rather overcast almost raining, a perfect day for pickerel, I decided to go get a mess as we hadn't had any all Summer, and were about fed up on salmon and smelts.

"I took a pork rind or two (we could always get one on that, then we

[7] *Exeter News Letter*, Sept. 7, 1841. Cf. "A Jug of 'Bass'," *Joe Allen's Fireside Tales* (New Bedford, Mass., 1941), pp. 15–16.

used a pickerel belly bait), and went down to the ponds. But fish as hard as I could no pickerel would bite.

"As I was casting around some lilypads I saw a small frog swimming along. Like a flash right out from under those pads darted the biggest pickerel I ever saw, and grabbed that frog. Well I just figured another frog and that fish was mine.

"But, to find a frog I couldn't and I was about to give it up as a bad job and come home when I saw a big black water snake swimming in-shore with a frog in his mouth. I sneaked up on that snake and grabbed him just back of the head and what an argument we had, but he wouldn't give up the frog.

"All at once it came to me that some of my good old New England rum might do the trick, I put my knee on the back of that snake, took the cap off my flask and poured a little of the contents into his mouth.

"With many a shudder and wiggle he let go of the frog. 'Now for the fish,' say I, but do you believe that before I could get that frog to work I felt something rubbing against my legs and what do you suppose. It was that snake back with another frog." [8]

Like the coon who told Davy Crockett not to shoot, he would come down, a wise fish gave himself up when hooked by a renowned Izaak Walton.

Tom Rodman's grog was held to be the best in the County. Squire Hooper and his old crony, Gran'ther Holland, differed on this point alone, for Gran'ther Holland always upheld the peculiar merit of Elisha Watson's drink. These two rumsellers were keen rivals in the groggery business, both managing to keep their customers in debt, and in the end taking even their farms at forced sale. In short, they were a precious pair. The story runs that one foggy summer morning, Gran'ther Holland sent word to Squire Hooper that it was a likely day to go tautogin' on Peaked Rock. They often fished together, and were the best of friends, quarreling only on the point of drink. So, taking their heavy chestnut saplin peeled poles, they went down to the Peaked Rock, then still standing upright on the ledge where Whimsy Cot, now the property of Mrs. Irving Fisher, of New Haven, stands overlooking the rock. The day turned out badly — hot and hotter till the sun burned off the fog, so the tautog got shy and lay swinging in the tide waiting for the twilight; the anglers lost their bait, and their tempers also; now and then by chance they "stole" a chogset, pest of the tautog fisherman. Most of these wily thieves dropped back, and of course told their friends below, *who* was after them. A few were saved for the frying-pan. No fish has a finer flavor, when properly fried. Along about noon Gran'ther Holland growled out, "Le's give up, and go on home, no use

[8] *Portland Telegram*, July 23, 1934, by Leander A. Dole, Sebago Lake, Me. I have heard this story orally from "Slick" MacQuoid of Wilton, Me., in July, 1942.

brilin' here any longer." "All right," says Squire Hooper, "I'll jest fish up my last crab." So he tied her on good and solid, and hadn't more'n got his line down when he felt a big one take holt, and bore down hard on his big pole, to hist him out. The big tautog, soon's he felt the pull, sung out with fright, "Chogsetties, who in hell has got hold of that thar dam pole?" "Squire Hooper! ole boy, Squire Hooper!" Hearing this, the big fish groaned out, "Good-bye, boys, I guess I'm a goner. *I'll be to Tom Rodman's afore sunset.*" [9]

Perhaps the classic American fish story concerns a trout who was tamed.

GRANT'S TAME TROUT

The sage of Beaver Camp sat sunning himself on the bench beside the cook camp, the bench so widely known as the scene of countless weary hours of that perpetual toiler. He seemed to be smoking an old black pipe, whereas he was only dropping matches into its empty bowl at intervals of three minutes, agreeable to the terms of his contract with the American Match trust.

As he so sat and pondered, the writer, at the time a recent arrival, approached and said: "Mr. Grant, I wish you would give me the true history of your wonderful success in taming a trout. I have heard of it in all parts of the world but I have always longed to hear the story direct from headquarters."

"Well, it really ain't so much of a story," replied the famous chronicler. "It was this way. Nine year ago the eleventh day of last June, I was fishin' out there in the pads, and right under the third yaller leaf to the right of the channel — yes, that one with the rip in it — I ketched a trout 'bout six inches long. I never see a more intelligent lookin' little feller — high forehead, smooth face, round, dimpled chin, and a most uncommon bright, sparkling, knowin' eye.

"I always allowed that with patience and cunning a real young trout (when they gets to a heft of 10 or 15 pounds there ain't no teachin' them nothin') could be tamed jest like a dog or cat.

"There was a little water in the boat and he swims around in it all right till I goes ashore and then I gets a tub we had, made of the half of a pork barrel, fills it with water and bores a little small hole through the side close down to the bottom and stops the hole with a peg.

"I sets this tub away back in a dark corner of the camp and every night after the little fellow gets asleep I slip in, in my stockin' feet and pulls out the peg softly and lets out jest a little mite of the water. I does this night after night so mighty sly that the little chap never suspected nothin' and he was a-livin' hale and hearty for three weeks on the bottom of that tub as dry as a cook stove, and then I knowed he was fit for trainin'.

[9] Thomas R. Hazard, *The Jonny-Cake Papers of "Shepherd Tom,"* With a Biographical Sketch and Notes by Rowland G. Hazard (Boston, 1915), pp. 399–400, note 34.

"So I took him out o' doors and let him wiggle awhile on the path and soon got to feedin' him out of my hand. Pretty soon after that, when I walked somewhat slow (I'm naturally quite a slow walker some folks think) he could follow me right good all round the clearin', but sometimes his fins did get ketched up in the brush jest a mite and I had to go back and swamp out a little trail for him; bein' a trout, of course he could easy follow a spotted line.

"Well, as time went on, he got to follerin' me most everywhere and hardly ever lost sight of me, and me and him was great friends, sure enough.

"Near about sundown one evening, I went out to the spring back of the camp, same one as you cross goin' to Little Island, to get some butter out of a pail, and, of course, he comes trottin' along behind. There was no wind that night, I remember, and I could hear his poor little fins a-raspin' on the chips where we'd been gettin' out splits in the cedar swamp. Well, sir, he follered me close up and came out onto the logs across the brook and jest as I was a-stoopin' down over the pail I heard a kee-plunk! behind me and Gorry! if he hadn't slipped through a chink between them logs and was drownded before my very eyes before I could reach him, so he was." Here a tear started from the good old man's eye on a very dusty trip down his time stained cheek.

"Of course I was terribly cut up at first — I couldn't do a stroke of work for three weeks — but I got to thinkin' that as it was comin' on cold (it was in late November then) and snow would soon be here and he, poor little cuss, wasn't rugged enough for snow-shoein' and he couldn't foller me afoot all winter no how, and as he couldn't live without me, mebby it was jest as well after all he was took off that way. Do you know, Mister, some folks around here don't believe a word of this, but if you'll come down to the spring with me, right now, I'll show you the very identical chink he dropped through that night, so I will. I've never allowed anyone to move it. No, sir! nor I never will."[10]

Strong men. Fact and legend blended in tales of pioneer strong men. Homemaking in the wilderness had stimulated physical performances that more tender generations recalled with awe and retold with relish. Most of these feats had to do with lifting great weights. Benjamin Tarr of Rockport, Massachusetts, lifted an anchor weighing 800 pounds.[1]

[10] In *The Tame Trout and other Backwoods Fairy Tales*, narrated by Ed Grant, chronicled by Francis I. Maule (Farmington, Me., 1941). Gary Cooper told this story when playing Wild Bill Hickok in the motion picture, "The Plainsman." Professor Arthur M. Schlesinger has told me the tale as he heard it from "Turtle Dan" in Xenia, Ohio, nearly fifty years ago. Cf. Charles E. Goodspeed, *Angling in America* (Boston, 1939), pp. 315–316.

[1] Lemuel Gott, *History of the Town of Rockport* (Rockport, Mass., 1888), p. 43.

Two men at a muster in Deerfield, Massachusetts, raised a cannon to their shoulders and marched with it around the common.[2] Kilburn Hoyt of Dunbarton, New Hampshire, ran a race with a 225-pound man on his back and a handicap of half the distance and won.[3] Ethan Allen Crawford, the giant of the White Mountains, carried bears, exhausted climbers, and barrels of potash on his back; once when a gust of wind toppled his load of hay as he was driving through the Notch, he leaped to the ground and caught it on his shoulder to prevent it falling over the precipice.[4] David Cass of Hinckley, Maine, could lift a heavy bateau to his shoulders as easily as an Indian could a canoe, and once ducked two thieving Indians, one in each hand, at the same time.[5] Captain Ben Dudley, the strong man of Douglas, Massachusetts, turned a timber six men could not raise, applying such pressure he forced both heels through his boots.[6] Joe Montferrat of Woonsocket, Rhode Island, raised his plow from the furrow to point a direction.[7] "Stout" Jeffrey Hazard carried for some rods a blue stone weighing 1600 pounds; he had a sister who used to take a full cider barrel by the chines and lifting it aloft drink at the bung.[8] George Burroughs had been proclaimed a wizard in Salem because he made nothing of taking up a gun of seven foot barrel and holding it out with one arm like a pistol, or carrying off barrels filled with molasses and cider.[9] The wonder is that more village titans were not explained as wizards. Deacon Leathers, a man of giant strength of whom wonderful stories were told, once at a raising righted a huge timber some thirty-five feet long and nearly a foot square which had been set wrong end to, unaided.[10]

Of course if verification were needed to convince unbelievers, that could be supplied by an eyewitness of equal integrity with the deponent.

[2] Francis M. Thompson, *History of Greenfield, Mass.* (Greenfield, 1904), II, 1010.
[3] C. C. Lord, *Life and Times in Hopkinton, N.H.* (Concord, N.H., 1890), p. 275.
[4] *History of Coös County, N.H.* (Syracuse, N.Y., 1888), pp. 440-441.
[5] Minnie Atkinson, *Hinckley Township* (Newburyport, Mass., 1920), pp. 17-20.
[6] William A. Emerson, *History of the Town of Douglas, Mass.* (Boston, 1879), pp. 17-20.   [7] *Rhode Island: A Guide to the Smallest State* (Boston, 1937), p. 101.
[8] Thomas R. Hazard, *The Jonny-Cake Letters* (Providence, 1882), pp. 175-176.
[9] *Salem Witchcraft*, Samuel P. Fowler, ed. (Salem, Mass., 1861), pp. 285-286.
[10] John W. Hayley, *Tuftonboro, N.H.* (Concord, N.H., 1923), p. 74.

A STRONG MAN FOR A HEAVY LOAD

Many are the tales of the strong men who inhabited the Moosehead Lake region in the early days. These stories, told and retold in the glow of campfires, probably have lost nothing in the telling. If they are true, even in part, Samson would have been but a babe in the woods in the days of "long-lumbering," in this section.

Most of these narrations or yarns are drawn from the period before the advent of King C. Gillette to the north woods, when full beards were worn for protection against the cold or the projection of weak chins. And it may be that these whiskers had the same strengthening qualities as did that proverbial growth of Samson's.

But all that is aside from the tale which one of these "pillars of power" modestly related, as follows:

"In the year 18--, I was one of a crew of drivers located at Seboomook Dam. In those days about the only things that could get over the three mile tote-road from Seboomook to Seboomook Dam were moose-birds and black-flies. One day the boss said that a boat had left a shipment of much needed boom chains at Seboomook wharf. He wanted them at once but did not know how he was going to tote them. Well, I always like to be accommodating so I told him to forget it and leave the transporting of them boom chains to me.

"The next morning I started for Seboomook wharf and upon arriving there found a sugar barrel full of boom chains. As I shouldered the barrel, I noticed the weight marked on it was 1600 pounds, and I decided that I would have to rest a couple of times before reaching the Dam. But after I got started I didn't notice the weight much because I was busy watching my step to keep from getting into the mud and water knee-deep.

"Just as I came within sight of the camp, I met an old friend and as we had not seen one another for a long time, we found plenty to talk about. Conversation drifted from one thing to another and before I was aware it was so late, I heard the dinner call at the camp. Well, sir, I looked at my watch and discovered that we had been standing there gabbing more than an hour, and I had completely forgotten that barrel of boom chains on my shoulder, which the boss wanted at once. Needless to say I hurried along."

As the speaker modestly finished his story, some of the impolite audience jeered as if to doubt the truth of his words, whereupon the strong man turned to a friend and asked, "Ain't that true, Joe?"

And Joe, without hesitation, replied, "Damright, and well I remember it, for I came in right behind you with the head-works on my back."[11]

There were superwomen too in those days.

A person called at the house of John McNiel, of Londonderry, in consequence of having heard of his strength and prowess. McNiel was absent,

[11] William Harris, *Northern*, VII (September 1927), 13. Cf. Stanley F. Bartlett, *Beyond The Sowdyhunk* (Portland, Me., 1937), pp. 111–116.

which circumstance the stranger regretted (as he informed his wife, Christian, who inquired his business), since he had traveled many miles for no other purpose than to "throw him."

"And troth mon," said Christian McNiel, "Johnny is gone, but I'm not the woman to see ye disappointed: an' I think if ye'll try, mon, I'll throw ye meself." The stranger, not liking to be bantered by a woman, accepted the challenge; and, sure enough, Christian tripped his heels and threw him upon the ground. The stranger, upon getting up, thought he would not wait for "Johnny;" but left, without deigning to leave his name.[12]

One renowned strong man, Gunpowder Beal of Beals Island, Maine, created no little stir in popular story and song.

> When Maine could boast of giant pines
> And brain and brawn in huge designs,
> Manwaring Beal begot a son
> No less than a phenomenon.
>
> Mere five feet folk were puny lot,
> And six feet people somewhat squat,
> For Barney Beal was six feet plus,
> With seven inches fabulous.
>
> He knew no fear and slight restraint,
> When others frothed or made complaint,
> But settled every quarrel quick,
> With energetic kick or lick.
>
> His fingers touched the sanded floor
> Whene'er he entered neighbor's door
> And sat him down to chat a bit
> And swear and boast and often spit.
>
> 'Tis said the women folks well knew
> Their kitchen chairs would fall in two
> Unless they tucked them out of sight
> And left stout bench to take his height.
>
> All up and down the coast of Maine
> He roved. A human hurricane
> They came to call Gunpowder Beal
> And let alone from head to heel.
>
> 'Twas when the British tried their luck
> And ran across his Yankee pluck
> That Barney Beal made history
> Not often known on land or sea.

---

[12] Caleb Stark, *History of the Town of Dunbarton, N.H.* (Concord, N.H., 1860), pp. 142–143. Cf. the giantess Widow Jewett, "about whom innumerable stories still survive." in Fannie S. Chase, *Wiscasset in Pownalborough* (Wiscasset, Me., 1941), p. 25.

They said he'd fished too near their shore,
He musn't do it any more;
In fact, no less than an arrest
Would their authority attest.

Five men then tried the bold affront
To Barney's fame. He faced the brunt
Of battle, broke one sword,
Tossed the leader overboard,

And sent the other hostile four
Asprawl upon the vessel's floor,
With clothes ripped off to gory skin
And muskits smashed, to their chagrin.

With toss of head and wave of hand,
Gunpowder Beal gave his command;
"You'd best go back," he swore with might,
"Or so much worse will be your plight!

"I'll rip the planks from off your boat!
I'll stuff your words right down your throat!
You think you'd try for my arrest —
You'd better plan your own inquest!"

His thirst for blood for once had stay
When Portland staged a grog affray.
He came out best, as you may ken,
Saloon all smashed, and fifteen men

Laid out to rue the bitter hour
That put them once within his power.
These tales they tell down Jonesport way,
Between their passing time of day.[13]

The centrifugal force of myth building shaped swirling bits of legend toward something like connected saga, and occasionally incipient saga heroes arose, clothed in fairly complete life histories. Such a one was George Washington Briggs, the Dighton Sampson.

Born June 27, 1776, member of a family noted for extraordinary physical strength in both boys and girls, "product of a state of society that has disappeared forever," Stout George grew famous in local story

[13] Alice Frost Lord in the *Lewiston Journal*, Nov. 1, 1938. See also Henry Buxton in the *Bangor News*, Oct. 25, 1938; *Maine: A Guide 'Down East'* (Boston, 1937), p. 233; Herbert G. Jones, *Maine Memories* (Portland, 1940), p. 197. The above piece is thus prefaced: "This broadside from the Washington County coast belongs to pioneer days and figures which have not grown less heroic with passing years."

for feats of might and daring. In his youth a seaman, he once put to rout, in the port of Valparaiso, an armed press gang from a British man-of-war with only a heavy club, killing five of the Englishmen — a fact that he later always remembered with regret. Challenged in Liverpool by the strongest stevedore of the city to a trial of strength, Briggs asked the two hundred pound Irish champion to sit on his shoulders, and then proceeded to lift off the ground the huge ship's anchor that the other had just been able, unhandicapped, to raise. In later life, settled down on his farm near the Upper Four Corners, Briggs became the object of considerable attention from passers-by who wished to view the famous strong man. One stranger persisted in seeking access to the titan about whom he had heard so much: "Well, my friend," said George, "now you have seen me, you may as well trot along about your business, and I will help you over the wall." And so saying he seized his surprised visitor by the coat collar and slack of his trousers and tossed him over the wall into the middle of the road. In time the story had it that Briggs had thrown the man's horse over after his rider. Not the passage of years but fearful work adjusting heavy stones at the bottom of a river for bridge pier foundations finally wrecked the magnificent constitution of Stout George. But still, when an old man on crutches, he lifted a stone that two or three ordinary men could not budge. Bordering the road along his farm stands a Cyclopean wall, built unaided by the Dighton Sampson, whose massive cap-stones still astonish travelers.[14]

Strong men prospered in village oral tradition among a handful of folk, comic demigods like Paul Bunyan have soared into national prominence largely through literary treatments; occasionally in American myth making the second type is rooted in the first.

The soil. In New England as in other sections local pride and shame have attached to the soil. One line of extravagance has deplored its complete and unequalled sterility — particularly in New Hampshire.

[14] *History of Bristol County, Mass.*, D. Hamilton Hurd, compiler (Philadelphia, 1883), pp. 251–253. Other similar strong heroes, Joe Call of Keeseville, N. Y., and Peter Francisco of Buckingham County, Virginia, like Beals and Briggs bested Englishmen; Francisco also pitched a horse and rider over a fence, and the Tuftonboro, N.H., history, pp. 76–77, gives the same folk incident.

An aged native of Manchester recalls the grasshopper found on the
pine plains wiping tears from its swarthy cheeks; when a sympathetic
traveler inquired the wherefore the animal replied, "The last mullen
leaf is wasting, and I see nothing but certain death by starvation."[1]
Pigs were so poor and lank they fell over in plucking a spear of grass;
it took two to make a shadow; unless their tails were tied in knots
they crawled out through the cracks in the pen.[2] A wagoner piloting
sportsmen through the abandoned mountain township of Kilkenny
related a dismal tale.

I was drivin' stage through this piece o' woods some years ago, when
I come all to once on a rabbit settin' on the brush fence an' cryin' as if
his heart would break. Bein' a good-natured man, an' fond of askin'
questions, I spose, — jest as you are, — I stopt the hosses, and said, "What
ails ye there? kin a feller do anythin' to help ye through yer trouble?"
The rabbit wiped his eyes with his tail as well as he could, and said to
me, "Stranger, my father died last week and left me two hundred acres
of this land, an' I've got to get my livin' off on it;" and then he bust out
cryin' ag'in. "G'lang," said I to the hosses, "can't do a thing to help ye,
if it's as bad as that."[3]

But on another, more frequent tack Yankee talk ran to lush bottoms,
plenty, luxuriance, size and fertility of unexampled proportions. Saw-
mills ran by buttermilk;[4] the sixteenth peeled layer of a forty-pound
onion encircled a four gallon demijohn;[5] a squash on a sandy farm
grew so heavy it sank through to China;[6] potatoes less than tea kettle
size were not picked;[7] enormous puddings crushed people to death in
accidental tumbles;[8] knee-high frogs twanged melodiously like guitars
and mosquitoes jabbed with bills large as darning needles.[9] Perhaps
astounding reports of Western loam brought back by Yankee travelers

[1] C. E. Potter, *The History of Manchester*, N.H. (Manchester, 1856), p. 8.
[2] *The Londonderry Celebration*, Robert C. Mack, compiler (Manchester, 1870), p. 72;
Yankee, III (May 1937), 39, quoting an 1854 issue of the *Lowell News*.
[3] *Granite Monthly*, XXXII (March 1902), 162.
[4] *Saturday Rambler*, Aug. 28, 1847 (vol. II).
[5] *Union Jack*, July 29, 1848 (vol. II).
[6] Jeremiah Digges, *Cape Cod Pilot* (Provincetown, Mass., 1937), p. 61.
[7] Sidney Perley, *Historic Storms of New England* (Salem, Mass., 1891), p. 213.
[8] William C. Hatch, *A History of the Town of Industry, Me.* (Farmington, Me.,
1893), p. 271; Clifton Johnson, *What They Say in New England* (Boston, 1896), p. 248.
[9] *The History of Milton, Mass.*, A. K. Teele, ed. (n.p., n.d.), p. 106.

aroused New England envy and evoked a regional rebuttal. For Yankees were visibly impressed at the Western scale of things.

THE HOOSIER AND THE YANKEE

'Wal now, stranger,' said the Yankee, 'suppose you tell us about your own country; you're the only man I ever seen from west, that didn't die of fever n'agur.'

'Well, old Yankee, I'll just tell you all about it. If a farmer in our country plants his ground with corn and takes first rate care on it, he'll git a hundred bushels to the acre; if he takes middlin' care of it he'll git seventy five bushels to the acre; and if he don't plant at all he'll git fifty.

'The beets grow so large that it takes three yoke of oxen to pull a full sized one; and then it leaves a hole so large, that I once knew a family of five children, who all tumbled in a beet hole once before it got filled up, and the earth caved in upon them and they all perished.

'The trees grow so large that I once knew a man, who commenced cutting one down, and when he had cut away on one side for about ten days, he thought he'd just take a look round the tree; and when he got round on t'other side, he found a man there who had been cutting at it for three weeks — and they never heard one another's axes.

'I have heard tell, yet somewhat doubt *that* story, that the Ohio *parsnips* have sometimes grown clean through the earth, and have been pulled through by the people on t'other side.'

'Wal now,' says the Yankee, 'I rather guess as how you've told enough, stranger, for the present. How'd you like to trade for some clocks to sell out west?'

'Never use 'em — we keep time altogether with pumpkin-vines. You know they grow just five feet an hour, and that's an inch a minute. Don't use clocks at all. Its no use, old Yankee, we can't trade, no how.'

The Yankee gave up beat, and suddenly cleared out.[10]

A Yankee in his turn could boast of properties inherent in his home soil.

A GOOD BRAG

In many parts of New England, says the Philadelphia City Item, bayberry is very common, especially on poor lands. The berries are abundant, easily gathered, and yield, on being thrown into boiling water, a tallow, which brings a higher price than beeswax. A good deal is made on a tract in Worcester county, Mass., called No-town.

A Yankee sat one day in a bar-room in Western New York, listening to some farmers bragging of their rich wheat lands. At length one of them taking occasion to sneer at New England soil, the Yankee broke in:

[10] *Exeter News Letter*, Oct. 19, 1841.

"Wal, now, gentlemen, you're greatly mistaken about the soil in the Old Bay State. Fact they wouldn't *have* such land as your'n in Massachusetts. Why, there is a piece of land so poor that nobody won't own it, and they call it No-town, because nobody don't live there, and yet even there the land is so rich that taller grows on the bushes. It *is* a fact, gentlemen, though I won't say as some do, that the old women of the neighboring towns go over there after a rain to dip candles in the puddles, but it is a fact that taller grows on the bushes, and I've sot by the light of candles made of it." The New Yorkers owned beat.[11]

Counterevidence demonstrating the fertile properties of New England soil somehow centered on large pumpkins.

BIG CONNECTICUT PUMPKINS

Dear Mr. "Spirit."— As you and your worthies have talked much about "races" and "tarnal wonders," allow me to present to you and the readers of the "Spirit," a "fast one," and which I will tell on my own responsibility. To some people, there seems to be no place like unto the old-fashioned State of Connecticut, notwithstanding all the hard stories told about it. As I had heard so much about it, I felt anxious to see it, so after I retired from the sanctum, I left seashore and salts, and *marvelled* at once into the interior of Connecticut, where once flourished wooden nutmegs, mahogany hams, horn gun-flints, oak cucumber seeds, pork and beans, blue-laws, etc. As I was somewhat acquainted with a venerable old gent who, it was said, couldn't be beat in telling a good story, I made for his mansion as fast as steam and fast nags saw fit to carry me, and on my arrival there, all things seemed to work for my goodly aims.

After leaving a bountiful table, where I had indulged over several cups of strong green tea, and partaken freely of griddles, flap-jacks, gormandisers, blackberry snaps, Indian bread, fresh butter, new cheese, and hot johnny-cake, I got the old gentleman fairly at it at once, by first introducing a story myself. As a *chum* of mine in Gotham bade me to get him to tell about the wonderful power of old Connecticut soil, I in due time opened my battery, and fired away boldly, thinking that I could defeat him in a discussion in regard to soil. The first thing I did was to crack up the noble farms and the enormous crops of Connecticut, as being a little ahead of anything in the Union, which in a twinkling caused a rejoinder from my friend, of "That's a fact." I then made an exception by remarking that, after all, I feared the Rhode Islanders had produced, by the aid of guano, soil so rich that the Connecticut people were *nowhar*. With an anxious heart, he urged me to tell him at once what I knew on the subject, as he feared I was laboring under a gross mistake.

I then began to tell him of a certain cucumber story that he had probably seen and read in print, where a certain Rhode Islander took a half bushel

[11] *Saturday Rambler*, Feb. 12, 1848 (vol. III).

of imported guano and put it into a hole in the ground, after which he dropped into the hill a dozen cucumber seeds, which he had no sooner done than a cucumber vine made its appearance, causing the man to drop his hoe and run for his life, as the vine was fast curling about him, like a serpent. By the time I had got thus far with my story, the old farmer crossed his legs and sighed. I went on, and told him that after the man had run for three-quarters of a mile, more or less, his legs became so entangled with the vine, that he fell to the ground, and was unable to extricate himself. Finding himself in such a "precarious situation," he at once endeavored to obtain his jack-knife from his pocket, but when he put his hand in said pocket, he found *a big cucumber already gone to seed.*

Having finished my story, the old gentleman slightly changed his position, and quietly remarked —"I do not doubt the truth of your story, my young friend, but listen, while I relate to you the wonders of the *native* soil of Connecticut.

"In my garden, where, I dare assert, a body might dig down four-and-thirty feet, and there find the same rich soil, more powerful than seventeen cargoes — yes, seventeen thousand cargoes — of your guano, I have seen wonders. It has been my family garden, it was my father's, and even his father's father's; in short, it has been a family garden more than a century. Well, when I was a boy, I was hoeing one morning with my good old father, in the garden, for a breakfast spell. I happened to be hoeing round a pumpkin vine, and was about to dig it up, when the old man said, 'Stephen, don't dig it up, my son, let it grow, and see what it will eventually become.' I obeyed, of course, yet could see nothing so very wonderful about it. Now don't you think," said he, earnestly, "that in time the vine grew so as to run over the north end of the garden wall, on the outside of which a very heavy ox-sled had been placed flat-ways, so as to keep it out of the sun during the summer months. This pumpkin vine eventually passed right under the sled, thence over another wall, thence through a cabbage patch and orchard, thence over a piece of meadow a hundred and fifty yards wide, thence down a long hill, and at last crossed a stream of water four rods wide. Now the soil of the garden being of such a powerful and unsurpassed nature, a pumpkin in time got under the sled; and it got to growing at such a thundering rate, as to raise that heavy ox sled an inch every night! In a very short period of time it had got the big sled on a *pize*, and we were obliged to prop it on the weak side, so as to keep the mammoth sled from tipping over. One day an old sow was looking for ground nuts on the opposite side of the stream, when she espied the pumpkin vine, and tracked it to the water's edge; thence, by some mystic movement, she crossed the stream *on the pumpkin vine*, and coursed it along, until she found the pumpkin itself, when she went at it deliberately, and ate four-and-twenty days out of it. One night, my father fearing that we were to have an old-fashioned black frost, he ordered all hands, and invited the neighbors to lend a hand, to get the mammoth pumpkin under cover.

"Well, we got the big stone drag down to the scene of action, and, after a while, two yoke of oxen and one horse made out to get it up to the back door. It was so big that it was an impossibility to get it in, so we took it round to the front door, which, as you have observed, is a wide old-fashioned one; and here we were obliged to rip off the door-casings, and then the pumpkin just rubbed through, on a tight squeeze at that. Well, sir, it was weighed right in this big square front room, after a fashion, and allowing good honest Connecticut weight, it weighed just *twenty-three hundred and seventeen pounds!* And in ten days, don't you think, full fifteen hundred people came from here, there, and yonder, to see this wonderful pumpkin! Now *whar* is *poodle* Rhode Island?" asked the old farmer.

Reader, what could I say now? could I do less than offer him my hat? "Sir," said I, "you are indeed *pumpkins to the core!* I have heard about being 'pumpkins,' but, Squire, the State of Connecticut is indeed that same renowned, and wonderful place." I went on extolling him to the "upper skies;" also the glorious State in which he had always lived, until the fire of energy and the spirit of *soil*ism, aroused him boldly for another "Connecticut whopper." Taking a pinch of snuff, he scratched his head, and then began again.

"Man may ascend mountains, and dive into the bowels of the earth, but after all his travels the State of Connecticut will be found *ahead*. Now I'll just tell you," said he, "another story, to show you the wonderful power of Connecticut *soil*. When spring came round a nephew of mine happened to be down here on a visit from the northern part of the State, and when he got all ready to go home, I made him a present of a dozen of these pumpkin seeds, knowing that the soil on any part of his small farm was very powerful and rich. I couldn't spare him no more, as I had even sold some single ones as high as a dollar and seventy-five cents a piece. Wal, my nephew went home and planted a dozen hills, one seed in each, and eventually up came the vines, and on they grew rapidly — so much so, that the fellow's eyes began to stick out like two peeled onions in a pail of water, for it seemed as though the vines were bent to run all over creation.

"In the fall of the year I visited him, having a pretty fast nag, full of the sap of life, and it took me just nine days to reach him. Well, I hadn't been there fifteen minutes before up drove, in haste, the widow Holmes, who lived about a mile and a quarter right north of my nephew's farm. Says she, in a passion, 'Be you agoing to take your pumpkin vines off my premises, or do you want me to destroy them?' Of course, I at once mistrusted, and asked right off what all this meant, when I soon found out that the trouble was all about the *pumpkin seeds I gave him to plant!* She told my nephew that she shouldn't come again, and off she drove as spunky as a North East wind. Now you see," said the old man deliberately, while I was roaring in laughter, "the pumpkin vines were running miles and miles in length, and the very devil was to pay with the neighbors. One would come from one way and complain, and another from this point of the compass, until my nephew wished them all in Halifax"———

"The *soil* must have been very, very rich?" said I, in a sober tone, interrupting him in his remarks.

"Oh yes, oh yes! — altogether richer, if anything, than my family garden. Any how, I can soon show you the power of Connecticut *soil*," and so the old gent took a pinch of yellow snuff, and then crossing his legs, began: "Now, when I got ready to start for home, I rode down the long lane and soon passed on to the turnpike. Well, 'Gid,' my young horse, hadn't more than struck the turnpike before I observed, along the road wall, a very thrifty pumpkin vine, which I knew to be one of my nephew's, as the place where he had endeavored to 'fence in' the plaguy vines when they first came up was visible to the eye. I drove on, whistling in my natural way — and after going a few miles, darn my eyes, there was the pumpkin vine! This puzzled me; I at once reined up 'Gid,' and away I rushed it over the Bunkhard-good turnpike, expecting to pass the *end* of it every instant. Well, now," said he, "don't you think I didn't pass the *end* of that pumpkin vine until just about twenty minutes before the hour of four in the afternoon! On I drove, and when night overtook me I put up at the Dutch tavern. On the second morning off I started again, but lordy! I *smelt* the pumpkin vine in a wink of a jiffee, just as soon as I struck on the turnpike. At it we went, and it was sundown before I overtook the *end* of it. Before stopping for the night I drove on some nine miles ahead, but when I pushed for home on the third morning, lo, and behold! there was the pumpkin vine! Then," said the old man, vehemently, I was wrathy, vexed — yes, mad. The way 'Gid' did take up his legs was a caution to any of your Third Avenue horses, now I tell you. He spun out full sixty-five miles that day, but to do our best, we didn't overtake the *end* of the pumpkin until just about twilight. I began to feel a little frightened, as well as being mad, yet knowing the almighy power of real Connecticut *soil*, I drove along, endeavoring to keep it off my mind as much as possible. On the sixth day I didn't overtake the end of it at all. On the seventh I conquered just about dusk — then drove on eleven miles ahead before I put up for the night, intending to have a good *start ahead of the vine* on the morrow. But you see," said the farmer, "it would make out to *pass me nights while I was asleep!* And I swear the pumpkin vine would have beat me home, if a *stout black frost hadn't killed it on the ninth night!!*"

Then I roared, laughed, and fairly yelled, until two fussy old maids got up, and advised us, from the head of a flight of stairs, to go to bed. I left for home in the morning, completely convinced that Connecticut *soil* and Connecticut stories, stood unsurpassed upon the annals of history.

Yours, comfortably,

J.D.V.[12]

---

[12] *Spirit of the Times*, XXI (Sept. 13, 1851), 350. Cf. "A Great Pumpkin Story" [N.H.], *ibid.*, XIV (Jan. 25, 1845), 568; "A Bit of a Punkin," *Yankee Blade*, Dec. 4, 1847 (vol. IV).

The sea serpent. Unparalleled in celebrity among fictitious creatures
fed by native fancy, unequaled as a theme for jubilant extravaganzas
and mock alarms, a deep-sea monster lurked off the New England coast
through the American centuries. Voluminous entries in all types of
popular publications noted his ubiquitous and terror-inspiring appearances, entries that ranged from eye witness reports issued with pious
conviction to lurid burlesques and gorgeous intentions. The hoax is
of ancient vintage; the monster surfaced off Cape Ann in 1641.

Some being on ye great beache gathering of clams and seaweed wch had
been cast thereon by ye mightie storm did spy a most wonderful serpent a
shorte way off from ye shore. He was as big round in ye thickest part as a
wine pipe; and they do affirme that he was fifteen fathom or more in length.
A most wonderful tale. But ye witnesses be credible, and it would be of
no account to them to tell an untrue tale. Wee have likewise heard yt at
Cape Ann ye people have seene a monster like unto this, wch did there
come out of ye sea and coile himself upon ye land mch to ye terror of them
yt did see him. And ye Indians doe say yt they have manie times seene a
wonderful big serpent lying on ye water, and reaching from Nahauntus to ye
greate rock wch we call Birdes Egg Rocke; wch is much above belief for yt
would be nigh upon a mile. Ye Indians, as said, be given to declaring wonderful things, and it pleaseth them to make ye white peeple stare. But
making all discounte, I doe believe yt a wonderful monster in forme of a
serpent doth visit these waters. And my praier to God is yt be not ye olde
serpent spoken of in holie scripture yt tempted our greate mother Eve and
whose poison hath run downe even unto us, so greatlie to our discomforte
and ruin.[1]

Off Cape Cod in 1719:

Boston. From Cape Cod we have the following remarkable Relation, That
on the 17th Instant there came into that harbour, a very strange and unusual Creature, which had a Head like a Lyon with very large Teeth, Ears
hanging down, a long Beard, with curl'd hair on his Head, his body about
Sixteen foot long, a round Buttock with a short Tail of a Yellowish colour,
who invited the Whale Men in their Boats to give him chase, he was very
fierce and gnashed his Teeth with great rage, when they attackd him, he
was shot at three times and wounded, and when he rose out of the Water, he
always faced their Boats in that angry manner; the Harpaniers struck at him,
but all in vain, for after five hours chase of him, he took to the Sea again;
there was none of the People there that had ever seen his like before.[2]

[1] Journal of Obadiah Turner, entry for Sept. 5, 1641, quoted in Fred A. Wilson,
Some Annals of Nahant Mass. (Boston, 1928), p. 161.
[2] *Boston News-Letter*, Sept. 21–Sept. 28, 1719.

In New London Harbor in 1769, when British customs collectors were plaguing colonial cargo vessels:

New-London. There has lately appeared off this Harbour, an ill-looking voracious Sea Monster, which has put all our Coasters upon a sharp look out, to steer clear of its devouring Jaws. It has been observed to devour whole Vessels at once; but some it has disgorged within an Hour after it has taken them; some of it has kept down a Day, some two, and some a Week. But its Constitution is such, that it can keep down nothing long, which may perhaps be owing to some bad Vermin inhabiting its Stomach. It is particularly fond of all sorts of West-India Produce, Rum, Molasses, Sugar, Cotton, Coffee, Cocoa, &c.

When it was first observed from Shore, by a great Number of People, there were various Conjectures what it could be: Some said that it was an old Shipwreck'd Hull with a TON on it. One said when he first saw it, it look'd like a P then like an AX with a clumsy Handle, and then like a TON, for it kept altering every Moment. Another said it look'd like a TEMPLE, but after viewing it through a good Prospective Glass, they all agreed that there was nothing in it that look'd like a Temple. Then an old aboriginal Native who had been on a Hill for some Time viewing it, said he thought it looked like ROBINSON Crusoe and his Man Friday be-KNIGHTED. After some Time it drew near to the Shore, when they could observe it quite plain, they found it was a rotten Burch Log, with a broken REED sticking in it for a Mast.[3]

With the manifold opportunities in nineteenth-century newspapers, periodicals, and humor compilations for printed expression, the sea-serpent fable burgeoned forth into a thousand fragmentary tales. The creature was sighted in many waters, even in inland lakes; his shapes, colors, limbs, and movements received detailed description; periodic visits to New England shores brought in their wake flooding rumors, scientific speculations, and organized expeditions to effect his capture.[4] Some accounts were soberly factual, others induced suspicion.

THE VERY LATEST GLIMPSE O' THE GREAT SEA-SARPENT, THAT
FOR THE LAST FIFTY YEARS HAS HAUNTED NA-HANT!!

Certified Affidavit o' Squire Varmifuge Vampose, o' Varmount.

L.S.   Seal o' State.

PARSONALLY appeared afore me, *Jeremiah Jehosaphat*, a Justice o' the Peace o' the County aforesaid, Mister Squire Varmifuge Vampose, who deposeth as follers: —

[3] *Essex [Salem] Gazette*, May 9–May 16, 1769.
[4] See e.g. Daniel Remich, *History of Kennebunk* [Me.] (n.p., c. 1911), pp. 394–397;

"On Monday mornin', a little atween sunshine an' clock-strike, as I war swimmin' off Egg Rock, I heerd a precussion in the water. I looked up, an' I seed a figger o' a big snake, that looked more like a worm, rise up, shake its head clean down to the eend o' its tail, an' head a kind o' circumbendibously for Egg Rock. Its body in diam'ter, in close kalk'lation, war as thick round as you could see, an' its length, from the head tu the tail, an' back, war' abeout as fur as from here to yander; the size o' its head war abeout fero-cious, its eyes war like tew large augur-holes, bored through darkness intu daybreak, an' its back looked like a train o' freight rail-cars, head up with stone-coal. He just gin' a flirt, an' then a spurt, an' then a squirm, an' the hull sea war turned intu sich a sink o' soap-suds, that the fish actooally slipped down each other's throat, without a swaller. Thar' war a big ox walkin' along Lynn Beach, the sarpent tuck aim at him with his eyes, an' he walked right intu his throat by suction, like a worm intu a horned trout, an' then picked his teeth with a wrecked mainmast that floated by. It now begin tu storm like Sodom, an' a thunder-bolt bolted right down his throat; he spit the bolt right out, all chawed up, flung a summerset, turned his tail intu his mouth, jumped deown his own throat, an' then *vanquished*."[5]

For all the ridiculing heaped upon the hoax, both in uncovered frauds and obvious lampoons, it would not die. Notoriously tenacious of life, the reptile writhed into the twentieth-century and slithered up the Green Hills of Vermont. How did he travel inland? Eyewitnesses who sighted him in Lake Memphremagog explained that he visited the lake through a subaqueous channel, and returned by it whenever he desired, for the benefit of his health, to exchange fresh water for salt.[6] Whether or not the hypothesis was sound, inland the creature indisputably did go.

THE SEA SERPENT APPEARS
Seen in Dead Creek by Three Reliable Citizens

It has just leaked out that three men, while fishing for bull pouts recently, in Dead Creek, saw a terrible water monster that gave them a scare that got onto their nerves pretty bad. They claim it was the real thing in a sea serpent and they hadn't touched a drop, except Fairfield water, since every-thing went to St. Albans. They are loath to talk about what they saw, "as no one will believe us," one of the party remarked. "But it is gospel truth, though," another member of the party chimed in as they owned up and consented to talk, with the understanding that we would keep their names

---

Herman A. Jennings, *Provincetown, or Odds and Ends from the Tip End* (Yarmouth-port, Mass., 1890), pp. 172–175. The *Idiot, or Invisible Rambler* (1818) abounds in sea-serpent yarns; but all the standard dailies and weeklies for the period yield tales.

[5] *Jonathan Jaw-Stretcher's Yankee Story All-My-Nack,* 1852 (Boston, n.d.).

[6] John R. Dix, *A Handbook for Lake Memphremagog* (Boston, n.d.), p. 48.

out of the Courier. Still laboring under considerable nervous tension the three managed to give the story in fragments substantially as follows:

"The three of us were in a boat not far from Indian Point. We had out lanterns, a can of nice fat worms and two lines apiece, intending to make a night of it and land a lot of pouts before morning. We got all fixed up just before dusk and settled down for a little smoke and visit before the bull pouts got along. You know the Missisquoi Bay pouts are pretty particular and never take hold good until it gets dark. They are the best that swim though, and prices are all right now. So we had quite a bit of time before the first run got along. You may not know it, but Dead Creek is about as cheerful as an old cemetery, with flat gray marble slabs, about the time the sun sinks out of sight for the night, over beyond the marsh, and queer, dark shadows come stealing through the trees and brush. I don't like to own it, but it always makes me feel creepy with twisted dark streaks eating right into me. One of the boys kept telling funny stories to keep things kinder pleasant until the pouts got busy and took our 'tention. All of a sudden there was the darndest noise just around the point, a splashing and sputtering and gurgling and in between a sharp snapping sound, for all the world just like a big steel trap springing together. At first we thought it was one of them cussed motor boats in a fit. Pretty soon the racket stopped and we heard something coming our way. A swashy, glide motion and real fast, faster than the 'Swastika' when she has plenty of gasolene and Homer Brown at the engine.

"Do you believe it, when the noise got around the bend and right opposite to us, in the deepest part of the creek, it wasn't a fussy power boat, but something sure alive and squirming. It was as big around as a sugar barrel, maybe a little bigger, we wouldn't exactly tell. It stopped right near us, too blamed near, but somehow didn't seem to see us. He smelled us all right for he stuck his head out of the water about 10 feet, maybe 12, and sniffed a good deal like a bird dog. The top of the head was black and hairy and shaded down to the ears to a dirty moss green. We saw shiny gray scales, about the size of a baseball on the throat, with big ones down towards the belley. When it opened its terrible mouth we could see several rows of glittering white teeth 10 inches long, maybe 12. A yellowish flat tail, twice as big as the rudder of the 'Siesta,' away back of the head about 80 feet, maybe 100, kept swishing around quiet like, just as a cat does before it jumps for a bird. 'What did we do?' You remember that big pepperage tree right on the edge of the creek? Well, we just backed out of that boat mighty quick and quiet and shinned up the pepperage, but it seemed as if we never would get to the top. It is the tallest tree in the marsh, but it wasn't tall enough by a hundred, maybe two hundred feet. We never said a word, we were so scart, just clung on all night, praying for the sun to come back on the other side of the marsh, bringing brightness and warmth. That big thing seemed to be fooling around a long time, but it was so dark we couldn't see just what it was up to. It was nosing around the boat sure, for we heard the lantern tip over and then it munched on the worms, can and all, eat up our extra coats, and a pair of rubber boots, licked up the kerosene, gnawed the handles off both oars and then went on up the creek. Some time in the night it went by like the devil and the last we heard, it was out in the bay and seemed to be headed for Lime Kiln Point.

My, we were glad to get home and set on the granite again and sun ourselves with the rest of the boys. No more bull pouting for us this year, you bet. Front of the bank is good enough for us. Now whenever anyone mentions Dead Creek it makes us feel creepy and just as sick to our stomachs as can be.[7]

[7] *Swanton [Vt.] Courier*, June 3, 1909.

V

LOCAL LEGENDS

Many native twice-told tales depend for their interest not simply on plot but on associations with specific landmarks and places. Unusual features of the landscape provoke story, or unusual story distinguishes a particular spot. Certain tale types have natural roots in geography: over mountain peaks and cliffs leap distraught lovers; in caves and creeks, under trees and rocks lie buried treasure caches; deserted houses shelter phantom guests; names of localities derive from traditionary incidents alleged to have occurred within their bounds. The rolling tide of folk history loosens these particles of lore from their anchorage in the past and floats them forward over new areas of time.

Thus firmly lodged in township saga, place legends show definite relations with folktale movements. Their simple motives, hidden treasure, the death of lovers, haunted crime spots, are universal story themes. Wandering popular tales frequently become localized in community traditions. And an original fiction once told, like colonial marvels or Indian tragedies, may by sufficient repetitions in regional histories and newspapers become firmly established as a place legend. Josselyn's secondhand yarn of the merman three centuries later is still being broadcast in a Sunday newspaper feature (*Portland Telegram*, July 10, 1938) about Peak's Island, Maine: "The most familiar legend connected with the island is said to have come from the lips of Michael Mitton, a huntsman with the propensities of Baron Munchausen." Continually retold, orally and in print, local legends reveal themselves the hardiest of native prose narrative types.

Indian tragedies. While the tribal stores of myth and folktale possessed by the red man never bridged the wide culture gap between Indian and white civilizations, perversely the noble savage himself became a part of his conquerors' folklore. Not his myths but his historical traditions, or those imputed to him, attracted the white man's fancy; Indian braves and comely maidens became folk property, like Yankees and witches. Popular legend dovetailed with literary treatments of the Indian, themselves a force for legend; both painted a fated primitive creature, governed by a crude theology and primal passions and yet often moved by unselfish instincts to heroic actions. Where white folks spelled cities and progress, the aborigines belonged to nature and the past; as befit these romantic concepts, the red man entered place legends associated with mountains, lakes, islands, rivers, caves, waterfalls, trees, and rocks, that commemorated a melancholy event of colonial or pre-colonial days — the death of lovers, the sacrifice of a maiden, the fate of a warrior.

Indian tragedies that passed into tradition contained a high content of literary and invented elements. Longfellow in *The Song of Hiawatha* (1885) employed a metrical and thematic arrangement that skilfully refracted the popular attitude toward the savage, and briefer imitations flowed into local history, exercising poetic license on a slender or non-existent thread of legend. The sum total of Indian place legends, however, must be recognized as a genuine body of American folktale: internal evidence in some of the legends reveals that they had previous oral life; fancies largely composed by a single person have been repeated and dispersed in local lore; the majority of the legends, regardless of their provenance, display similar and characteristic motives. And the most fanciful sentimental tales of heartbroken lovers, tribal conflicts, and the Manitou's vengeance may be at the core pure Indian folk narrative.

The events recorded in this legend belong far back in the dim past. I heard this story as it fell from the lips of a wrinkled old squaw in the White Hills, who sold beaded and braided baskets, and who claimed to be a direct descendant of the Penacook Indians. She told it as it had been handed down in the tribe for more than five hundred years. No history has chronicled the acts set forth in the story of the old squaw; only in the traditions of the red men do they find a place.[1]

Within the conventions of mournful romance that found congenial material in the vanishing American, no theme surpassed the attractiveness of tragic death, and in particular tragic death linked to blighted

---

[1] Charles H. Glidden, *The Legend of Wonalansett. A Tale of the White Hills* (Boston, 1914), p. 3.

love. Natural features of the land frequently marked the untimely graves of Indians or Indian and white lovers whom fate had sundered by devious means. One technique of preventing the desired union allowed the wrong rival to triumph in a contest for the maiden. Across Wahconah Falls in the Berkshires two braves leaped for the hand of a maiden both loved, and when the one she cherished failed to reach the opposite bank she followed him into the rushing waters, calling out his name — Wahconah.[2] In what is now Jackson Valley, a young warrior and his lover plunged to death over a cataract after he had lost her hand in a shooting contest with his rival, and they had endeavored to flee together. Two airy forms are sometimes seen ascending through the mists of the falls.[3] Treachery affected the outcome of some contests. Attached to Wood Island, Maine, is the tradition of a duel between two warriors for a girl who, refusing to name her preference, stated that she would marry the braver. Unknown to either she paddled across the bay to observe the combat. As they stood side by side, awaiting the signal to be flashed by the rising sun, one stepped forward and faced the east, his arms extended to invoke the aid of the Great Spirit in accord with Indian ethics. To her surprise and horror the other drew his knife and stabbed him through the back. When the girl made known the crime to her tribe, a chieftain slew the assassin on the very spot where he had murdered his rival, and had his body thrown into the sea.[4] A similar occurrence is associated with Bayard's Point, Maine, where once dwelt a party of Penobscot Indians and a French youth, Pierre Gaudin, only survivor of a wrecked French sloop. Adopted by chief Hahatan, he fell in love with the chief's daughter, Minnecoma; the match was approved and wedding plans under way when the powerful chief of all the Penobscots, Pocomic, arrived to visit his kinsmen. The chieftain's son, Wonnewok, smitten with Minnecoma, refused to join in the games or be civil to his fellows until he had the promise of her hand. Heartsick Hahatan did not dare offend the powerful chief, and took refuge in a conciliatory decision:

[2] Ella S. Brown, "Wahconah Falls — Their History and Traditions," *Collections of the Berkshire Historical and Scientific Society* (Pittsfield, Mass., 1906), pp. 270–271. The story is described as an "unwritten legend."
[3] *History of Carroll County, N.H.*, Georgia D. Merrill, ed. (Boston, 1889), p. 131.
[4] *Portland Sunday Telegram*, July 22, 1923.

his daughter should wed the warrior bringing her as a wedding present the skin of the man-killing panther whose lair lay at the head of the pond. Accordingly Wonnewok and Pierre, equally armed with hunting knife and rifle, paddled up toward the rocky heights at the head of the pond. Pierre had landed on the east side and edged through the thick underbrush, when he heard a rifle shot followed by a snarl and a scream. He plunged through to the clearing of a little beach and saw the panther leap through the air at Wonnewok and knock him to the sand. Forgetful of their enmity, Pierre raised his rifle and fired; the mortally wounded beast closed with him and bore him to the ground. Wonnewok staggered to his feet, and watched with folded arms until writhing man and beast lay prostrate on the bloody sands. Then he skinned the panther and returned to the settlement. At the council meeting that evening Minnecoma, who had been found unconscious at the bottom of her drifting canoe, confronted Wonnewok with the facts she had surreptitiously witnessed; frenziedly she plunged a knife into his breast, then turned it into her own. When the Penobscot chief returned that fall on a less friendly visit he found the point deserted.[5]

Races with a maiden as prize united the thrills of sport and love. A tragic canoe race involves the Penacooks, the Merrimac River, and the Amoskeag Falls. For the hand of the winsome Winneona, admirers competed to see who could match the fleetness of her canoe — among them Kohass the Pine, whom she feared, and Aurayet the Sunbright, whom she loved. At the race's start word spread that Aurayet had been slain. Startled Winneona overtook the others and edged slowly past Kohass, the leader. But then the spirit of Aurayet rushed swiftly to meet them in a canoe propelled by some strange power; all three toppled over the falls, but Aurayet had lifted Winneona into his canoe that they might share their fate together.[6] A like disaster lacks the overtone of treachery. Walahassee and his wealthy rival, young chief Moosguntik, joined in a canoe race to overtake

[5] *Bangor Daily News*, July 24, 1937. As told by Carleton Walker living near the old Indian encampment.
[6] Laconica, "The Bride of the White Canoe. A Legend of Amoskeag Falls," *Granite State Magazine*, V (1908), 209–216.

comely Naginscot. She had planned to allow her love, Walahassee, to overtake her, but looking back to make sure he was in the lead, she forgot the approaching falls and came within their fatal vortex; Walahassee followed her to destruction.[7] In another variation of the tragic race, both rivals meet death through exhaustion. Along a beach at Rogue Bluffs, Maine, coquettish Golden Wing, daughter of an Abenaki chief, decided to have her two equally favored suitors, Black Wolf and Flying Fox, run in a contest of speed for her hand. One crumpled on the beach before he reached the mark — the maiden herself — and the other, unaware that his distanced competitor had fallen, also ran his heart out to perish in her arms. Ever since the beautiful but cruel beach has been known as "The Race Course."[8]

Once a departure from the standard plot permitted a happy ending. Nessacus, the handsome young stranger, wooed lovely Wahconach, daughter of the old chief Miahcomo and idol of the Pequot remnant inhabiting the village of Dalton in the Berkshire Hills. But complications came in the presence of a burly Mohawk chieftain, smoke-dried, scarred, and scalp-laden Yonnonongah, who demanded the maiden for his fourth wife in a suit favored by the crafty priest Tashmu. According to the interpretation of supernal signs and portents by the priest, an ordeal of arms was frowned upon; the Great Spirit had decreed that the spirit of the stream should decide the issue. On each bank of the stream a rival would stand, an unguided canoe would be set adrift toward a rock that cleft the waters, and to the one whose side it passed would go the human prize. The night before the test Tashmu and the Mohawk could have been seen tugging at certain heavy rocks, which they place in the water so as to direct the current toward one bank. Yet when the fateful canoe was launched, an inconstant current carried it by the feet of Nessacus. Had the handsome brave witnessed the midnight labors of the conspirators and rendered them abortive?[9]

[7] Orvel Weaver, "The Legend of the Falls," *New England Magazine*, n.s., XXXI (September 1904), 20–23.

[8] In Ernest E. Bisbee, *The State O' Maine Scrap Book* (Lancaster, N.H., 1940).

[9] Joseph E. A. Smith, *Taghonic: The Romance and Beauty of the Hills* (Boston, 1879), pp. 269–282: "There is a tradition about these falls which I heard, long years

Not only in combats and contests, but also by simple violence, spurned and unwelcome suitors brought death to lovers. A Mohegan brave and his Mohawk rival hurtled over Ahwannega Rock, New Hampshire — Indian for "The Lover's Leap" — in a death struggle for White Fawn. Daughter of a Mohawk chieftain, she had fled from the tribal match arranged by her father to the side of her Mohegan lover; when her kinsmen pursued the pair, she fought alongside her lover and escaped with him to the banks of the Connecticut. But one day the jealous rival stole on them unawares, to precipitate a fatal struggle. Not long after, White Fawn lay still on the grave of her loved one, and even today the wind sometimes carries the echo of her wild death song.[10] When the Penobscots visited the hunting grounds of the weaker Wee-weenocks, a son of their sachem became enamored of a Wee-weenock girl already betrothed. On a hunting excursion up a mountain rising boldly from the western shore of the lake he met the maiden whom he coveted, and when she spurned his persuasions, in high rage he flung her down a craggy precipice. Because the Wee-weenocks were inferior in strength the broken-hearted lover had to stifle his desire for revenge; but when the two tribes gathered at the annual feast upon Mount Kinnes, in view of the great Kataadn and in honor of the good Spirit who watched over their hunting grounds, he could no longer contain himself and with a blow of his war club laid the murderer dead at his feet. In the resulting fray all the Wee-weenocks were massacred save for a few of the boldest warriors who chose to take their own lives by leaping headlong down the rugged precipice toward the still waters of the lake. To this day Indians cannot be prevailed upon to ascend the mountain, which they imagine haunted by the souls of the warriors slain in the presence of the Great Spirit of Kataadn.[11] Ignoring the rightful claim of the young chieftain

ago, from a young Indian of the civilized Stockbridge tribe, who had come back from the western exile of his people to be educated at an eastern college" (p. 269).

[10] *New Hampshire Folk Tales*, Mrs. Moody P. Gore and Mrs. Guy E. Speare, compilers (n.p., 1932), pp. 7–11: "Legend of Ahwannega." Told by Mrs. George H. Sawyer to her Campfire girls in Whitefield, as she had heard it many years previously from an aged squaw.

[11] *New-Bedford Daily Mercury*, Feb. 24, 1840, "A Leaf from 'Down in Maine'." Credited to the *Knickerbocker*. "My guide, though a man of few words, and those few of the purest Yankee dialect, had often listened to the traditions of the few wandering red

Tecola upon his beautiful daughter, the miserly trader Nelson sold her to an infamous Indian agent. Tecola, learning of the scheme, planned to foil it, but before he could spirit Laura away the agent had forced her into his canoe, paddled out over the waters of Sebago Lake (Maine), and plunged a knife deep in her breast. Short-lived was his revenge, for Tecola slew the cowardly wretch on the bank and left his body for carrion birds and wolves. Over the grave mound of Laura, Tecola often kneeled, communing with her spirit, and since he has rejoined her their names are linked in the memories of the villagers.[12] A stone cairn rising from the bed of Lake Hoccomocco in Westboro, Massachusetts, recalls a murderer's death spot, for whenever Indians passed over the place in their canoes they dropped a stone, to dishonor the memory of the villain. On the eve of her marriage to the tribal chieftain, a beautiful Indian maiden sped playfully across the pond in her canoe, to hide in a leafy bower at the end; underneath the water swam her rejected suitor until he reached the canoe, then with an agonized shriek the maiden sank beneath the surface. But for three anniversaries of the death day the murderer was impelled to the shores of Hoccomocco, there to embark in a phantom canoe, see his victim materialize from blue flame, and hear again her dying shriek. On the third repetition, knowing it to be the last, he confessed his sin to the gathered tribe, then rode in the fatal boat to the middle of the pond, whence he vanished in a vivid lightning flash.[13]

An unwanted husband enjoyed prerogatives denied the preferred wooer. In a cove of Squam Lake, New Hampshire, a block of granite resembling the draped figure of a woman (now removed), mutely memorialized the Legend of the Stone Squaw. Mamon, an old, wise, and famed sachem, eyed the beautiful Amata with longing, and though her heart was given to the young warrior Moowis, the chief her father

---

men who, during the hunting season, are still found in the vicinity of the lake; and while floating listlessly upon the water . . . I gathered from him the incidents of the following story."

[12] "Tecola: or the Wrought Belt. A Legend of Sebago Lake," *Yankee Blade*, Oct. 9, 1847 (vol. VII). Told to St. Clair by an aged man dwelling near the lake.

[13] *History of Worcester County, Mass.*, D. Hamilton Hurd, compiler (Philadelphia, 1889), II, 1354–1355; H. P. DeForest and E. C. Bates, *The History of Westborough, Mass.* (Westborough, 1891), pp. 5–6. Told by an old Indian who used to come to the house of Horace Maynard for cider.

desired an alliance with his friend Mamon. After the wedding banquet sad-faced Amata returned to the wigwam of her aged husband, who, surfeited with food and drink, fell promptly asleep. The curtains of the lodge flapped apart, a hand touched her forehead, and a well-known voice spoke in her ear, bidding her fly with him. But as they fled into the stormy night the sagamore awoke, and by a flash of lightning recognized the fugitives. From the shore he discharged his arrow at the pair struggling to escape in the water, and Moowis sank with a cry, crimsoning the waters. Amata reached a ledge and, struggling upon the rock, stretched her round arms to the shore. "Let Manitou make of her a signal and example to coming time," prayed Mamon, and even as he spoke a vivid flash of lightning and a crash of thunder shook the earth. For ages after, Indians roaming near the lake pointed out the crouching stone figure as a judgment by the Great Spirit for her wanton flight.[14]

Tribal ethics in other instances ignored the demands of just love that had transgressed arbitrary ethical codes on penalty of death; Manitou, not the jealous lover, sealed the tragedy. So in the Legend of the Blowing Cave at Kennebunkport, Maine, the young brave and the Pocasset maiden whom he wooed contrary to the "Great Spirit's Decree" thereby forfeited their lives. For none of alien tribes could wed until his voice, roaring over the ocean, should rend in twain the giant cliff that overhung their trysting place. Despairingly, on the day they must part, they donned their festival garments, ascended the towering cliff and, chanting their death song and clasped in each other's arms, plunged to the bottom. When morning dawned the mighty rock had fallen, and the ocean tide washed its fragments over the spot where the lovers had died.[15] Impious love likewise met a retributive fate in the romance of Shoon-keek and Moon-keek, Mohegan cousins who lived in the Pontoosuc (now Pittsfield) valley in the olden time. Forbidden each other's company by a stern tribal edict against incestuous passion, they stole time together in the sedgy shores of islands on the lake. When jealous Nockawando spied their

[14] Fred M. Colby, "Asquam Lake and Its Environs," *Granite Monthly*, X (February 1887), 77–79.
[15] Annie P. Brooks, *Ropes' Ends: Traditions, Legends and Sketches of Old Kennebunkport and Vicinity* (Kennebunkport, Me., 1901), pp. 18–20.

clandestine meetings, he informed Moon-keek's father of her ill conduct; the now-alarmed lovers determined to flee to a neighboring tribe with a laxer marital code. Before leaving the island they solemnly vowed, if unsuccessful in their purpose, to meet beneath the waters of the lake and part no more. As Shoon-keek glided stealthily to the island in his canoe, an arrow from the bow of Nockawando pierced his body, which fell heavily into the lake, but his form still directed the canoe at more than mortal speed past the island. Waiting Moon-keek saw it pass, and with a wild death-song leaped into her own canoe and darted madly from the shore. Nockawando started in pursuit, but as he came near he saw that the maiden, like her lover, was a shade. He returned to camp a gibbering idiot. And across the lake that bears their name, the phantoms of Shoon-keek and Moon-keek continue to call and search piteously for each other in obedience to their unlawful pledge to constant union that Manitou has decreed can never be ful-filled. Sometimes keen eyes detect a spectral canoe flitting across the waters of Lake Shoon-keek-Moon-keek.[16]

Only a slight erotic element is present in the sacrificial legend of Monument Mountain in Southern Berkshire. A towering line of an-cient rocks rears a frowning front toward the heavens, so perpendicular that a chill seizes the awestruck beholder at the sight; behind this height once dwelt a tribe of Stockbridge Indians, and when one among them violated the tribal code he must plunge or be plunged over the frightful precipice. A beautiful squaw transgressed by marrying into another tribe, and although she had courage sufficient to face death in marrying, she could not commit the required self-sacrifice. Accordingly her limbs, save for her hands, were bound; she was borne to the verge and cast over. But here a thing occurred which had never been known before; in her downward flight the squaw came in contact with the long branch of a protruding pine, and grasping it with the clutch of death succeeded in staying her fall. There she hung for two days and two nights, without any hope of rescue, while the dusky forms above mocked her in her agony. On the night of the second day a fierce storm arose, and a thunderbolt struck the pine, setting it on fire; parted from the cleft of the rock, it spun round and round so swiftly that no one

[16] Joseph E. A. Smith, *Taghonic*, pp. 67–74.

could distinguish tree or squaw, and whirled up into the blackness of the sky until it seemed no bigger than a star, then winked out entirely. In council the Indians decided this was the work of the Great Spirit, and raised a monument of stones to which every visitor, if he or she be conversant with the traditional cause, adds one more.[17]

Death that separated lovers sometimes resulted from unforeseeable mischance. Good intentions governed the brothers of Winota, the Princess of the Pines, when they met with Lewara, her handsome chieftain lover, to discuss his suit. What happened could only later be surmised, for when the impatient braves sought out their tardy chiefs, they found Lewara and the brothers in the mute embrace of death. Winota poured out her grief from the fountains of her lustrous eyes; her tears fell faster and faster, bigger and bigger, gathering and swelling and rolling onward down the valley until they had reached the bosom of the sea. And so, through the tears of the Indian maiden, was born the silver-voiced Connecticut.[18] No vengeful rival but a panther destroyed the lives of the fair daughter of wizard Passaconway *(sic)* and her lover chieftain from Newichwanic; he sought, found, and grappled to the death with the tawny beast that had crushed her body in his absence. Beside his wigwam doorway Passaconway set and tended a wild rosebush on which bloomed two beautiful white roses; when at last they faded he preserved every petal and laid the bush secretly away. It was said that the spirits of the lovers had blossomed on the rosebush to a sweeter, purer life.[19] Pure accident caused its share of tragedy. Trevaldos, the hermit of Indian Cave, last of the redmen around Lake Sunapee, chose there to remain in self-imposed solitude that he might linger near the spirit of the dusky maiden whom a cruel whirlwind had cast beneath the waves.[20] Bethel Rock in Woodbury, Connecticut, is chargeable with two deaths in a case of unrequited love. Waramaukeag, graceful, manly, and highly intelligent, cultivated

[17] "Monument Mountain. Strange Legend of an Indian Maiden," *Berkshire Hills*, vol. II (March 1, 1902).

[18] G. Waldo Browne, "The River of Tears. An Indian Legend of the Connecticut," *Granite Monthly*, XXIV (March 1898), 171–172.

[19] W. D. Spencer, "Passaconway," *Granite Monthly*, XVII (December 1894), 371–374.

[20] C. F. Browne, "A Legend of Sunapee Lake," *Granite Monthly*, XXXVIII (July 1906), 209–211.

a close acquaintance with his white pastor, Mr. Walker, and in so doing fell smitten with Sarah Walker, his innocent and fetching niece. Gently she rejected his advances, and in kindly fashion the pastor explained to Waramaukeag the impropriety of his desire. Neither saw the crestfallen sachem for some time until one Indian summer at dusk when Sarah, as was her wont, wandered out to Bethel Rock for her evening devotions. Suddenly the Indian appeared at her side; startled, she stepped back in alarm and fell with violence on the jagged rocks below. When found the next morning her disordered tresses had been smoothed and her body composed, while nearby lay the mangled corpse of Waramaukeag, who had chosen deliberately to follow her unintended plunge.[21]

Suicides and sacrifices accounted for a certain percentage of lovers. A pile of igneous rock presenting a façade forty feet sheer overlooks Lake Munson in southern New Hampshire; it is named "Lover's Rock" from a melancholy tale. Many years prior to the French and Indian Wars adventurous French Canadian voyageurs penetrated deep into New England forests and consorted amicably with the redmen; occasionally one wed a brown warrior's daughter. Le Clair, a trader from Mount Royal, had long been a welcome guest at the island home of Hanoket, powerful sachem of the Wanokets, and one time he brought his son, gay young Antoine, who speedily became enraptured of the graceful sylph Mamomish. On the day for their departure the boy announced his love to Le Clair, who sternly refused to countenance such a mésalliance. After the two had gone, Hanoket, musing before his tent, heard a low, piercing wail that gained in intensity; glancing for the source he perceived Mamomish standing with outstretched arms on the rocky eminence; even as he watched she flashed downwards into a cloud of spray. The maiden had sought and found her Lethe.[22] The grafting of fancy onto fact in a Lover's Leap legend is shown in a tragedy that occurred on Mount Megunticook, Maine, in 1862. A certain perpendicular ledge facing the lake bears the

[21] William Cothren, *History of Ancient Woodbury, Conn.* (Waterbury, Conn., 1854), 1, 90–92. "The legend has been variously related, both orally and in printed accounts" (p. 90).
[22] Edward W. Wild, "Lover's Leap. An Aboriginal Legend of Southern New Hampshire," *Granite Monthly*, XXV (August 1898), 79—81.

name Maiden Cliff because an eleven-year-old child, Eleanor French, toppled from it to her death when she reached for a bonnet the zephyrs had blown from her head. A local poet immortalized the incident in verses entitled "The Fair Maid of Megunticook," wherein the girl, wooed by King Boreas, dropped into his outstretched arms to be his queen; and the poetized version replaced the actuality in the minds of the sentimental public.[23]

How romantic interest is supplied to what might well have been originally an accurate tale of simple sacrifice appears in the growth of the legend of Lake Pocotopaug. When Wangunk braves drowned in the lake and a plague ravished the settlement, the tribe convened in council to decide what actions of theirs had angered the god Hobomoko. Sadly the medicine man returned from his conclave with the angry god; sorrowfully he described his wrath that only one costly sacrifice would appease — and here he paused until chief Terramaugus bade him speak — the fairest daughter of the tribe, Na-moe-nee, daughter of Terramaugus. The chieftain waited but a moment to settle the furious struggle that gripped his breast; then quietly he announced, "The will of Hobomoko shall be obeyed." With heavy heart he led his brave child, eager to be the instrument that would relieve the sufferings of the tribe, to the summit of the ledges on the east shore of the bay; after he bound her ankles and wrists, she tumbled over the edge of the cliff. From that day Hobomoko relented from torturing the Wangunks, and even white men escaped harm from the lake until the spell was broken by a drowning in 1885. So ran the tale until two subsequent twentieth-century versions altered its plot. In one the jealous Cochicha, resentful of the love Amawan bears Osweenee, curses her rival so that, to save Amawan from the evil spirits of the lake, she must give herself in sacrifice. A second rendering has Na-moe-nee behold her lover and her sorceress rival storm-battered while crossing the lake in a birch canoe; fearing the malediction about to be fulfilled, she leaps into the lake from her point of vantage. Thereupon the storm subsided and a spell of safety from drowning in the lake lasted for a considerable period. These modern revisions illustrate a revealing shift in emphasis: in the early tale, which is described as

[23] *Camden [Me.] Herald*, Nov. 21, 1935.

long current in pioneer firesides and probably closely akin to what the Indians actually believed, the germinal incident lies in an exacted sacrifice to appease an angry god and save the tribe; in the later ones, a human love triangle replaces the god-tribe relationship as the situation that leads to the sacrifice.[24] Here a clear reworking of oral tradition into fabricated legend indicates the superimposed tastes of white on Indian folk history, in a fashion that presumably has shaped similar material in a similar way.

While most Indian tragic legends concern lovers, others deal with vengeful deeds of Manitou on faithless tribes, with prophecies, curses, and malicious spirits. Where Lake Mashapaug in Union, Connecticut, now reflects the sun formerly stood a majestic mountain; at its foot reveled and feasted a once warlike people, grown soft, cowardly, and impious. For the fair young queen Nokemo heeded not the warnings of the prophetess Nakentis, who dwelt near the summit of the mountain, of the rising wrath of the Great Spirit; and she continued to lead her people on in their wickedness. During one of their wanton revels, a black tempest arose that caused rocks to heave and the ground to tremble; as Nakentis had prophesied, a white swan descended from the sky, sung its death song, and died at her feet. Then Nokemo knew vengeance had come for the evil she had encouraged; the mountain sank, water poured in torrents over its grinding edges, and of all the tribe only Nakentis was left standing on an island, praying for her wayward people. Thus was Mashapaug created, and the fisherman still can see beneath him, when the light shines through the water, wigwams and trees.[25] A similar prophetically announced catastrophe swept away Swan Island in Saco Pond, to warn the impenitent Pequawkets of the coming of the white man. Old Scawesco had told his people angry Manitou would blast their maize fields, dry up their

[24] Carl F. Price, *Yankee Township* (East Hampton, Conn., c. 1941), pp. 15–22. The modern versions referred to are "The Legends of Lake Pocotopaug," by Eleanor M. Buell, the *Penny Press*, Middletown, June 16, 1910; "Lake Pocotopaug and Its Moods and Legends," by O. Adella Clark, fourteen page poem printed in pamphlet form by the author in 1925.

[25] Charles Hammond and Harvey M. Lawson, *The History of Union, Conn.* (New Haven, 1893), pp. 20–24. The opening verses picture a setting wherein an old Indian warrior tells the legend to young braves around the campfire, that they may repeat it to their children as his forefathers had given it to him.

brooks, drive away the deer and, before the next coming of the Moon of Leaves, send the white man among them. And so it happened; a hurricane lashed tremendous waves against the island of the White Swan until the sandy shores were washed from their rocky foundations. When the Moon of Leaves shone over the valley the rangers came and smote the Pequawkets, killed their chieftains and the flower of their warriors.[26] So too the prophet Pascagora had confided to the daughter of Manesquo of the coming of the white man; when she relayed the prophecy to the assembled braves, Manesquo hurled his hatchet in defiance. It struck a tree, glanced off, and buried itself in the breast of his daughter. In remorse he heeded her warning, and the warriors marched off to the setting sun. But he returned to be buried by her side.[27]

Extinction of the tribe occurred not only as an explicit act of retribution by Manitou, but also to fulfill a fatalistic prophecy or condition. No vengeance is stated in the Kennebunk legend of the Flying Island. Disease, fire, and water thinned away the tribe until only Samoset remained to ponder over the departed days of the red man's glory. At last he was observed to grow wilder, his eye brightened unnaturally and he talked in a flighty style about a voyage he was to make at sea. One morning visitors discovered him on the beach, gravely dressed in red feathers, beads, and shells and smoking his great pipe. He sat and stared at the Flying Island, on that day distinctly visible. (In tribal belief the Flying Island was the abode of the blessed, an Elysian spot to which the brave and heroic were transported after death to participate in unending joys; on a clear day in autumn, late in the afternoon, the figure of a bright green island could be seen in the east, its woods and mountains resting upon the blue waters of the distant horizon — perhaps an oceanic mirage of the kind sighted by sailors.) When Old Samoset perceived the apparition he sprang to his feet, uttered a solemn parting to the spectators, and with newfound strength hurling aside the dozen men who sought to dissuade him, set his birchen skiff in motion over the dancing surf. Even as

[26] John S. Barrows, "A Legend of Swan Island," *New England Magazine*, n.s., XIX (January 1899), 606–608.
[27] C. E. Potter, *The History of Manchester, N.H.* (Manchester, 1856), pp. 29–30.

he left a heavy thundercloud stretched over the valley, and a hurricane deluged the land. When the storm had passed, the whole valley was found to be strewed with ruins, and nothing more was ever seen of Samoset or the Flying Island.[28] In the legend of the Smoking Pine at Bombahook, the prophecy of tribal doom involves no supernatural ill will. Tired of war, Assonimo and his Wawenocs return to their old homes on the Kennebec to live in amity with the whites. Then the Great Prophet, a very old Indian, prophesied that as long as water flowed in the Bombahook, the Wawenocs would smoke the pipe of peace with the white men. Soon after an August cyclone annihilated the Indian camp. Years later a number of young pines covered the scars, and an old man excitedly discovered they were exactly the same in number as the lost Wawenocs, and furthermore that a spectral vapor ascended from one (a phenomenon still observable in Hallowell on certain days). "I believe those pines are the lost Wawenocs come to life again, and it will be a bad day for any man who lays axe to one of them." But as the pines grow older and the land is cleared around its head springs, the water grows less year by year in the streams, and the fulfillment of the prophecy comes nearer; when the last pine of the Wawenocs totters to its fall, then the last drop of water will ooze down the bed of the Bombahook.[29] A sad memory clings to the "Weeping Rocks" between Pownal, Vermont, and Williamstown, Massachusetts. For a persecuted Indian tribe seeking refuge from powerful enemies, confident in a tradition that said they should never be conquered until *the rocks wept*, read their fate in this mysterious formation. (An aqueous composition of lime and slate gravel causes water to drip continually.) When their pursuers fell upon them they offered no resistance and were wholly annihilated.[30]

Where Manitou did not extinguish the irreverent tribe, he dreadfully warned its members. To show his wrath and power, the Great Spirit turned rivers and monsters to stone. According to Indian chiefs and medicine men, Coos Canyon on the Swift River, the place of

[28] In *A Shillings Worth of Fun, or, Laughter For The Million* (New York, 1846).
[29] Edward P. Norton, *Legends and Otherwise of Hallowell and Loudoun Hill* (Augusta, Me., 1923), pp. 23–27.
[30] *Vermont Historical Gazetteer*, Abby M. Hemenway, ed. (Burlington, Vt., 1867), I, 213, quoting the *Williams Quarterly*.

"Petrified Waters," had so been formed. When in the long ago the tribe that made yearly trips up the river to spear trout suddenly began searching the river bed for gold nuggets that would bring rum, powder and ball, and calico, their action angered Manitou, who caused a terrible thunder storm to descend upon the valley. Out of the black clouds descended a huge ball of fire, which struck the troubled waters of the river and threw up a great geyser of steam. When the terrified Indians returned the next day, they found no water in the place where they had fished and sought gold; it had been turned to stone. Offerings and medicine during the winter months induced the Great Spirit to relent, so that on their pilgrimage up the river the following summer the tribe found an opening in the rock, now known as Coos Canyon, through which water flowed. But a large section of the stream-bed has remained solid rock to remind them of their folly, and needless to say they have since confined their activities to spearing fish.[31] Years ago the Penobscots, the St. Francises, and the Norridge-wocks inhabiting the Moosehead region fell to quarreling over their rights to the rich game lands. Bloody wars and cruel slaughters grieved the Great Spirit, who determined to send his children some great affliction as a sign that they must cease their warfare and obey his divine will. Accordingly he sent to earth a mighty monster, who tore up oak-trees with its claws, split stones with its teeth, blew storm-winds from its nostrils, and depopulated the woods of game. In remorse the redmen promised Manitou to live together in love and friendship if he would take the beast away; in answer to their prayer another, mightier creature appeared and gave chase to the first. In a fierce convulsive struggle both tumbled into the lake, and as the water touched them turned to stone. Kineo today stands a solemn warning to nations, old and new, to live and love as brothers.[32]

Spirits of the mountains, equally with Manitou, affected Indian destinies. Stories about Pamola, the malicious spirit of Mt. Katahdin,

[31] *Lewiston Journal*, Aug. 3, 1940 and Jan. 11, 1936. Told by an Indian, Johnny Tallash, to Stanley F. Bartlett.

[32] *Lewiston Journal*, Jan. 30, 1937. The legend was versified by Ellen A. Warren from a telling by Dr. E. A. Thompson of Dover, who had heard it while fishing and hunting at Moosehead from his guide Louie Annance, a St. Francis Indian. Mrs. W. A. Hinckley of Phillips sent in to the *Journal* an "age-yellowed copy" of the verses.

differ in incidents but agree on the central motive of abduction. A hunter wandering too near the forbidden mountain, faint with hunger, called in desperation on Pamola. A gigantic warrior pushed the branches aside and conducted the Indian in friendly manner to the summit at incredible speed. Through a large opening they descended to the interior, furnished like an immense wigwam; this was the lodge of Pamola, where he dwelt with his comely sister. In spite of his comfortable surroundings, the hunter chafed at his confinement, and obtained permission to return for a short visit to the lodges of his people. But once free he forgot his promise to the mountain spirit and prepared to wed a bright-eyed maiden of his people. During the wedding feast the bridegroom disappeared and never again was seen; Pamola had exacted his due. Another tale told by old Penobscots recalls the seizure of a beautiful girl, accompanying a small party of the tribe out hunting meat, by a splendidly bedecked warrior who suddenly appeared at her side while she gazed at the crests of Katahdin. Alarmed by her outcries the hunters endeavored to follow the trail of the abductor straight up the side of the mountain. But tons of boulders hurled by some supernatural power compelled them to retreat, and the party returned helplessly to camp, aware that Pamola had chosen their fairest flower for his bride.[33]

Not all Katahdin legends feature Pamola. In one tale the Mountain King conspired with his lovely but wilful daughter Lightning to keep the hero Kinaldo in their mountain hall. At a great feast in his honor, she gave him a potion that clouded the memory of his former life, and they lived together in happiness until the tears of Kinaldo's favorite sister, Winona, broke the spell; the hero left the mountain fastnesses to rejoin his tribe, ignoring the King's warning that he who had tasted the wine of Katahdin could no longer live among men. Next evening a storm gathered over the mountain and the Thunders, giant warriors who served the Mountain King, closed about Kinaldo. He saw his loved one among the Thunderheads; then a blinding streak of lightning reached out and seized the hero. When the storm cleared Katahdin was bathed in glittering light and the dead warrior lay as

[33] John C. Warren, "Pomola, the Spirit of Mt. Katahdin," *New England Magazine*, n.s., LII (April 1915), 276–277.

asleep at the foot of the mountain. A favorite story of Abenaki squaws tells of a girl who loved the mountain, and returned after an absence of three years bearing a beautiful baby boy with eyebrows of stone. As the boy grew in beauty and stature, his marvelous power of killing game by merely pointing his finger at bird, beast, or fish excited his tribesmen's curiosity; they plagued the mother and made insinuations about the father until, angered by their cruelty and ingratitude, she burst forth: "Fools, your folly kills you! You must have known from his eyebrows that this was Katahdin's son sent to save you." So saying she departed with her god child, and from that time the Abenakis were doomed, for the white man stole their hunting grounds and put them to flight.[34] The Katahdin legends are striking examples of congenial folktale passing directly from Indians to whites: this passage can be inferred by comparing modern fictions with aboriginal texts; and it can be directly viewed in Indian retellings of Pamola stories to white auditors.[35]

Mount Washington similarly is credited with a spirit being. An Indian living on the mountain possessed a daughter whose beauty brought many suitors to her feet. One day she disappeared, but was later observed at the pool below Glen Ellis Falls, in a tall man's embrace. Then her aged parents knew she had wed the god of the mountain; and by way of compensation for their loss, whenever they went to the pool and called for a deer, moose or bear, the animal would swim against their spear points.[36]

While the coming of the white man served as a prophetic retribution against Indian evil-doing, Indians in turn cursed the nefarious white man, and their curses were not without effect. Chocorua, a Pequawket brave, was forced to leap, or shot so that he fell, from the summit of the mountain that bears his name by a settler whose family he had murdered in mistaken reprisal for the supposed murder of his own son; his dying curse seemed fulfilled by the Great Spirit when disease struck the cattle

---

[34] *Maine: A Guide 'Down East'* (Boston, 1937), pp. 313–314.

[35] See Fannie H. Eckstorm, "The Katahdin Legends," *Appalachia*, XVIII (December 1924), 39–52, for pristine myths; but the orally transferred legends are much simpler and may merely cite the supernatural strength of Pamola (see the *Lewiston Journal*, Oct. 15, 1927; *Portland Telegram*, June 18, 1939; Chapter I, p. 8).

[36] Samuel A. Drake, *The Heart of the White Mountains* (New York, 1882), p. 128.

of the white man.[37] Likewise the curse of the chieftain Squando exacted annual toll from the white people who had brought death to his baby boy, from its utterance in 1676 until its formal expiration in 1928. Leader of the Sokokis who camped near Saco, Maine, Squando had preserved amity with the settlers, until in 1676 a boatload of English sailors ascending the Saco River threw his baby into the water, to test an old story rife in England that an Indian child could swim by instinct. The squaw recovered her child, but it died a few days later from exposure, and the heartbroken Squando no longer restrained his followers, long agitated by King Philip to drive out the white man. War began in sight of Cow Island near the Saco wharves where the child was thrown overboard, and the Indians burned nearly every house in Saco and Biddeford. In addition Squando laid a curse on the river, that it should take three lives each year; and thenceforth lumbermen, fishermen, and pleasure sailers paid the annual forfeit, and more. Between 1676 and 1878 over seven hundred persons drowned in the Saco; mothers forbade their boys to swim in the river until the third life had been claimed. But the historical committee appointed to observe Saco's tercentenary, June 28, 1931, decided that in view of the clear record for the previous three years, townsfolk need no longer fear the curse of Squando.[38]

Haunts. Where tainted death had occurred, perhaps of infamous persons, perhaps in an infamous way, signs remained long after of

[37] Some early references and versions of this widely printed legend are given in John Anderson and Stearns Morse, *The Book of the White Mountains* (New York, 1930), pp. 145–154; see also Frederick W. Kilbourne, "Chocorua: The Complete Mountain," *Appalachia*, n.s., VIII (December 1942), 162–164. Science decided that muriate of lime in their drinking water caused the disease to cattle in Burton (now Albany), N.H.; that such refutation was made testifies to the credence accorded the tradition.

[38] "Indian Curse on River at Saco Broken," *Portland News*, June 6, 1931. Other twentieth-century newspaper stories about Squando's Curse are in the *Portland Press Herald*, July 26, 1931; *Biddeford [Me.] Record*, Sept. 9, 1916. The immersion and subsequent death of Squando's papoose are credited by historians with causing the Saco Indian uprising in 1676; see e.g. Herbert M. Sylvester, *Indian Wars of New England* (Boston, 1910), II, 273n; George Folsom, *History of Saco and Biddeford* (Saco, 1830), pp. 153–154. Squando himself was regarded, like Passaconaway, as a powwow with magical powers accustomed to have converse with the Indian devil; see e.g. William Hubbard, *The History of the Indian Wars in New England* (Roxbury, Mass., 1865), p. 270; "Margaret Smith's Journal," *The Prose Works of John Greenleaf Whittier* (Boston and New York, c. 1892), I, 30–33.

troubled and uneasy spirits. Shades of the unhappy dead tormented and alarmed persons hardy enough to visit or venture near their death sites; phantasmal forms, strange lights and sounds, unnatural happenings, and telltale signs recalled the nefarious deed, often in periodic recurrences on its anniversary. Taverns, cottages, factories, farmhouses, ships, and plots on the open soil where such phenomena occurred became objects of somber superstitions. Ghosts that walked a traditional beat marched through the years in local legends.

Murdered travelers or strangers secured some slight if tardy satisfaction from the nuisance value of their ghosts. A popular region for killing travelers seems to have been the Berkshire Hills. About 1820, in a wayside tavern in Savoy, a strange traveler was seen to ride up and alight one evening — but he never was seen again, although his horse was found roaming at large the next day, with a frightful gash in his neck. Some thought that the tavern keeper had killed and robbed the stranger, then maimed his horse and turned it loose to make it appear that the man had encountered robbers on the highway. It was also said that bloodstains dyed the stairs leading to the chambers in the old tavern, which could never be erased; and that on dark and stormy nights the gory specter of the murdered man stared out the chamber window where he was killed. At any rate the tavern was soon abandoned and fell into ruin, but the locality continued to be prominent for fatal happenings. One of a gang of haymakers in an adjoining meadow was thrown from a haywagon when one of the team suddenly started up, landed on his head and snapped his neck. He was interred in a small burying lot nearby, and for many years afterward workmen cutting grass in the meadow insisted they could see his ghost standing at the head of his grave watching them work.[1]

Concealment and camouflage never could completely stifle the dark act of villainy. Many years past a pedlar arrived at the foot of Mount Tom, in Arcadia, Rhode Island, knocked at a lonely farmhouse, and

[1] *Berkshire Hills*, vol. II (May 1, 1902). Cf. *The Berkshire Hills*, Federal Writers Project (New York and London, 1939), pp. 255-256. "Just as almost every town on Cape Cod has a sea-serpent story, Berkshire abounds with tales of missing travelers. At every second town, some unfortunate wayfarer has disappeared, never to be seen again. Of all these legends, the most gruesome is the tale of the traveler who haunted the tavern in Savoy" (p. 255).

offered to sharpen knives for a night's lodging. When the farmer's daughter retired, she heard a commotion, and coming down found evidence in broken and damaged furniture of a struggle; the pedlar's pack and silver lay on the floor, while her father was patting the hearthstones back into place. Aware that she had divined his action, he burned out her tongue to ensure secrecy — a secrecy impossible of preservation. Long after weird noises issuing from the hearthstones led to the discovery of the pedlar's bones — since called the Moaning Bones of Mount Tom.[2] Haunted Valley in Wells, Maine, owes its name and notoriety to a comparable episode. On the old Post or Stage Road formerly stood a public tavern where suspicious and mysterious characters indulged in gambling and hilarity. One dark, stormy night a Jewish gambler and pedlar called for a night's lodging; Maxwell, the proprietor, who liked to gamble asked the Jew to play with him, and before the night was out the Jew owned the tavern. He was never seen to leave it. After his body was found in the woods, tongues wagged and stories flew of strange lights and noises seen and heard; folks ran rather than walked through the woods of the Valley. A Mr. Kimball and his young son who ventured into the woods heard an odd noise and descried a weird form, resembling a headless bear, which moaned and cried and ran after them — a mystery of the Haunted Valley still related, with kindred incidents, to the younger generation.[3] At the base of a high, rocky, and densely wooded ridge of land known as the "Ledges," not far from the ancient village of Saccarappa, Maine, runs an old, deserted road. Two brothers named Proctor once lived there and hired men every winter to haul considerable timber from the "Ledges." One winter they employed an Englishman named Kronk or Cronk, a stranger with no friends or acquaintances in that part of the country. When spring came, being discharged with the other men, he requested his wages that he might return to his native land. Several times he vainly asked for a settlement, and finally threatened to commence legal proceedings. After this threat the Proctors promised to

---

[2] *Rhode Island: A Guide to the Smallest State*, Federal Writers Project (Boston, 1937), pp. 109–110.

[3] Florence D. Myers, "Spooks Patrol Valley Where Man Met Death," *Sanford* [*Me.*] *Tribune*, Jan. 28, 1932.

pay Kronk in full upon the completion of one more day's work. He last was seen entering the woods with the brothers, who in response to queries stated that he had immediately left with his wages for Portland, intending to take passage for England. There being no proof to the contrary, this story was accepted without question for some time. At length, however, teamsters who frequented the road began to report horrible noises coming late at night from the direction of the Proctor lot. "I have heard an intelligent man say many times that he has heard strange noises which appeared to resemble the tones of a human voice calling for help and ending in a low melancholy gurgle, growing fainter and fainter until it was lost in silence and then was repeated after a short interval." Unpleasant rumors arose, but searching parties failed to locate any remains of the missing man whose supposed cries for vengeance continued to be heard for many years. When one of the Proctors, while driving an ox team, fell from the cart and dislocated his neck, the cries were heard less frequently. A few years later, when the other brother was instantly killed by a falling tree, they ceased entirely.[4]

Desperate characters lived beyond their normal span as tortured specters. Along Pirate's Creek, a century ago the rendezvous for smugglers who hid their contraband in the woods along the sequestered inlet of Johnson's Bay, in Maine, a spook patrolled ever since the night a white horse, half sea mammal, had come for Black Dick. The Dominie had often reproved Black Dick for his profane outbursts, and warned him that the Devil would surely get him as he had Tom Walker (see Chapter II, *The Devil*). On a wild November night a knock on his door aroused Black Dick: "You're wanted, Dick," a voice said. Thinking the message came from his accomplices, Dick dressed and followed the voice to the edge of the creek. A long arm or claw reached out of the waves and dragged him onto the back of a fearsome sea monster. Later residents said that on the anniversary of his disappearance hollow sounds and peculiar noises came from under the rotting piers of the old bridge. A new steel culvert and two earthwork fills were expected

[4] "Lonely Wood Road At Base of Westbrook 'Ledges' Once Haunted, Declares Legend," *Portland Telegram*, Jan. 13, 1935. The writer (not named) states: "The following legend was commonly believed in my boyhood, and there are several people now living who give credence to it implicitly."

to smother the noises permanently.[5] A painful penance prolonged the activities of two deceased New England pirates in similar legends. People in York, Maine, learned with relief of the death of "Trickey," a suspected pirate who lived alone down by Brave Boat harbor and was held in awe because he possessed an "evil eye" and had surreptitious dealings with the Devil. Since the possessor of an evil eye held power to return and haunt the living, the pastor of York bound Trickey for a thousand years; for three hundred of these he has been busy making rope of sand; when a storm is brewing and the sea moans low, folks look out over the oily swells and say that Trickey is crying, "More rope, more rope."[6] On the bar of Ipswich, Massachusetts, where he had sent many a ship ashore, Harry Main, wrecker, smuggler, pirate, and blasphemer, twined ropes of sand, or some said shoveled the sand back into the sea. Whenever his rope broke, his roar of rage could be heard for miles. When the tide and a gale are rising together people who hear the moaning from the bar say, "Old Harry's grumbling again."[7] No one knows the previous history of the Headless Pirate, who has often been seen flying up and down the road below the Nubble on Bailey Island, always around Christmas time and always astraddle a milk-white horse.[8] On the other hand, the background of the "Harbor Boys" whom inhabitants of Block Island hear crying for help on stormy nights is common knowledge. For they are a ghostly crew of "Refugees," desperadoes who had deserted from both armies during the Revolution and devoted themselves to plunder. Sometimes a band of these marauders would pass over from the mainland to the island in a light rowboat — known as a "Shaving Mill" because it tossed like a shaving upon the waves — that eluded the swiftest sails. On one night when a galley of these roughs descended on the armed and expectant Islanders, the seas rolled high as the wind increased, and the darkness thickened, until finally the Shaving Mill was lost to sight. Above the angry tones of the sea rang out a thundering command, "Row! boys, row for your lives!" But as the Refugees approached the shore, the Shaving Mill went to pieces,

[5] "Laying Ghost of Pirate's Creek," *Bangor Daily News*, July 13, 1937.
[6] "Old York; the Forgotten City of Maine," *Portland Telegram*, July 29, 1923.
[7] Charles M. Skinner, *Myths and Legends of Our Own Land* (Philadelphia and London, c. 1896), II, 13.
[8] Alfred Elden, "Ghosts of Bailey Island," *Lewiston Journal*, Oct. 25, 1941.

and only the drowning cry, "Help! Help!" pierced the night. Over many years the same words have echoed in the ears of the Islanders.[9]

Not only pirates but their victims returned to plague the living. On White Island off the New Hampshire coast a wraith sits on a huge rock and gazes silently out to sea. For this is the shade of Ann Brock fulfilling her promise to the pirate Blackbeard to stand guard over his treasure till Doomsday. When the half-breed Spaniard left the island in his pirate ship to overtake a sail running northeast from Cape Ann, he mockingly exacted that pledge from the eighteen-year-old captive who had learned to love him. But the innocent sail turned out to be a British man-of-war; a direct hit on the pirate magazine blew up both craft and Blackbeard went down with his ship. But Ann Brock remains faithful to her vow.[10] From a richly laden Spanish ship captured by English pirates off Marblehead, a beautiful English lady was seized and cruelly murdered near the rocks at Oakum Bay. Taking her a little way off shore, the pirates flung her into the sea, and as she clung to the gunwale they hacked at her hands with cutlasses. Startled fishermen heard her cry, "Lord, save me! Mercy! O, Lord Jesus, save me!" Next day they interred her mangled remains; and on every anniversary of the date for 150 years her screams and cries affrighted the citizens of Marblehead.[11]

Tortured and revengeful shades clung to buildings within whose walls or under whose foundations fiendish deeds had taken place. All the inhabitants of Great Chebeague Island in Casco Bay, Maine, believed the Peabody Ghost House at Deer Point haunted from the day it was built. About a hundred years ago, some time before its construction, two fishermen had resolved to settle a dispute over an island belle by rowing to lonely Deer Point and fighting it out. Only one came back, in terrible condition, his eyes blackened, his nose broken, one ear nearly torn off. "But you ought to see Doughty," he was reported as saying. That was the trouble; nobody ever did see Doughty again. Fishermen passing Deer Point at night saw strange dancing lights, and heard

[9] S. T. Livermore, *Block Island* (Hartford, Conn., 1886), pp. 61–63.

[10] Earl Newton, *Granite Monthly*, LVIII (March 1925), 100–102; Henry J. Finn and others, *Whimwhams* (Boston, 1828), pp. 135–150.

[11] Samuel Roads, *The History and Traditions of Marblehead* (Marblehead, 1897), pp. 37–38.

terrifying cries of hate and anguish. These stories persisted for half a century, at which time Mrs. Mary Peabody of New York decided to build a handsome summer cottage on thickly wooded Deer Point. Native workmen would not work a moment after the shadows began lengthening in the afternoon, and soon after the house was completed troubles ensued as they had predicted. A cousin visiting the Peabodys heard a baby wailing, its mother soothing, then the sound of heavy feet and the frantic screams of a woman fighting for her life. But when after a period of deathly silence he crept down stairs to find the bloody corpse, everything was as he had left it. The cousin suffered a nervous reaction from which he never fully recovered. Another time a woman guest saw a snow-white figure, clad in a diaphanous mantle, come straight down through the roof and fade away into nothingness before her eyes. Other persons sighted a woman holding a baby in her arms who dodged here and there about the cottage always just out of reach. John Calder, a fisherman-farmer at Great Chebeague, made just one trip on foot through the eerie woods to Deer Point. As he gazed out to size up fishing conditions for the morrow — Crash! Down came the brick chimney on the Peabody cottage in a cloud of dust. Calder walked back to ascertain the damage, and the chimney was in its usual place.[12] Similar legends cling to Pickering Island, Maine, where one Dr. Davis of New York City who had bought the isle erected buildings and brought patients to it every summer — always women. He seemed averse to meeting people, came and went alone in his boat, discouraged visitors, and kept two savage dogs on the premises. After about ten years rumors circulated that cries of terror and imploring shrieks for help were heard by passing fishermen. Finally it dawned on the community that no one was ever seen to return with the doctor or to leave the island. When a clear outcry of "Murder, Save me, Help me before he comes back and murders me" was reported by passing boats, the sheriff descended on the island to investigate. He found the house a veritable prison, windows and doors barred and with narrow slits for observation of the victims, in an outhouse an oven with quicklime and an underground passageway leading to the sea. The Doctor was arrested

[12] Alfred Elden, "The Ghost House of Chebeague," *Lewiston Journal*, Feb. 13, 1937.

and sentenced, but hearsay asserts that groans and cries still issue from the house.[13]

Witchery and unnatural accidents plagued the inmates of haunted houses from the seventeenth century to the twentieth. Increase Mather collected cases dating from the 1670's and 80's of dwellings mysteriously hexed; large stones crashed through their windows, kitchen utensils misbehaved, furniture, ashes, cow dung flew about striking people and spoiling the food. Nicholas Desborough of Hartford, Connecticut, "was strangely molested by stones, pieces of earth, cobs of Indian corn, &c., falling upon and about him, which sometimes came in through the door, sometimes through the window, sometimes down the chimney."[14] Two daemon-possessed houses became famous in folk history, the William Morse house in Newbury, Massachusetts,[15] and the George Walton house in New Castle, New Hampshire,[16] scenes of extensive antic performances and ludicrous tricks. Post-Mather times continued the tradition of the *hausgeist*. In Dighton, Massachusetts, weird stories clustered about the Colonel Richmond house. An Irishman named Sleepy Bill heard a long procession of carriages rumble past it one night; another time he heard a terrific crash in the front hall, as if the staircase had fallen down. A boarder once saw several people dressed in old-fashioned costume dancing a "break-down" in the front dooryard.[17] In Portsmouth, New Hampshire, a certain residence became known as a rendezvous for witches and wizards, who would sally forth from the house, throw a horse's bridle over a passer-by, thus transforming him into a horse, and ride the animal until daylight; in the morning the horse became a man again, but bore the prints of horse nails on his hands and feet and marks of bridle bits on the sides of his mouth. In

---

[13] Anne E. Perkins, "Pickering Island, Now Haunt of Naturalists, Has Gruesome Tale," *Lewiston Journal*, Oct. 17, 1936. Also Alice F. Lord, *Bangor News*, Jan. 14, 1939.

[14] Increase Mather, *Remarkable Providences Illustrative of the Earlier Days of American Colonisation* (London, 1890), p. 113.

[15] Mather, *Remarkable Providences*, pp. 101–110; E. Vale Smith, *History of Newburyport* (Newburyport, 1854), pp. 28–33.

[16] Mather, *Remarkable Providences*, pp. 114–116; Richard Chamberlain, *Lithobolia; or, the Stone-Throwing Devil* (London, 1698); John Albee, *New Castle Historic and Picturesque* (Boston, 1884), pp. 43–47; Mary R. P. Hatch, "The Stone-Throwing Devil of New Castle," *New England Magazine*, n.s., XXXII (March 1905), 57–65.

[17] *History of Bristol County, Mass.*, D. Hamilton Hurd, compiler (Philadelphia, 1883), pp. 223–224.

the nighttime strange noises isued from this house, as of many voices intermingling, and lights would be seen passing quickly from chamber to chamber.[18] Tenants left a house in Corinth, Vermont, declaring it was haunted; spinning wheels were heard in the attic, lights flashed in the front windows, and moaning as of a dying person was heard in the front hall. It was whispered that an expert carpenter who had built the entire set of farm buildings did not get his pay and suddenly disappeared. An eight-year-old boy, son of the owner, stayed in the house one Halloween and traced his scares to a loose clapboard which vibrated to resemble the whir of a spinning wheel and a large age-weakened lilac bush that scraped against the garden fence and seemed to say "O dear." Nevertheless for many nights in his dreams the boy saw himself back in the house, where ghosts with pumpkin-lantern features rattled dead white bones, danced on stilts in the front hall, and called out, "Yes, you found the groan, come and dance with us."[19] Above Sanford, Maine, another house of ill omen has bred its stories of chilling occurrences ever since the time a cattleman, laden with the money for his disposed cattle, asked the farmer for a night's lodging and never reappeared. Subsequent inmates told of falling china that did not break, of bedclothes pulled off in the dark by a gliding hand and then returned, of candles blown out by a mysterious breath of air, like a sigh from an unhappy woman, only to be lighted again as a faint gruff voice echoed in a nearby hallway.[20] An old, overgrown two-storied dwelling house that before its demolition in 1829 adjoined the courthouse in York, Maine, was said to have been haunted by an evil spirit incarcerated in one of the apartments. "After a certain period of years, this spirit was ...to be 'laid,' and permitted to depart, when it would proceed to walk thrice around this burying-yard, and evoke the denizen of this grave to join it. After this, both were condemned to form a penance by travelling a thousand years on the face of this mundane sphere." But when the spirit became unduly troublesome to the inmates, they performed

---

[18] Charles W. Brewster, *Rambles About Portsmouth, Second Series* (Portsmouth, N.H., 1869), pp. 212–213.

[19] "CORINTH HAD GHOST HOUSE 62 YEARS AGO. People Feared to Live in the Stately Old Structure. 8-Year-Old Boy Solved Mystery. But He Went Through Terrifying Experiences in Meantime." *Barre [Vt.] Daily Times*, Nov. 8, 1935.

[20] *Sanford [Me.] Tribune*, Jan. 28, 1932.

the "allaying" ceremony and released him before his allotted time.[21] In the wake of the *Palatine* shipwreck sprang a sequel legend, the haunted house of Simon Ray on Block Island where several of the dying passengers received hospitality. Unnatural sights and sounds abounded in the enchanted home, but the chief marvel was a Dancing Mortar, fashioned by the islanders from blocks of lignum vitae the *Palatine* had left them for making mortars to crush their corn. Inheriting the curse of the ill-fated ship, it acted queerly; untouched by human hand, it threw itself from a standing position to its side, then rolled from one side of the room to the other. Men, women and children dodged from the rolling mortar lest they too should be infected with its witchery. After the rolling the mortar righted itself and began to dance; it bounded from the floor to the joists and floor overhead, up and down, up and down, in various parts of the room. Only one explanation of the phenomenon ever was advanced, that the late owner of the house had been an opium eater. Yet several aged and trustworthy Islanders, consulted separately (1876), testified to the authenticity of the legend.[22]

Factories and mills were not impervious to haunts. In the Rhode Island Census for 1885, the Ramtail Factory Haunt receives official confirmation. Ramtail was a cotton cloth factory located near Foster, owned by the Potter brothers and Peleg Walker, the night watchman. After a falling out over money matters, Walker was discovered one morning hung from the pull rope. Thereafter the bell would ring out at midnight, even when the pull rope had been removed. Taking the bell away only incited the spook to new mischief; he drove the mill wheel backwards; once the empty factory ran at top speed. On one occasion a curious nocturnal visitor descried a white figure swinging a lantern who resembled Peleg Walker.[23] In Hollis, Maine, the vengeful ghost of a dispossessed owner checked all attempts to run a sawmill. One John Livingston, strange to the town, jumped at the chance to make a surprisingly cheap investment in the abandoned mill. But no one would work in the mill at night, so he was obliged to tend it him-

[21] George A. Emery, *Ancient City of Gorgeana and Modern Town of York* (Boston, 1874), pp. 176–178 (quotation from p. 177).

[22] Livermore, *Block Island*, pp. 89–92.

[23] J. Earl Clauson, *These Plantations* (Providence, c. 1937), pp. 95–98.

165

self into the small hours of the morning. Then peculiar derangements began to upset the machinery. With the floodgates hoisted and a full head of water the water wheel would scarcely move. Though the wheel was well oiled and free from obstructions, it would not turn fast enough to run the saw. Again, without any cause the wheel would fly round at lightning speed. The dogs which fastened the big logs to the carriage that fed the saw would become detached; the levers which controlled the water gate would fly back; the lanterns would go out. One night a peculiar noise came from the machinery, and the saw almost stopped. Livingston went to the wheel pit to ascertain the cause of the trouble, but seeing nothing returned to find a man tampering with the machinery. Quickly seizing a cant dog he advanced on the intruder with the order: "Get out of here!" When the figure remained motionless, Livingston swung the cant dog with all his might on the head of the saboteur. It passed through the form and against the lever controlling the flow of water with such force as to close the gate and stop the water. At the same time the saw became detached from its fastening and fell on the log with a crash. Groggy by now, Livingston demanded of the figure his name and the reason for his visit. It turned its face to him, and he recognized a former owner of the mill who, according to tradition, had been wronged out of his property shortly before he died.[24] An old mill in Somerville, Massachusetts, likewise houses a ghostly tenant, although in this instance he is doing penance rather than seeking revenge. A captive Acadian maiden, disguised as a youth, fled from her cruel master and sought refuge with the old miller. He gave her his only vacant room, the dismal, dusty mill loft. Her master, having traced her hiding place, induced the miller with smooth speech and specious story to unlock the mill. Clumsily he clambered up the ladder, reached the loft, and tried to seize his victim; in the darkness he lost his foothold, plunged to the mill floor, and clutched at a rope to break his fall. It was the mill rope; the great fans moved, the millstone rolled hoarsely around, and soon all was over.[25]

[24] "Hollis Had Only Haunted Sawmill," *Bangor Journal*, April 10, 1931, and Jan. 9, 1937.

[25] *Somerville Past and Present*, Edward A. Samuels and Henry H. Kimball, ed. (Boston, 1897), p. 42. In Charles M. Skinner, "The Old Mill at Somerville," *Myths and Legends of Our Own Land* (Philadelphia and London, c. 1896), I, 249–251, the mill

One kind of spectral memorial took the form of the ghost ship. From Freeport, Maine, the proud *Dash* set sail in 1812 and vanished with her complement of sixty men. In time the legend evolved that when a dear one of any of the sixty came to die a phantom ship sailed in from the sea and bore the departing one into the beyond. When all the relatives and friends and lovers of the doomed crew have thus been borne away, the Dead Ship will glide no more into the Bay.[26] John Winthrop noted in 1647 an apparition of a vessel that perplexed New Haven colony.

> There appeared over the harbor at New Haven, in the evening, the form of the keel of a ship with three masts, to which were suddenly added all the tackling and sails, and presently after, upon the top of the poop, a man standing with one hand akimbo under his left side, and in his right hand a sword stretched out toward the sea. Then from the side of the ship which was from the town arose a great smoke, which covered all the ship, and in that smoke she vanished away; but some saw her keel sink into the water. This was seen by many, men and women, and it continued about a quarter of an hour.[27]

Like a good historian, Cotton Mather secured corroborating and embellishing details which gave the marvel a rational explanation. According to the judicious, this was undoubtedly a spectral reconstruction of a Rhode Island ship that had sailed from New Haven in January, 1647, a ship so walty that its captain said it would prove their grave. News of the ship had not reached the good people of New Haven by the ensuing June, so that they prayed the Lord to let them know what He had done with their friends. This replica in the air which formed after a great thunderstorm in the northwest, sailed against the wind for half an hour, and then dissipated gradually from her maintop to her hulk was the Lord's answer — so said the Reverend Mr. Davenport.[28]

Where these specter ships connoted natural tragedies of the sea, the annual reappearance of the flaming *Palatine* signified a heinous man-made disaster. Sailing from Holland in 1719 or 1720 for Philadelphia

serves as a trysting place for lovers; unwilling that his daughter should marry beneath her, the wealthy farmer entered the mill during their tryst, and in the pursuit has his arm ground between the millstones; his profane ghost still explodes curses in the mill.

[26] Florence G. Thurston and Harmon S. Cross, *Three Centuries of Freeport, Me.* (Freeport, 1940), pp. 63–64.

[27] *Winthrop's Journal "History of New England," 1630–1649*, James K. Hosmer, ed. (New York, 1908), II, 346.

[28] Cotton Mather, *Magnalia Christi Americana* (Hartford, 1855), I, 84.

with a passenger list of thrifty Dutch merchants, the *Palatine* was delayed by icy seas and a whipping gale. When the captain died — some say he was murdered — the brutal crew seized control of the ship, imprisoned the passangers, extracted from them extortionate sums for food and water, and finally took to the boats, leaving the unguided ship and its wretched people to their fate. They never reached a harbor. Drifting aimlessly, the ship struck on Block Island, where wreckers stripped her of everything valuable and set her on fire; as she drifted out to sea the screams of a maniac woman left on board shrilled across the waves. Every twelfth month later, until 1832, the ship loomed off the island, flames lapping at her rigging and smoke billowing from her sails, and burned to the water's edge, while maniacal screams issued from the vessel.[29] Still other, less celebrated traditions center on death ships. Each Midsummer Eve a Phantom Fleet rises in the waters of Cape Cod, vessels lost and wrecked that sail again this one night in the year; so too sunken Gloucester fleets rise on the Night of the White Review.[30] Ghost ships merge with treasure legends. Spectral vessels commanded by Kidd periodically sail to Clarke's Island, in the Connecticut River, and up the Kennebec to Hallowell, Maine, to revisit caches.[31] A phantom privateer, manned by grinning pirates, sailed straight into Plum Island off the Massachusetts coast and melted by a certain rock; an onlooker concluded that treasure was hidden there but found only clamshells.[32]

In certain sharply delimited areas, unwholesome zones scrupulously avoided by their communities, witches, headless specters, bogies and such invisible beings brewed in a devilish cauldron. So late as the Revolution, inhabitants of East Hartford, Connecticut, believed that

[29] William P. Sheffield, *A Historical Sketch of Block Island* (Newport, 1876), pp. 38–46; Samuel T. Livermore, *A History of Block Island* (Hartford, 1886), pp. 92–118; Edward E. Pettee, *Block Island, R.I.* (Boston, 1884), pp. 96–106. These accounts draw upon an article by Dr. Aaron C. Willey in the *Parthenon* in 1811 that scientifically describes the peculiar illumination linked to the legend. Livermore, after a thorough analysis of the legend, concludes "*that* it consists of two parts — *Facts*, and *Fiction*" (p. 104).

[30] Elizabeth Reynard, *The Narrow Land* (Boston and New York, 1934), pp. 310–314; see Chapter VI, *Holman Day*.

[31] Clifton Johnson, *New England: A Human Interest Geographical Reader* (New York, 1917), p. 129; *Lewiston Journal*, Jan. 6, 1938.

[32] Charles M. Skinner, *American Myths and Legends* (Philadelphia and London, c. 1903), II, 285–287.

a gigantic specter haunted the Hockanum Causeway, an apparition higher than the tree tops who cleaved the midnight air with a vast shadowy sword. Headless horsemen were seen wandering aimlessly in the nearby swamp.[33] "Dogtown" in Rockport, Massachusetts, did not decline until after the Revolution; by 1830 it was a deserted village, the abode only of witches who lived together in groups and made their living from curse tolls and fortune telling. Peg Wesson and Tam Younger were the most famous of many witches and odd characters; "for the number and weirdness of its sayings, traditions, witches and ghosts, nothing in all New England can equal Dogtown."[34] In North Kingstown, Rhode Island, gruesome stories cling to "Swamptown," location of Indian Corner, where an Indian skull found by a road-mender leered on a leech barrel until called for by its owner; to Hell Hollow, where spooks held moonlight dances, and Goose Nest Spring, a resort for witch carnivals; to the Kettle Holes, into one of which a cow fell and was not seen till two days later off Beaver Tail, making her way to shore. A horrified spectator passing through the dreaded locality once beheld a headless negro boy revealed in a column of phosphorescent light; the traveler dug a hole the next day to mark the spot, and strange to say, it never fills with leaves.[35] "Northeast," in Greenfield, Massachusetts, knew of many witcheries. Ezekiel Bascom who owned a gristmill there asserted that one night a horseshoe came into his room and performed various evolutions; the mill wheels sometimes stopped and could not be induced to go. Mr. Bascom's cattle and cart stopped in the road and would not move until a fox came out from under the cart. "In fine, Northeast was a sort of enchanted ground, the residence of witches and hobgoblins, and furnished many stories for the credulous."[36] A particularly ill-spoken ground belongs to Medway, Massachusetts, known as Dinglehole. By a tall pine tree, whose topmost branches are twisted together into a fantastic crown, Satan and his witches were wont to meet. This scary place, a large pit with dank, stag-

[33] Joseph O. Goodwin, *East Hartford: Its History and Traditions* (Hartford, 1879), p. 240.
[34] George W. Solley, *Alluring Rockport* (n.p., n.d.), p. 103.
[35] George W. Gardiner, "Swamptown — A Queer Locality," *Facts and Fancies Concerning North Kingstown, R.I.* (North Kingstown, 1941), pp. 66–72.
[36] Francis M. Thompson, *History of Greenfield, Mass.* (Greenfield, 1904), II, 982–983.

nant water at the bottom, owes its name to the dingling or tinkling of a bell heard there on misty summer evenings, rung, it was believed, by hobgoblins. Strange globes of fire played about Dinglehole; and the benighted traveler would be petrified to meet a headless man who would lead him along the circular road about the glen without advancing him a step on his journey. Anciently the townsfolk muttered prayers on approaching Dinglehole in the night, for on certain words the bell would cease to tinkle, the lights vanish, and the headless specter disappear in the deepest recesses of the woods, there to await a more ignorant and less pious traveler.[37]

In distinction to the miscellaneously haunted plague spots, specific places had special personal haunts. On a limestone ledge on the Felt farm in Holyoke, Massachusetts, appeared a specter who declared that Tim Felt's bones could be found underneath where his father had buried them; people remembered the irascible temper of the father who beat and shot his neighbor's cattle, and the mysterious disappearance of the son.[38] Search never did locate his bones, but the discovery of bones under a barn in Troy, New Hampshire, gave rise to many ugly suspicions, confirmed with reports that "marvellous phenomenas" had been seen in and about the barn.[39] About the upper reaches of Mount Moosilauke scurries a form, well known to Summit House crews, that uncannily resembles a recluse doctor who formerly dwelt there and devoted his researches to alchemy.[40] Only strangers go near the Haunted Pool of Bailey's Hill, ever since Goodman Huntington wrestled there with a pack of werewolves who fled when he uttered the name of Jesus; next morning Goody Martin's back was covered with strange bruises, and the sheriff bore her from Amesbury.[41] Associated with the Crying Bog in the Narragansett country is a mournful haunt legend. For here at nights

[37] *The History of Medway, Mass.*, E. O. Jameson, ed. (Millis, Mass., c. 1886), pp. 13–14.

[38] Clifton Johnson, "Tim Felt's Ghost," *What They Say in New England* (Boston, 1896), pp. 249–252.

[39] M. T. Stone, *Historical Sketch of the Town of Troy, N.H.* (Keene, N.H., n.d.), pp. 235–238.

[40] Landon G. Rockwell, "Concerning the Strange 'Doctor' of Moosilauke," *Appalachia*, n.s., VII (June 1941), 338–343.

[41] H. G. Leslie, "The Haunted Pool of Bailey's Hill," *Granite Monthly*, XXXIII (September 1902), 195–198.

issued a doleful weeping and wailing, from the conscience-stricken
ghost of Manouna, an Indian squaw of the Narragansett tribe, who had
murdered her two children and buried their bodies in the bog. At times
the wretched specter could be seen sitting under some willow trees
about twenty rods from the Crying Bog, rocking and moaning; when
a stranger once accosted her there, she ignored his words until he rolled
a stone against her feet, on which she vanished from sight, uttering
such unearthly shrieks that he could not force his horse to pass the spot.
After her nights of woeful lament, the ghost murderess would depart
toward a wooded islet in Kit's Pond, screaming as she coursed close to
the surface of the water until she reached the island, when all again was
still.[42]

In lieu of the shades of murdered men that return to haunt their
slayers, symbolic red stains might linger or reappear annually on dese-
crated spots, an ineradicable blood smirch that colored the ground or
dyed vegetation that rooted in the soil. Good reason there is for the red
spot in the center of the apple known as the Micah Rood, or the Mike,
from its originator. In 1679 Micah Rood removed to West Farms, Connecticut, and located in Peck Hollow. Upon his farm he had an apple
tree which bore large, fair fruit — since a great favorite in the vicinity —
but always with a red globule, like a clot of blood, near the center of
each apple; and the "story of its origin handed down from father to
son for over a hundred years, has at length grown to be a fixed tradition,
implicitly received." Once a pedlar had entered the town, vending costly
and luxurious ware; dazzled by the display, Micah had invited the
pedlar to his house, and in an evil moment plunged a knife into his
heart as they stood beneath the apple tree, so that his lifeblood flowed
down and mingled with the roots. But lo! the next spring its blossoms
changed from white to red, and in August when the apples, large and
yellow and juicy, came tumbling down, each had within a drop of
blood. Horror stricken, the simple-hearted Micah grew into a morose

[42] Thomas R. Hazard, *Recollections of Olden Times* (Newport, R.I., 1879), pp.
123–124. "Many other stories analagous to these used to be told in connection with 'the
ghost of the Crying Bog,' in my younger days" (p. 124). An Indian ghost haunt of the
White Mountains, appearing annually on a certain crag, arrayed in black bearskin war
robe and carrying a bloody stone tomahawk and broken hornbeam bow, is mentioned
in John H. Spaulding, *Historical Relics of the White Mountains* (Boston, 1855), p. 31.

and melancholy man, unable to escape the memory of his crime; he neglected his business, and sank from a prosperous farmer to a town pauper, whose keep and burial in 1728 is noted in the community records. "In face of the facts, who shall pronounce the story of Micah Rood a fiction, or think it too strange that Nature should thus record her horror of human crime?"[43]

Among the tales told by Uncle Marky in his store on Matinicus Isle (see Chapter I), that of the Bloody Beach centered on a recurrent death stain. This account had come down to Uncle Marky from his great-grandfather, one of the original settlers on the island. In February of 1770 the British corvette *Alden*, which had been terrorizing the Maine coast, one wild night lost her bearings and struck a rocky ledge west of Green Island inside Monhegan. With killing labor the boats were lowered into the boiling sea, and the frozen and blinded crew started driving before the wind. Till dawn they pulled; all perished save one boat of twenty-five which sighted the foaming shores of Matinicus. Before it reached shore and beached in the cove at the easterly end of the island, life left all but two, a man and a boy whom the islanders carried to their houses. The boy died within the hour, and the man's legs were frozen so that they snapped off at the knees when touched, but he lived and was taken to the mainland by a passing Nova Scotian. The corpses of the twenty-four frozen seamen were buried just above the beach on which they struck. When the ground thawed the following spring, Abraham Young noticed a red discoloration on the sand, and since then, every spring when the sun warms the sand, the red blood of the frozen men oozes through the drifts and smirches the white beach a dark crimson. "Blood that is spilled on the ground," said Uncle Marky with great earnestness, shaking his gray head portentously, "always leaves its stain, and it never comes out never!"[44]

Similar traditions testify to plaguing memories of villainous acts. A Bristol, Rhode Island, slaver sometimes put down his morning cup of coffee because he seemed to see blood on the surface of it — blood that

[43] *History of Franklin, Conn.* (New Haven, 1869), pp. 60–61; note D to "Historical Address" by Ashbel Woodward. For a different, longer, literary version see *Harper's Magazine*, XXI (August 1860), 477–479.

[44] Joseph W. Porter, "The Wayfarer Papers," bk. III, p. 38 (in the Maine Historical Society, Portland).

brought stark into his mind the picture of a smallpox-stricken slave tossed from a boat and attempting to clamber back over the gunwale, prevented by hands that severed his hands with an axe.[45] On Chebeague Island, Maine, near the oldest house on the island, grows a queer white moss which turns blood-red one day a year. Botanists have been unable to name it. Is it pure coincidence that an Indian massacre once took place near the spot?[46] For killing a deerskin pedlar, Captain William Carter was hanged in gibbets at Rochester, Rhode Island, and his body left dangling until it dropped piecemeal from the irons to the ground beneath; for years after the soil and verdure were rank and dark with blood.[47] In Mast Swamp in eastern Connecticut, which in the spring blazes with rhododendrons marked by strong crimson centers, a band of Pequots took refuge from the English in 1637. There they held out until starvation forced them to capitulate; the chief, Putaquaponk, was shot to death beneath a gorgeous rhododendron. Before dying he cursed the fatal swamp that had forced his people to surrender, and he cursed the English for their craving for human blood. Since his curse the golden hearts of the rhododendrons show blood-red hearts on the anniversary of the massacre as a reproach to the white people. If the flowers are transplanted from the swamp they show yellow centers again.[48]

Buried treasure. Just why a certain class of popular fictions propagate with undiminished vigor through the years may be explained by a recent United Press dispatch.

COLEBROOK, N.H., Aug. 15 (U.P.) — Discovery of a century-old treasure trove buried at Pilgrim's Beach at Plymouth, Mass., was revealed today by Ben Lay.

Mr. Lay said that he and his son, Fred, were skipping stones at the beach a few weeks ago when the son picked up an old silver dollar. They soon found several more coins and then noticed the corner of an old box protruding from the sand.

[45] M. A. DeWolfe Howe, *Bristol, Rhode Island: A Town Biography* (Cambridge: Harvard University Press, 1930), p. 66.
[46] *Lewiston Journal*, Jan. 7, 1939.
[47] Thomas R. Hazard, *The Jonny-Cake Letters* (Providence, 1882), pp. 188–189.
[48] Charles M. Skinner, *American Myths and Legends* (Philadelphia and London, c. 1903), I, 129–131, "Bloody-Heart Rhododendrons."

Without attracting the attention of hundreds of bathers in the vicinity, they covered the spot with sand and went away. They returned and salvaged all the coins that the box contained.

An inventory included 400 silver half-dollars, 38 silver dollars, $50 in gold coins and forty-six foreign pieces. The oldest gold coin was dated 1834 and the oldest silver piece, 1795.

The treasure in the box was wrapped in an old Boston newspaper and was believed to have been buried at about the time of the Mexican War, 1846-47. Mr. Lay is said to have been offered $2,000 for the collection.[1]

In the hope of just such a find or strike, searchers for buried wealth have followed leads, tips, hunches, and dreams that produce little more than a never-ceasing crop of underground rumors, and some unshakable place legends. The ubiquitous Captain Kidd is responsible for a host of such rumors; all six of the New England states received visits and conceal deposits made by Kidd. "Shepherd Tom" Hazard, the gossipy annalist of Rhode Island lore, recalled that every well-informed man in South Kingstown knew the old Thomas B. Hazard house to have been a great resort for American and West Indian pirates "among whom was the famous Captain Kidd, who, as is well known, was in the practice of burying his treasures along the American coast in holes dug in the ground, with which he always buried one of his men (generally a nigger, because they are the most honest,) to keep guard over it."[2] Such a guardian ghost posed a problem to eager diggers for Kidd's gold, for if he provoked outcries from the startled searchers, they forfeited their chance by breaking the spell of silence imposed by the sporting pirate captain. In Weare, New Hampshire, feverish excavations took place on Jesse Hadley's farm, and Dr. Grant just missed the jackpot when something in the earth broke his iron bar and he exclaimed, "Good God! the spell is broken." Men who saw the clean break in the bright iron said the ghost of Kidd had bit it in two.[3] On Jewell's Island, Maine, an herb doctor dug by the full of the moon, when a sow and her litter of pigs emerged from the hole. Biting the doctor in the leg, the ferocious sow forced out a "Damn," whereupon the pigs vanished, the hole filled up, and the treasure trovers found them-

---

[1] *New York Times*, Sunday, Aug. 16, 1942.

[2] Thomas R. Hazard, *The Jonny-Cake Letters* (Providence, 1882), p. 272.

[3] William Little, *The History of Weare, N.H.* (Lowell, Mass., 1888), p. 652.

selves sitting on the ledge at the mouth of the Punch Bowl with the incoming tide lapping their feet.[4] Clarke's Island in the Connecticut River hides a Kidd chest of gold — although how Kidd and his men ascended three falls with so ponderous a load is puzzling. One Abner Field, learning the site from a conjurer, resolved to tempt the ghost of the pirate sacrificed by his fellows to guard the cache. He and two confederates formed a triangle at midnight under a full moon about the designated spot, and all began to work silently and energetically, for the task must be completed before the cock crew. One mighty stroke of the crowbar clinked against an iron lid: *"You've hit it,"* exclaimed one involuntarily, and withal the chest settled beyond reach, while the disturbed ghost flitted about. Then Satan himself, full six feet tall, rose from the bank, crossed the island "like a wheel," cut right through a haystack, and plunged into the river with a yell and a splash. When the story was later told around the evening fire, some maliciously insinuated that Oliver Smith and an accomplice had impersonated the ghost and the Fiend. But the diggers ever after insisted that only an untimely exclamation had deprived them of riches.[5]

Various towns in Connecticut were honored with the presence of Kidd. When cruising up Long Island Sound in 1699, he strode down the street of Milford one evening about seven o'clock, entered a house and boldly kissed a young lady — according to a letter found in an old garret: "when he came in the room he put his arms about my waiste, and kyssed me, wh. made Jacobeth laugh and Thomas Welsh cough."[6] At Stratford Point a slave lay on a high bluff in the moonlight watching for wild fowl on the rocky shore below; he saw a large boat come ashore and men bury a heavy chest in the sand. Since then many have looked for Kidd's treasure in "The Gold Diggings."[7] The pirate captain likewise tarried at Wethersfield, where in a hollow known as "Tryon's Landing" he buried some loot. At that spot the pirate chieftain in anger killed one of his mates with a water bucket, whose ghost still keeps

[4] "Islands of Casco Bay Offer Great Diggings for Treasure Seekers," *Portland Telegram*, Dec. 27, 1931.
[5] J. H. Temple and George Sheldon, *History of the Town of Northfield, Mass.* (Albany, N.Y., 1875), pp. 18–19.
[6] *History of Milford, Conn.*, Federal Writers' Project (Bridgeport, Conn., 1939), p. 37.
[7] William H. Wilcoxson, *History of Stratford, Conn.* (Stratford, 1939), pp. 648-649.

watch; in the first quarter of the nineteenth-century no inhabitant would pass Tryon's Landing after ten P.M., even for five dollars. Men came long distances to dig there, and Amos Wilcox once came upon two earnest diggers who, seeing him, placed their hands over their mouths as a sign to him not to utter a word.[8]

On the coast or far inland Kidd left his traces. His spirit keeps vigil over a cache of jewels and doubloons hidden on Cape Cod [9] — more specifically, a box of gold on Hogg Island.[10] He bore part of his gold to Antrim, New Hampshire, and buried it on the shores of Rye Pond, where hunters probed rooty bog and rocky soil.[11] When two Spanish silver dollars of very early date were excavated in 1839 at Bellows Falls, Vermont, by some workmen near the head of the canal, speculation immediately produced the theory that the noted pirate had sailed up the river till he reached the falls and there hid the treasure until such time as he could return.[12] But in particular stories of Kidd abound on the Maine coast. Prior to the disastrous voyage to the coast of east Africa in 1696-1698, whence he returned to be haled before the Boston authorities and then shipped to England for hanging, legend avers he deposited gold at a number of coastal points. Hundreds have dredged and dragged the waters around Musselridge Channel near Twobush Island; campers on Codlead Marsh, where Marsh Creek joins Penobscot River six miles inland from its junction with Penobscot Bay, have shoveled enough earth to build embankments and fill cuts for the grading of a railroad twenty miles in length — work that at regular railroad pay would have earned $30,000, instead of the few battered coins whose discovery in 1798 resulted in such a dissipation of human energy. A more romantic burial spot yet is where Stony Brook empties itself into Penobscot River a mile above Fort Point Lighthouse; for here Kidd, sensing his coming disaster, took the treasure he had looted from East Indian mer-

[8] Henry R. Stiles, *The History of Ancient Wethersfield, Conn.* (New York, 1904), I, 689.

[9] Clipping from *Colonial Newspaper*, November 1936, in the Hyannis (Mass.) Public Library.

[10] Jeremiah Digges, *Cape Cod Pilot* (Provincetown, Mass., 1937), p. 154.

[11] Warren R. Cochrane, *History of the Town of Antrim, N.H.* (Manchester, N.H., 1880), pp. 316-317.

[12] Clipping from an article by L. S. Hayes in the *Bellows Falls [Vt.] Times* in the Vermont Historical Society, Montpelier (Rockingham Scrapbook, I, 119).

chantmen, in a rowboat manned by four African slaves, and buried it at the mouth of Stony Brook in four comic opera chests, heavily clasped and padlocked. Then the Captain ordered his slaves into the hole above the boxes and shot them to death, after which he cross-piled the bodies, muttered an invocation over them, refilled the hole with dirt, and rowed back to his ship alone. A hundred or more residents of Waldo and Hancock counties in the past century and a half have dug at Stony Brook for Kidd's gold, but all have been frightened away by the ghosts of the murdered African slaves. Sometimes a tidal wave that swept in from the bay flooded the hole and made further work impossible. Or when the points of the spades grated on the steel trappings of the treasure chests, a ghostly blue light illuminated the pit and a smell of burning sulphur overpowered the searchers. On five or six occasions the skeleton guardians came to life and hit about them so vigorously that the intruders fled with bleeding faces and aching bodies.[13]

In a former day Hallowell throve as a port and shipbuilding center, but now little vestige of her quondam activity remains, save for a Kidd legend. Under a ravine on the Chelsea side of the Kennebec River, which, due to some air current, is cased in a drift of fog, the Captain buried part of his loot; and there, amid the phantoms of ships sunk in distant waters that return on the tide, swells the sail of Kidd on foggy days and wintry nights. For the Captain and his ghostly crew have returned to watch their treasure.[14] A legend of Monhegan Island recalls a treasure quest that failed only because the seeker was a poltroon. In a dream a tall, thin, scarfaced man with gold-hooped earrings informed the widow, Eva Marshall, of treasure buried under mottled pebbles, marked by three spears of grass, on the windswept rise in her yard; she should dig for it alone at midnight. Kidd had killed its guardian, the man of the dream, two hundred years before, and now that his term was served, it belonged to the owner of the property. Mrs. Marshall told her son Joe, who went with his friend Jed at the hour; they located the spot, but a sudden lashing rainstorm frightened them

---

[13] *Bangor Daily News*, Feb. 22, 1932, "tales told by old codgers down along the coast."

[14] *Lewiston Journal*, Jan. 6, 1938. Mrs. Grace M. Ames of Gardiner, Me., submits verses with an explanation that "the enclosed legend was told me by my grandfather."

away, and subsequent seekers never found the mottled pebbles or the three spears of grass. In the village store, an old man spun yarns of his boyhood; pausing in his narrative, he gesticulated with his thumb at Joe Marshall striding toward the woods with an axe on his shoulder: "He got skeered." And emitted his cud of tobacco.[15]

An unusual variation from the typical legend connects two of the most famous fortunes of all time, the ill-got wealth of the notorious Captain Kidd and the vast holdings of the Astor family. When a comparatively unknown fur trader, John Jacob Astor (according to the tale) purchased the treasure from one of his trappers for a small sum and sold it in London for more than a million dollars. Some fifty years ago the then owner of Deer Isle, author-architect Frederick Law Olmsted, discovered in a cave on the extreme south end indentions in the form of a cross. Curiosity led to excavation, which disclosed, fifteen inches below the surface, the perfect imprint of a heavy chest, even to the row of bolt heads around the edge. Olmsted undertook inquiries to probe the mystery, and discovered that a French Canadian trapper in the employ of Astor, Jacques Cartier, had lived on the island in extreme poverty until 1801 when he returned from his annual trip to New York with abundance of money. General suspicion as to its source caused his sudden departure, and the only clues ever forthcoming were partially burned fragments of paper in his cabin, one with the signature of John Jacob Astor and another with the words, "absolute secrecy must prevail because ———."[16]

Besides legendary treasure imputed to Kidd, which never seemed to materialize, chance treasure finding could and did occur, and stimulated explanatory fictions. Captain Stephen Grindle was plowing up some alders with a yoke of oxen when one of the oxen stepped into a small hole and pulled out its foot with a Spanish coin stuck to the hoof. "That's fine, old boy, try it again," whooped the captain, and the ox repeated the action with the same result. Grindle rushed back to his barn for a shovel and unearthed enough coins to fill a ten-quart pail,

[15] Leela Richards, "A Monhegan Legend. A Captain Kidd Treasure That Was Never Found," *Lewiston Journal*, May 22, 1937.
[16] W. Whidden Johnson, "Is Astor Fortune Founded on Pirate Treasure on Deer Isle—" *Portland Express*, July 16, 1934 ("one of the most persistent legends of America").

six hundred dollars' worth of Spanish and French coins and Pine Tree shillings.[17] Similarly, while plowing on his intervale field in Dunstable, New Hampshire, Colonel Bancroft struck a stone — a matter so rare that he sent his boy at once to the barn with the team and turned his labors to digging. Shortly he unearthed a pot of money, supposedly placed there by an Indian trader named Cromwell; for many years after excavations were secretly made in the field.[18] A sudden turn in the affairs of Captain Kit Pennel of Orrs Island, Maine, whose eleven boys had barely been able to eke out the meanest kind of living, is credited to their turning up a pot of pirate gold while plowing on Harpswell Neck; at any rate the Captain paid spot cash for a fifty-acre farm, acquired three fishing schooners, and when he died left much land and money and a fleet of fishing craft. Likewise a shiftless resident of Bailey Island, John Wilson, sailed into Mackerel Cove one day sole owner and skipper of a very fine sloop. Not for months did he reveal that while winter duck shooting on a little rocky reef between Ram and Elm's Islands his foot had slipped into a hole; on looking within he lifted from the seaweed a copper kettle full of strange gold coins. This Spanish gold he exchanged in Boston for $12,000 in American money. In 1855 a farmer and his two sons plowing on Richmon Island discovered a stone pot at the bottom of a furrow containing twenty-seven silver coins dating from the reign of Elizabeth, and a gold wedding signet; they are still in the possession of the Cummings family, inherited from the original finders.[19] An old hemp-spinner of Portsmouth, New Hampshire, who suddenly retired to a life of ease was credited with finding the gold hidden by Myrick, a rich Englishman, beneath a boulder near the old cellar of his imposing house before he returned to England.[20]

But since these accidental finds could not be anticipated, deliberate treasure hunting relied on special paraphernalia, divining rods and stones, to divulge the location of hidden riches. (Invariably, however, science failed where chance had succeeded.) Black Dinah Rollins, a

[17] Henry Buxton's column, *Bangor Daily News*, Oct. 7, 1937.

[18] John B. Hill, *Bi-Centennial of Old Dunstable* (Nashua, N.H., 1878), p. 123.

[19] Alfred Elden, "Stories and Legends of Pirate Gold and Buried Bullion Attract Treasure Seekers," *Bangor Commercial*, June 22, 1940.

[20] Charles W. Brewster, *Rambles About Portsmouth* (Portsmouth, N.H., 1859), pp. 173–174.

sorcerer and money digger of local repute in York, Maine, bequeathed before her death an elaborate apparatus she had employed, consisting of an "indicator" and a divining rod. The indicator, a small quantity of metallic mercury sewed up in sections in a piece of black velvet, would be held in a horizontal position near the likely place; should a sympathetic agitation be induced, the mercury changed position. Thereupon the rod, which differed from a common walking cane only in being longer and having a pointed, silver-tipped ferrule one quarter of its length at one end, came into play; the operator stuck this end into the ground designated by the indicator, and if either silver or gold were present, it gave forth a peculiar sound and transmitted a definite sensation.[21] Fully detailed, if badly spelled, directions for ferreting out the elusive metal with modern devices are preserved in the notes of Silas Hammond, a leading spirit in such affairs round about Whitingham, Vermont.

A METHOD TO TAK UP HID TREASURE (viz).

Tak Nine Steel Rods about ten or twelve Inches in Length Sharp or Piked to Perce in to the Erth, and let them be Besmeared with fresh blood from a hen mixed with hogdung. Then mak two Surkels Round the hid Treasure one of Sd Surkels a Littel Larger in surcumference than the hid Treasure lays in the Erth the other Surkel Sum Larger still, and as the hid treasure is wont to move to North or South East or west Place your Rods as is Discribed on the other sid of this leaf.[22]

Divining instruments figure prominently in popular tales of treasure hunts. A party sallied forth from Essex, Vermont, led by a "juggling doctor who carried in his hat the mystical stone in which he could see the precise locality and enormous quantity of the concealed precious metals, or held nicely poised upon his fore-finger the charmed stick which was certain to become mightily agitated and decline from its horizontal position at the presence of gold or silver." While the mystic stone and the charmed stick brought the sought-for treasure within sight, premature outcries of joy caused it to disappear.[23] A resident of

[21] George A. Emery, *Ancient City of Georgeana and Modern Town of York, Me.* (Boston, 1874), pp. 202–204.

[22] Clark Jillson, *Green Leaves from Whitingham, Vt.* (Worcester, Mass., 1894), p. 119.

[23] *The Vermont Historical Gazetteer*, Abby M. Hemenway, ed. (Burlington, Vt., 1867), I, 784–785 (quotation from p. 785).

Shirley, Massachusetts, named Sherman Willard, owned a rod which would turn when there was silver beneath; doubters buried spoons and other silver on a hill, but the rod easily detected the spot. Tradition avers that a buried treasure lay under Willard's taproom, for the rod turned there; some say he murdered a wandering Indian and buried him there, no doubt as the guardian.[24] "Wint" Getchel of Weare, New Hampshire, as a young man acquired the power of "rhodomancy" or "dowseying" with a witch hazel rod. He could discover water and precious metals in the earth by means of the rod, which would turn in his hands of itself and point down when he came to the right place. A midnight treasure hunt, guided by the rod, nearly proved successful; but when a spade struck a ringing rock, one of the party cried out, "Thank heaven! we have found it!" and Kidd's ghost promptly spirited the gold away.[25] One prized divining rod has remained in the Heath family for one hundred and fifty years; once on Gott Island, Maine, the heirloom, then in the possession of Frank J. Heath, showed signs of attraction, which promptly led him to dig. Next day a strange schooner anchored off the little island, and an aged, enfeebled man was lowered into a boat and rowed ashore. He sat on a log and pointed to a spot, whereupon members of the crew began to dig alongside the hole excavated the previous day. When Mr. Heath examined their traces, he found the rod had pointed accurately. "At the bottom of this new hole was the imprint of an iron chest, with patches of rust that remained on the earth. All the way to the beach were marks where the heavy chest had been dragged to the shore."[26] A notorious charlatan, Rainsford Rogers, executed a successful fraud on certain credulous citizens of Exeter, New Hampshire, by promising to locate a vast subterranean treasure provided he could purchase a superior divining rod. The interested parties entrusted him with several hundred dollars to obtain the equipment in Philadelphia, and Rogers departed with it from Exeter, permanently.[27] Among marvelous traditions reported from Groton,

---

[24] Ethel S. Bolton, *Shirley Uplands and Intervales* (Boston, 1914), p. 93.

[25] Little, *History of Weare, N.H.*, p. 589.

[26] Henry Buxton, "Treasure Divining Rod Used Over 150 Years in Search for Pirate Gold on Coast," *Bangor Daily News*, May 22, 1937; see also his *Assignment Down East* (Brattleboro, Vt., c. 1938), pp. 168–172.

[27] Charles H. Bell, *History of the Town of Exeter, N.H.* (Exeter, 1888), pp. 411–414.

Massachusetts, as deserving appendixes to Cotton Mather's fourteen examples of "Thaumaturgia," one dealt with supernatural treasure finders. Nathaniel Sartell and others enjoyed the gift (devil-granted it was said) of divining the underground location of water springs and mineral ores, by the aid of steel or witch hazel rods wound about with cords and prepared with incantations. But when pious Christians dug for the pots of gold and silver thus pointed out, as they approached within an inch of the objects, a hideous daemon or a saucer-eyed night-bird rose to mock them, or on some slight whisper the chest would rumble off into the earth. So the handlers of the rods came to be regarded as no better than imposters, duped by the devil.[28]

Sybils and sorcerers added their black art to the power of the divining rod. To trace the pagan treasure of St. Francis (rifled by Rogers' Rangers from the church of St. Francis, then hidden somewhere in the White Hills when its curse led them to death, and ever and anon sighted in a vision of a glittering church altar by a benighted traveler), a party of adventurers solicited the aid of an old fortune teller. An herb gatherer, possessor of a marvelous stone, who lived in a mud hovel, she burned drugs, uttered mystic words, and divined that on the ensuing night the stars would be favorable for locating the silver image. She led them up the mountain to the place designated by her magic; but in the course of digging, shattering thunderbursts and liquid lightning frightened the rash hunters into headlong flight down the mountain. But the fortune teller, gripped by avarice, continued to dig frantically in defiance of the powers of earth and darkness. A twinkling blue flame spread a ghostly light over the black rocks, and a giant form arose from the mist, hurled over the precipice kettle and phial and then, in a flash of electric fire, dragged the old fortune teller by her hair towards the brink of the cliff. Such was the last view of her beheld by the fugitives; today around that spot strange wailings may be heard when the wind is high, and some believe that in a dark cavern the hag dwells in torment.[29] In more recent times a resident of Norfolk, Connecticut, consulted a noted fortune teller in Burlington, Vermont, with respect to a store robbery

---

[28] Caleb Butler, *History of the Town of Groton* (Boston, 1848), pp. 256–257.
[29] John H. Spaulding, *Historical Relics of the White Mountains* (Boston, 1855), pp. 38–48.

involving several hundred dollars; the soothsayer looked through her stone and instantly informed him the precise location of the money. Reactions to the story veered between belief in the sybil's power of second sight and suspicions that the middleman had obtained a perfectly good first sight.[30] A faithful treasure digger on Fort Point Cove, Maine, Captain Rufus Harriman, followed the directions of his clairvoyant wife; according to information from a spirit imparted to her in a trance, he dug for a pot of gold under an Indian clam shell heap on the shore for many nights, but without success.[31]

Spirits often provided important assistance in treasure finding. In his Maine travels Henry Buxton heard a Down-Easter declare that a ghost had haunted his farm and urged him through a series of rappings to dig up a pot of gold buried in the eighteenth-century by the swashbuckling pirate, Captain Jack Gibbs, whose career ended on a New York gallows.[32] Beneath a gigantic oak in Woburn, Massachusetts, by the side of a pond, a ghost zealously guarded a large sum of money hidden under the roots by a robber. Persons often saw a light dancing over the water, which, if they ventured nearer, moved toward the oak and glided up and down its huge branches. Samuel Caldwell, as he was passing the tree on his way home from courting Esther Johnson, saw the ghost rise out of the pond like a ball of fire and approach him with dreadful cries; next morning he found a lock of his black hair had turned gray, while his hat looked as if it had been scorched on top. A boy driving cows to pasture let them drink at the pond; he happened to wander near the tree, when one of the cows became violently agitated, and ran out of the water with her tail up; the terrified lad saw the ghost on the cow's back, holding onto her tail, but as the cow ran past the tree, it glided from her up the trunk and disappeared in the branches. Tradition said that the ghost thus frightened off intruders because it could only be released from its guardianship by Deacon Wright. In a dream the ghost visited the Deacon, and set a rendezvous at the old oak, at which time he revealed himself as the shade of the Deacon's father, who had hanged

---

[30] *New Bedford Daily Mercury*, Nov. 2, 1831, from the *Hartford Mirror*.
[31] *Bangor Daily News*, Feb. 6, 1937.
[32] *Bangor Daily News*, Mar. 1, 1938; for Gibbs see Buxton, *Assignment Down East*, pp. 174–175.

himself from the oak on April 29, 1763; if the son acquired legal title to the property, he could secure the treasure and the tormented specter could depart; if he sought to seize the gold prematurely, the guardian would smother him in a deadly gas. But alas for the Deacon, an unscrupulous third party discovered the secret, successfully exorcised the ghost, and made off with the treasure. Next year the oak, after over a century of sturdy life, withered away and died.[33]

Dreams, with or without the coöperation of spirits, furnished goads for treasure search. In the crude notebook kept by Silas Hamilton of Whitingham, Vermont, recording nearly fifty rumors and reports of hid treasure or lost mines, seventeen begin in dreams.[34] "Mother Worcester's Cave" near Campton, New Hampshire, owes its existence not to natural but to human causes; for here the townsmen of Mother Worcester (a character famous for her dreams) vainly tunneled after gold she had dreamed lay in the ledge on the far bank of Beebe River at the base of a waterfall.[35] More foundation seems to have existed for the dream of Ashbel Tucker, although results were equally disappointing. Thrice Ashbel dreamed he crossed Ayer's Brook and met a man who told him he had buried money. Thereupon he awakened, went down to the spot and saw the man of his dream walking about, but dared not accost him. Tucker revealed his dream to others, who procured a mineral rod and began the search. When they neared the treasure the pot moved, for the ground was seen to rise and fall in the direction it departed. At another time several men cornered the money within a small space hedged about by old scythes stuck upright in the ground to prevent its escape. But Silas Flint, jealous that the diggers should gain the prize (he was said to have always believed that he would die rich) pulled up one of the scythes, and immediately the money escaped through the opening.[36]

Perennially clues to deposited wealth or tales of near strikes excited human avarice, yet in most treasure quests, the actual and the legendary,

---

[33] Parker L. Converse, "The Haunted Oak. A Legend of Wright's Pond, Woburn," *Legends of Woburn, Second Series* (Woburn, Mass.), pp. 140–150.

[34] Jillson, *Green Leaves from Whitingham, Vt.*, pp. 115–119.

[35] "Mother Worcester's Dream," *New Hampshire Folk Tales*, Mrs. Moody P. Gore and Mrs. Guy E. Speare, compilers (n.p., 1932), pp. 203–204.

[36] H. Royce Bass, *The History of Braintree, Vt.* (Rutland, Vt., 1883), p. 46.

men chased rainbows that never led to pots of gold. For sixty years a regularly organized stock company in Bristol, Vermont, promising each donor $100 for every dollar in money or equipment invested, methodically probed for rich ore on a slender lead. A secretive stranger, a Spaniard named DeGrau, claimed to have accompanied a group of Spanish explorers to the region around 1800; they had discovered a rich vein of silver, walled it up in one of the numerous caves, and covered it over with natural vegetation. None ever returned save DeGrau, who could not precisely determine the spot because a landslide, so he said, had changed the face of the cliff. On the strength of this story digging persisted through the years; Richard Brown started to dig as a young man and continued, in spite of argument and ridicule, until in old age death ended his search. Hundreds of holes dug in solid rock in "Hell's Half Acre" testify today to the credulity of man and the persistence of human hope.[37] Constant excavating similarly followed the cryptic words of Manuel Caton, who in an unguarded moment was believed to have said that "Money Hill," the dismal looking mound on Province-town's beautiful bathing beach, concealed gold taken from the very pirate ship that landed Manuel. Yet all the efforts of zealous investigators have unearthed nothing more than a tiny silver anchor, probably fashioned by the hand of some seafaring bucko in an idle moment.[38] In local legends paralleling Kidd tales, treasure might come within grasp, but unseen powers decreed it should not reach human hands. Tradition in Wiscasset, Maine, preserves the hunt of old William More-len for a pot of gold supposedly holed up near the dyke in the shore of Finley Creek. By his story, when one day he thrust his crowbar into the ground hoping to pry out the prize, it bounced back over his head, and he heard coins jingle as witches seized the pot of gold, and hoofs beat as they crossed the bridge at the north.[39] One summer day in the late 1850's two women of Gott's Island decided to catch a mess of fish to vary their fare. By a submerged shoal off Bass Head they dropped their hooks and waited; by and by one felt a weight like a bunch of

[37] "Bristol's 'Money Diggings' Unique Chapter in History," *Burlington Free Press*, July 31, 1936.
[38] "When Pirates Sailed Into Provincetown," *Yarmouth Register*, Sept. 30, 1933.
[39] Fannie S. Chase, *Wiscasset in Pownalborough* (Wiscasset, 1941), p. 619.

rockweed, and pulling in the line was excited to see on the hook a small canvas bag, tightly tied. Clutching hands reached for gold coins, but as the bag surfaced the bottom burst and the contents sank beyond reach, leaving them only the empty bag to prove this was the treasure thrown overboard by an English privateer long before.[40]

Did hunters never find hidden riches? It were better that treasure eluded searchers, for tainted gains brought a curse upon their possessors. A chain of calamities ensued from the accidental discovery of pirates' gold on Norton's Point in Penobscot Bay. Sandy Duguid had first settled there; coming one day on three cairns of rocks, he measured off thirty paces from each, and on the spot where his paces met he dug. Under a flat rock rested an oak chest, bound with copper bands and filled with Spanish gold and silver coins. But also within the chest he found a parchment bearing the words, "A curse on the man who removes this chest, and upon the region. Let him beware, misfortune will follow him to the end of his days." Duguid laughed off the curse, but from that day misfortune shadowed him. Storms washed away his nets and destroyed his traps; a blight ruined his garden, early frost killed the buds on his fruit trees, a strange sickness crippled him, and a bolt of lightning struck and burned his house. On the site of the burned structure Patrick Collins, ignoring warnings, built for himself and his family a commodious house from lumber of the ship whose wreck cast upon the island. Storms, blight, and disease likewise visited Collins; shortly after he closed his house lightning struck and burned it to the ground. About a hundred years ago a man rummaging in the rubbish of the deserted cellar found a Spanish gold coin dropped by Sandy Duguid. On his way home he passed the Old Harbor Quarry just as a blast was touched off; a fragment of granite shattered his right leg so that it had to be amputated. He loaned the coin to a friend who happened to have charge of the blasting in that quarry; the next day the new possessor was blown up and blinded for life. Another friend borrowed it to show his family; he went mad, killed a fellow quarryman and threw himself off the pier. Finally a professor wished to place the coin in the museum of his college, but before he could do so he drowned in a side-wheel ship

[40] Mrs. Seth S. Thornton, *Traditions and Records of Southwest Harbor and Somesville, Mount Desert Island, Me.* (n.p., 1938), pp. 326–327.

which sank just off Vinal Haven. So ended the history of the coin with its trail of enigmatic misfortunes.[41]

Disaster and death trailed the ill-begotten gold of Black Bellamy, the pirate, who sailed away from bewitching Maria Hallet and Eastham with a brazen promise to return and lay riches at her feet. Years passed and he did not return; a child was still-born to Maria, whom the select-men placed in jail, then finally allowed to roam at will beyond the town. The pretty girl grew into the surly, stringy-haired witch Goody Hallet, who was seen dancing in the hollows amid the dunes and singing on the bluffs during a storm; men avoided looking toward her cabin on the beach and muttered a prayer as they passed it by. People said that her voice heard shrieking above the surf called curses on the pirate who had left her alone in Eastham. Then in the great storm of 1717 Bellamy's ship, the *Whidah*, struck the bars off South Wellfleet, bringing death to all but two of its cutthroat crew, while Goody Hallet stood on the bluffs and cackled hideously. But Bellamy and his former sweetheart were destined to meet once more; several years after the wreck, a minister lost on his way up the Cape from Truro found himself outside the hut of Goody Hallet, where the witch and a villainous stranger held alterca-tion. Bellamy, for it was he, demanded of her the whereabouts of the *Whidah*'s treasure; she led him to the shore, and showed him several rotted leather bags, empty save for a few gold coins left in the corners. "There, you can see for yourself," came Goody Hallet's voice trium-phantly, "the leathern bags are still here. I have never seen the treasure." From his point of concealment the minister heard a bubbling shriek; he peered over the bluffs and saw the witch, flat on her back, arms spread awry, and her throat gashed from ear to ear. Five days later the drowned body of Black Bellamy washed up on the shore. The *Whidah*'s gold had destroyed its owners and its seekers.[42]

[41] *Rockland* [*Me.*] *Courier-Gazette*, Mar. 22, 1938, "The Power of a Curse. What Happened to Finders of Pirate Gold — Scene Laid in Penobscot Bay."

[42] Oliver Knowles, "Goody Hallet's Treasure. A Legend of the Pirate Bellamy," *Cape Cod Beacon*, XLVIII (March 1937), 11–14, 22. Cf. Elizabeth Reynard, *The Narrow Land* (Boston and New York, 1934), pp. 160–161, 208–217, notes to "The Black Bellamy," p. 323; Jeremiah Digges, *Cape Cod Pilot*, pp. 193–197; Hildreth G. Hawes, *The Bellamy Treasure: The Pirates of the "Whydah" in the Gulf of Maine* (Augusta, Me., 1940).

Place names. Catalogue the names of local points in any community, and the chances are favorable that many intriguing titles will appear.

Gloucester: Goose Cove, Barberry shore, Samp Porridge Hill, Two Penny Loaf, Turtle-pond hill, Dog-town common, Cart-wheel heaven, Seven-star lane, Happy valley, Portuguese Hill, Breakheart Hill, Judy Milletts' parlor, Granny Berger's lane, Done Fudgin.

Portsmouth: Christian Shore, Pull-and-beD-d Point, Windmill Hill, The Gut, Boiling Rock, Point of Graves, Mandlin Lane, Gravelly Ridge, The Pound, Pumpkin Island, Bread-and-Cheese Rock, Breakfast Hill, Barberry Lane, Half-Moon Pond, Eel Pot, Devil's Den, Windmill Lane, Whales Back, Grave's End, Commercial Alley, Smutty Nose, Haymarket Square, Frenchman's Lane, Hog Island, The Dump.[1]

Popular tales became fixed in local legend when they contributed names to roads, brooks, hills, rocks, swamps, ponds, caves, falls, and sundry spots made memorable by an incident that had transpired in the vicinity. Since an unusual or provocative name evokes a prompt inquiry by the curious into its origin, tales thus synopsized into permanent labels for natural landmarks live on in folk history; since oral memory flickers, doubts shroud the original story and give rise to hazarded surmises or speculative interpretings. While many place-name stories are simple historical tradition, many also fall within the various types of imaginative fictions, supernatural and humorous.

Satan, so conspicuous a personality in New England folktale, left his calling card in innumerable communities that boasted a Devil's Den, Devil's Armchair, Devil's Pulpit, Devil's Corncrib, Devil's Garden, Devil's Kitchen, Devil's Basin, Devil's Jump, and, preëminently, a Devil's Foot. But a fraction of the geological formations named for the Evil One are still linked to story; such name histories as survive doubtless indicate the nature of those that have not. Behind the large indentation resembling a human footprint that onlookers in many localities gazed at apprehensively lay an obvious explanation that yet failed to explain all; Satan had stepped there, but why?

If legend can be relied upon, the banks of the Mousam River were once visited by a personage whose fame has been known in all ages of man's existence and through all inhabited lands. There was a large boulder a few

---

[1] Portsmouth Scrap Book, IV, 18 (clipping dated May 4, 1889), in the New Hampshire Historical Society, Concord.

Local Legends

rods below the village saw-mill which bore a mysterious imprint, said to be the impress of the cloven foot of his Satanic majesty. He must have bounded upon it with a heavy tread or placed the limb there while the once molten rock was yet soft and pliable. . . . Whence this legend is not known, nor is it easy to imagine what could have induced the old fellow to visit this locality in person. He was not interviewed.[2]

DEVIL'S ROCK is the name given to a large rocky island about midway of the second, or Factory dam. The traditional origin of the name is as follows: In the early settlement of the place, a man and his wife occupied a lone house a little way back from the river, on the Topsham side. This man was very superstitious, and probably addicted to the habit of taking both frequent and deep potations. One day during an ice freshet, as he was sitting at his window watching the ice go by, he imagined he saw Satan, *in propria persona*, floating down the stream on a log, and that he could hear the clanking of his chains as he climbed the rock. He informed his wife of this imaginary occurrence, and after the waters had subsided, the pair visited the rock and found the footprints left there by his supposed Satanic Majesty.[3]

Some facetious wags avowed that the Fiend had stepped across to Devil's Foot on the Rhode Island mainland from Conanicut Island bound Westerly-way, or perhaps he was heading from Massachusetts to Connecticut to continue his labors; he passed through so quickly because (1) he realized there was no chance of proselyting in that state; (2) it was already his.[4] Most informed persons knew, however, that the Devil had merely trod here or there or wherever it might be in the ordinary pursuit of his business.

Tradition has handed down to us the important intelligence (we do not, however, vouch for its truth), that Major George Leonard — the first of the name in town — made a league with the Devil in order to acquire great wealth; and, as a return for the services rendered, Leonard promised to give his body to the Devil when he called for it. Accordingly, in 1716, while Mr. Leonard was sick with a fever, of which he died, the old imp came, claimed his body, and actually carried it off! As he left the premises with it, he made a tremendous jump, and landed on some rocks situated thirty or forty rods back of the house, where he came down with so much force as to make his foot-prints in the rock, which are to be seen at the present day! At the funeral, the corpse was not to be seen, of course; and the family gave out word that it was not proper to be seen: but, in reality, there was nothing

[2] Daniel Remich, *History of Kennebunk* (n.p., c. 1911), p. 428.

[3] George A. and Henry W. Wheeler, *History of Brunswick, Topsham, and Harpswell, Me.* (Boston, 1878), pp. 78–79.

[4] J. Earl Clauson, *These Plantations*, (Providence, c. 1937), p. 99.

189

in the coffin but a log of wood, put in to lull all suspicion that the body was not there.[5]

On the west side of the highway leading from Wickford to East Greenwich, where the railroad from Davisville to Quonset now crosses, is a ledge of rock known as Devil's Foot. The legend connected with the naming of this rock is quite fantastic.

In the early days of the Puritan Colony in Massachusetts, there lived an Indian squaw, who by some trickery, had forfeited her soul to the Devil. She afterward tried to escape from his presence by fleeing into Rhode Island. The Devil gave chase leaving the first print of his long foot in this ledge of rock. His second stride landed him on Chimney Hill and his third on Block Island. Here he found his victim and returned her to the Puritan Colony to answer for her treachery.

It is said that footprints of the Devil's dog can be seen near by and that the Devil's chair made of rock stands higher up on the ledge.[6]

The Devil displayed a peculiar fondness for Rhode Island — more than to be expected of one who was simply passing through. His soil-searing footprints inspired even versified legend. Lovely Polly of Apponaug consented to elope with a teamster, who did a quick change.

> In an instant the form of a monster he took;
>   The maid with affright and astonishment shook
> As she gazed at his face with eyes full of tears.
>   His nose like the claw of a lobster appears,
> A shock of thick eel-grass surrounded his head,
>   His beard of fine coral, a bright, flaming red,
> His teeth like barnacles that cling to a ship,
>   To which beauty now add a very thick lip,
> And two clamshells immense which served him for ears
>   And you have the ensemble exciting her fears.

But it was too late for Polly to renege, and so Apponaug lost its prize beauty.[7] "Purgatory," an evil-looking fissure at Middletown, Rhode

[5] George F. Clark, *A History of the Town of Norton, Mass.* (Boston, 1859), p. 532.

[6] Anna S. Nugent, "The Legend of Devil's Foot Rock," *Facts and Fancies Concerning North Kingstown, R.I.* (North Kingstown, 1941), p. 90. Henry Buxton reports a triple footprint legend told him by a Down-Easter: "There is an old saying that the devil came ashore at Penobscot, made a stride of eight miles to Sargentville and another stride of eight miles to a point on the beach on Deer Isle. At both Sargentville and Deer Isle are said to be footprints that are identical to the one here at Penobscot." (*Bangor News*, Oct. 7, 1937.) Likewise while in pursuit of some high offender the Devil jumped from Step Rock in Saugus to Step Rock in North Woburn, and thence to Mt. Mianomo and Mt. Towanda, leaving his foot mark wherever he stepped (Parker L. Converse, *Legends of Woburn, Second Series*, Woburn, Mass., 1896, p. 33).

[7] Clauson, *These Plantations*, p. 101.

Island, commemorates an adventure of the Indian Satan, Hobomoko. Accosting an Indian squaw who had murdered a white man, he grasped her by the waist, made one or two fierce stamps on the ground, and flew with her toward Purgatory. When the squaw showed fight, the Devil bumped her head against a boulder, and chopped it off with his tomahawk; he then ran up on the ledge with the body and threw it in the chasm. Bowl-like depressions in the rock show where he bumped the squaw's head, ax marks where the tomahawk struck, and footprints in the vein of stone where he ran with his victim's body to the edge of Purgatory.[8]

Besides Faustian legends, other activities accounted for the Devil's tracks. Purgatory Falls, in Mont Vernon, New Hampshire, is a wild and rocky gorge distinguished by a footprint seven feet long and a hollow resembling a bean pot. There the Devil lived, and lured the godly men of Mont Vernon Hill to his lair with the promise of a bean supper. But when the elders were all seated, awaiting the repast, the Evil One forgot to turn off the heat, and as his great foot sank in the soft rocks, his imprecations so terrified his guests that they hastily fled.[9]

Not all Devil place-name stories revolved around footprints. Devil's Rock in Salisbury, New Hampshire, commemorates the exorcising of Satan from his rendezvous with an old lady whose soul he had purchased (see Chapter II, *The Devil*). Saddleback Mountain in Derry, New Hampshire, is so called for a strange fiction that involves the Evil One. A huge horseman rode up and down the mountain in days past, breaking shrubs and snapping rock fragments in his mad rides; one night a fearful storm arose, and on the flame-lighted mountain top the wicked giant could be seen battling one still more wicked. Unhorsed, the giant disappeared through a chasm that suddenly yawned beneath him; his steed too began to sink, but the sides of the gulf closed before he had slipped from sight. After the storm, spectators saw that the horse had been changed to stone, with his upper parts

[8] *Rhode Island: A Guide to the Smallest State*, Federal Writers' Project (Boston, 1937), pp. 419-420.
[9] "Purgatory Falls," *New Hampshire Folk Tales*, Mrs. Moody P. Gore and Mrs. Guy E. Speare, compilers (n.p., 1932), pp. 181-182.

visible above the earth. Now at long distances may be viewed in outline the petrified saddleback of the gigantic horse.[10]

Hoax tales which carried the Devil into nineteenth-century humor
also named places for posterity. In his Jonny-Cake stories, Tom Hazard
reveals the escapade that gave a cleared spot in Wilson's woods the
appellation "Devil's Ring." While crossing that spot, Richard Cory
found himself suddenly seized by a great horned monster, who promised to spare him on condition that he bring to the Ring, next day, a
bigger liar than himself. Cory promised, and sought out Paris Garner,
whom he attempted to cajole to the designated place with a story of
Kidd's treasure, but Paris declared Cory was such a liar he couldn't
believe him, and flatly refused to go — being the Devil himself. Thereafter Richard went the long way round Wilson's woods.[11]

Dark and tragic legends linger on on in place names. Heartbreak
Hill in Ipswich, Massachusetts, signifies the tedious hours an Indian
girl spent on this eminence awaiting the return of her sailor lover who
never came back; some say his ship foundered in her sight and he
drowned before her eyes.[12] Nix's Mate is the beacon in Boston Harbor
named after the mate who was accused on hearsay evidence of murdering Captain Nix; on the gallows, erected on an islet in the bay, he laid
a curse that the island might sink to prove his innocence; today the
beacon marks where the island once stood.[13] Several traditions ex-

[10] *New Hampshire Folk Tales*, pp. 180-181, "A Legend of Saddleback Mountain in
Derry." ("Last year I met an old man ... who repeated the story of the horrible conflict
between the imprisoned horseman and The Evil One and, told in his quaint dialect, the
tale was doubly interesting.")

[11] Thomas R. Hazard, *The Jonny-Cake Letters* (Providence, 1882), pp. 270-273. A
tale also based on a tribute by the Devil to an expertly devilish human being relates the
dreams of two cronies in Eaton, N.H., described to the village store audience. Eli Snow
dreamt he was Amandus and went to Hell, where the Chief Devil greeted him warmly
and offered him the highest seat. As a counter, Amandus told how he dreamed he was
brother Snow and went to Hell, where the Chief Devil gave him a sulphur match — a
torch as big as a drum major's baton — to start a Hell of his own. (Cornelius Weygandt,
New Hampshire Neighbors, New York, c. 1937, pp. 174-176.) Cf. also Simon L. Bradbury, *Corn Tassel Tales of New England* (Meadville, Pa., c. 1931), pp. 16-17, "Zeke Wuz
Sartinly Tough."

[12] "Heartbreak Hill," *The Poems of Celia Thaxter* (Boston and New York, 1896),
pp. 54-57. "In Ipswich town, not far from the sea, / Rises a hill which the people call /
Heartbreak Hill, and its history / Is an old, old legend, known to all" (p. 54).

[13] Edward R. Snow, *The Islands of Boston Harbor: Their History and Romance*

plain the naming of Haunted Lake, New Hampshire; the most likely
holds that a young man was murdered and buried near where the mill
was afterwards built, and that his spirit haunted the spot with nightly
groanings and cries.[14] On Rachel's Curse, a rock near Plymouth,
Massachusetts, foundered the brig of pirates who had burned the house
of Aunt Rachel, a reputed seer, who cursed their ship in revenge.[15]
Vexation Hill in Wethersfield, Connecticut, recalls the suicide of an
old Negress in that quarter; the people buried her body on top of the
hill in the twenty-rod highway (a survival of the old custom of burying
murderers and suicides at a road crossing, with a stake driven through
the body); it was said that the suicide's ghost haunted the spot. The
highway in question was never used except for drawing wood.[16] Carbuncle Pond and Hill in Coventry, Rhode Island, evoke the memory
of a somber Indian treasure legend. A great snake with a brilliant carbuncle in the center of its head lived on the hill; the Indians captured
it after a violent struggle in which its tail cleft in two a large rock, still
so marked. When the white men came they coveted the stone, whose
increased glow warned its possessors of impending attack; only the
Indian chief survived the battle, and he hurled the carbuncle into the
middle of the pond that carries its name.[17] Fiddler's Reach is an elbow
bend in the Kennebec at the lower extremity of Long Reach where,
according to tradition, a fiddler had drowned. As the sloop he was on
passed through the bend of the river, the people on board became
greatly elated at viewing a reach of water four miles long; to lend a
festive note the fiddler went out on the bowsprit to play a tune, when
the wind slat the jib and knocked him overboard.[18] Dead Indians tell
tales. Whist Pond in Goshen, Connecticut, bears the name of an
Indian who, warned not to slide on the ice, said, "I will have one more
slide," went through the ice and drowned; a drunken Indian named

(Andover, Mass., c. 1935), p. 326, which cites the *Boston News Letter and City Record*,
Dec. 16, 1826.

[14] W. R. Cochrane and George K. Wood, *History of Francestown, N.H.* (Nashua,
N.H., 1895), p. 433.

[15] Charles M. Skinner, *Myths and Legends of Our Own Land* (Philadelphia and
London, c. 1896), I, 306-307, "Aunt Rachel's Curse."

[16] Henry R. Stiles, *History of Ancient Wethersfield, Conn.* (New York, 1904), I, 708.

[17] *Rhode Island: A Guide to the Smallest State*, pp. 106-107.

[18] Parker M. Reed, *History of Bath and Environs* (Portland, Me., 1894), p. 74.

Lewis, about to capsize in his canoe over a waterfall, stood up in the boat and shouted that it should thenceforth be known as Lewis Falls.[19] Wonsqueak Stream, on the eastern side of Schoodic Peninsula, Maine, is also locally called One Screech. A jealous Indian took his squaw out in a canoe and threw her overboard; before the waters closed around her she gave one screech.[20]

Certain folktales explain the coinage of road names connected with eating and drinking. Drinkwater Road in Hampton Falls, New Hampshire, was christened by a man who traveled the whole length of the road asking for a drink of cider and was in every case given water; he expressed his chagrin by saying, "This must be the drink-water road."[21] Johnny Cake Lane in Chelsea, Vermont, has been so called since a pedlar went down a certain street at noon hour and remarked that every family had the same dish—"Why, it's a regular johnny cake lane."[22] A road in Stratham, New Hampshire, is known as Frying-pan Lane because the early settlers owned only one frying pan between them and planned their days for frying by passing the pan in turn amongst themselves.[23] When a flood destroyed the gristmill and fire consumed the Loveland homestead, no one remained to explain how the abandoned thoroughfare came to be called "The Johnnycake Hill Road." One story ran that farmers in that region working on the road for a few days were puzzled by one of their number who always went off by himself to eat his lunch. Seizing an opportunity they investigated his dinner pail and discovered that it contained only johnnycake.[24]

Odd descriptive names generate from domestic incidents, local accidents, word plays, and ludicrous episodes. Squabble Hill in Torrington, Connecticut, memorializes family rows that disturbed the neighbors of a certain house at the foot of the hill.[25] Dingit Corner in Boscawen,

[19] A. G. Hibbard, *History of the Town of Goshen, Conn.* (Hartford, Conn. 1879), pp. 51-52; *Maine: A Guide 'Down East,'* Federal Writers' Project (Boston, 1937), p. 162.
[20] *Maine: A Guide Down East,* p. 276.
[21] Warren Brown, *History of the Town of Hampton Falls, N.H.* (Manchester, N.H., 1900), p. 387.
[22] *Yankee,* III (April 1937), 5.
[23] New Hampshire's Daughters, *Folk-lore Sketches and Reminiscences of New Hampshire Life* (Boston, c. 1911), p. 34.
[24] Edward C. Smith and Philip M. Smith, *A History of the Town of Middlefield, Mass.* (Menasha, Wis., 1924), pp. 320-321.
[25] Samuel Orcutt, *History of Torrington, Conn.* (Albany, 1878), p. 245.

New Hampshire, according to tradition consecrated a domestic turmoil. The wife seized the skillet; the husband cried, "Ding it! Ding it!"[26] Scenes of catastrophes are appropriately called "Breakneck Road," "Break Neck Hill," "Tail-down Hill," "Tumble-Down Dick" (a cliff over which a blind horse tumbled), "Tubwreck Brook;" this last has an unorthodox history.

Tubwreck Brook, which rises in the Great Spring, is the northerly source of the Neponset River. Its name celebrates a humorous incident. One spring, when the brook was unusually swollen, Capt. James Tisdale attempted, in a half hogshead, to sail down the stream, preparatory to gathering flood cranberries. The tub became unmanageable and capsized. Captain Tisdale's friends made much of this event. A quantity of ship-bread, together with such other articles as might be washed ashore from the wreck of a merchant ship, were left at his door; and the neighbors gathered in large numbers, and celebrated his rescue from the wreck. An original poem, telling this story, was repeated for many years around Dover firesides. From that time the stream was called Tubwreck Brook.[27]

Happier pictures are evoked by names suggested by drinking mishaps. Punch and Wigwag Brooks indicate successive drinking stops by a company of men carrying a keg of rum.[28] Scribner's Dock pays tribute to one Scribner who, having partaken liberally of the horn, lost his balance on a bridge, tumbled backwards head-foremost into the stream, and stuck in the soft muddy bottom.[29] Dog Hill has pleasant associations; when a farmer's vicious dog was shot by a neighbor, the owner brought suit for damages; a large crowd and the justice declared for the defendant, who decided that the dog's skin should be stuffed and auctioned, with the proceeds to be invested in rum for the crowd. A hilarious party resulted for, like Davy Crockett's coon, the skin was

[26] *The History of Boscawen and Webster*, Charles C. Coffin, compiler (Concord, N.H., 1878), p. xxiii.

[27] Frank Smith, *A History of Dover, Mass.* (Dover, 1897), pp. 5-6; W. S. Tilden, "The Legend of Tubwreck Brook," *Dedham Historical Register*, IX (July 1898), 80-85. The earlier names are given, respectively, in Harvey M. Lawson, *The History of Union, Conn.* (New Haven, Conn., 1893), p. 29; Joseph Fullonton, *The History of Raymond, N.H.* (Dover, N.H., 1875), p. 10; C. C. Lord, *Life and Times in Hopkinton, N.H.* (Concord, N.H., 1890), pp. 270-271; *History of Carroll County, N.H.*, Georgia D. Merrill, ed. (Boston, 1889), p. 102.

[28] John J. Dearborn, *The History of Salisbury, N.H.* (Manchester, N.H., 1890), pp. 20-21.

[29] Edmund Wheeler, *The History of Newport, N.H.* (Concord, N.H., 1879), p. 225.

sold and resold many times.[30] What lies behind the curious title of Rumstick? Tradition improvises an answer: a barrel of rum floated high and dry upon the beach; while Indians were removing it, the hoops broke, the barrel burst, and spirits of rum and red men sank into the sand, provoking the lament, *"Rum stick here! Rum stick here?"* [31] Religion as well as rum made contributions to place-name tales. Bible Hill commemorates an unministerial descent of an icy hill with the Word of God as a sleigh; the Reverend slid easily down on the ponderous tome he was carrying.[32] Horse-heaven Hill compliments the forbearance of an unknown man who had labored mightily to draw a heavy load up the hill; as he saw his horses disappear over the side of the road and fall to the jagged rocks below he remarked, in place of the more usual phrase, "Go to Heaven."[33] Sometimes a title embodied narrative action. Point Judith repeats the command given by an aged skipper whose dim eyes could not pierce the sullen weather; he placed his daughter beside him at the helm to spy for land, and when the wind drowned her voice cried, "Point, Judith! Point!"[34] A dim tradition anent Mount William reports that a man on horseback was journeying by the mountain, accompanied by an Indian guide; the gentleman, seeing he was tired, pitied him and said, "Mount, William."[35] Squopenik Peninsula signifies, corruptedly, a melancholy mishap: Squaw-broke-her-neck.[36]

Tall tales lie behind innocent place names. Bangerstown neighborhood mocks an extravagant story teller who, expatiating on his travels in York State, was asked if he had ever been to Bangerstown, and at once proceeded to give a full description of it.[37] Salmon

[30] *Rhode Island: A Guide to the Smallest State*, p. 108.

[31] Thomas W. Bicknell, *A History of Barrington, R.I.* (Providence, 1898), pp. 36-37.

[32] *More New Hampshire Folk Tales*, Mrs. Guy E. Speare, compiler, (Plymouth, N.H., 1936), p. 265.

[33] Lyman S. Hayes, *History of the Town of Rockingham, Vt.* (Bellows Falls, Vt., 1907), p. 108.

[34] Hazard, *The Jonny-Cake Letters*, pp. 335-336; Charles M. Skinner, *Myths and Legends of Our Own Land*, II, 35.

[35] William Little, *The History of Weare, N.H.* (Lowell, Mass., 1888), p. 4. The author states that Zephaniah Breed claimed to have heard this story from an old woman long deceased.

[36] Shebnah Rich, *Truro — Cape Cod* (Boston, c. 1883), p. 225.

[37] John Q. Bittinger, *History of Haverhill, N.H.* (Haverhill, N.H., 1888), p. 412.

Falls River perpetuates the tradition that salmon crowding up the stream to spawn wedged so tightly between the banks that Indians walked over them as on a natural bridge.[38] Wolf Bog in the Narragansett country of Rhode Island is a simple title that conceals the wildest of Tom Hazard's whoppers. A big gray wolf gave chase to an "old slab-sided, long-bodied, sharp-nosed sow." Just before she reached the edge of the bog, the wolf grabbed the end of her tail with his teeth, which caused the terror-stricken old sow to increase her speed so marvellously that old Jim Newberry, who was passing by, said the two animals could not be separately distinguished. In her heedless course the sow plunged directly through a maple tree two feet in diameter, dragging the wolf after more than half his length, when he was caught by the rebound and held secure just forward of his hips. Then Jim came up and easily dispatched him with his wood axe.[39]

Moose Brook in Hancock, New Hampshire, mutely attests the tough moose yarn of Moses Morrison. With his brother-in-law, Duncan, Moses trailed a big moose up in the bog, killed and dressed it. Brother Duncan being very hungry cooked and ate a whole quarter, and put another on his back; Moses loaded himself with the remaining two quarters. (A full-dressed moose will weigh several hundred pounds.) Pretty soon Duncan began to feel sick, and gave Moses the other quarter and his gun to tote. Then the dog tired, and Duncan placed him on top of the load. Before the end of the bog loomed, Duncan became too sick to go further, so Moses, fearing wolves might get him, told him to mount a stump and climb aboard. Then Moses steamed to terra firma carrying the dog, guns, moose, and his brother-in-law.[40]

Buck Plain, a level area in Dighton, Massachusetts, covered with a growth of scrub oaks, commemorates a heroic feat. When Samuel Briggs, an active young man, was crossing the plain one day, he came upon a large buck lying fast asleep under a rock among the scrub oaks.

[38] Gore and Speare, *New Hampshire Folk Tales*, p. 5. Cf. the same tradition in *The Jonny-Cake Letters*, pp. 346-347, where two young ladies going to a ball are obliged to dismount and cross the jammed stream of striped bass on foot.

[39] *The Jonny-Cake Letters*, pp. 384-385.

[40] William W. Hayward, *The History of Hancock, N.H.* (Lowell, Mass., 1889), pp. 73-74. Moses Morrison was a well-known fabulist; see Speare, "The Tall Story Club of Peterborough," *More New Hampshire Folk Tales*, 195-197.

Having no gun, he crept cautiously up to the sleeping deer, sprang upon its back, and seized one of its horns in each hand. The astounded buck leaped to its feet and raced headlong toward the river, more than a mile away, with Briggs holding on as best he could, dodging bushes, briers, and scrub oaks. Reaching the river the panic-stricken animal plunged with his rider into the water, but the doughty Briggs managed to drown him and secure his prize. According to the tale, Briggs was stripped of clothing by the end of the ride, save for his shirt collar and wrist bands. Mazeppa's ride becomes tame by comparison.[41]

[41] *History of Bristol County, Mass.*, D. Hamilton Hurd, compiler (Philadelphia, 1883), pp. 224-225. Some doubt exists as to whether Samuel Briggs or Matthew Gooding performed the exploit.

VI

LITERARY FOLKTALES

POPULAR TALES of the types described trickle into literary works —
novels, poems, and sketches. Such literary folktales bind together
folk and culture literature in a significant relationship; a fertile folklore
eventually infiltrates into and nourishes creative writings. And literature thus fertilized serves as a further printed source for the entry and
stimulation of traditional fictions.

New England authors and poets have utilized folk narratives in two
fashions: consciously, in an endeavor to exploit native legendry as
material for a national literature; and unwittingly, unaware that local
stories dredged up from memory and association might be folklore.
Such traditional tales again are employed in two ways: they may be
introduced in a storytelling scene within the action, much as they
originally were told; or they may form the basis for incidents of the
story proper — parts of a long, the whole of a short, work. Where the
conscious folklore user, like Whittier and Brainard, reshapes and selects
his material to secure conventional moods and effects (witness their
preference for the sentimental and slight of the comic tale), the un-
selfconscious regional writer, like Rowland Robinson or Holman Day
or George Wasson, reproduces yarns, milieu, and speechways of folk
raconteurs with verisimilitude. Contrasted with the romantic method,
this unpretentious realism presents a truer transcript of the American
scene and thus a maturer note of literary nationalism.

John G. C. Brainard

Among the well-known activities of Whittier in directing attention
to New England folk legend, not the least significant concerned his
interest in the poet Brainard. This interest was expressed in a lauda-
tory memoir Whittier wrote to one edition of his poems,[1] in his frequent

---

[1] *The Literary Remains of John G. C. Brainard, With a Sketch of His Life* (Hartford:
P. B. Goodsell, c. 1832).

references to and quotations from Brainard (e.g., in his essays on *Supernaturalism of New England*), and in his use of legendary themes previously employed by the Connecticut poet.

John Brainard (1790-1828) passed his short life wholly in Connecticut; he was born in New London, educated at New Haven, and had business ventures at Middletown and Hartford. A poet of minor stature much in the spirit of his times, plaintive, melancholy, and characterized by sensibility, he yet brightened for posterity a handful of pieces retelling local legends in a new vein. If his merit in his own day was greatly overrated (even Poe, in one of his salutatory deflations, conceded "it is not that Brainard has not written poems which may rank with those of any American, with the single exception of Longfellow"[2]), the tribute to his native quality appears justified.

Brainard has recommended himself to his countrymen as a truly *American* poet. His topics, his imagery, his illustrations are mostly of native growth. There is a raciness about them which cannot be mistaken. The reader on this side of the water is familiar with the scenes, the associations, or the incidents to which he is introduced. Most of the common-place of poetry is avoided. The mountains, lakes, rivers, trees, animals,—the characters, pursuits, pastimes and superstitions, which are touched by the pen of the bard, are American. A foreign reviewer has expressed the opinion, concerning a volume of Selections from American Poets, designed especially to convey strong impressions of the characteristics of the New World, that it conveys no such impression at all,—that, with slight exceptions, one is surprised to find it so truly English,—that its beauties and defects are so similar to the poetry of the parent land. However true this may be in general, yet in regard to Brainard, who is one of the poets from whom selections were made, it cannot be admitted. Scarcely a page is there but shows the American in the topic, the allusion, the scenery, or the characters. He is more truly American, than some English bards are English.[3]

In employing popular traditions current in his vicinity as the subject matter of poems, Brainard did strike an authentic native note.[4] To

---

[2] *The Literati: Some Honest Opinions About Autorial Merits and Demerits* (New York, 1850), p. 140.

[3] *The Poems of John G. C. Brainard* (Hartford: Edward Hopkins, 1842), pp. lvi-lvii, from a "Memoir of Brainard" by Royal Robbins. Whittier, in *Literary Remains*, p. 35, says substantially the same thing.

[4] The one volume of his poetry to be published during Brainard's lifetime, *Occasional Pieces of Poetry* (New York: E. Bliss and E. White, 1825), omits one legendary ballad, "The Money Diggers."

these versified legends he prefaced notes, explaining their background, which indicate his desire to utilize genuine folktale. From these we learn that "The Black Fox of Salmon River" transcribed an Indian legend of a ghostly fox who incited hunters to a constant pursuit they could never successfully terminate; that "The Shad Spirit" was based on a prevalent superstition that a "Yankee bogle," in the shape of a bird, led the shad from the Gulf of Mexico to the Connecticut River fishermen every season; that "The Newport Tower," around which he wove a prophecy of Indian extermination — when the last stone had fallen, the last Indian would perish — had only conjectural associations; that "The Money-Diggers" owed its inspiration to a factual report about two Vermonters who, in 1827, dug by the side of one of the wharves in New London for a box of dollars packed edgewise which an old woman had distinctly seen through her magic stone.[5] (To this note Brainard added, "For the story of the Spanish galleon that left so much bullion in and about New London, see Trumbull's history of Connecticut,[6] and for Kidd, enquire of the oldest lady you can find.") A solitary instance of the humorous tale appears in his "Sonnet to the Sea-Serpent," which closes with the admonition

> But go not to Nahant, lest men should swear,
> You are a great deal bigger than you are.[7]

Some of these tales belong to familiar types previously discussed, the tragic prophecy of Indian extinction, the hidden treasure revealed through a magic stone, the sea serpent hoax. Less usual are the bogle superstition, which however can be placed with numerous traditions in history and literature about "guiding animals" who perform services for man,[8] and the enchanted fox, although a comparable legend ap-

---

[5] *The Poems of John G. C. Brainard* (Hartford: S. Andrus & Son, 1847), pp. 124, 71, 100, 189.

[6] Benjamin Trumbull, *A Complete History of Connecticut* (New Haven, 1818), II, 298-300, describes the mysterious disappearance of a valuable cargo deposited with the collector of the port by a wrecked Spanish vessel; these facts gave rise to many treasure tales.

[7] *Poems* (1847), p. 107. See Fred A. Wilson, *Some Annals of Nahant, Mass.* (Boston, 1928), pp. 167–169, for the association of the sea serpent with Nahant.

[8] See the detailed discussion on "Guiding Animals," by Alexander H. Krappe, in the *Journal of American Folklore*, LV (October-December 1942), 228-246.

pears in an Indian tragedy from the Suncooks, in New Hampshire. Vainglorious Lewana, against the chieftain's advice, hunted with the magic bow of the lightning-riven oak, and slew all animals in the chase until a silver fox crossed his path. Baffled, the hunter trailed him to the riven oak, but his charmed bow missed the mark and struck the tree; instantly the fox vanished, and in his place stood the white wraith of Lewana's father. His tribesmen, searching, found Lewana's lifeless body beneath the oak.[9]

One well-known place legend found its way into Brainard's verse, the story of "Matchit Moodus" (in Indian, "Place of Bad Noises"). Speculations about the rumbling growls that issued irregularly from the bowels of the mountain in East Haddam had, from their first settlement in 1670, engaged the attention of white hearers, who gave some heed to its Indian explanation as the vocal anger of Hobamocko.[10] A more ingenious fancy, adopted by Brainard, linked a treasure search to the Moodus noises. Early settlers of East Haddam, terrified at the sounds, repaired to a learned and erudite man from England, a Dr. Steele, to allay their fears; to this end he set up his quarters in a blacksmith's shop, excluding all from admittance, and worked through the night at occult operations. He did vouchsafe the admission that the noises proceeded from a great carbuncle in the heart of the mountain, and would cease with its removal until another carbuncle had grown in its place. Obviously the interest of the wizard lay in possessing the treasure rather than in quieting the noises.

> Loud and yet louder was the groan
> That sounded wide and far;
> And deep and hollow was the moan,
> That rolled around the bedded stone,
> Where the workman plied his bar.

[9] "The Enchanted Bow. A Legend of the Suncook," *Granite State Magazine*, V (January-December 1908), 284-289. The author, "Laconica," in a note (p. 284) speaks of other Indian legends where a fox represents a spirit of evil.

[10] Carl F. Price, *Yankee Township* (East Hampton, Conn., c. 1941), pp 170-171. Chapter xi, "Matchitmoodus Noises" (pp. 169-181), gives a detailed, documented history of the legend, which draws largely upon Charles B. Todd, *In Olde Connecticut* (New York, c. 1906), ch. xi, "Mount Tom, A Haunted Hill" (pp. 142-152). Todd and Price quote a letter of Aug. 13, 1729, from the Rev. Mr. Hosmer, first minister of Haddam, to a Mr. Prince in Boston, that reveals early wonder about the noises. See also W. Harry Clemons, "The Legends of Machimoodus," *Connecticut Magazine*. VII (February and March, 1903), 451-458.

Then upward streamed the brilliant's light,
　　It streamed o'er crag and stone: —
Dim looked the stars, and the moon, that night;
But when morning came in her glory bright,
　　The man and the jewel were gone.[11]

But the wizard did not live long to enjoy his prize, for on his hasty return voyage to England the ship bearing both sank in a storm, and the carbuncle now rests on the ocean bed.[12] The tale here given has close resemblances to the carbuncle story associated with the White Mountains and given literary dress by Hawthorne. While Hawthorne, as usual, employed the legend only "to frame a tale with a deep moral," he credited its inspiration to a "wild" and "beautiful" Indian tradition, which he had seen in Sullivan's history of Maine.[13] He no doubt refers to the following passage.

There was an early expectation of finding a gem, of immense size and value, on this mountain: it was conjectured, and it is yet believed by some, that a carbuncle is suspended from a rock, over a pond of water there. While many in the early day of the country's settlement believed this report, each one was afraid that his neighbor should become the fortunate proprietor of the prize, by right of prior possession. To prevent this, credit was given to the tale of the natives, that the place was guarded by an evil spirit, who troubled the waters, and raised a dark mist, on the approach of human footsteps.[14]

In Maine the Nicatous noises have excited uneasy imaginations and given rise to legends.

Most intriguing of all the rumors which have drifted out of the eastern wilderness in recent years is a tale from the regions beyond Nicatous Lake, of a river gorge where horrible noises may be heard, uncanny even to the ears of men accustomed to all the ordinary sounds of the woods. The ac-

---

[11] *Poems* (1847), p. 64.

[12] See Brainard's note, *Poems* (1847), p. 62, which claims as authentic tradition all but the final disaster. This version appears in the *Connecticut Gazette*, Aug. 20, 1790 (reprinted in Todd, pp. 149-150), as a credited account some twenty or thirty years old; both the prose and Brainard's verse narrative are repeated in Hosford B. Niles, *The Old Chimney Stacks of East Haddam, Conn.* (New York, 1887), pp. 28-31.

[13] "The Great Carbuncle. A Mystery of the White Mountains," in *Tales of the White Hills and Sketches* (Boston and New York, c. 1894); cf. "Sketches from Memory" in the same book, pp. 67-68.

[14] James Sullivan, *The History of the District of Maine* (Boston, 1795), pp. 74-75. Cf. J. S. English, *Indian Legends of the White Mountains* (Boston, 1915), ch. v, "The Great Carbuncle"; the carbuncle legend of Coventry, R.I., Chapter V, *Place names*.

count recalls Indian traditions of strange monsters who haunted lonely valleys and hillsides, far from human habitations, traditions which may have had a distant origin in a tribal memory of prehistoric beasts, handed down from generation to generation, or in an effort to explain noises which were inexplicable from their daily experiences.[15]

Whittier in an extensive note to Brainard's poem lists testimony by a number of authors and travelers relative to strange mountain noises. His instances cover Brazil, Mexico, and the Lewis and Clark expedition in Missouri, and the exploding treasures include nuts encasing jewels, precious stones, and coal mines.[16]

While Brainard levied on popular tradition only for themes congenial to his tastes and times — supernatural local legends rather than comic popular tales — he early recognized the interest of such narratives for native audiences, and the part the poet could play in giving them artistic dress and some measure of permanence. The body of Brainard's poetry has been forgotten, but the half-dozen Connecticut legends he preserved still thrive in folk history. These he either originally set in print, as seems to be the case with the Black Fox of Salmon River,[17] or supplied with another link of transmission in a chain already forged, as with the Moodus Noises; for pioneering in these activities he deserves remembrance in our literary history.

John Greenleaf Whittier

> The aged crone
> Mixing the true and doubtful into one,
> Tells how the Indian scalped the helpless child
> And bore its shrieking mother to the wild.
> How drums and flags and troops were seen on high
> Wheeling and charging in the northern sky. —
> How by the thunder-blasted tree was hid
> The golden spoils of far famed Robert Kid;
> And then the chubby grand-child wants to know
> About the ghosts and witches long ago.[1]

[15] "Weird and Inexplicable Noises Haunt Region of Nicatous Lake," *Portland Herald*, June 29, 1936.   [16] *Poems* (1847), p. 65.

[17] Price, *Yankee Township*, pp. 36-42, is the latest to reprint the prose legend with Brainard's verse. Oddly Brainard, in his original note to the legend that has appealed to readers for over a century, spoke of it as limited in oral currency by its lack of interest. If this is true, then his artistic reworking gave it new life.

[1] Quoted by Whittier on the title page of *Legends of New England* (Hartford: Han-

Rarely has a creative artist finding stimulus from popular sources left clearer evidence and documentation of his indebtedness than the Quaker poet John Greenleaf Whittier (1807-1892), himself a source to large audiences who would never have known native legendary tales. This evidence takes three main forms: the slender volume of *Legends of New England*, printed when the poet was only twenty-four, that assembled pieces in prose and verse elaborating or simply recording germs of legend;[2] *Supernaturalism of New England*, a series of essays which interpolated observations and parallels among a collection of folk-history narratives;[3] and the annotated New England fictional ballads in the final corpus of his poetry.[4] Whittier's intimacy with colonial legend is further demonstrated in his superb re-creation of Puritan· New England, *Margaret Smith's Journal* (1849), which bulwarks the diary account of Puritanic bigotry with supporting superstitious myth.

Actually, then, Whittier was both an amateur folklorist and a regional poet utilizing native folklore. As collector and creative artist his common motive was "to present in an interesting form some of the popular traditions and legends of New England. The field is a new one — and I have but partially explored it. New-England is rich in traditionary lore — a thousand associations of superstitions and manly daring and romantic adventure, are connected with her green hills and her pleasant rivers."[5] As these last phrases indicate, Whittier relished local legends with sentimental implications; our interest lies in where he found and how he treated this material.

Whittier's sources for folktale. Unquestionably Whittier had contact

---

mer and Phelps, 1831), from Brainard's poem, "The Connecticut River," with many discrepancies from the text given in editions of Brainard's poetry.

[2] This volume is critically evaluated in Frances M. Pray, *A Study of Whittier's Apprenticeship as a Poet 1825-1835* (Bristol, N.H., 1930), pp. 71-89. Only two of these youthful ballads survived in the Cambridge edition of his poetry ("Metacom" and "The White Mountains"— reprinted as "Mt. Agiochook"— both fancies about the vanishing red man), while the theme of a third, a local legend of spectral Indians, links "The Spectre Warriors" to "The Garrison of Cape Ann."

[3] New York and London: Wiley and Putnam, 1847.

[4] *The Complete Poetical Works of John Greenleaf Whittier*, Cambridge edition (Boston and New York: Houghton Mifflin and Company, c. 1894), in the sections titled "Narrative and Legendary Poems" and "The Tent on the Beach."

[5] *Legends*, p. iii.

with the reservoirs of oral tradition fed by pioneer families and community historians. In his first book he reveals his familiarity with pioneer storytelling habits.

It was in very deed a fearful time. The old gossips of the neighborhood gathered together every evening around some large, old-fashioned fire-place, where, with ghastly countenances whitening in the dim fire-light, the marvellous legends which had been accumulating for more than half a century in the wild woods of the new country, were related, one after another, with hushed voices and tremulous gestures. The mysteries of the Indian worship— the frightful ceremonies of the Powwaw — the incantations and sorceries of the prophets of the wilderness, and their revolting sacrifices to the Evil Being, were all made subjects of these nocturnal gatherings.[6]

While most of the notes to the *Legends* refer to printed sources, some credits are given to oral information. "A Night Among The Wolves," a tale of pioneer danger from animals of the kind common in town histories, derives from the lips of old settlers in Vermont.[7] Similarly in a headnote to "The Unquiet Sleeper" Whittier states, regarding the strange death of a New Hampshire villager a half century previously: "There is a story prevalent among the people of the neighborhood, that, on the evening of the day on which he was found dead, strange cries are annually heard to issue from his grave! I have conversed with some who really supposed they had heard them, in the dead of the night, rising fearfully on the Autumn wind."[8] A well-known ballad that presents an unfamiliar legend about Jonathan Moulton appears to be taken directly from oral narrative. In his headnote to "The New Wife and the Old" he announces having heard the story as a child from a "venerable family visitant."[9] A genealogist of the Moulton family, discussing the saga encrusted about the illustrious General, inserts a note from Whittier that amplifies this statement.

General Moulton was a man of wealth and influence and was a noted character. Many curious stories about him have been handed down by old folk's lore. He is said to have bargained his soul to Satan for a boot full of gold and then to have cheated old Nick by removing the bottom of the boot so that it could not be filled. After his death the ghosts of himself and wife were thought to visit the old mansion by night, he thumping up and down

[6] *Legends*, pp. 80-81.
[7] *Legends*, p. 105, 111.
[8] *Legends*, p. 51
[9] *Supernaturalism*, p. 31, *Poetical Works*, p. 21.

stairs with his heavy gold headed cane and his wife moving about with
rustling silk gown. The ghosts were formally exorcised and "laid" with
impressive ceremonies and afterwards walked no more. Whittier's poem
"The New Wife and the Old," is founded upon one of these traditional
tales.*

* The following letter from Mr. Whittier refers to the poem:

Oakland, Danvers, Mass., May 14, 1888.

"A. F. Moulton, Esq. I only heard the tradition of General Moulton's first and second
wives but did not know their names. There are many stories relating to the General.
It was said that he haunted the old mansion and used to tramp up and down stairs in his
military boots. Parson Milton of Newbury was sent for to 'lay' him.

Thine truly,
JOHN G. WHITTIER."[10]

In the *Supernaturalism* essays Whittier related many anecdotal legends, ranging over haunted inns and mills, spectral warnings of death,
buried treasure and fortune telling, witches and Satan, "Pumoolah" the
Indian spirit of Katahdin and Passaconaway the Penacook conjuror;
some of these seem to be lifted directly from oral currency. One ghost-
prank tale Whittier tells in the best manner of the nineteenth-century
yarnspinners. After Aunt Morse died and left a handsome little property with no will for its disposal, Squire S., who was believed to have the
document, one day saw before him a familiar figure. Puffing vehemently
at a stubby tobacco pipe, the crooked little old woman in the oil-nut
colored woollen frock with the sharp pinched face flatly refused to
return to the burying ground until the Squire promised to do justice
to her will. Then, after requesting the trembling Squire to relight her
pipe, she pulled her blanket over her head and hobbled off. Some scof-
fers averred that a living heir and not a bloodless ghost had intimidated
the malfeasant.[11]

A proof that the legendary ballads frequently had inception in living
folklore is seen in their stirring active currents of folktale. Twenty-five
years after writing "The New Wife and the Old," Whittier received a
letter from a then resident in the Moulton house adding new ghost
tales about the General and his wife.[12] Two years after he had written

[10] *Some Descendants of John Moulton and William Moulton, of Hampton, N.H.,
1592-1892*, Augustus F. Moulton, compiler (n.p., n.d.), p. 18.
[11] *Supernaturalism*, pp. 13-15.
[12] *Poetical Works*, p. 517. The Moulton House ghost stories are revived, and Whittier's ballad reprinted, in Marion Lowndes, *Ghosts That Still Walk* (New York, c. 1941),
pp. 99-107.

"The Palatine" from a description of the fireship given him by Joseph P. Hazard of Newport, a ninety-two-year-old correspondent related a very similar vision of the spectral vessel —"a full-rigged ship, with her sails all set and all ablaze."[13] Whittier's ballad thus grew from one and evoked a second oral tradition.

If Whittier was acquainted with native traditional story in its oral form, most of his topics came from printed texts. Familiar works, the bibles of colonial literature, supplied him with themes for the legendary tales and ballads. From the *Magnalia*, Cotton Mather's treasury of colonial antiquities, he garnered the Haunted House of Newbury and the spectral Indian warriors at Gloucester; [14] Upham's study of witch-craft furnished information about Moll Pitcher;[15] he plucked from Samuel Peters' dubious history of Connecticut the exorcising of an Indian powwaw by an Episcopal clergyman at Stratford;[16] Josselyn's Indian tradition concerning spirit-dwellers of the White Mountains caught his eye;[17] from Brainard he borrowed the ghostly fox of Salmon River and the Moodus Noises.[18] Even in using printed sources, how-ever, Whittier showed appreciation of underlying folktale movement; he realizes that the report to Cotton Mather about the two-headed snake of Newbury crystallized a floating tall tale.

[13] *Poetical Works*, p. 523, and *History of Newport County, R.I.*, Richard M. Bayles, ed. (New York, 1888), p. 847; Samuel T. Pickard, *Life and Letters of John Greenleaf Whittier* (Boston and New York, 1894), II, 527-528. For a list of references to other beholders of the flaming ghost ship see Albert Matthews, "The Word Palatine in Amer-ica," *Publications of the Colonial Society of Massachusetts*, VIII (Boston, 1906), 220, n. 2.

[14] The sources are *Magnalia Christi Americana*, bk. 6, ch. vii, third example (Hartford ed., 1855, II, 450-452); bk. 7, art. 18 (II, 620-623). The compositions are "The Haunted House," *Legends*, pp. 55-74; "The Spectre Warriors," *Legends*, pp. 76-78.

[15] Source: Charles W. Upham, *Lectures on Witchcraft* (Boston 1832), pp. 229-230, partially quoted in the tail note to the composition *Moll Pitcher, A Poem* (Boston: Carter and Hendee, 1832). In the Cambridge edition of the poems this survives in truncated form as "Extract from 'A New England Legend'."

[16] Source: Samuel A. Peters, *A General History of Connecticut* (New-Haven, 1829), pp. 167-168. Composition: "The Powwaw," *Legends*, pp. 79-85.

[17] Whittier in his head note to "The White Mountains" (*Legends*, p. 112) ascribes this to *New-England's Rarities*, but while that work does mention the White Moun-tains (Boston, 1865, p. 36), the tradition is given in the same author's *Account of Two Voyages to New-England* (Boston, 1865, p. 105).

[18] "The Black Fox," *Legends*, pp. 116-124, and "The Human Sacrifice," *Legends*, pp. 93-97, credit Brainard's poems on the same themes.

Far and wide the tale was told,
Like a snowball growing while it rolled.

. . . .

Stories, like dragons, are hard to kill.
If a snake does not, the tale runs still.[19]

Amphisbaena, like the sea serpent, did keep wriggling through popular story.

Newbury. A Serpent was kill'd here this Week, about two foot long, with two perfect Heads, one at each end; in each Head two Eyes and a Mouth, and in each Mouth a forked Sting, both which he thrust out at the same time with equal fierceness. The manner of his defense was, raising up his Heads about two Inches from the ground, he always kept one directed towards his Adversary, thrusting out both his Stings at once; the Lad that kill'd him affirm'd that when running, if his Motion was obstructed one way, he would run directly the contrary way and never turn his Body. One Head was something bigger than the other, and from the biggest to the other his body was somewhat Taperwise, but in a far less proportion than in common Snakes. I the Subscriber with several others saw said Serpent just after he was kill'd, and can testify to all above written, except his Motions described by the Lad, who only saw him alive.

Nath. Coffin

P.S. The colour of the said snake was not much differing from that of many common streaked Snakes, but neither of it's Heads any ways like them.[20]

In general such supernatural stories, place legends, and pioneer traditions more or less in the air as Whittier converted to literature could easily be located by the sympathetic observer; his contribution lies not in adding to knowledge of native folktale but in enlarging the circle of those who possessed such knowledge. His rewritten legends supplanted their sources and acquired authority of their own in local folk history.[21]

[19] *Poetical Works*, p. 62. Like Brainard's "Sonnet to the Sea-Serpent," this ballad represents a unique excursion into popular humor. Whittier no doubt saw the letter of Rev. Christopher Toppan to Cotton Mather, describing the marvel, as printed in Joshua Coffin, *A Sketch of The History of Newbury, Newburyport, and West Newbury* (Boston, 1845), p. 195. For notes on this letter see George L. Kittredge, "Cotton Mather's Scientific Communications to the Royal Society," *Proceedings of the American Antiquarian Society*, n.s., XXVI (1916), 54; Clifford K. Shipton, *Sibley's Harvard Graduates*, IV, 116.

[20] *New-England Courant*, June 24-July 1, 1723.

[21] Essex County, Massachusetts, and the coast region of New Hampshire are chiefly indebted to Whittier for literary legends, although he drew meagerly upon the other New

Jonathan Draws the Long Bow

Whittier's literary treatment of folktale. In making literature of legend Whittier was not motivated by an original appreciation of native folktale — he missed the richest part of it — but rather by a wish to emulate the literary nationalism of English and Scotch writers. In the introduction to *Supernaturalism of New England*, he acknowledged that he had collected "the present superstitions and still current traditions of New England, in the hope that . . . it may hereafter furnish materials for the essayist and poet, who shall one day do for our native land what Scott and Hogg and Burns and Wilson have done for theirs."[22] Whittier himself performed this task, choosing for his form the literary ballad, modeled roughly on the Scotch and English traditional ballads, which he had praised Brainard for using;[23] functionally the popular ballad was designed to tell a bare story, tragic, sentimental, or humorous, usually tinged with pathos.[24] Whittier's verse narratives eminently fitted this description, narratives of unhappy death and frustrated or triumphant love linked to the supernatural. Ghost ships particularly attracted American romanticism; three New England states yielded Whittier "The Spectre Ship,"[25] "The Palatine," and "The Dead Ship of Harpswell," while a fourth contributed the phantom ship of New Haven in which Bryant, Irving, and Longfellow all showed interest.[26] Witches cursed and ranted in several of Whittier's folk poems: "Moll Pitcher" concocts a lovers' near-tragedy about the celebrated sorceress of Lynn; "The Wreck of Rivermouth" issues from the

England states. See William S. Kennedy, "In Whittier's Land," *New England Magazine*, n.s., VII (November 1892), 275; and David L. Maulsby, "Whittier's New Hampshire," *ibid.*, n.s., XXII (August 1900), 646-647.

[22] *Supernaturalism*, p. vii.

[23] "There is much of the true spirit of the old English Ballads in the Black Fox, Matchit Moodus, the Shad Spirit, and other poems of this description." *"The Literary Remains of John G. C. Brainard* (Hartford, c. 1832), p. 34.

[24] Metrically as well as thematically Whittier followed the genuine ballad tradition. See Gay W. Allen, *American Prosody* (New York, c. 1935), p. 139.

[25] Whittier erroneously ascribes this early effort (*Legends*, pp. 86-92) to the *Magnalia*, following the facetious credit given in an article, "The Spectre Ship of Salem," signed "Nantucket," in *Blackwood's Magazine*, XXVII (March 1830), 462-465, reprinted in the *Salem Gazette*, Apr. 20, 1830; Whittier's poem initially appeared in the *Essex Gazette*, May 1, 1830; and was reprinted in Freeman Hunt, *American Anecdotes, Original and Select* (Boston, 1830), II, 40-44.

[26] Samuel A. Drake, *A Book of New England Legends and Folk Lore in Prose and Poetry* (Boston, 1884), p. 420.

curse of Goody Cole, the notorious Hampton witch, and "The Change-ling" traces the substitution of Goody Cole's imp for Anna Dalton's handsome baby;[27] "Mabel Martin: A Harvest Idyl" spins out a lovers' tale wherein Esek Harden defies the prejudice that excommunicates the daughter of Goody Martin (an old woman of Amesbury, Massa-chusetts, actually executed for witchcraft); "The Witch of Wenham," based on a tradition that a witch had escaped from her jail in Amesbury through the aid of the Evil One, allowed fair young Ann Putnam, labeled a witch, a romantic rather than supernatural egress from the prison by the assistance of her lover. Indian tragedies appealed to Whittier; the long poem, "The Bridal of Penacook," and several pieces in the *Legends* set forth the death of a lover or the prophecy of tribal extinction.

Both in matter and in form, however, Whittier's legendary ballads reveal a sharp individual twist. Having given the outline of the legend in his notes, the poet felt no obligation to project it exactly. Rather, as in several of the witch plots above, he used motives from the tradition as a frame about which to construct a fancy. Thus a juvenile story in the *Legends*, "The Haunted House," originates with the *Magnalia* account of infernal doings in the Newbury house, but the conventional plot includes none of the antics that distinguished Mather's relations: a witch haunts the dwelling of the girl her son loves; he stands guard and puts her to flight in a midnight fracas that causes him a severe knife wound, but ends in her death. Similarly in "The Human Sacrifice," he strays considerably from Brainard's story of "Matchit Moodus" and uses the mountain's rumble as a device to save a white girl about to be sacrificed by Indians; delivered at the opportune moment, it frightens into flight the red men who believe the sound to be the angry voice of the

[27] Goody Cole is well known in folk history. "History tells us among her strange doings she was accused of bewitching a promising infant of Goody Marston, assuming before its death the likeness of an ape. Among the mourners at its funeral, following close behind was seen 'a little old woman dressed in a blue cloak and petticoat,' who bore a strong resemblance to old Goody Cole, notwithstanding she was confined in Ipswich jail, miles distant." Rebecca I. Davis, *Gleanings from Merrimac Valley: Sheaf Number Two* (Haverhill, 1886), p. 65. Other witcheries are described on pp. 65-66. Whittier brings these tales into "Margaret Smith's Journal" (*The Prose Works of John Greenleaf Whittier*, Boston and New York: Houghton Mifflin and Company, c. 1892), I, 84–89.

Great Spirit. "The Bridal of Penacook" expands a comic episode, recorded in Thomas Morton's *New-English Canaan*, into a pathetic fiction. Weetamoe, daughter of the famed Passaconaway, married a Saugus chief and never returned to visit her father because neither sachem felt it his duty to provide the escort. In the situation finally reported by Morton, the offended dignitaries had reached an impasse wherein each preserved his dignity at the expense of the poor girl.

> So much these two Sachems stood upon tearmes of reputation with each other, the other would not send for her, least it should be any diminishing of honor on his part that should seeme to comply, that the Lady (when I came out of the Country [1630]) remained still with her father; which is a thinge worth the noting, that Salvage people should seeke to maintaine their reputation so much as they doe.[28]

From this predicament Whittier lifted his heroine by implanting in her breast the resolve to undertake the return voyage unescorted up the ice-laden Merrimac.

> On that strong turbid water, a small boat
> Guided by one weak hand was seen to float;
> Evil the fate which loosed it from the shore,
> Too early voyager with too frail an oar!
> . . . .
> Down the white rapids like a sear leaf whirled,
> On the sharp rocks and piled-up ices hurled,
> Empty and broken, circled the canoe
> In the vexed pool below — but where was Weetamoo?[29]

Besides altering legends with invention, Whittier showed tendencies to the subjective moral commentary that places Hawthorne's art beyond the range of folkloristic literature. "The Garrison of Cape Ann" followed closely

> A wild and wondrous story, by the younger Mather penned,
> In that quaint *Magnalia Christi*, with all strange and
>   marvellous things,
> Heaped up huge and undigested . . .[30]

[28] Publications of the Prince Society edition, Charles F. Adams, ed. (Boston, 1883), p. 157. Adams regards the story as "not only highly inconsistent with what we know of Indian life and habits, but also at variance with facts and dates" (p. 155n.).

[29] *Poetical Works*, pp. 32-33.

[30] *Poetical Works*, p. 53. Cf. p. 208, note 14.

that recounted a weird experience of colonial soldiers with phantom
Indians impervious to leaden or even silver bullets. But the poet ends
the story by reading into it symbols and a moral; these phantoms are
none other than specters of the mind, springing from vanities of the
spirit, which must be combated with the pure strength of prayer and
faith. In versifying the "Palatine" marvel of the phantom fireship,
he intrudes into the straightforward narration with these personal
thoughts.

> Is there, then, no death for a word once spoken?
> Was never a deed but left its token
> Written on tables never broken?
>
> Do the elements subtle reflections give?
> Do pictures of all the ages live
> On Nature's infinitive negative,
>
> Which, half in sport, in malice half,
> She shows at times, with shudder or laugh,
> Phantom and shadow in photograph?[31]

In the final stanza the poet self-consciously refers to this "sidelong
moral squint" and admits that "here is a bit / Of unrhymed story, with
a hint / Of the old preaching mood in it"; such subjective intrusions
to point moral lessons — the wrecking of the "Palatine" was a criminal
deed done in secret, the ghostly reënactment its public confessional —
sharply distinguish the psychology of the literary from the popular ballad. The same note of covert sin revealed through supernatural evidence
sounds in "The New Wife and the Old," where the meek dead wife
haunts the young bride of the sinner; the fatal price of vanity provides
the moral for "The Bridal of Penacook"; in "The Black Fox," Whittier
elaborates on Brainard to interpret the deathless fox as a mighty chief
accursed by Hobomoko and doomed to wander ever for some un-
spoken crime.

While Whittier thus openly tacked on his moral, and never made it
the pulse of his tale as did Hawthorne, his sentiments at times closely
echo those of the writer who lived in Salem, Concord, and Lenox. His
symbolic interpretation of Satan could easily have been written by

[31] *Poetical Works*, p. 259.

Hawthorne: "And what is the fiend himself, but the evil which all men see in others, and feel in themselves — a monstrous embodiment of the terrible idea of sin?"[32] Hawthorne employed popular traditions merely as canvas on which to paint his sensitive abstractions;[33] Whittier consciously set out to transmit traditional story, but could not keep it proof against the aesthetic and ethical revisions that divide literary from folk art.

Daniel P. Thompson

In the stilted language and Scott-Cooper techniques of the Vermont novelist, Daniel Pierce Thompson (1795-1868), a strange mixture unites old "romantic" literary manners and an upthrust of popular folk comedy. In his regional fiction, Thompson leaned heavily on Vermont social and historical settings, and incidentally incorporated local folktales into his historical romances.

Local legends. In two tales Thompson elaborated plots about simple buried treasure motives. Both attribute their factual inspiration to a counterfeit ring established by the notorious Stephen Burroughs, a rascal infamous throughout northern New England whose activities had generated countless stories, joined with a tenacious treasure tale of silver dollars buried by adventurers from Mexico in Camel's Hump, a conspicuous peak in the Green Mountains. In "The Counterfeiter," a treasure legend told by his son and a treasure dream related by a lame stranger stimulate farmer Bidwell to digging; his daughter Kate learns that the coins discovered through the stranger's assistance have been salted to simulate age.[1] An organized company sets out after a cache in "May Martin, or The Money Diggers," guided by a professional treasure finder who possesses a magic stone.[2] (In a note Thompson states that a woman in central Vermont had some years previously attracted wide attention through the use of such a stone.) The counter-

---

[32] *Supernaturalism*, p. 71; see also p. 70, for transcendental comments on supernaturalism.

[33] In *Legends of New England* (1877), *Tales of the White Hills* (1877), and *Legends of The Province House* (1877).

---

[1] In *Centeola; and other Tales* (New York: Carleton, 1864), pp. 252–312.

[2] In *May Martin, and other Tales of the Green Mountains* (Boston: Benj. B. Mussey & Co., 1852), pp. 7-160.

feiter describes it as "the same thin, oval, yellow, speckled kind of stone I used when I discovered the pot of money on Cape Cod that they supposed Kidd buried there." While holding out high promise for finding the treasure, he admonishes "we may have to fight dead men and devils before we get fairly hold of it." And a spurious ghost effectively puts to rout the seekers on one occasion. Thompson here transmutted a Green Mountain treasure legend, equipped with familiar appurtenances, into a literary tale relying in the main on the suspense and excitement of the quest.[3]

Popular tales. Thompson's attention to folkstory and folk types, early for his time and medium, is tentative and limited, but none the less authentic. A chapter in one novel, *Locke Amsden, or The Schoolmaster,* (1847), is pure folktale. Locke goes to a district schoolhouse to apply for a vacant teachership, and finds a court trial in progress. The plaintiff, a grocer named Bill Bunker, asserts he sold a cheese to a customer, the defendant, who vigorously denies ordering or receiving any cheese. Bunker offers for proof his personal books which, because he was illiterate, required a special system; every item sold had a picture of it alongside a likeness of the customer. Sure enough a circle indicating a cheese appeared opposite the drawing of the defendant. Finally the customer explains that, because of Bunker's hot accusations, he had not previously cleared up the matter; the fact was he had ordered a grindstone, and the grocer had simply forgotten to draw the hole. This tale is widespread in American folklore; yarners have told it of New Hampshire village characters, in Maine logging camps, in the Berkshire Hills, in the California gold rush country, and it forms one of the key stories in the Paul Bunyan cycle.[4]

[3] The *Vermont Historical Gazetteer*, Abby M. Hemenway, ed. (Burlington, Vt., 1867), I, 784-785, gives the legend substantially as Thompson summarizes it in his introduction to the revised edition of *May Martin.* Cf. "Cave Near Bristol Still Conceals Buried Treasure," *Burlington Free Press and Times*, May 31, 1938.

[4] *Sun-Up*, March 1932, p. 29; *Berkshire Hills*, vol. II (May 1, 1902); *More New Hampshire Folk Tales*, Mrs. Guy E. Speare, compiler (Plymouth, N.H., 1936), pp. 31-32; G. Ezra Dane, *Ghost Town* (New York, 1941), pp. 21-23; many Paul Bunyan publications. The illiterate shopkeeper and the customer are always actually known and named characters. Thompson's chapter is bodily lifted out of the novel and reprinted in the *Green Mountain Gem*, VI (1848), 281-283, as "Bill Bunker's Blunder," an interesting recognition of its essential independence.

Thompson's novel of woodland scenes and characters, *Gaut Gurley*, contains rich nuggets of folk humor. A leading character, Comical Codman, is a Vermont rendition of the frontier roarer; he capers, clowns, tells stories, and even crows like his prototype:

> Comical Codman on his distant perch straightened up, and triumphantly clapping his sides like the boastful bird whose crowing he could so wonderfully imitate, raised his shrill, loud, and long-drawn *kuk-kuk-ke-o-ho* in a volume of sound that thrilled through the forest and sent its repeating echoes from hill to hill along the distant borders of the lake.[5]

He tells tall tales: the trout in the lake are so thick a hook and line could not be drawn through it without getting into some of their mouths; he is superstitious as well as a braggadocio, and narrates a curious devil story, wherein a farmer harrassed with rocky land read a Black Art book which procured for him devils to clear his soil of stones; but they shied at pulling stumps.[6]

Other characters in *Gaut Gurley* spin backwoods yarns. One Phillips, designated the "Old Hunter," tells how he once caught a black duck and a seven pound nine ounce trout by hand; the fish had fastened onto the leg of the bird so fiercely that it could not rise from the water, and Phillips simply paddled within reach and pulled both aboard.[7] One camping-out scene in the novel recreates a storytelling session with full narrative texts, following the proposal that "you professional hunters...each give us a story of one of your most remarkable adventures in the woods."[8] While the renditions suffer from the inability of Thompson to handle salty speech, the stories in their pristine setting satisfactorily mirror woodsmen's yarning habits. Codman, the "Trapper," described a beaver trial he had witnessed from a lake shore, where two offenders were tried by the beaver colony before a judge and,

[5] *Gaut Gurley; or, The Trappers of Umbagog* (Boston: John P. Jewett & Co., 1857), p. 120.

[6] *Gaut Gurley*, p. 109.

[7] *Gaut Gurley*, p. 163.

[8] *Gaut Gurley*, p. 179. Thompson's biographer comments on this scene, "It is rather unfortunate that so much that is real in the book should be sacrificed for melodramatic effect," and describes it as a grave flaw in treatment, because the stories are "highly colored"! This observation is typical of literary historians totally ignorant of the nature of the folktale; actually, of course, the scene is a fine piece of realism. (John E. Flitcroft, *The Novelist of Vermont*, Cambridge: Harvard University Press, 1929, p. 151.)

largely through the influence of one particularly spiteful beaver, sentenced to death and executed with slaps from the other beavers' tails. Codman took pleasure in shooting the spiteful one. Phillips, the "Old Hunter," he of the fish story, now produced a detailed account of a fierce bear and panther fight, which terminated in a fantastic manner; the fleeing bear swam across a stream to an islet, dug a hole in the sand, scrambled into it, turned over on his back, and heaped sand around his sides. The pursuing panther jumped on the prostrate bear, who calmly slashed his opponent's exposed under flanks to ribbons. For his story the "Amateur Woodsman," Carvil, contributed a moose hunt in which he had fired consecutively at two moose who never stirred from their positions; had they mistaken his gunshots for thunder? were they paralyzed with fear?[9] A factual source for this last character and his yarn is credited by a Vermont local historian to Judge Isaac Parker, a hunter and scholar resident in the Lake Memphremagog region.

He was a fertile story teller, especially in hunting tales. One I will mention here. Once when his hunting camp stood near a deer lick, where that game was plentiful, he spied a fine buck. He grabbed his gun and proceeded to load or charge it while on his way to intercept the stag. He came up with his quarry and fired. The deer leaped high in the air and fell dead. He carried him to camp, dressed it, but was unable to discover any wound, or place where the bullet had penetrated, which puzzled him very much. But when about to retire that night he put his hand in his vest pocket and found the identical bullet he had hastily placed there preparatory to charging his gun; in his haste he had evidently neglected to put it in the gun. Here was the full explanation of the absence of a wound. His solution of the mystery was that the animal had died from fright. A queer case surely and very exceptional.

Judge Parker was the hero character in "Grant Gurley,"*(sic)* one of Thompson's later and best novels. He figured there under the pseudonym of "Carvil the Hunter." The facts upon which the story was founded (being a history of his student life) having been given the author by Judge Parker.[10]

Patches of genuine popular storylore intersperse the novels and tales Thompson wrote about Vermont pioneer life. His sympathetic use of native folktale foreshadowed more effective literary transcriptions by

[9] *Gaut Gurley*, pp. 180-199.
[10] William B. Bullock, *Beautiful Waters* (Newport, Vt., 1926), p. 213.

craftsmen whose style and form aided instead of hindered similar sympathies.

Harriet Beecher Stowe

Alone among the New England female writers producing local color fiction, Harriet Beecher Stowe (1811-1896) touched the wellsprings of native folklore. In two novels embodying much local incident about Natick, Massachusetts, and Orr's Island, Maine, Mrs. Stowe introduced twin storytellers with the familiar traits of the village Munchausen; and in a later book, realizing an affinity between the teller of folktales and the writer of literary tales, she merged their two techniques, projected herself within the psyche of Sam Lawson, and recounted his idle legends in deliberate fashion.[1]

Storytelling. Mrs. Stowe knew the eerie tales and the manner of their relation directly from her husband, a fecund yarner, and from the mores of "Oldtown" life.[2] Her description of pioneer narrative art duplicates other such accounts by local historians.

Life in New England, in those days, had not the thousand stimulants to the love of excitement which are to be found in the throng and rush of modern society, and there was a great deal more of story-telling and romancing in real life than exists now. . . . Hence, in those days, chimney-corner story-telling became an art and an accomplishment. Society then was full of traditions and narratives which had all the uncertain glow and shifting mystery of the firelit hearth upon them. . . . Then the aged told their stories to the young,— tales of early life; tales of war and adventure, of forest-days, of Indian captivities and escapes, of bears and wild-cats and panthers, of rattlesnakes, of witches and wizards, and strange and wonderful dreams and appearances and providences.[3]

Accompanying the storytelling impulse and opportunity come the master narrators. Sam Lawson, village jack-of-all-trades, and Captain Kittredge, retired mariner, spin gossipy legends of the community and windies of far places with a proficiency that entrances, without perhaps convincing, their neighbors. Comment had it that the old sea captain, if no one else, believed the long bows he drew so fluently.

---

[1] *The Pearl of Orr's Island* (1862), *Oldtown Folks* (1869), *Sam Lawson's Oldtown Fireside Stories* (1872).

[2] Forrest Wilson, *Crusader in Crinoline* (Philadelphia, c. 1941), p. 164.

[3] *Oldtown Folks* (Boston: James R. Osgood & Co., 1877), p. 166; *Oldtown Fireside Stories* (Boston: James R. Osgood & Co., 1872), pp. 2-3.

The Captain himself was a welcome guest at all the firesides round, being a chatty body, and disposed to make the most of his foreign experiences, in which he took the usual advantages of a traveler. In fact, it was said, whether slanderously or not, that the Captain's yarns were spun to order; and, as, when pressed to relate his foreign adventures, he always responded with, "What would you like to hear?" it was thought that he fabricated his article to suit his market. In short, there was no species of experience, finny, fishy, or aquatic,— no legend of strange and unaccountable incident of fire or flood,— no romance of foreign scenery and productions, to which his tongue was not competent, when he had once seated himself in a double bow-knot at a neighbor's evening fireside.[4]

Among the church-going folk who consumed the Captain's productions, doubts arose as to the integrity of a character that would so dally with the truth — particularly in the mind of his wife, who best could observe the "variations and discrepancies of text which showed their mythical characters."[5] Moralists viewing the problem — perhaps the author herself — concluded that the Captain, known for honesty in his contractual dealings with fellow men, might be entitled to poetic license in his yarnings, which indeed bordered on the creative arts. For their fictional elements rendered them into "marketable fireside commodities" whose entertainment value surely atoned for any venial sins in the composition.

In the pages of Mrs. Stowe evidence for literary as well as oral transmission of folktales presents itself. One scene depicts a direct conjunction of both methods.

... my grandmother produced her well-worn copy [of the Magnalia]; and, to say the truth, we were never tired of hearing what was in it. What legends, wonderful and stirring, of the solemn old forest life,— of fights with the Indians, and thrilling adventures, and captivities, and distresses,— or encounters with panthers and serpents, and other wild beasts, which made our very hair stand on end! Then there were the weird witch-stories, so wonderfully attested. ... Of all these fascinating legends my grandmother was a willing communicator, and had, to match them, numbers of corresponding ones from her own personal observation and experience; and sometimes Sam Lawson would chime in with long-winded legends, which, being told by flickering firelight, with the wind rumbling and tumbling down the great chimney, or shrieking and yelling and piping around every

---

[4] *The Pearl of Orr's Island* (Boston and New York: Houghton Mifflin Co., c. 1890), p. 28.

[5] *The Pearl of Orr's Island*, p. 29; cf. p. 65.

corner of the house, like an army of fiends trying with tooth and claw to get in upon us, had power to send cold chills down our backs in the most charming manner.[6]

So potent an agency was the *Magnalia* for the sowing of legend that skepticism of its wonders amounted to heresy: "Why, Aunt Lois don't even believe the stories in Cotton Mather's 'Magnalia'."[7]

Stories. References to local legends by Oldtown or Orr's Island characters implement the visual scenes of storytelling. Miss Ruey's aunt tells of a haunted cradle, found after a dreadful storm during which a baby was heard to cry; ever after, when a gale blew, the cradle rocked, and a "spirit-seeing" visitor saw a white-faced woman rocking it; Aunt Lois promptly split it for kindling, and heard a baby scream.[8] People on Orr's Island had heard that a Harpswell baby can swim from birth, and will dent a rock with its head. The testing of this belief on an Indian papoose by drunken sailors initiated a war and a curse.[9] Oldtown folk know the legend anent the romance of Sir Harry Frankland and barmaid Agnes Surridge, and Sam Lawson testifies to rumor that the ghost of Sir Harry still walks in his red cloak.[10] Still other specters of the unhappy dead are reported by village folk.[11]

Most Oldtown and Orr's Island fictions stem from the fertile tongues of Captain Kittredge and Sam Lawson. The Captain awes the children and alarms the elders with various wonderful tales: of Old Polly Twitchell from "Mure P'int" who brewed storms and went to sea in a sieve; of a bespangled merman who asked the Captain to move the anchor dropped before his door, as it prevented his mer-family from going to meeting; of prodigious catches at the Grand Banks, when he stood up to his knees in fish after half an hour's fishing; of critters, trees, plants, and pearls on the bottom of the sea; of polar bears on icebergs, so hungry water runs from their chops in a perfect stream.[12]

---

[6] *Oldtown Folks*, p. 285.

[7] *Oldtown Fireside Stories*, p. 139; Cf. p. 23: "What would become of all the accounts in Dr. Cotton Mather's 'Magnilly' if folks were like you?"

[8] *The Pearl of Orr's Island*, pp. 43-44.

[9] See Chapter V, in *Indian tragedies*, the legend of Squando's curse on the Saco River.

[10] *Oldtown Folks*, pp. 81-82; see Samuel Roads, *The History and Traditions of Marblehead* (Boston, 1880), pp. 52-57; "Agnes," in *The Complete Poetical Works of Oliver Wendell Holmes* (Boston and New York, n.d.), pp. 72-79.

[11] *Oldtown Folks*, pp. 81, 140.

[12] *The Pearl of Orr's Island*, pp. 140, 117-118, 127, 60-61, 128.

But the Captain's prize yarn topped even these adventures. One of the children had asked if the wind blew at the Banks.

"Why, yes, my little girl, that it does, sometimes; but then there ain't the least danger. I've stood it out in gales that was tight enough, I'm sure. 'Member once I turned in 'tween twelve and one, and hadn't more'n got asleep, afore I came *clump* out of my berth, and found everything upside down. And 'stead of goin' upstairs to get on deck, I had to go right down. Fact was, that 'ere vessel jist turned clean over in the water, and come right side up like a duck."[13]

Handy man Sam Lawson likewise spun entertaining yarns, seemingly weighted with more tradition and less invention. In his introductory appearance to readers, Sam recounts a comic courtship, a ghost tale of a weeping woman in white, and a typical treasure chase where Dench dives for a great carbuncle which slips from his grasp when Jake yells prematurely, "There, you got it!"[14] In a later presentation Sam dominates the scene in a volume contrived around his local narratives delivered to a youthful audience. These conform in matter to conventional village traditions, although the manner of their telling is embroidered and dramatized beyond the bald outlines of antiquarian history. Here are ghostly visitants, Captain Kidd's cache, a hoax involving the Devil, an absent-minded local character, such as the Natick town historian might have recorded.[15] In *Oldtown Fireside Stories*, Mrs. Stowe makes fictional capital of local folklore that crept incidentally into her earlier books.

Rowland E. Robinson

While popular story from the Green Mountain country filtered into Thompson's stilted and conventionalized fiction in relatively slight amount, in the work of another Vermont author it found extensive and memorable recording. In a casual, unhurried, plotless, but carefully wrought series of vignettes portraying the folkways of a Vermont pioneer community, Rowland E. Robinson (1833-1900) harmonized form and material with results unequaled, in this genre, anywhere else in

[13] *The Pearl of Orr's Island*, p. 127.
[14] *Oldtown Folks*, pp. 176-177, 190, 191-193.
[15] The Natick town histories, being for the most part too early and too churchly, do not contain any of these tales.

American literature. His sketches capture the atmosphere of the raising and the paring bee, the turkey shoot, the militia training, the town meeting, the traveling circus, the sugaring party, the camping trip; his monologue and dialogue catch rhythms and accents of homespun talk preeminently concerned with farming, hunting, trapping, and fishing. Authors of the forewords and prefaces to the centennial edition of Robinson's works,[1] according him a tardy due, have pointed out his skilful reproduction of Yankee and Canuck speech, his richly humorous, unsentimental character portraits, his thorough knowledge of early Vermont society, his limning of fields and woods with the fidelity and sharpened sense of sound and color that perhaps only a blind man possesses. But none of these critical tributes has recognized, except in a general way, a value in Robinson's writings made possible by these virtues, his artistic and authentic presentation of native folktale.

The very title of the book that introduced Danvis and its characters to literature indicated a storytellers' rendezvous. "Uncle Lisha's Shop" served as an after-supper meeting place for a convivial group in Danvis (probably Vergennes in the Green Mountains), notably Uncle Lisha himself, the shoemaker autocrat of the assembly, Antoine Bissette, a Canadian wag who equally murdered English and the truth, and Sam Lovel, something of a Vermont Natty Bumppo. For these and kindred wits the shop served as

a sort of sportsmen's exchange, where, as one of the fraternity expressed it, the hunters and fishermen of the widely scattered neighborhood met of evenings and dull out-door days "to swap lies." Almost every one had a story to tell, but a few only listened and laughed, grunted, or commented as the tale told was good, bad or of doubtful authenticity.[2]

In a sequel volume, *Danvis Folks*, further such storytelling sessions occur in the shop, and in later books about camping and outing trips they originate around the campfire. These yarn-swapping scenes are presented with illuminating details that give complete little histories of each: the congregation of the group; the preliminary discussion on

[1] Published by the Tuttle Company, Rutland, Vermont, 1933-1934, in seven volumes. The first book about Danvis people (*Uncle Lisha's Shop: Life in a Corner of Yankee-land*) initially appeared in 1887.

[2] *Uncle Lisha's Shop and A Danvis Pioneer* (Rutland, Vt.: Charles E. Tuttle Co., c. 1933), p. 137.

some topic of immediate interest, a fox hunt or a hooting owl, that leads
easily into a story which leads into another suggested by the subject or
some related aspect, and that into yet another; the actual delivery of
the tales, which projects with almost phonographic exactitude the word
sounds and word coinages of their rural narrators; the interjected reactions and post-comments from the attentive audience. But besides
drawing a faithful picture of old settlers' storyspinning, Robinson in
giving many full narratives contributes original texts to the known
store of American folktale.

Supernatural stories. Superstition and supernaturalism, while less
evident than trickster and exaggerated humor, engendered stories told
by Uncle Lisha and his friends. Thus a fatalistic morality of retributive
justice, invisibly manipulated, pointed some backwoods fictions. In his
tale, "The Hard Experience of Mr. Abijah Davis," Uncle Lisha listed
calamities that befell crabbed Bije after he gave a boy a wild green turnip on the pretense that it was a sweet ground apple. Bije laughed at
the boy spitting and sputtering as if his mouth was full of bumble
bees, but from that day things went badly at the mill; he fell through
an icy pond and thereafter suffered from rheumatism, and finally met
his death by falling from his invalid's chair in a rage when the boy
shoved a wild turnip under his nose. The same string of disasters, supplemented with a spectral reminder of his evil deed, befell Noah Chase
for cruelly slaughtering a fawn-laden doe yarding inside the crusted
snow.[3]

Metamorphosis occurs in a brace of Canuck tales. From memories of
his Canadian childhood Antoine summoned a conte of the dreaded
loup-garou, who once chased his grandfather, impervious to his whip
lashings, right up to the door of a priest; the holy man transformed
the killer-wolf into a man who was seen to bear whip cuts on his face.[4]
Another of Antoine's tales, evoked by talk of fishing, dealt with a man
who fished so much, to the detriment of his work, that the priest turned
him into a kingfisher who could fish all the time; when winter came

[3] *Uncle Lisha's Shop*, pp. 210-212, 205-207.
[4] *Danvis Folks and A Hero of Ticonderoga* (Rutland, Vt.: Tuttle Company, c. 1934),
pp. 123-124. Cf. Paul A. W. Wallace, *Baptiste Larocque: Legends of French Canada*
(Toronto, c. 1923), pp. 42-46, "A Tale of the Loup-Garou." If the *loup-garou* bleeds,
he will never run again.

the bird kept on fishing instead of flying south, and dashed his brains out flying into the frozen surface of the river.[5] Here magic motives, moral lessons and the power of the priest indicate tales extraneous to American culture.

Ghosts and the Devil performed in yarns strongly tinctured with nineteenth-century comedy. A spurious ghost that protects an estate recalls Whittier's anecdote of Aunt Morse. Bijer Johns put in a false claim on Uncle Ebenezer's estate, but retracted it when he mistook the sloshing of a hen in the swill barrel for Eb's ghost.[6] In a sly fiction aimed at the notoriously wretched fit of Uncle Lisha's cobbled shoes, Antoine employs the familiar jest of a dreamed visit to the Devil. While sitting around in hell, he sees an old shoemaker approach the Devil and ask for work. Satan holds out his feet, one foot a man's and the other a cow's, and tells him to fashion just one boot; the shoemaker decides to fit the human foot, but his finished boot will only go on the bovine foot.[7]

Place legends. Buried treasure on several occasions stimulated the energies and tongues of the Danvis folk, who display acquaintance with all the rituals of the treasure hunt. Portentous Solon Briggs professes to have the power of divination, given suitable equipment; referring to an unsuccessful treasure seeker

"I should admire tu know if he ever tried the myraculous paower of a witch hazel crotch," said Solon. "I c'n find veins of water with 'em onfalible, an' the' hain't no daoubt 'at they hev jest as paowerful distraction tow-ards gold and silver, hid artificial, or growin' nat'ral in the baowels of the airth. Mebby he did find it an' spoke afore he got his hand on 't an' it moved. It sartinly will, ef you speak a audible laoud word. The' is allers a sperit a-guardin' bairied treasure, an' ef you speak afore you lay your hand on 't, it gives the sperit paower to move it, the' 's no tellin' haow fur."[8]

To confirm Solon's words, two actual attempts to recover treasure that unfold in the sketches are thwarted by the tabooed outcry from an overeager digger when his shovel clinks against the chest.[9] One of

[5] *Uncle Lisha's Outing, The Buttles Gals and Along Three Rivers* (Rutland, Vt.: Tuttle Co., c. 1934), pp. 154-155.   [7] *Uncle Lisha's Shop*, pp. 193-194.

[6] *Danvis Folks*, pp. 125-127.   [8] *Danvis Folks*, pp. 121-122.

[9] *Sam Lovel's Camps and Other Stories Including In the Green Wood* (Rutland, Vt.: Tuttle Co., c. 1934), "The Camp on the Lake," ch. 8, "The Treasure-Diggers," p. 162; *Danvis Folks*, ch. 17, "Treasure Seekers," p. 164.

these results directly from a local story told by Uncle Lisha, which incidently revived the tenacious tradition of Rogers' Rangers and the silver image of St. Francis. Half-cracked old Bart Johnson lugged off and buried his loot at Tater Hill, or so he thought when he returned determined to find it; chased one night by wolves, he scrabbled up a tree and clung desperately to a limb — only to find, in the morning, he was clasping a root.[10] Solon and Antoine laugh at the yarn, but secretly set out on their own after the Ranger's treasure.

Fool and trickster yarns. A knot of Danvis yarns centered around ludicrous mistakes, of the kind frequent in Yankee stories. Sam Lovel adopts Irish brogue to tell about newly landed Paddies who hunted skunks they mistook for birds or cats, with expected consequences; in another tale he describes a wrathful search by a New York businessman owning lumbering interests in the Green Mountains for a trespassing sawmill whose buzz is simulated by a saw-whet owl; Joseph Hill related "How Zene Burnham Come It On His Father" by setting a cabbage on the end of a sweep outside the window and egging on the old man at dusk to blaze away at the hoot owl.[11] This trio of narratives, besides sharing a common folktale motive, the mistaken animal or object, incorporate native character types that reappear endlessly in nineteenth-century anecdotal fiction, the ignorant Irishman, the city tenderfoot, and the Yankee trickster. In the same vein Antoine tells, in his tale of "Le Feu Follet," a gaucherie of his own that had cost him a wife; seeing a light on his father's farm, and suspecting a thief, he followed it through a swamp which so muddied his clothes he could not go courting that night, whereupon a rival suitor won out; the light came from a firefly.[12]

Deception likewise provided the theme for a story-swapping entertainment during an outing trip. After eating their self-prepared meal,

[10] *Danvis Folks*, pp. 120-121. For traditional accounts of Rogers' Rangers and the silver image see John H. Spaulding, *Historical Relics of the White Mountains* (Boston, 1855), pp. 38-40; Samuel A. Drake, *The Heart of the White Mountains* (New York, 1882), pp. 263-266; Charles M. Skinner, *Myths and Legends of Our Own Land* (Philadelphia and London, 1896), I, 220-222; John Anderson and Stearns Morse, *The Book of the White Mountains* (New York, 1930), pp. 95-98.
[11] *Uncle Lisha's Shop*, pp. 148-149, 152-153, 151-152.
[12] *Uncle Lisha's Outing*, pp. 68-69. Cf. Wallace, "A Tale of the Fi-Follett," *Baptiste Laroque*, pp. 47-51.

the campers drifted idly into talk of soup making. Uncle Lisha remembers a case where a vagrant offered to make the suspicious housewife a bowl of soup from a stone, and while stirring continually demanded additional ingredients to improve the flavor, until a hearty meat and vegetable soup had been concocted. Antoine then recalls an ingenious pea soup made by a poor provider who added to his one pea a chunk of meat purloined from his neighbor, and then blandly informed his wife she had never used the right kind of pea before. Still on the topic of chicane, Sam Lovel volunteers an anecdote of a town sot who, bereft of funds, secured his rum by offering to buy a pint and then, when denied credit, returning a concealed pint bottle filled with water.[13] The first of these innocently presented campfire yarns is an old European folktale.[14] The last represents an extensively traveled native folktale linked to scalawags and scapegraces in many states. In mid-nineteenth-century humor, in twentieth-century folk gossip, artful rascals employ the dodge for gin, brandy, or rum, with various embellishing twists, from the White Hills of New Hampshire to Mississippi in the Deep South.[15]

Tall tales. Most of the fictions spun by the Danvis yarners were of the long bow order. In keeping with their woodland habitat, these dealt mainly with b'ars, hunting, shooting, and fishing — the stock themes of the long bow. Talking with his friends about cases of conjugal infelicity, Uncle Lisha cites an example of domestic difference — or indifference — in which Bruin played a conspicuous role. An old couple on the outs had long preserved a stony silence; one night hearing a rumpus in the sheepfold the man goes out to investigate; when he is long in returning the woman follows and finds him clinched with

[13] *Uncle Lisha's Outing*, pp. 130-132.

[14] The writer remembers his mother telling him this story in his childhood. This is Type 1548 in Antti Aarne and Stith Thompson, *The Types of the Folk-Tale*, and Motif 112.2 in Thompson's *Motif-Index of Folk-Literature*. Cf. the *American Magazine of Wit* (New York, 1808), pp. 222-224, "Stone Soup."

[15] See "How to Get a Drink," *Spirit of the Times*, XIV (Jan. 25 1845), 569; and "How Big Lige Got the Liquor," *ibid.*, XX (July 27, 1850), 266; "Gen. Tay," *New York Atlas*, May 20, 1860; *Berkshire Hills*, vol. II (April 1, 1902); Cornelius Weygandt, *The White Hills* (New York, c. 1934), pp. 144-147, and *New Hampshire Neighbors* (New York, c. 1937), p. 213; Harold W. Thompson, *Body, Boots and Britches* (Philadelphia, 1940), pp. 281-282.

a great bear. "Go it, ol' man, go it, bear," says she, "it's the fust fight
ever I see 'at I didn't keer which licked." This yarn, captioned "Life in
Kentucky," rests in a nineteenth-century jokebook, persists in Wisconsin, and is credited to the "walking, stalking library of stories," Abe Lincoln.[16] Another bear folktale is given as a real happening. Uncle Lisha
has set a spring gun in the cornfield ready to be discharged by a marauding bear; the gun goes off, Lisha runs to the kill, and in the confusion
at close quarters mistakes the bear's entrails for his own insides and believes he is dying, until the doctor informs him of the facts.[17]

Shooting and hunting feats allowed the exuberant imagination of
Antoine free play. In the tradition of the curved shot and the one bullet
bag, he boasts of winning a turkey shoot where the bird was hidden
behind a hillock, by firing up into the air at the sound of the gobble at
an angle that permitted the bullet to drop home on the other side; and
he credits to his "father's brother-in-law" the exploit of killing ten
wolves and wounding five others by the simple expedient of trailing
from his sleigh a rope rubbed with hog's blood, and then sighting along
the rope at the quickly assembled sniffers. Once having trailed a panther to his den, Antoine tied a knot in his tail which protruded behind
a rock, and then boldly marched into the cave, to the consternation of
his companion, and shot point-blank at the beast. Antoine's classic
hunt, however, was after coons; many coon tracks led to holes under
an enormous rock, which rose and fell with the breathing of numerous
racoons sleeping underneath.[18] Here Antoine has related a variant of a
widespread American whopper.

MAJOR BROWN'S COON STORY

"I was down on the crick this morning," said Bill Gates, "and I seed any
amount of coon tracks. I think they're agoin' to be powerful plenty this
season."

[16] *Danvis Folks*, p. 191; *The American Joe Miller* (London, 1865), p. 207; Charles E.
Brown, *Bear Tales* (Madison, Wis.: Wisconsin Folklore Society, 1944), "The Bear Fight."
Samuel E. Morison, *Builders of the Bay Colony* (Boston, 1930), p. 248 (the quoted phrase
is from Carl Sandburg, *Abraham Lincoln: The Prairie Years*, New York, c. 1926, II, 298).

[17] *Uncle Lisha's Shop*, pp. 128-136. Cf. R. M. Dorson, "Just B'ars," *Appalachia*, n.s.,
VIII (December 1942), 178-179.

[18] *Uncle Lisha's Shop*, p. 167; *Danvis Folks*, pp. 122-123; *Sam Lovel's Camps*, pp.
59-60; *Uncle Lisha's Shop*, pp. 220-221.

"Oh, yes," replied Tom Coker, "I never hearn tell of the likes before. The whole woods is lined with 'em. If skins is only a good price this season, I'll be worth somethin' in the spring, sure's you live, for I've jest got one of the best coon dogs in all Illinois."

"You say you never hearn tell o' the like o' the coons?" put in Major Brown, an old veteran who had been chewing his tobacco in silence for the last half hour. "Why, you don't know ennything 'bout 'em! If you'd a come here forty years ago, like I did, you'd a thought coon! I jest tell you, boys, you couldn't go amiss for 'em. We hardly ever thought of pesterin' 'em much, for their skins weren't worth a darn with us — that is, we couldn't get enough for 'em to pay for the skinnin'.

"I recollect one day I went out a bee huntin'. Wal, arter I'd lumbered about a good while, I got kinder tired, and so I leaned up agin a big tree to rest. I hadn't much more'n leaned up afore somethin' give me one of the allfiredest nips about the seat o' my britches I ever got in my life. I jumped about a rod, and lit a runnin', and kept on a runnin' for over a hundred yards; when think, sez I, it's no use runnin', and I'm snake bit, but runnin' won't do enny good. So I jest stopt, and proceeded to examine the wound. I soon seed it was no snake bite, for thar's a blood-blister pinched on me about six inches long.

"Think, sez I, that rether gits me! What in the very deuce would it a bin? Arter thinkin' about it a while, I concluded to go back, and look for the critter, jest for the curiosity o' the thing. I went to the tree and poked the weeds and stuff all about; but darned the thing could I see. Purty soon I sees the tree has a little split a runnin' along up it, and so I gits to lookin' at that. Dreckly I sees the split open about half a inch, and then shet up agin; then I sees it open and shet, and open and shet, and open and shet, right along as regular as a clock a tickin'.

"Think, sez I, what in all creation can this mean? I know'd I'd got pinched in the split tree, but what in thunder was makin' it do it? At first, I felt orfully scared, and thought it must be somethin' dreadful; and then agin I thought it moutn't. Next I thought about hants and ghosts, and about a runnin' home and sayin' nothin' about it; and then I thought it couldn't be enny on 'em, for I'd never hearn tell o' them a pesterin' a feller right in open daylight. At last the true blood of my ancestors riz up in my veins, and told me it 'ud be cowardly to go home and not find out what it was; so I lumbered for my axe, and swore I'd find out all about it, or blow up. When I got back, I let into the tree like blazes, and purty soon it cum down and smashed into flinders — and what do you think? Why, it was rammed and jammed smack full of coons from top to bottom. Yes, sir, they's rammed in so close that every time they breathed they made the split open."[19]

[19] Scrap Book AC 040.1, P873g (VIII, 87-88), in the Vermont Historical Society, Montpelier. Cf. "Cale Lyman's Coon Story," *Spirit of the Times*, XVI (Oct. 10, 1846), 389; *Tennessee Folklore Society Bulletin*, V (October 1939), 57-58 (coons); *Hoosier Folklore Bulletin*, I (1942), 14 (mice); 52-53, (coons); 66 (bees).

Accompanying tall hunting stories were equally outrageous fishing adventures. Antoine's most successful catch netted a string of trout who, in anxiety to reach the worm on his hook, swallowed the tail of a nearer fellow until a long procession had formed; but the string broke on a slim fish in the middle as Antoine was dragging in the line and he lost its hind end. Disappointed, the trout then began to jump at his dish of worms on the bank, and when he took it up and scooted for home, they jumped right out of the water and followed him to his house so that he had to shut the door in their faces. Uncle Lisha at once countered with a true story of bullpouts so plentiful in a frozen Wisconsin lake that when a fisherman chopped a hole in the ice they kept spilling through over the surface onto the shore, and people for twenty miles around came with their sleds and teams to fetch them away for hog feed and manure; the whole country smelt like a fish kettle all summer. To the query "You'll see dat, Onc' Lasha?" the narrator replied faithfully, "Wal, no; it happened the winter afore I went there, an' I did n't ezactly see it, but I smelt it." [20]

Tall tales fastened to other themes besides occupational activities. From their well-stocked memories the Green Mountain raconteurs drew forth narratives about an overzealous breadcutter who sliced himself and a bystander clean in two, although they were fortunately patched up again; of a partridge that flew into Antoine's mouth, whereupon he bit its head off and spent two hours picking the feathers out of his teeth; of a strong-jawed man who, when his horse broke away from his wagon, hung on to the lines with his teeth and the wagon with his hands for over a mile until he brought the animal to a stop; of a stubborn old couple who separated for three years over a dispute whether a passing rodent was a rat or a mouse, and promptly resumed it

---

[20] *Danvis Folks*, pp. 171-172. The first part of Antoine's fiction is matched by an anecdote, "Catching Wild Geese," in *The American Comic Almanac, 1833* (Boston, n.d.), p. 33: "An Irishman much accustomed to marvellous narrations, and also attached to sporting, was one day silenced by a gentleman presenting him with the following method of catching wild geese. 'Tie a chord to the tail of an eel and throw it into the fens where the fowl haunt. One of the geese swallowing this slippery bait, it runs through him and is swallowed by a second and third, and so on till the cord is quite full. A person once caught so many in this way, that they actually flew away with him'."

on reuniting, then parted permanently.[21] This last tale suggests a comparable example of a stubborn spouse.

WASN'T SHE SPUNKY?

A couple who had lived together for some years in seeming contentment, one day went a fishing, and tied their boat by a rope to a post in the water. All of a sudden the boat went floating down the stream, and a contest of words immediately arose as to the real cause of the parting of the rope. The wife said it must have been cut with the scissors, but the husband, an unfeeling old fogy, stoutly maintained that it was a knife that did the business. Scissors! said the wife. Knife! said the husband. Scissors, Knife, Scissors, Knife, said both, but at last the husband losing his temper, cried out: "If you say scissors again, I'll duck you."

"Scissors!" said the wife, determined to hold out to the last.

Away went the old woman into the water, and as she came up the first time, she bellowed "Scissors," at the top of her voice. The old man pushed her down again.

"Scis-sors!" sputtered she, in fainter tones, as she rose again, but the old fellow had her by the head, and plump she went down for the third time. Now she rose more slowly, and as her waterlogged form neared the surface, having lost the power of articulation yet determined never to give in, she thrust her hand out of the water, and imitated with the first and second fingers *the opening and shutting* of a scissors.

The old man was then convinced that it was useless to try to fetter a woman's speech.[22]

The many superb yarns that flavor Robinson's writings of Vermont backmountain folk entitle their author to a special place in American literary history, for bringing into literature a wide range of living native folktale.

Holman F. Day

Three volumes of homespun ballads by Holman Day (1865-1935) provide an unexampled source for Maine popular tales. Written early in his career, before he turned to writing a spate of novels, these stories in verse tap native folktale at first hand in much the same manner, if in different form, as the prose sketches of Robinson. Day's ballad is

[21] *Uncle Lisha's Shop*, p. 139; *ibid.*, p. 159; *Uncle Lisha's Outing*, p. 30; *Danvis Folks*, p. 191.

[22] *Yankee Blade*, Dec. 17, 1853 (vol. XIII). Cf. Herbert Halpert, "Folktale and 'Wellerism' — A note," *Southern Folklore Quarterly*, VII (March 1943), 75, for American versions and European references to The Obstinate Wife.

not the literary imitation of the popular ballad used by Brainard and Whittier for consciously prettifying legends, but straightforward rhyming that intensifies the rhythms of storytelling speech, and suits its homely folk material. Lore from wells now dry that Day has saved is otherwise largely unobtainable: the saga of loggers on the Kennebec in the boom days of the 1880's; of salts and skippers who sailed from once busy Maine ports; of "home folks" in the pre-industrial Maine small town. While humorous character portraits occupy much of the balladry, nearly all the well-known types of native popular tales and legends find representation: supernatural stories and place legends of witches, haunts, and spirits; tall tales and trickster yarns in abundance.

Supernatural stories and place legends — Witches. "Rid By A Witch," a narrative of witch mischief played on old Ezry, includes many motives previously observed. The witch afflicted Ezry with the usual malpractices: she galled the oxen's shoulders, swatted him with the cows' tails at the milking, and strangled a Jersey calf across a beam. To fend her off he trimmed the ears and tails of his critters. But in revenge the witch took to visiting him of nights, slapped a bridle around his jaws, flipped onto his back, and rode him about the village in company with her sisters engaged in similar sport. And for proof he showed his sores and squeaky joints.[1] At the logging camps witch belief obtained; "Fiddler Cured The Camp" hinges on the lifting of a witch spell.

> Old Attegat Peter said we was bewitched,
> He said that he seed the Old Gal when she twitched
> A fistful o' hair out the gray hosses' tail
> For a-makin' witch tattin'. She'd hung on a nail
> The queerisome web, so he said, an' the holes
> — They were fifty — they stood for the whole of our souls.
>
> An' there we would swing, an' hang there we must,
> Till the hoodoo was busted. . . .[2]

But a lively fiddler chased the hoodoo and the blues out of camp.

Ha'nts. In one of the ambling prose passages that link together the

---

[1] *Kin O' Ktaadn* (Boston: Small, Maynard & Co., 1904), pp. 153–156. Cf. the same charm used against the witch Molly Bridget, cutting off and burning the tips of tails and ears of bewitched pigs (Charles W. Brewster, *Rambles About Portsmouth: Second Series*, Portsmouth, N.H., 1869, p. 344); also *ante*, Chapter II, *Witches and wizards*.

[2] *Up in Maine. Stories of Yankee Life Told in Verse* (Boston: Small, Maynard & Co., 1902), pp. 132-133.

poems in *Kin O' Ktaadn*, the woods boss dogmatizes on forest haunts
to a group of lounging loggers.

There are certainly ghosts in the woods — says The Boss. There is a
store camp up in the Sourd-na-hunk woods that we all know is ha'nted.
It is built on a man's grave an' that man was killed in the dam sluiceway
at the Abol falls. The stones rolled down on him. Stand out in front of
that camp in the night an' you can hear the stones come tumblin' an'
boomblin' down like thunder bumpin' acrost the sky. There's a song about
that camp that runs this way:

> Oh, I went, boys, I went to old Jumper Joe's grave,
>   Clank, clank your chains, you old devil, you!
> Says he, Boost me up from hell-fire to save,
>   Clank, clank your chains, old Joe.
>
> He rattled underneath, and he rattled overhead,
>   Whew! smell the brimstone down there below!
> I did not darst to lie down in that bed,
>   Where they laid out old Joe.[3]

Equally with the red men the lumberjacks feared the spirits of Katahdin,

> But we hain't afraid of ownin' that we fellers hunt
>   our holes
> When Pamola sends her devils chasin' out to catch
>   our souls.[4]

On Isle au Haut ghosts still walk, whose shameful pasts are known to
the grandma knitting by the window. One is Tom Davis's gal; when
she went to the city with his child inside her, he burned the home
where they had planned to live as man and wife.

> And she? In her sin and shame she died
> In the spring 't would 'a' made her an honest bride.
> And nights when the sky is blind with snow
> And the ghosts are walkin' on Isle au Haut
> She beats at the winder and trails the train
> Of her robes o' sin acrost the pane,
> Huntin' and peerin' nigh and fur
> For the little home Tom built for her.
> Feelin' with hands so white and thin
> And moanin' alwa's "I can't get in!"[5]

[3] *Kin O' Ktaadn*, p. 136.
[4] *Kin O' Ktaadn*, p. 139.
[5] *Kin O' Ktaadn*, p. 171, from "When The Nights Are Long On Isle Au Haut."

On Christmas eve can be heard the clanking of an endless chain, for then Club-Foot John pays penance for the dozen lives he lost when he wrecked the *Stormy Jane* off Isle au Haut in a drunken fury.[6] Specter and curse ships haunt Maine waters. "The Night of the White Review" tells the somber legend of ghost ships manned by Gloucester fishermen which issue forth annually in a phantom procession past the Grand Banks.[7] A curse sits on the *Mary of the Mist* as she rots in port; no Banksman will ever sail her until the Wah-Hooh-Wow has claimed its towage fee of four lives; the "conjer" man who called up the monster from the sea to tow the becalmed ship paid part of the fee with his own life, but three more men must die before the Hoodoo is lifted.[8]

In some haunt tales old supernatural dreads mingle with new extravagant fantasies. Into this category fall ferocious mythical beasts.

> For even in these days P. I.'s shake
> At the great Swamp Swogon of Brassua Lake.
> When it blitters and glabbers the long night through,
> And shrieks for the souls of the shivering crew.
> And all of us know of the witherlick
> That prowls by the shore of the Cup-sup-tic.
> Of the Side Hill Ranger whose eyeballs gleam
> When the moon hangs gibbous over Abol stream;
> — Of the Dolorous Demon that moans and calls
> Through the mists of Abol-negassis falls.[9]

A prank haunt frightens in "The Ha'nt of Aunt Ann Dunn," where the mysteriously boiling kettle has a very rational unnoticed cause in tobacco juice squirted onto the stove, there to fizz explosively, by Uncle Nial as he calmly rocks in his chair and hums a song about Old Beals' skinny hog.[10]

Yankee characters. Many of the ballad stories deal with eccentric

[6] *Kin O' Ktaadn*, p. 173.

[7] *Pine Tree Ballads. Rhymed Stories of Unplaned Human Natur' Up in Maine* (Boston: Small, Maynard & Co., 1902), pp. 63–67.

[8] "The Awful Wah-Hoo-Wow," *Pine Tree Ballads*, pp. 79-87.

[9] "Ha'nts of the Kingdom of Spruce," *Up in Maine*, p. 157. Cf. Charles M. Skinner, "Maine's Woodland Terrors," *American Myths and Legends* (Philadelphia and London, c. 1903), I, 34-40. Grotesque beasts are common in nineteenth- and twentieth-century folklore, and become attached to the Paul Bunyan cycle. See e.g. the Haggletopelter in "A Marvellous Hunting Story," *Spirit of the Times*, XXVI (Sept. 27, 1856), 392; George P. Krapp, *The English Language in America* (New York, 1925), I, 111-113.

[10] *Kin O' Ktaadn*, pp. 51-55.

characters standard in folk humor. Day's Yankee portraits include such stock types as the ugly man, the absent-minded man, the pig-headed man, the skinflint, the trickster, the ignoramus, whose traits and scrapes yield folktales identical or similar to those attached to "orig-inals" elsewhere.

Ugliness has formed a fertile theme for folk jokes and anecdotes. In "John W. Jones" the title character describes himself as the homeliest man in town; driving along the road his cart locked wheels with the cart of an incredibly homely stranger; John Jones abruptly leaped on him and threw him down after a fierce wrestle. Gasping and groaning the stranger asked the reason for the assault.

> Said I, 'I've sworn if I meet a man that's homelier 'n what I be,
> I'll kill him. I reckin I've got the man.' Says he, 'Please let me see?'
> So I loosened a bit while he struck a match; he held it with
> trembling hand
> While through the tears in his poor old eyes my cross-piled
> face he scanned.
> Then he dropped the match and groaned and said, 'If truly
> ye think that I
> Am ha'f as homely as what you be — please shoot! I want to die.' [11]

This twist to the many drolleries about comparative ugliness is an old folktale — told even on Lincoln.[12]

Absent-mindedness, treated by Day in "The Off Side of the Cow" (the hired man gives the horses his luncheon pail and eats their hay), and "Absent-Minded Heseki' Shaw," inspired endless folk jokes.[13] Ab-sent-Minded Amos, sketched by Cornelius Weygandt in his White Mountain chronicles, poured the Sunday milk into the mash for the cows, and brought the guests a pail of water; sometimes he would hang the milk pail on a hook and start milking into the lantern; once he put his overalls over his good pantaloons and then began looking for them; after his funeral the Baptist deacon said he hoped some kindly angel would start Amos up the road to heaven so he wouldn't go down.[14]

[11] *Pine Tree Ballads*, pp. 8-9.
[12] "Ugly vs. Ugly," *Yankee Blade*, Jan. 21, 1854 (vol. XIII); Alexander K. McClure, *Lincoln's Yarns and Stories* (Chicago and Philadelphia, n.d.), p. 17.
[13] *Up in Maine*, pp. 61-62; *Kin O' Ktaadn*, pp. 59-63.
[14] *New Hampshire Neighbors* (New York, c. 1937), pp. 276-279.

Nineteenth-century comic almanacs, literary weeklies, and jokebooks vied in supplying absurd performances by absent-minded people.

Bill Jones's absence of mind was somewhat remarkable.— I saw him once in a bar-room, lighting his Havana with a live coal; as soon as the fire had communicated itself to the cigar, he clapped the coal into his mouth and threw the cigar into the fire! And another time, being considerably sprung, he laid a piece of wood upon his leg to divide it with a handsaw, but unfortunately forgot to stop till he had sawed his leg entirely off! He was known frequently to put pepper and salt into his coffee, and pour milk and sugar upon his beef steak — and once, while reeling drunk, he mistook his eyes for a couple of oysters, gouged them out, and swallowed them. Poor Bill's absence of mind at last proved his ruin — going one night to a well to draw water, he placed his bucket and hat near the brink, and hanging himself by the upper jaw upon the hoop pole, lowered himself into the well, and was drowned.[15]

A gentleman from the west informs us of an instance of absence of mind, where a Yankee speculator, while engaged in speculation, fell to whittling his fingers instead of a stick, and did not discover his mistake till he had whittled off his first two fingers, and sharpened the third to a point. This is beaten by a farrier in this city, who, in making horse-shoe nails, instead of taking a nail-rod, deliberately put his own hand into the fire heating it red hot, hammered each of his fingers into nails, and the thumb into a toe-calk, and did not discover his mistake till the horse was shod and gone.[16]

This is Mr. Jones — everybody knows Mr. Jones. Intending to open a large oyster, and swallow the fish, he was suddenly seized with absence of mind, when he set the oyster up in the easy chair, opened the dressing-room door, and swallowed his wife. He did not perceive his mistake until he missed the regular scolding when he brought home company the next day.[17]

A young man in Bangor intending to go in swimming with bladders last week, lay his clothes on the bladders and took two large stones which he tied to his neck. He discovered his error when he swam to the bottom.

A man going a-fishing in Connecticut river, with his wife, put his clam on a rock, and put his wife on a hook for bait. She was so homely that the fish wouldn't bite; and he discovered his error when he had frightened them all away.

A young girl intending to fasten on her bustle to go to church and carry a bag of corn to mill, tied the bag of corn on behind her, and took the

[15] *The American Comic Almanac, 1838* (Boston, n.d.), p. 22.
[16] *The National Comic Almanac for the year 1838* (n.d., n.p.).
[17] *Turner's Comic Almanac, 1842* (Boston, n.d.).

bustle to the miller. The miller soon discovered the error as the bustle was so much larger than the bag of corn.[18]

Meanness, with ugliness and absent-mindedness, afforded fruitful opportunity for lampooning Yankees. Shamefully mean men in "Uncle Benjy and Old Crane," "Old 'Ten Per Cent,' " and "Mean Sam Green" (whose soul was one ten-millionth the size of a fly's eyebrow),[19] are brethren to the extortioners, skinflints, and gross materialists conspicuous in Yankeeland. In "Aunt Shaw's Pet Jug," Uncle Elnathan Shaw takes a violent tumble downstairs while carrying the prized jug; he might have caught at the cellar shelves and saved himself, but he clung to the jug; on hearing the clatter his wife indignantly yelled "Dod-rot your hide, did ye break my jug?" and kept yelling until Elnathan picked himself up and smashed the precious crockery against the wall.[20] Jokelore can supply an even more vivid illustration of Yankee materialism.

THE RULING PASSION

Before the Connecticut schooners were forbidden the liberty of carrying corn brooms, onions, and poultry to the West Indies, one Joe Swain resolved to go to sea; and accordingly proceeded to New London, and shipped as a green hand on board the *Charming Nancy*, for Barbadoes and a market. The whole of the family, father, mother, brothers, and sisters, were concerned in an adventure of fowls committed to his charge. On the passage home, in a violent gale, Joe fell overboard, and all attempts to save him were vain. The vessel arrived at New London: the father of the unfortunate sailor repaired to the sea-shore to meet his son, and learn the result of the family speculation. The *Charming Nancy* was riding at anchor, her colours streaming mournfully from half-mast. He hailed her from the beach — *"Halloo, there — is that the Charming Nancy?"* "Ay, ay, sir!" *"Is there one Joe Swain aboard there?"* "No, he's drowned!" *"Drowned?"* "Yes, drowned, I tell you." *"Fowls drowned too?"*[21]

A further addition to the gallery of Down East odd sticks, the mule-headed man, emerges in "Dan'l and Dunk." Fast friends, Dan'l and

---

[18] *Yankee*, Aug. 24, 1844 (vol. I). A sheaf of inventions similar to the foregoing is given in "Remarkable Cases of Absence of Mind," *The American Joe Miller* (Philadelphia, 1847), pp. 117-123.

[19] *Up in Maine*, pp. 11-12; *Pine Tree Ballads*, pp. 136-139; *ibid.*, pp. 140-146. Cf. "The Meanest Men on Record," *Saturday Rambler*, July 21, 1849 (vol. 4); "The Stingiest Man on Record," *Spirit of the Times*, XXIV (Aug. 5, 1854), 300.

[20] *Up in Maine*, pp. 3-5.

[21] *The American Joe Miller* (Philadelphia, 1839), pp. 125-126.

Dunk fell into their first quarrel while out sailing in their jointly owned smack, the *Pollywog*. Determinedly Dunk divided the deck with a chalkline, then retired to the stern and the wheel; grimly Dan went forward and hoisted the anchor overboard. "The bow-end's mine," yelled Dan to Dunk, "now steer if ye want to, blast yer soul!" Both men swore they would never give in; and nothing more was ever seen of Dan'l or Dunk or the *Pollywog;* perhaps Dunk sank or Dan burned his half.[22] A recurrent yarn portraying similar obstinacy involves two travelers who meet on a narrow road and resolutely stand their ground; the impasse terminates when one of the two proves the more persistent newspaper reader.[23]

Sharpsters and tricksters perpetuate saws and sells of the kind habitually associated with Yankees. The hero of "B. Brown — Hoss Orator" coaxes trades with all the silver-tongued craft of the horse jockey; "A. B. Appleton, 'Pirut,'" fleeced at the fair, turns fleecer by barking an exhibit of a giant Americanized Cock-a-too and an infant white African anaconda, and then abruptly absconding before the customers see the domestic hen with dyed tail feathers and the angleworm; Ozy B. Orr, stripped to his last dime, advertises "A Jig-Dancing Turkey," and produces as good as he boasts — although the audience does not realize the gobbler is shifting uneasily on a tin platform under which, concealed, a confederate holds a kerosene lantern.[24] The world of Day's balladry is peopled with the same Yankee types that throng mid-nineteenth-century humor.

Tall tales. Munchausens in Day's ballad sagas spin yarns as tall as the pine and the spruce trees against which they are framed.

> 'Twould make an ox curl up and die
> To hear how Zek'l Pratt would lie.
> — Why, that blamed Zeke
> Could hardly speak
> Without he'd let some whopper fly.[25]

[22] *Pine Tree Ballads*, pp. 76-79.

[23] "A Quaker Race," *Saturday Rambler*, Oct. 2, 1847 (vol. II); Thomas R. Hazard, *The Jonny-Cake Letters* (Providence, 1882), pp. 75-76.

[24] *Up in Maine*, pp. 181-184; *Pine Tree Ballads*, pp. 156-160; *ibid.*, pp. 122-127. This last sell is identical with a sketch, "The Yankee's Turkey Show," in the *Yankee Blade*, Feb. 16, 1856, credited to *Harper's*.

[25] "Zek'l Pratt's Harrycane," *Up in Maine*, p. 89.

Maine youth grew up on a diet of fierce inventions. "Grampy's Lullaby" entertains a "leetle barby" with American wonder tales: how spry Ebenezer Cowles ran up an unsupported ladder, and before it could teeter straddled out on air, raised it another length above him and skittered up it again; how two-hundred-pound Samuel Strout once lugged a rock so heavy he sunk to his knees in the ground at every step; how Athanial Prime twitched right out of its bark a log that two argumentative chaps tending sluice were standing on, so neatly that the arguers thought it was still there and kept jawing on it till dark. In "Grampy Sings a Song" the same incorrigible fabulist informs little sis how Chester Cahoon of the Tuttsville Brigade, "The Thund'rinest fireman Lord ever made," stood at the second floor window in a blazing flame, a stove and a bed in his arms, a bureau balanced square on his head, his hands loaded with crockery, rolls of quilts wreathed around his neck, and Mis' Jenkins' old aunt suspended from his teeth; he called for the stream, and when it came, hooked his legs around the water as if it were rope and eased himself down the slope.[26] Grampy's tales all contain traditional motives. Babe the Blue Ox, Paul Bunyan's consort, attained such bulk she sank to her knees in walking across solid rock. A "moron" joke in a currently popular cycle revolves about the marvelous descent: two morons fleeing from the booby hatch are puzzled how to descend the high wall; one carrying a flashlight offers to focus it on the ground and allow the other to climb down the beam; oh no, replies the other, you will snap the light off when I am halfway down.[27] Ascending an unsupported ladder is a feat previously narrated in tall-story circles, although in one story-matching contest it loses to the exploit of a nameless hero who at a raising ran the whole length of the ridge pole and five paces beyond, then turned round and ran back.[28]

[26] *Up in Maine*, pp. 23-26, 80-82.

[27] These moron jokes enjoy a current vogue in urban society. The above was told me by William B. Gresham in Boston in February, 1943.

[28] W. R. Cochrane and George K. Wood, *History of Francestown, N.H.* (Nashua, N.H., 1895), p. 473. Cf. Charles E. Trow, *The Old Shipmasters of Salem* (New York and London, 1905), pp. 21-22, for the ladder feat. These tales suggest the well-known American windy of shingling a house in a fog so heavy shingles are laid several feet beyond the roof onto the fog: for New England versions see Daniel L. Cady, *Rhymes of Vermont Rural Life: Third Series* (Rutland, Vt., 1926), p. 22, "A Vermont Liar"; *Berkshire Hills*, Oct. 1, 1901; Edward C. Birge, *Westport, Conn.* (New York, c. 1926), pp. 68-69; Robert Kempt, *The American Joe Miller* (London, 1865), 57-58.

Extricating a log from its bark without disturbing sitters is in its turn an intersectional accomplishment. A Cincinnatian is acquainting an English traveler with the impudence of frontier thievery.

"Just to give you an idea how they can steal out there," continued Case, sending a sly wink to the listening company, "just to give you an idea — did you ever work in a saw-mill?"

"Never."

"Well, my brother, one day, bought an all-fired fine black walnut log — four feet three at the butt, and not a knot in it. He was determined to keep that log, anyhow, and he hired two Scotchmen to watch it all night. Well, they took a small demijohn of whiskey with them, snaked the log up the side-hill above the mill, and then sat down on the log to play keerds, just to keep awake, you see. 'Twas a monstrous big log — bark two inches thick. Well, as I was saying, they played keerds and drank whiskey all night — and as it began to grow light they went to sleep a-straddle the log. About a minute after daylight my brother went over to the mill to see how they got on, and the log was gone!"

"And they sitting on it?"

"Sitting on the bark. The thieves had drove an iron wedge into the butt end which pointed down hill, and hitched a yoke of oxen on, and pulled it right out, leaving the shell and Scotchers setting a-straddle of it, fast asleep."

The Englishman here rose, dropped his cigar stump into the spittoon, and looking at his watch, said he thought he would go on deck, and see how far we'd be down the river before morning.[29]

Other Down East artists with the long bow tell folktales. "Cy Nye, Prevaricator," owned a setting hen a keg of powder couldn't shake off her nest; Cy said he got so mad he fed her hemlock sawdust mash, but she kept right on setting and hatched a brood of wooden-legged chicks. In parallel yarns a sow whose hind legs are smashed by a truck is patched up with a rolling truck, and when she farrows, her piglets all have little trucks in place of their hind legs; a captured partridge is tied by the leg to a frying pan but manages to escape, and is seen the next summer with a family similarly anchored to little frying pans.[30] Disgusted at hearing Talleyrand B. Beals boast about his hired man Jim, Ben Haskell explained to the store gathering why Jim suddenly left town one day. Ben had seen him climb a poplar tree, coat his boots

[29] "Log Rolling," *Yankee Blade*, July 22, 1854 (vol. XIII).

[30] *Up in Maine*, pp. 8-10; Carl Carmer, *Listen for a Lonesome Drum* (New York, 1936), p. 380; A. F. Ayer, Moosehead, Me., "The Anchored Partridge," *Portland Telegram*, July 23, 1934.

with mutton tallow, grab his boot-straps and pull himself up in the air. When Talleyrand interrupted to assert belligerently that even if Jim hadn't gone off that way, he was easily strong enough to lift himself if he wanted to, Ben cut short the coming flow of encomiums with a further explanation; the prince of hired men had chosen that way to leave the earth in order to escape his mean master, old Beals — and so saying Jim had hoisted himself out of sight.[31] This fantasy matches the disappearance in a mid-nineteenth-century sketch, "Where Joe Meriweather Went To," which has Joe, fancily dressed in buckskin breeches with straps under the boots, caught in a drenching rainstorm; drying himself by the fire, Joe suddenly begins to elevate, and shoots up past the trees; he managed to cut one strap but then the other leg shot up and Joe whirled out of sight.[32] An anonymous raconteur testifies to the enduring quality of "The Pants Jemimy Made." Aunt Jemimy Brown fed her sheep on the toughest straw and spun the thread from their wool with a double twist; the farmer, ploughing rocks and stumps out of his field, ploughs right through a maple stump that snaps back and catches his pants by the slack — the pants Jemimy made; the oxen strained, the farmer grasped the handle-bars, a living link between plough and stump; and the stump comes out.[33] This again is a twice-told tale.

"A HASTY PLATE OF SOUP."

A Tough Story.— Our Uncle Ezra is in the habit sometimes of "stretching the truth" a little — a vicious sort of a propensity from which the rest of the family are singularly free. We heard him tell Snooks a rather severe tale one day last week, which we have concluded to give to the world.

"When I lived in Maine," said he, "I helped *break up* a new piece of ground; we got the wood off in the winter, and *arly* in the spring we begun to think of ploughin' on't. It was so consarned rocky that we had to get forty yoke of oxen to one plough — we did, faith — and I held that plough for more than a week — I thought I should die. It e'en a'most killed me, I van. Why, one day I was holdin', and the plough hit a stump, which measured just nine *foot* and a half through it — hard and sound white oak. The plough split it, and I was going straight through the stump, when I happened to think it might snap together again, so I just threw my feet out,

---

[31] "Jim's Translation," *Pine Tree Ballads*, pp. 195-199.

[32] A convenient reprinting of this story is in Constance Rourke, *American Humor* (New York, c. 1931), pp. 46-48.

[33] *Pine Tree Ballads*, pp. 204-208.

and I had no sooner done this, than it snapped together, taking a smart hold of the seat of my pantaloons. Of course, I was tight, but I held on to the plough handles, and though the teamsters did all they could, that team of eighty oxen couldn't tear my pantaloons — nor cause me to let go my grip. At last though, after letting the cattle breathe, they gave another strong pull altogether, and the old stump came out about the quickest; it had monstrous long roots too, let me tell you. My wife made the cloth for them pantaloons, and I haint worn any other kind since."

The only reply Snooks made to this was, — "I should have thought it would have come hard on your suspenders."[34]

Strong men perform in traditional fashion in the ballad stories. Zibe Haines, "a tough old rip" with whiskers so long he had to stuff them in his chest, ran up against a barbed wire fence one day; he didn't climb over or crawl through, but bit the wire right in two; when a tooth ached he borrowed a spike, grabbed a maul, and pegged the tooth out; when his toe sprouted a corn, he whacked it off with a mallet and chisel and threw it a mile.[35] Cy Nye, the prevaricator, claimed he had bought a whole side of beef up to Johnson's store, tucked it underneath his arm, and then forgot all about it as he sauntered on his way pondering Bible texts; suddenly remembering he had meant to get some meat, he hustled back to the store and bought another side.[36] Another strong man boasted a set of double teeth with which he could bite in two a shingle nail or crunch a bullet or lift up a keg of pork by the chine. Once while shingling the Baptist meetinghouse his ladder buckled under him and he quickly gripped the eaves with his jaws, still holding bundles of sheaves under his arms; when deaf Skillins passed down the street he hollered at him, and then resumed his dental grip before he had a chance to tumble. This last touch improves on the version rendered by Rowland Robinson.[37]

A fruitful category of American whoppers, comic sea stories, is fully represented in the Pine Tree Ballads. Sea songs tell about memorable voyages: in "The Tale of the Kennebec Mariner" the steamboat *Ezry Johnson*, lost in a fog, sailed eight miles across country in a heavy dew;

[34] *Spirit of the Times*, XVII (July 31, 1847), 265. From the *Yankee Blade*.

[35] "Old Zibe Haines," *Kin O' Ktaadn*, pp. 207-209.

[36] *Up in Maine*, pp. 9-10.

[37] "Had a Set of Double Teeth," *Up in Maine*, pp. 20-22; *Uncle Lisha's Outing* (Rutland, Vt., c. 1933), p. 30.

"The Cruise of the 'Nancy P.'" celebrates the feverish pumping activities of the crew who, not realizing the ship had left her bottom in Sheepscot Bay, brought her into Boston harbor with the cargo of plank intact in the hold, having tried to pump the Atlantic Ocean dry.[38] Uncommon sharks and whales breed salty fictions. There was the shark who starved to death, although she swallowed all the refuse of the fishing schooner and even her heftiest seaman; on cutting her open seamen found a cask inside her belly, through whose open end had passed all the food properly destined for the stomach.[39] A kinder fate met the shag-eyed shark who inopportunely happened along to frighten away a bait-hungry mackerel school; the Old Man had him hoisted aboard, told the cook to rip him open, cut out his liver, sew him up again, and toss him back into the sea. Next day the liverless shark herded a huge school of mackerel up to the *Sarah Ann*, then turned his stitched-up side toward the Old Man with an imploring look; the skipper had the tackle set up, the noose lowered, and the fish raised, poured the shark and all hands a drink of rum, then instructed the cook to take the liver out of the scuttle butt and restore it to its proper place.[40] Fishermen on the Grand Banks know well the pranks of the jolly Jeehookibus whale, who once caught a fisherman blown out of his dory by a gale, stood on his tail and juggled the man like a ball till his oil "petticuts" filled out and floated him in the air; then the fan-fluke whale lowered him back into the dory.[41] Travelled folktale crops up in the sea whoppers. In "Skipper Jason Ellison," the famed Gloucester sea captain infallibly tells the exact location of his ship by tasting the bottom soil on the sounding lead; only once in the memory of men did he err — and then he really hadn't made a mistake. During a sky-splitting storm the skipper tasted the lead, howled that the tidal wave had tossed the ship over the Widow Abbott's garden in Gloucester. Observers later discovered that the plummet had scraped against a pail of herbs set in dirt from the widow's garden. Commonly this windy is told of Nantucket.[42]

[38] *Up in Maine*, pp. 117-120; pp. 99-100.
[39] "Tale of the Sea-Faring Man," *Up in Maine*, pp. 101-106.
[40] "Tale of a Shag-Eyed Shark," *Pine Tree Ballads*, pp. 48-53.
[41] "The Great Jehookibus Whale," *Pine Tree Ballads*, pp. 54-57.
[42] *Pine Tree Ballads*, pp. 87-93. Cf. "Tupper's Hill," *Exeter News Letter*, Dec. 28, 1841; Arthur C. Watson, *The Long Harpoon: A Collection of Whaling Anecdotes* (New Bed-

Literary Folktales

Day chose to put the folklore he had collected from Maine life into verse, verse with considerable bounce and a rugged sea- and earth-smelling language. He himself deprecated any literary pretensions in his rhymed stories, and abruptly ceased to compose them after publishing three volumes within five years. What he did leave in this vein has a unique quality for students of the borderland area between American literature and folktale. For his Pine Tree Ballads prove that the oral folk humor whose printed expression in newspapers and almanacs ceased with the Civil War never died, but lay available for future literary translation.

George S. Wasson

Totally neglected by the literary historians who faithfully exhume female local colorists and "handkerchiefly" novelists, Massachusetts-born George Wasson (1855-1932) caught the sea talk of a Maine coastal village much as Rowland Robinson transcribed the yarnings in a Vermont mountain township.[1] In many ways the two men reveal similar talents and tastes: both possessed artistic skill and supplemented their localized fiction with their own drawings; both reproduced dialect with an uncanny phonographic exactitude that impedes readers; both resorted for their fictional genre to informal local sketches united merely by scene and personalities and constructed largely around the patterns of folk gossip — the speech of men close to the elements and tightly grouped; both mined, unawares, the lode of living folktale. In Wasson's key book, as in Robinson's, the title explains a storytelling setting; *Cap'n Simeon's Store* duplicates *Uncle Lisha's Shop* as a backdrop for unfolded yarns that exhibit the wisdom and lore and edged humor of lounging townsfolk.

A professional knowledge of sail and the coastal sea infuses the sketches of Killick Cove (actually Kittery Point, where Wasson lived

ford, 1929), p. 147; James T. Fields's "Ballad of the Alarmed Skipper," in *Poems* (Boston, 1849), pp. 79–81; the *New Yorker*, July 21, 1945 (Captain Titus of Phenix, R.I.).

[1] Fannie H. Eckstorm has recently written a fine factual article, "George Savary Wasson, Artist and Writer, 1855-1932," in *The Essex Institute Historical Collections, LXXIX* (January 1943), 47-59. Of Wasson's three books of fiction, only *The Green Shay* (1905) contains a serial plot, and even this is loosely jointed.

many years), and an obsolete vernacular permeates their talk. Cap'n Simeon and his fellow-skippers think nautically even on land: "she hove in sight ahead sailin' up the road with her par'sol set"; they depend on sea terms and homely similes: "krawm," "tanto," "nail-sick," "no bigger than a trawl-kag"; "Blow my shirt ef he didn't tread up to the counter here same's a chicken doos to a dough-dish"; "what blame' ole eel-rut have you been crawled up into the last five year, anyhow?" Beneath this surface realism of coastal manners emerge deeper truths, the shrunken horizon of the ingrown community, the decay and defeat, ignorance and immorality of a once-active fishing and trading port. With these details in the village tapestry seemingly so accurate, the emphasis on yarning as a main recreation for the fisherfolk appears correctly drawn.

At the outset of his Maine pieces, Wasson emphasizes the villagers' relish for the leisurely conversation at Cap'n Simeon's store the long winter evenings, which supplied for Killick Covers their lecture, concert, and theater entertainment. Many of the oral narratives that climax the evening's talk embody supernatural legends. Two sessions revolve about local witches, spiteful man riders who hove their dreaded bridles on offending persons, and a skilled necromancer rendered tributes of tobacco, snuff, and tea by departing mariners. Skipper Job Gaskett relates how his wife once had her mare "teched" by a witch she visited so that the animal could not move, whereupon she reached out of the wagon and jabbed a long pin into the charmer's arm, so that the blood gushed forth; immediately the mare started up like a bullet out of a gun. Job further testifies that he has actually seen witch bridles still hanging in two Cove houses, and describes in detail one his father found plastered up in the wall of his house, woven of tow, horsehair and yellow birch bark.[2] A famous Cove tradition, slyly elicited from the witch authority Job by the store circle for yet another telling, involved Skipper Nate Spurshoe and a parcel of fly-by-nights. When Skipper Nate rudely denied old Sairy Kentle some stripped halibut he was lugging home, trouble instantly commenced: the lashings on his bundle of halibut came off and would not stay tied; Sairy, hiding in

<hr />

[2] *Cap'n Simeon's Store* (Boston and New York: Houghton, Mifflin & Co., 1903), pp. 57-59, 85.

the bushes, threw a bridle at him, and Nate, knowing he had to cross water or a stone wall to avoid being ridden, streaked up the road and leaped over a wall just as the bridle brushed his shoulder. (The turn in the road atop the hill thenceforth bore the name "Devil's Gap.") But at home the witch works continued; Nate's cow kept getting mired in the hackamatack swamp, and his wife could not make the butter come; one windy night the Devil called for Sairy, who whisked away leaving a shiny black cat sitting in her place (Mrs. Job Gaskett had seen this); then a screeching troupe broke into Spurshoe's barricaded house, bridled him up and rode him twenty miles through the rain and mud; for a month after the Skipper lay sick abed.[3]

Most of the yarnings dealt with eerie sea happenings, spectral sailor-men and cursed vessels. Strange works beset the schooner *Harvester;* Skipper Rufus Hulldown would tell of a short, chunky-built fellow, wearing a fur cap and knitted jumpers, whom he spied on deck one night; but the figure never spoke nor stirred, and Rufe clasped only air when he sought to seize him. Before the voyage was out the un-wanted guest had proved his worth, however, for Rufe and his brother Ephe heard an unseen voice warn them to make sail from the treacher-ous bight where the *Harvester* lay anchored, just before a fearful storm broke that would have lashed her to pieces against the island. On returning to Burnt-Coat Harbor, where he had bought the ship, Rufus learned that the former owner, whose widow had disposed of the packet immediately after his death, still stood anchor watch aboard his ship.[4] A differently motivated specter caused the works on the square-rigger *Falls of Ettrick,* nee the *Gertrude Spurshoe* before she was sold to Eng-lishmen for the Quebec–Liverpool run. Yarning in the store, Uncle Rufe tells how he had sailed on her in both her roles of Yankee barque and English timber drogher; it was in the latter stage that Rufe beheld a man-figure plummet from aloft and thud bloodily beside the sullen Dago at the wheel. No one on board could identify the body, and no one would touch it to heave overboard except McLaren the Dago, who suddenly declared, "I've handled him once, and I can ag'in"; but when he grasped hold of the bloody mass, it stretched two writhing arms

---

[3] *Cap'n Simeon's Store,* ch. 5, "The Witch-Bridle."
[4] *Cap'n Simeon's Store,* ch. 7, "The 'Works' on the Schooner Harvester."

about him and both dove over the rail together. Later Rufe learned from the *Gerty's* former captain that McLaren had been suspected of cutting the rigging under a crewmate who had fallen to his death from aloft.[5] Other haunt yarns concern two ghostly reprobates, rum-drinking, chantey-singing loafers, whose profane oaths and lusty songs still sound over the river emptying into the bay and always herald a heavy breeze;[6] "ructions" at deserted Wreck Island, mysterious footprints and rappings that followed the uncovering of three island graves by a pounding storm, and led the two rugged islanders to flee precipitately;[7] a talking hagdon (a species of seagull) who spoke with the voice of Skipper Nate Kentle — the Skipper whose ship with all its crew had gone down off Matinicus Rock, after a rat had been seen to shin ashore on a breast line at the wharf.[8] Cursed ships disport strangely. When Aunt Polly Futtock "teched" the *Vesper*, in response to pleas of her youthful crew for a one-day holiday, it stood upright on the gravelly beach with no visible supports, balancing on its narrow keel, and the martinet skipper dared not lay a hand to her until she behaved more normally the next morning.[9] No more Jonah'd vessel ever sailed out of Killick Cove than the oak-built *Heart's Desire*, whose trail of misfortune began with her very launching and submerged several owners in its wake; hearing her story the hardiest cynic could not deny that luck inheres in wood and iron.[10]

Omens and superstitions weave into the daily lives of the fisherfolk. Various kinds of "forerunners" — portents of impending tragedy — intersperse the memorable experiences relived in Cap'n Simeon's store. Job Gaskett brilliantly interpreted the six thumps he heard issue from the empty oil-can, as indicating the limit of sister Jane's life; sure enough the series of thumps decreased by one each month, until finally when

[5] *Cap'n Simeon's Store*, ch. 6, "Who Fell from Aloft?"

[6] *Home From Sea*. (Boston and New York: Houghton, Mifflin & Co., 1908), ch. 2, "The Two Chanty-Men." Stranded on the beach by the ebb tide, the precious duo refused to quit: "be jiggered ef the pair wouldn't lay right back on them thwarts and dig their oars into them mudflats so spiteful 't would start the clams a-squirtin' for all they was wuth, everywheres inside a dezen boats' lengths!" (p. 56).

[7] *Cap'n Simeon's Store*, ch. 9, "The Wreck Island Ructions."

[8] *Cap'n Simeon's Store*, pp. 66-68.

[9] *Cap'n Simeon's Store*, ch. 12, "The 'Teching' of the Vesper."

[10] *Cap'n Simeon's Store*, ch. 11, "Deacon Spurshoe's Jonah."

they ceased altogether in the sixth month, sister Jane passed away. A mystic affinity bound Sim Kentle and the crooked little apple tree close to his house; as Skipper Sim's liver shrunk, its blossoms and leaves dropped off; but when the Doctor implanted a new liver in Sim, the buds and blossoms instantly began to cover the bare poles, and grew apace with the sprouting liver. A rattling and banging fit to stave in the house of Skipper Job Gaskett apprised his mother that her mate at sea would not return, and sure enough nineteen sail from Killick Cove went down that night in a master storm. Conversely, while at sea, Skipper Job's father had once heard a burst of heavenly music and seen the stars shine through a sudden rift in the mud-thick fog; and at his home, just at that time, Job and his twin brother were born. "Sho, you!" exclaimed Sheriff Windseye. "I don't doubt but what the ole sir was some tickled to find it wasn't no wuss!"[11]

Superstitious beliefs and primitive practices revolved about cures and remedies, charms and observances. Sail a hitch to the nor'ard on your first spring trip out of the Cove to insure a fair voyage; kill pork at flood tide unless you want the carcase to shrink one-quarter; fill your bucket with ebb tide seawater to bathe those with rheumatism, if you wish to draw it out successfully; place a black cat under a washtub to hinder a ship from sailing.[12] Even love succumbed to a potent spell. Aunt Polly Futtock specialized in projects calculated to ensnare the most obdurate lover; the tragedy behind the pitiable invalidism of once handsome Robert Henderson was due to an untimely heaving of the project by Aunt Polly, at the request of lovelorn Susy Mary May, for he was at sea in the *Heart's Desire*, aloft in the rigging in a hard blow, when the project took hold; he lost his grip and plummeted to the deck, smashing his hipbone but somehow surviving, to be consoled through the years by a grief-tortured Susie May.[13] Bodily as well as spiritual ailments yield to proper treatments. After eating a cake made from a finely powdered, fresh-caught rat, at the behest of Roweny Kentle, a deformed sickly girl grew into a stout healthy woman. Feeling his

---

[11] *Cap'n Simeon's Store*, ch. 4, "Superstitions of the Cove."

[12] *Cap'n Simeon's Store*, pp. 76-77, 79-80, 80-81; *Home from Sea*, p. 280.

[13] *Home from Sea*, ch. 9, "Heavin' the Project" (casting a specially prepared witch-spell). Job Gaskett exhibits a scar caused by a project (p. 289).

blood sluggish and foul, Captain Simeon Roundturn simply jabbed a
jackknife into the calf of his leg and bled out his impurities; to straighten
out a crooked finger he set it on a flatiron and hammered it periodically
— a process that pained considerably less than the misery doctors
would inflict, physical and financial. Old Doc Gaskett once operated on Jake Kentle's sore tooth by placing him on the floor across
a doorway, jamming the door against his neck with his knee, and then
yanking out the tooth with his cant-dog; inadvertently Doc pulled out
two teeth and a big chunk of jawbone, but since he only charged for
one Jake did not complain.[14]

A lesser strain of humor mingles with the flow of supernatural yarns.
Eccentric characters misbehave: obstinate Uncle Sylvane, to escape the
summer "rusticators," had his house moved by boat to a forsaken
island;[15] a miserly woman sent her children with letters to the rusticators begging food for the winter and in a postscript offering to buy
a canary bird.[16] A bashful Yankee suitor emerges in Skipper Haultaut,
who upon much persuasion sallied forth to court a rusticator with a
mild eye, but shortly gave up the chase; damning evidence of the "toni-
ness" he suspected had presented itself, for on passing the widow's
quarters he had spied, in the window, a gleaming "toothbresh."[17] One
hardy folktale about a fool mistake creeps into an evening session; a
woodchopper gashes his boot with his axe and spying his red stockings
through the cut, thinks he is bleeding to death. Holman Day and the
Saturday Rambler contain like confusions, while the *Yankee Blade*
can cite a case of a man who put two stockings on the same foot and
in great agony summoned a doctor to treat the swelling.[18]

In Wasson's slender writings the arts of folk and literary narration
overlap. With Day and Robinson, he represents a strain of American
literature that has naturally drawn sap and vitality from soil enriched
by a popular lore.

[14] *Cap'n Simeon's Store*, ch. 10, "Doctors, Both Human and Veteran." Cf. Holman
Day's "The Ballad of Doc Pluff," *Pine Tree Ballads* (Boston, 1902), pp. 181-185, for
similar surgical severity.
[15] *Home from Sea*, pp. 105-109.　　　　[16] *Cap'n Simeon's Store*, pp. 33-34.
[17] *Home from Sea*, ch. 5, "Skipper Haultaut's Wooing."
[18] *Cap'n Simeon's Store*, pp. 31-32; Holman Day, *Up in Maine* (Boston, 1902), pp.
188-192; "Power of Imagination," *Saturday Rambler*, Sept. 25, 1847 (vol. II); "Reducing
a Swelling," *Yankee Blade*, April 28, 1855 (vol. XIV).

Literary Folktales

Robert P. Tristram Coffin

A confirmed regionalist describing Maine rural life in autobiography, biography, history, fiction, and poetry, Mr. Coffin has known and used local popular tradition from oral and written sources. A revealing account of the process whereby folk history fertilizes in the brain of the artist to emerge in a creative work has been set down by the poet himself. Years after reading the Indian captivity of John Gyles, without recourse to the source book (being in fact in England and denied access to it), Coffin wrote "The Schooling of Richard Orr" around the salient features that remained in his memory. Purely chance associations evoked the brightest images in his mind; some details were hazy; additions and alterations had to be made for purposes of artistic construction.[1] Between the historical tradition and the literary production, therefore, a notable hiatus exists; probably in more compact narratives the source, oral tale or written legend, is closer to the composition, but that revision, conscious and unconscious, transmutes folkstuff into "the substance that is poetry," the poet himself readily admits.

In the poems collected in *Maine Ballads*, Mr. Coffin has deliberately set out to present traditional material within a traditional form.

Folk living and folk speaking still go on, in spite of all our modern improvements. The materials for ballads are still being made up every day out of the whole cloth of human nature.... The stories are there for the ballads, and the words to them, for anybody who has eyes to see the shape of them and ears to hear the rhythms and the fall of the words. The words are there because there is still such a thing as oral literature: idioms and images, wise sayings, and words themselves that have not got into books much even yet, at least with much life in them. Maine is especially full of such idioms and words. And Maine is full of the makings of ballad stories, too.... It is such patterns of experience which I have tried to set down in this book, as I have seen them for myself, or heard them told, in a straightforward and spoken style but with that irreducible minimum of adornment which oral literature demands.

These verses ... are to be judged, both in style and in plot, by the principles of folk design.[2]

[1] *The Substance That Is Poetry* (New York: Macmillan, 1942), pp. 112–127. The ballad is in *Collected Poems of Robert P. Tristram Coffin* (New York, Macmillan, 1939), pp. 91–99.
[2] *Maine Ballads* (New York: Macmillan, 1938), pp. vii-viii. Quoted by permission of the publisher.

Folk design is manifest in both the form and the matter. Mr. Coffin is partial to the conventional ballad meter, alternate four plus three measures rhyming a b c b; his story is brisk and baldly told, usually with a strong suggestion of pathos. Mr. Coffin's regional balladry combines the literary pretensions of the Brainard–Whittier poems with the native gusto of Day's verse, and rings much truer than the diffuse and facile outpour of his non-regional ballad efforts.

Local legends. Supernatural motives have crusted into place legends mentioned in the ballad stories. Fisherfolk avoid the cove where Jethro hanged himself and from which his billy goat vanished without leaving even a hoofprint behind.[3] "The Cross-Roads Grocery-Store" is built over the grave of a flighty wife who, some two hundred years before, had taken her own life and been buried in usual witch fashion with a stake driven through her ribs, there to lie under pounding feet until Old Hairy should come to fetch her soul.[4] When Captain Jeremiah Sinnett did not return from his voyage as expected on Christmas day, his wife planted his name in green seed on the hill behind the house; each spring thereafter, regardless of plowings over by new owners, the letters reappeared in green.[5] Holman Day knew of a like gravemark, the heavenly crown that graced the shaggy head of Elias Rich, who through adversity had kept his faith in God; scrubbings of the marble slab could not remove the picture that grew deeper with the years.[6] Blaspheming Jim Bibber feared neither man nor God, and sneered at those who prayed in church; one foggy April Sunday he unscrewed the horn from his phonograph:

> And he went out upon his hill,
>   Tipped the horn up far
> And bellowed through it, "Hi thar God!
>   How's the fog up thar?
>
> "How's the weather, Old White-Whiskers?
>   Has it wet your lap?"
> And that instant there ripped out
>   An ear-splitting thunder-clap.

[3] In "Jethro's Pet," *Maine Ballads*, p. 19.
[4] *Maine Ballads*, pp. 53-54. Cf. "Vexation Hill" in Chapter V, *Place names*.
[5] "The Name Kept Green," *Maine Ballads*, pp. 57-59.
[6] " 'Heavenly Crown' Rich," *Pine Tree Ballads* (Boston, 1902), pp. 30-34.

A ball of fire, lobster-red,
Came down like a ship,
Hit the horn and melted it
To Jim's smoking lip.[7]

Jim repented. A place legend linked to Daggett's Rock in Phillips, Maine, preserves a parallel occurrence.

200-YEAR-OLD LEGEND ABOUT CLEFT IN PHILLIPS BOULDER

Every year it is estimated that at least 5,000 vacationists to the Rangeley Lake region visit or snapshot or climb Daggett's Rock in this town. It is not such a wonderful looking boulder altho it is credited with being second only to the famous Jockey Cap at Fryeburg, the largest boulder in New England.

It is the story that for two full centuries has been told and believed by many explaining how this great rock came to be split in twain that makes it a magnet of tourist attraction. Two hundred years ago there lived in a little log cabin near this boulder, which was then intact, a rough and ready woodsman named Daggett. He made and drank his own liquor and was a pronounced and offensive infidel.

One day during the progress of a terrific thunderstorm with jagged lightning bolts striking frequently, the blasphemous Daggett climbed to the top of the boulder. There, soaked to the skin by the rain, half drunk, he shook his fist at the black firmament overhead and with horrible oaths defied any Creator to strike him. Crash! A bolt from the ether followed almost instantly by a thunder peal that reverberated and reverberated from the near by mountain tops.

As if sliced by the irresistible knife of some Gargantuan the huge rock fell apart. Killed instantly Daggett's body plunged headlong into the gap and into a great hole at the bottom the bolt had ploughed out. A ready-to-order grave where the broken Daggett lay. Then came another lightning bolt and a slab was ripped from the cleft rock. It fell over the hole completely sealing and covering forever the infidel Daggett.

A lone trapper coming thru the forests got a glimpse of Daggett as he stood on the rock shaking his fist. He saw the death-dealing bolt and saw the body plunge forward and down. Partially stunned himself from his proximity to the stricken boulder he finally recovered and as the sun emerged from the clouds he got a clear view of the scene of the tragedy. It was easy to reconstruct what had happened.

Residents of the then sparsely settled region came to see and then it was that they bestowed the name of Daggett's Rock by which it has ever since been known. Parallel cases of death dealing lightning bolts to those who have defied the Creator to harm them may be found.[8]

[7] From "The Big Voice," *Maine Ballads*, p. 27. Quoted by permission of the publisher.
[8] *Lewiston Journal*, Jan. 23, 1936.

Other graphic legends in the ballads similarly follow familiar folktale types. A graphic Kidd treasure yarn, told by Cap'n Pye who saw the chest on the sea bottom, guarded by a boy holding his severed head upon his knee, Mr. Coffin recaptures both in prose and verse.[9] In "The Half-Quintal of Fish," Eph's grandma relates a plausible pioneer experience, of her own granny chased by wolves as she walked back through the woods from Harpswell to Brunswick carrying fifty pounds of bluefish and her grandchild piggy back; by tossing out the fish one by one, reluctantly, as she ran, she managed to appease the snapping wolves until the lights of Brunswick loomed.[10] This ballad tale derives from Brunswick folk history, but is a multiple pioneer experience.[11]

Yankee yarns. Strains of Yankee folk humor relieve the darker legends in the ballads. Earlier horse races with unexpected victors are recalled by "The Dark Horse"; prudish, gentle Deacon Raspberryhorn finds himself unexpectedly involved in a bitterly contested race between two tipsy, cursing ruffians who stream by his buckboard; the Deacon's horse, once a pacer at the fair, becomes infected with the racing virus, sweeps into the course, and willynilly brings the Deacon home a winner.[12] Caught red-handed, a sheepstealer is ready with a scapegrace retort; he claims the sheep bit him, and unabashedly continues on his way before his dumbfounded accuser.[13] Elsewhere in Yankee anecdotes the thief shows equal gall.

An old chap, residing here, who might be classed as of the genus 'Scalawag,' who was too lazy to work, but picked up a living by pettifogging, and other means more or less equivocal, was caught by a neighbor with a rail on his back, which he had just appropriated from said neighbor's fence for firewood.

[9] *Lost Paradise* (New York: Macmillan, 1934), pp. 207–213; "Ballad of Cap'n Pye," *Collected Poems*, p. 62-67.

[10] *Maine Ballads*, pp. 99-102.

[11] George A. and Henry W. Wheeler, *History of Brunswick, Topsham, and Harpswell, Me.* (Boston, 1878), pp. 88-89; "A Race with the Wolves," *New Hampshire Folk Tales*, Mrs. Moody P. Gore and Mrs. Guy E. Speare, compilers (n.p., 1932), pp 108-109; Scrapbook AC 040.1. P873 (vol. 5, pp. 60-61), in the Vermont Historical Society, Montpelier. Mr. Coffin told me he would have considered his story an unfaithful transcription if granny, smacking her lips at the thought of a bluefish dinner, had thrown the baby to the wolves. Actually one bear tale does contain a frightened woman's suggestion to throw Bruin the baby (Edwin Emery, *The History of Sanford, Me.*, Fall River, Mass., 1901, pp. 160-161).

[12] *Maine Ballads*, pp. 73-76.   [13] "Black Sheep," *Maine Ballads*, pp. 68-71.

'Hallo! you old scoundrel! what are you stealing my fence for?' was the salutation he received from the owner.

The old fellow turned around, rested one end of the rail on the ground, and replied without the least embarrassment, 'I ain't such an almighty sight older than you are, you meddling old fool.' Then deliberately shouldering the rail, he carried it home. Slightly on the 'wrong tack!'[14]

Yankees might be mean, cunning, ignorant, inquisitive, but above all else they were lazy. The shiftless Yankee is exposed in "Lazy-bones"; neighbors bring a cord of wood to the shivering Yanceys, who with their seven strapping sons huddle inertly around the empty fireplace of their slatternly hovel. In the evening Dan Yancey calls on Abel Leigh:

"Can't you send one of your boys
To saw my birch for me?"[15]

Folktales of the insuperably lazy Yankee fill native humor. Commonest is the starving idler who, proffered a bushel of corn, asks "Is it shelled?"[16] Other slothful Yankees exercise by weeding in the garden from a cushioned rocking chair with a pair of firetongs; dig potatoes with an all-day gusto that yields three — including one being dug and another about to be dug; hoe corn without touching hoe to earth — for one hill is not worth the hoeing, and another would never produce anything if hoed.[17] A champion lazy man, awarded ten dollars for supreme laziness north of the Massachusetts line, asked the committee to roll him over and place it in his back pocket; he missed seeings the sheriff's funeral because he was facing the wrong way in his hammock.[18]

[14] Nathan Daboll, *The New-England Almanac*, 1855 (New London, n.d.), p. 29, "Not So Old, Neither."

[15] *Maine Ballads*, p. 12.

[16] New Hampshire's Daughters, *Folk-lore Sketches and Reminiscences of New Hampshire Life* (Boston, c. 1911), p. 39; *More New Hampshire Folk Tales*, Mrs. Guy E. Speare, compiler (Plymouth, N.H., 1936), p. 283; Leonard A. Morrison, *The History of Windham in New Hampshire* (Boston, 1883), p. 242; *Yankee*, II (September 1936), 10; Marion Blake, "Helping the Shiftless," *Burlington Free Press*, Oct. 8, 1934; Amos Otis, "The Linnal Genealogy," *Barnstable* [Mass.] *Patriot*, May 1, 1886.

[17] "A New Bedford Fish Story," *Spirit of the Times*, XVI (Nov. 7, 1846), 433; Thomas R. Hazard, *The Jonny-Cake Letters* (Providence, 1882), pp. 54-55; *Yankee Blade*, Dec. 11, 1852 (vol. XII), "An Awful Lazy Case" ("Jabez, a great loblolly of a slab-sided dooless-looking whelp"); Simon L. Bradbury, "How Jonathan Buzzel Hoed His Corn," *Corn Tassel Tales of New England* (Meadville, Pa., c. 1931), pp. 36-37.

[18] Robert Davis, "Some Characteristics of Northern Vermont Wit," *Proceedings of the Vermont Historical Society*, n.s., V (December 1937), 330-331.

Jonathan Draws the Long Bow

In his sheaf of Maine ballads Mr. Coffin has avoided romantic designs without renouncing poetic craftsmanship. By adapting his literary form to the colloquial idiom of American popular tales, he necessarily strays far from the impossible model of the Child ballad Brainard and Whittier regarded as their guide.

Walter Hard

Vermont rural life forms the one subject of the free verse poet Mr. Walter Hard, who finds that the folkways of his state are not regionally or even nationally unique.[1] From personal observation and acquaintance he has etched compact life histories, prevalent social attitudes, speech manners and rhythms, sharp character portraits, and succinct episodes that in common limn a twentieth-century backwash society. The dominant tone in the poems is somber, and poverty is the most insistent note; if Mr. Hard is primarily a realist picturing an industrially bypassed, stagnant country, and a moralist as well whose verse stories are often moral fables, his ear is nonetheless acutely tuned for the folk humor that bubbles from such stony ground. His brief narratives, shaped into poetic contours of ordinary speech, move toward climaxes pointed by the barbed retort, the compressed phrase, and the casual lie of Yankee language; these stories about Vermont folk incidentally, almost necessarily, include Vermont folk stories.

Local legends. Few place legends enter into the corner store and village talk. Two place-name histories show sufficient oral vitality to reach Mr. Hard's poems. "Smuggler's Notch" mentions without explaining what must have been a lurid legendary association, for boulders stand on either side of the road "Jest as the Old Gent left 'em"; "Fiddler's Crook" is a bend in the road where Jimmy the fiddler used to sit and play, and where he died in a snowdrift.[2]

---

[1] In the course of a conversation Mr. Hard told me that while all of his material has come at first hand — much of it from experiences while working in his father's general store — he has received letters from other parts of the country and from abroad testifying to characters and incidents parallel with those in his poems. He ascribes these common elements to "the uniformity of rural living."

[2] *Vermont Valley* (New York: Harcourt, Brace & Co., c. 1939), pp. 21–22; *A Mountain Township* (New York, Harcourt, Brace & Co., c. 1933), pp. 215-216. Cf. Chapter V, *Place names*, "Fiddler's Reach."

Yankee stories. Yankee types, folk tricks, and sayings color the verse anecdotes. Dickers and swaps hinge on the literal contract. A sly trader admits his mare has two faults, one being that she is hard to catch; after the trade is concluded he reveals the other, that she is no good after she is caught.[3] Another hoodwinker replies to a complainant accusing him of lying about the unruly oxen he had sold, that his words had been strict truth: he had said the oxen never bothered him a mite, and they hadn't, because nothing bothered him.[4] Similarly in the folktale of the Kicking Cow, the trader disposes of a cow who habitually kicks over the milkpail, with some such remark as, "You will be able to handle her as well as I can."[5]

Varieties of shiftless, cunning, and stingy Yankees parade through the poems. Congenital laziness unfolds in several pieces: Tom refuses a job because he is helping Hiram — although Hiram isn't doing anything just then; Pat complains at being fired when it takes so little to keep him busy ("Pat Clark wasn't afraid of work. / He would lie right down beside it / And go to sleep any time."); Eph Applegate comes to town at dawn so he won't even have to hear about work; Ezra decides, after many failures, to raise hogs — because they can mostly raise themselves, and Cynthy can fetch the swill.[6] Scapegraces indulge in traditional knavery. When Zephaniah, whose saving habits had earned him the envy of shiftless neighbors, sold a yoke of oxen on a Sunday, the Board of Deacons labored with him on his wickness, and secured his promise to express in meeting his regret for selling cattle on the Sabbath. At meeting Zephaniah rose and said, "Wal, I will say I'm sorry it was Sunday / When I sold them cattle."[7] This concession suggests another unconvincing public repentance that has passed into folktale: a congenital liar, tearfully repenting in the meetinghouse, an-

[3] "Only Two Faults," *Vermont Valley*, pp. 73-74.
[4] "Botheration," *A Mountain Township*, pp. 161-162.
[5] Mr. William S. Piper of Worcester, Mass., has told me two versions of the Kicking Cow; Marion Blake gives another in her series "Vermont Oddities" (*Burlington Free Press*, Nov. 2, 1935, "Scarcely a Lie"), where the farmer admits his cow kicks one of her four legs; the buyer thinks he means "forelegs."
[6] *Walter Hard's Vermont* (Brattleboro, Vt.: Stephen Daye, c. 1941), pp. 121–122, "A Helping Hand"; *ibid.*, p. 151, "Anti Work"; *A Mountain Township*, p. 83, "A Gardener"; *ibid.*, pp. 173-174, "Hog Culture."
[7] *A Mountain Township*, pp. 163-164, "Zephaniah's Repentance."

nounces he has shed barrels and barrels of tears over his besetting sin.[8] Hard exposes two precious ingrates: a loafer who, given a quarter pound package of tobacco, says he usually gets a pound; and a skinflint who, loaned a horse after he had worked his own to death, complains that the borrowed animal overeats.[9] Elsewhere rascals show similar cheek. Asa Jenness went to the store doubting whether his picayune swap of an egg for a knitting needle would entitle him to the gill of rum that rewarded traders. The storekeeper allowed him the rum; Asa asked him for an egg in it; when the egg proved to be double-yolked, Asa demanded a second needle.[10] A suppliant wayfarer stopped at Perkins' tavern and asked the landlady for a few potatoes to eat with his cold meat. Since travelers frequently carried a portion of their provisions en route, she acceded. After nicely roasting them, he again approached the landlady and importuned for a little cold meat to eat with his roasted potatoes.[11] Yankee materialism comes to the fore in "The Last Wrong," where Liza refuses dying Hiram a piece of ham because she plans to serve it at his funeral.[12] A kindred Maine farmer registered regret when his wife hung herself in an apple tree, because she kicked off so many green apples.[13] New England parsimony did not retreat for death.

Senator Lodge, of Massachusetts, by way of pointing a moral of New England economy, spun this yarn the other day to three or four bystanders in the Capitol:

There was a funeral in one of the small farmhouses in the neighborhood of Cape Cod, and the friends of the deceased were gathering in the tiny parlor when there entered the room a typical New England female of the kind that mingles curiosity with sympathy. As she glanced around the darkened room, she said to the bereaved widow,

"Where did you get that new eight-day clock?"

[8] "Barrels and Barrels of Tears," *Berkshire Hills*, vol. II (March 1, 1902); Marion Blake, "An Exaggerator," *Burlington Free Press and Times*, Aug. 28, 1934. This story is also credited to "Oregon" Smith, an Indiana folk hero, by Herbert Halpert and Emma Robinson (*Southern Folklore Quarterly*, VI, September 1942, 166).

[9] *Walter Hard's Vermont*, pp. 91-92, "Looking a Gift Horse"; *A Mountain Township*, pp. 153-154, "Looking at a Gift Horse."

[10] Cornelius Weygandt, *The White Hills* (New York, c. 1934), p. 350; cf. *American Wit and Humor* (New York: Harper & Bros., c. 1859), p. 20.

[11] C. C. Lord, *Life and Times in Hopkinton, N.H.* (Concord, N.H., 1890), pp. 292-293.

[12] *A Mountain Township*, pp. 195-196.

[13] John Gould, *Farmer Takes A Wife* (New York, c. 1945), p. 70.

"We ain't got no new eight-day clock," was the reply.

"You ain't? What's that in the corner there?"

"That's the deceased. We stood him on end to make room for the mourners."[14]

The folk humor of indirection points Mr. Hard's choicest stories. A customer who had purchased a singularly tough side of beef returns and asks the butcher for a pair of galluses from the same critter; a buyer of spalt firewood comes back for another cord, explaining he has a contract to put out the fires of hell.[15] Crazy Williams, asked why he has so much trouble fighting off the Devil who does not disturb others, replies, "He don't never bother / them that he's sure of."[16] Eternally busy about other folks' business, Samuel Hickok observes to young Higgins as he drives past with a new team of Western horses, "That nigh mare interferes"; "Wal, thank the Lord, Sam Hickok, / She don't interfere / With nothin' but herself."[17] These and other verbal spears fall within the established conventions of acid Yankee dialogue.

Tall tales. Remembered corner-store conversations supply much material for Mr. Hard's poems, which frequently reveal his familiarity with storytelling scenes.

> It was a chilly day in spring
> And Frank drew a nail keg
> Up to the big chunk stove
> Where a brisk fire was crackling.
> He took out his jack knife
> And cut off a generous chew.
> The storekeeper filled his cob pipe
> And sat down in the black arm chair
> With its arms worn smooth by many elbows.[18]

Talk begins, and Frank tells the storekeeper what a good investment his old frayed sweater has been; it stretches so that every fall his woman

[14] "The Story-Tellers' Club," *Cosmopolitan*, XLIX (July 1910), 275.

[15] "Haberdashery," *Walter Hard's Vermont*, p. 34-35; "A Fire Extinguisher," *A Mountain Township*, pp. 207-208.

[16] "Crazy Williams," *A Mountain Township*, p. 92.

[17] "Interference," *A Mountain Township*, p. 69. A stock Yankee rebuff to inquisitive questions states that the quizzed traveler is journeying to draw his pension money; he gets a pension for minding his own business. ("Not So Green," *Yankee Blade*, Mar. 10, 1855; "A Good Story Well Told," *Expansion — Vermont's Industrial Magazine*, May 1906.)

[18] From "A Good Investment," *Walter Hard's Vermont*, p. 48. Quoted by permission of the publisher.

gets a sweater off the bottom for little Frankie, plus a pair of wristers from the sleeves. Side by side with tight-tongued Vermonters, Green Mountain Munchausens invent.

> Lin was no ordinary liar.
> He belonged to the romantic school
> Of fiction talkers.
> He used his overwhelming creative instincts
> Making ordinary events into things of interest.
> He began in his youth
> By telling tales of adventures
> In which he usually figured as hero.
> Later in life a creative memory
> Enlarged and enriched his field.[19]

From such "romanticists" the windies fly. To assist the storekeeper, berated by city folks for recommending an unsatisfactory man to build their chimney, Jim Slocum puts in a boost for the carpenter; he had built Jim a chimney that drawed so powerfully, it drew the wood right out of the stove.[20] When an officious New York summer resident inquired why hounds had outlandish-looking long ears, Elias Parsons civilly expatiated; the ears flopped around when the dogs ran after game, fanned the air up and down, and blew the scent into their noses.[21] Around the chunk stove at the store, discussion centered on startling weather changes; Smith Jameson recalled how, back in the early seventies, a sudden cold snap had frozen over Sand's Pond, where a flock of ducks had lit; in the morning the ducks rose and flew off with the whole pond.[22] The sudden cold snap has inspired many longbows.

A TRIO OF LONGBOWS

Some of our "river men" (says the Cincinnati Daily Columbian) are not slow coaches in telling long yarns. During these low times, the river folks have but little to do else than sample fluids and solids, whittle, smoke, and spin yarns. About a dozen of well known river captains, pilots, &c., congregated in ----- t'other day, when one led off with saying —

"Capt. Mac, thundering cool morning."

[19] From "A Romanticist," *A Mountain Township*, p. 90. Quoted by permission of the publisher.

[20] "A Chimney," *A Mountain Township*, pp. 88-89. A powerfully drawing chimney in New Hampshire is described in Robert Kempt, *The American Joe Miller* (London, 1865), pp. 4-5, "Hard Lying." [21] "Dog's Ears," *A Mountain Township*, pp. 209-210.

[22] "Weather Change," *Walter Hard's Vermont*, pp. 184-185.

"Cool," says Mac, "don't begin to be. Why boys, I've seen the weather so *cool* up the Missouri, that when I and Bob Graham got into a skiff to cross the river, a north wind swept down the stream and the water began to chill. 'Pull,' says I, 'Bob, stick in your paddle, it's going to freeze.'

" 'Tis freezing,' says Bob.

" 'Pull,' says I; and the ice began to get thick as window glass, afore we got ten yards out in the river. 'Pull,' says I, 'Bob'; but, Lord a massey, boys, before we got ten rods further, the ice was thick as a beefsteak, and though Bob and I kept a breaking up the ice and pushing the boat, it got so ahead of us, that we dropt the skiff; she was frize in; we got out on the ice, and run like – – – –, to get ashore before we froze to death!"

"Not so very cold that warn't, nuther," — says a weather-beaten pilot. "Now, there's Jimmy Gilfilian and I once were driving a flock of sheep across a big prairie, near the Illinois river; about the time we got half way across the prairie, one of them north winds swept down upon us, the sheep huddled together, we found that we were about to freeze, so we takes to our feet, and ran about two miles to a woods, where we started a fire, and laid up for the night. It was awful cool, a feller would roast one side to the fire and freeze t'other. Well, sirs, next morning we goes out to the sheep, they were all huddled together, we commenced starting 'em up, none of 'em would move, by thunder and Goliah, we found 'em all dead — froze fast together all in a lump."

"That sheep story," said a well known river man, who, with a dirk-knife, was giving the finishing touches to a pine dolphin, "is some; it is cold on the prairies now and then; but I can tell you of a cool snap I once knew, in the dead of summer time, here in Shelby, Kentucky."

"Cool snap in the dead of summer?" said one of the slightly incredulous.

"Why, yes; you see we were out harvesting; the frogs were mighty thick around there, and it came on to freeze and blow so in ten minutes that the ground got as hard as ever you see it in the middle of winter. Well, the frogs were so suddenly took by the cold snap, that they were frozen in the mud afore they could get their heads under, and we walked over an acre lot, and kicked off the heads of more than ten thousand frogs, frozen in that way."

A bystander volunteered to treat the crowd — he did it and sloped.[23]

Sitting around after the haying, the farmers start spinning yarns. Old man Peters boasts of having in his youth shucked a whole load of hay by straightening out his back under the axle. Cy remembers a strong man from the marble quarry who bet he could lift a tarnation big block with a crowbar; he strained so hard his feet sank two inches right into the solid ledge on which he was standing.[24] Vain of his grey

[23] *Yankee Blade*, Mar. 25, 1854 (vol. XIII).

[24] "A Little Careless with the Truth," *Vermont Valley*, pp. 172-174. Cf. *ante*, Day, "Grampy's Lullaby."

mare, Hiram Nichols bragged he could tell to a pound how much the mare could draw. A bystander picked out a log and bet a dollar against the animal. In spite of Hiram's conviction, the mare could not stir the log; knowing something was wrong, Hiram looked around, spied a pair of wet mittens left on the end of the log, threw them off, picked up the reins, gave the mare the word, and she drew it first try. This too is a traveled yarn.[25]

In one verse story the poet has a Green Mountain storekeeper describe a busy day; "Th' cow's a-calvin', th' sheep's a-lambin' / Th' sow's a-piggin', and I got t' git me a clerk." [26] In a Boston newspaper of 1764 we have observed coincidental births in a parallel windy.[27] American folktale has prospered throughout American history, and Mr. Hard is merely the most recent raconteur in a vital native tradition.

[25] "The Tale of a Mare," *Walter Hard's Vermont*, pp. 45-46. Cf. *Yankee*, VIII (June 1942), 18-19.
[26] From "A Busy Day at the Scotsville Store," *Vermont Valley*, p. 15.
[27] Quoted in Chapter II, *Marvels and prodigies.*

NOTE ON THE PRINTED SOURCES FOR
NEW ENGLAND FOLKTALES

While the following categories of source material are by no means exhaustive, they indicate the chief hunting grounds tracked for this study.

Town Histories. A rewarding percentage of these contain traditional tales. New Englanders have notably specialized in local and antiquarian history. Buttressing town are county, regional, and colonial general histories, which sometimes print legends.

Newspapers. For the eighteenth century the *Boston Evening Post* has proved most fruitful in outlandish items. For mid-nineteenth-century humor the *Burlington Daily Free Press*, the *Exeter News Letter*, and the *Rutland Herald* have been harvested; the index to the file of the first of these in the Billings Library of the University of Vermont, compiled by the Federal Writers' Project (1932–1940), immeasurably simplified the labor of examination. Regular newspapers yielded comparatively much leaner returns than the antebellum literary-sporting-humorous weeklies: the New York *Spirit of the Times*, the Boston *Yankee Blade*, *Saturday Rambler*, *Union Jack*, and the *Yankee Privateer*. For the twentieth century, sets of clipping books in the Maine State Library at Augusta have provided an unexpected avenue to local legends and tall tales in Maine newspapers, particularly the *Bangor Daily News*, the *Lewiston Journal* and the *Portland Herald*. The Vermont Historical Society at Montpelier has a convenient file of the free verse local stories, "Vermont Oddities," published by Marion Blake in the *Burlington Daily Free Press and Times* in 1934 and 1935.

Magazines. For New Hampshire Indian legends the *Granite Monthly* (1877–1905) and its successor, the *Granite State Magazine* (1906–1914), offer a fertile repository. The *New England Magazine* (1884–1917) is much less profitable. Maine woodsmen's yarns and tall stories continually crop up in the *Northern* (1921–1927) and the *Maine Sportsman* (1893–1908). The *Berkshire Hills* (1900–1906) is stuffed with regional gossip and folk anecdotes from western Massachusetts. *Yankee*

(1935–1942) reveals in frequent patches the continuing tradition of native folk humor. Its earliest predecessor is probably *The Idiot* (1818), a short-lived serial that brims with sea-serpent tales and other Yankee-isms.

Collections and Collectors. Folktale compilations vary widely in character and usefulness. Sometimes books that have "Folklore" or "Legends" in their title prove blind alleys, since the terms are so loosely employed. Collections of supernatural and local tales worth noting are the three volumes of historical and fictional family traditions compiled under the auspices of the New Hampshire Federation of Women's Clubs, *Folklore of New Hampshire's Daughters* (1911), *New Hampshire Folk Tales* (1932), and *More New Hampshire Folk Tales* (1936); the spiritedly written books of Charles M. Skinner, *Myths and Legends of Our Own Land* (1896) and *American Myths and Legends* (1903), both strong in New England local legends whose integrity is not noticeably injured in the dangerous process of stylizing; a dull presentation of literary legends by Samuel A. Drake, *A Book of New England Legends and Folk Lore in Prose and Poetry* (1884), which has some value as an anthology but little in its commentary; the diversified folklore gathered from oral sources in western Massachusetts by Clifton Johnson in *What They Say in New England: A Book of Signs, Sayings and Superstitions* (1903), which includes a section of local stories; two pamphlets published by Ernest E. Bisbee in Lancaster, New Hampshire, *The State O' Maine Scrap Book* (c. 1940), which draws from the once popular Boston *Youth's Companion*, and, less original, *The White Mountain Scrap Book* (c. 1939). What could have been a genuine contribution, *The Narrow Land: Folk Chronicles of Old Cape Cod* by Elizabeth Reynard (1934), suffers from an absurdly overwritten style and an unjustifiable fusion of oral and literary sources.

Humorous popular tales can be found in jokebooks, galaxies, almanacs, and booklets. Compilations of ante-bellum humor with New England selections are *The American Joe Miller* (1839, 1865), and *The Galaxy of Comicalities* (1841). The long files of Robert Thomas's *The Farmer's Almanack* (1792–) and Nathan Daboll's *The New-England Almanack* (1793–) contain sprinklings of folk jokes and anecdotes for some sixty years on, but boast no single issue equal to a unique Crockett-like effusion, *Jonathan Jawstretcher's Yankee Story All-My-Nack* for 1852. Twentieth-century tall yarns curried directly from verbal sources can be found in two booklets, *Fireside Tales Told on Martha's Vineyard* by Joseph C. Allen (1934), editor of the *Edgartown Gazette*; and *The Tame Trout and Other Backwoods Fairy Tales* by Edward Grant (1904), a celebrated guide of the Rangeley Lakes.

Some expert folktale collectors are more or less accidentally folklorists. Quite unwittingly "Shepherd Tom" Hazard wrote a prime source-book of living folktale from the Narragansett Country in Rhode Island, in *The Jonny-Cake Letters* (1880) — (see R. M. Dorson, "The Jonny-Cake Papers," *Journal of American Folklore*, LVIII (April-June 1945), 104–112). Cornelius Weygandt, longtime summer resident of Sandwich, New Hampshire, inserts many twentieth-century folk anecdotes and witticisms into his four volumes on folkways of the New Hampshire mountain country: *The White Hills* (1934), *New Hampshire Neighbors* (1937), *November Rowen* (1941), and *The Heart of New Hampshire* (1944). Creative writers like Rowland Robinson, Holman Day, and George Wasson should be counted with the most zealous deliberate preservers of native folktale.

INDEX

Index

Index

Index

"Major Brown's Coon Story," 227–228
Mammy Red, witch, 38
Manchester, N. H., 46n., 127
Manitou, Indian deity, 145, 146, 150, 151, 152, 153
Marble, Dan, Yankee actor and storyteller, 70n.
Marblehead, Mass., 5n., 38, 45, 161, 220n.
Margaret Smith's Journal, 156n., 205, 211n.
"Marine Munchausen, A," 108–110
Martha's Vineyard, Mass., 8, 30, 106, 112n.
Martin, Jeffrey, wizard, 42
Massachusetts, 19, 23, 30, 42, 50, 51, 57, 61, 95, 97, 103, 121, 122, 144, 152, 158, 159, 160, 163, 166, 168, 169, 170, 173, 181, 183, 189, 190, 192, 193, 197, 211, 218, 243, 253, 256
Matchet Moodus, legends of, 202–203
Mather, Cotton, folk historian, 25, 28–30, 167, 182, 208, 211, 212, 220
Mather, Increase, folk historian, 28, 163n.
Matinicus Island, Me., 7–8, 172
"May Martin, or The Money Diggers," 214
"Mean Sam Green," 236
Medway, Mass., 41n., 169
"Melting Story, A," 19–20, 89–91
Meredith, N. H., 35n.
Meriden, Conn., 4n., 38n.
Merrimac River, 45, 141, 212
Merrimac Valley, N. H., 40n., 41n., 211n.
Micah Rood Apple, legend of, 171–172
Middlebury, Vt., 12n., 21, 23
Middlefield, Mass., 194
Middletown, Conn., 200
Middletown, R. I., 190
Milford, Conn., 175
Milton, Mass., 127n.
Moaning Bones of Mount Tom, legend of, 157–158
Mohawk braves, 142, 143
Mohegan Indians, in legend, 143, 145–146
Moll Pitcher, witch, 42–44, 208
"Moll Pitcher, A Poem," 208n., 210
Molly Molasses, witch, 42
"Money-Diggers, The," 201
"Money Hill," legend of, 185
Monhegan Island, Me., 177
Monmouth, Me., 36n.
Mont Vernon, N. H., 191
Montferrat, Joe, strong man, 122
Montpelier, Vt., 23n.
Monument Mountain, legend of, 146–147

Moodus Noises, 204, 208
Moody, Parson Samuel, character, 99–100
Moose Brook, legend of, 197
Moosehead, Me., 239n.
Moosehead Lake, Me., 123, 153
More Wonders of the Invisible World, 60
Morelen, William, money digger, 185
Morton, Thomas, folk historian, 16, 212
Moses Morrison, storyteller, 197
"Mother Worcester's Cave," legend of, 184
Moulton, Jonathan, figure of legend, 52–53, 206–207
Mt. Agamenticus, 16
Mount Desert Island, Me., 186n.
Mt. Katahdin, Me., 8, 143, 153, 154, 155, 207, 232
Mt. Kineo, Me., 153
Mt. Megunticook, Me., 148
Mt. Mianomo, Mass., 190n.
Mt. Moosilauke, Me., 170
Mt. Tom, R. I., 157–158
Mt. Towanda, Mass., 190n.
Mt. Washington, 16, 45, 155
Mt. William, N. H., 196
Mousam River, Me., 188
Mum Amey, witch, 40
Munchausens, 5–8, 102–110, 219, 237, 258

Nahant, Mass., 133, 134, 201
"Name Kept Green, The," 250n.
Nantucket, Mass., 22, 66, 109, 242
Narragansett country, R. I., 170, 197
Natick, Mass., 218, 221
"Nehemiah Flufkin's Visit to the City of Notions," 72–74
New Bedford, Mass., 21–22, 253
New Castle, N. H., 7, 34n., 41n., 163
New England's Prospect, 16
New-English Canaan, 16, 212
New Hampshire, 7, 23, 43, 49, 52, 65, 66, 85, 111, 117, 126, 143, 144, 148, 161, 163, 170, 174, 176, 179, 181, 184, 191, 194, 197, 202, 206
New Hampton, N. H., 42n.
New Haven, Conn., 27, 29n., 167, 200
New London, Conn., 134, 200, 201, 236
New Salem, Mass., 95
"New Wife and the Old, The," 206, 207, 213
Newbury, Mass., 163, 207, 208, 209
Newbury, Vt., 36n.
Newburyport, Mass., 12n., 23, 163n.

270

Index

Index

Index